EXPERIENCING THE WORD

Through The Gospels

Marjie Schaefer

EXPERIENCING THE
WORD
Through The Gospels

with notes by
HENRY BLACKABY
Best Selling Author of *Experiencing God*

HOLMAN
BIBLE PUBLISHERS

Nashville, Tennessee

Experiencing the Word Through the Gospels
The Holman Christian Standard Bible™
Copyright © 1999 by Broadman & Holman Publishers

ISBN: 1-5581-9857-1

Printed in the United States
1 2 3 4 02 01 00 99
Q

Introducing

The Holman Christian Standard Bible

Bible study is the road God's people take to hear and obey our Creator and Savior. The Holman Christian Standard Bible™ offers believers in the third millennium an up-to-date translation designed specifically for the needs of students of Scripture. It seeks to provide a translation as close to the words of the Hebrew and Greek texts as possible while still maintaining the literary quality and ease of reading that invite and enable people to read, study, and obey God's Word. To reach God's people effectively, a translation must provide a reverent, exalted text that is also within reach of its readers.

Translating the Bible into English offers a double challenge. First, each language has its own vocabulary, grammar, and syntax that cannot be rendered exactly into another language. Second, contemporary culture so honors relativism and individual freedom that it distrusts claims to absolute authority.

PRECISION WITH CLARITY

The first challenge means that English translators must avoid creating a special form of the language that does not communicate well to modern readers. For example, John 1:6 in Greek reads, "was a man having been sent from God, name to him John." The English translator must provide a word order and syntax that follow the dynamics of the English language and that are familiar to English readers. In this instance, the Holman Christian Standard Bible reads, "There was a man named John who was sent from God." This accurately represents the Greek text but also presents it in a form readers should find inviting and natural.

On the other hand, the Holman Christian Standard Bible is not based on a theory of translation that considers completely dispensible the form of the original language. Rules governing word order are very different in Hebrew, Greek, and English. But English shares with Hebrew and Greek certain grammatical forms such as nouns, verbs, prepositional phrases, independent and dependent clauses, and so forth. In most cases these forms perform similar functions in English as they do in Hebrew or Greek. Therefore, since grammatical form is one way that language communicates, we have retained the grammatical form of the original whenever it can be rendered into English with sufficient accuracy and clarity. Nevertheless, this is not a strict word-for-word translation since it is often impossible to render one and only one English word for every Hebrew or Greek word. Language differences often require several English words to render one Hebrew or Greek word, and sometimes a Hebrew or Greek phrase may be more accurately and clearly translated by one word in English.

Introducing

COMMUNICATING WITH AUTHORITY

The second challenge, that of contemporary culture, means translators must hold firm to traditional beliefs about the authority of Scripture and avoid modern temptations to rewrite the Bible to say what modern readers want to hear. Translators must remember that the divine Author of the Bible inspired His Word for people today and for all time just as much as for the original audience. The Holman Christian Standard Bible stands on the authority of God and has attempted to provide an accurate and readable translation of the Greek text. The mission of the Holman Christian Standard Bible is to produce as precise a translation of the Hebrew, Aramaic, and Greek Scriptures as possible with the use of newly-published lexicons, grammars, and computer programs. The goal of this kind of translation is to encourage in-depth Bible study, but this translation also seeks to be highly readable (for public and private use) and also useful for personal memorization.

THE MAKINGS OF A NEW TRANSLATION

With these goals in view, an international and interdenominational team of more than eighty scholars has been formed to translate the Scriptures from the original languages. This translation project is being undertaken by Holman Bible Publishers, the oldest Bible publisher in America. Its origin can be traced back to a Philadelphia firm founded by Christopher Sower in 1743. Holman is spiritually grounded in the belief that the Bible is inerrant and is the sole authority for faith and practice in the life of a Christian.

In order to produce this translation, Holman Bible Publishers entered into a partnership with Dr. Art Farstad, former General Editor of the New King James Version. Art had been working on a new translation of the Bible for several years when in the Spring of 1998 he agreed to contract with Holman to complete the project. Art served as General Editor of this translation project until his death on September 1, 1998. His Assistant Editor and coworker, Dr. Ed Blum, former professor at Dallas Theological Seminary, picked up the mantle of leadership that Art left behind and now serves as General Editor of the Holman Christian Standard Bible.

HOW TO USE THIS EDITION

This presentation of the Gospels contains several helpful features of the Holman Christian Standard Bible. Notes immediately beneath the text of the translation refer to some of the variants in Greek manuscripts. Notes at the bottom of the page provide in significant places a literal rendering of the Greek text, other possible translations, explanations of biblical customs, places, and activities, and cross references to other passages.

Introducing

Word studies which explain the precise meaning and application of prominent Greek words found in the Gospels are another helpful element, complete with the pronunciation in brackets of each word that is featured. To help the reader in further study, certain word studies include the number of times the word occurs in the other three Gospels (if any). Other similar listings are included: In the Gospel of Luke, for example, a note appears when a similar word is found in the Book of Acts. In the Gospel of John, the same treatment is applied for words that appear in 1, 2, 3 John and Revelation. Additionally, in the text of the word studies themselves, references to parallel passages are indicated by an equal mark (for example, the temptation of Jesus; Mt 4:1-11 = Mk 1:12-13 = Lk 4:1-13), to clarify that the same word is used in two, three, or all four Gospels.

As a further aid to understanding and incorporating the Bible into daily life, Dr. Henry Blackaby has provided spiritual insights that explain and apply truths from the Gospels into daily Christian experience.

Bible Book Abbreviations

OLD TESTAMENT

Gn	Genesis
Ex	Exodus
Lv	Leviticus
Nm	Numbers
Dt	Deuteronomy
Jos	Joshua
Jdg	Judges
Ru	Ruth
1 Sm	1 Samuel
2 Sm	2 Samuel
1 Kg	1 Kings
2 Kg	2 Kings
1 Ch	1 Chronicles
2 Ch	2 Chronicles
Ezr	Ezra
Neh	Nehemiah
Est	Esther
Jb	Job
Ps	Psalms
Pr	Proverbs
Ec	Ecclesiastes
Sg	Song of Solomon
Is	Isaiah
Jr	Jeremiah
Lm	Lamentations
Ezk	Ezekiel
Dn	Daniel
Hs	Hosea
Jl	Joel
Am	Amos
Ob	Obadiah
Jnh	Jonah
Mc	Micah
Nah	Nahum
Hab	Habakkuk
Zph	Zephaniah
Hg	Haggai
Zch	Zechariah
Mal	Malachi

NEW TESTAMENT

Mt	Matthew
Mk	Mark
Lk	Luke
Jn	John
Ac	Acts
Rm	Romans
1 Co	1 Corinthians
2 Co	2 Corinthians
Gl	Galatians
Eph	Ephesians
Php	Philippians
Col	Colossians
1 Th	1 Thessalonians
2 Th	2 Thessalonians
1 Tm	1 Timothy
2 Tm	2 Timothy
Ti	Titus
Phm	Philemon
Heb	Hebrews
Jms	James
1 Pt	1 Peter
2 Pt	2 Peter
1 Jn	1 John
2 Jn	2 John
3 Jn	3 John
Jd	Jude
Rv	Revelation

Henry Blackaby Presents

SEVEN STEPS TO

Experiencing the Word

Do your morning devotions ever seem disconnected from the rest of your day? Do familiar Scriptures feel at home in the context of a worship service, but sound like wishful thinking the rest of the week?

It's true, you can *read* the words without *experiencing* the Word.

But it doesn't have to be that way.

Experiencing the Word can be an everyday, anytime event.

Few people have been able to communicate this concept with as much power, clarity, and commitment as Henry Blackaby, best-selling author of the *Experiencing God* book and study course and numerous other titles and resources, now selling in the millions of copies. His methods for seeking God's will, listening for God's voice, and obeying God's teachings have helped many people begin experiencing God in their own lives on a daily basis.

Now he brings this same kind of spiritual depth to your study of the Gospels. As you travel these pages, as you interact with the Scriptures, as you sense God speaking through verses both comforting and confrontational, you'll be joined by Dr. Blackaby's wise counsel, awakening your heart to God's loving plan for your life, discovering His genuine desire to use you in helping others draw nearer to Him.

What better place to begin than in the life and ministry of Christ, to hear from His own mouth how Jesus related to His Father, how He lived and practiced total obedience, how He surrendered the keys to human desire and ambition in order to willingly, humbly, consistently follow the path of selfless service.

Be watching for Dr. Blackaby's godly advice around these overall themes:

1 • Seek Relationship with God First
2 • Tune Your Heart to Hear God's Voice
3 • Live the Word Through Experience
4 • Surrender Your Rights
5 • Know God's Will by Knowing God's Heart
6 • Obey, Obey, and Keep on Obeying
7 • Relax—Let Witnessing Happen Naturally

Whether you catch them at random in your regular reading, or use the step-by-step outline on the following page, you will come away with proven principles that will help you align yourself in harmony with God's will, becoming a person God can use to touch others with His love. Both relationships—both the vertical and horizontal—will be perfected as you let God's Word have its way in your life.

EXPERIENCING THE WORD Through The Gospels

1. Seek Relationship with God First

Everything in your Christian life, everything about knowing Him and experiencing Him, everything about knowing His will depends on the quality of your love relationship with God.

2. Tune Your Heart to Hear God's Voice

You are going to have watch to see how God uniquely communicates with you. You will not have any other crutch. You will have to depend on God alone.

3. Live the Word Through Experience

When you obey His Word, God accomplishes something through you only He can do. Then you come to know Him in a more intimate way by experiencing God at work through you.

4. Surrender Your Rights

To live a God-centered life, you must focus your life on God's purposes, not your own plans. You must see things from God's perspective rather than your own.

5. Know God's Will by Knowing God's Heart

You never have to sense an emptiness or lack of purpose. He will always fill your life with Himself. When you have Him, you have everything there is.

6. Obey, Obey, and Keep on Obeying

Adjust your life to God in the kind of relationship where you follow Him wherever He leads you—even if the assignment seems to be small or insignificant.

7. Relax—Let Witnessing Happen Naturally

When the world sees things happening through God's people that cannot be explained except that God Himself has done them, then the world will be drawn to the God they see.

Pronunciation Guide
for Greek Words

CODE	EXAMPLE	CODE	EXAMPLE
a	HAT	oo	LOOK
ah	far, FAHR	<u>oo</u>	boot, B<u>OO</u>T
aw	call, KAWL		
ay	name, NAYM	ow	cow, KOW
b	BAD		out, OWT
ch	CHEW	oy	boil, BOYL
d	DAD	p	PAT
e, eh	met, MEHT	r	RAN
ee	sea, SEE	s	star, STAHR
	ski, SKEE		tsetse, SET see
ew	truth, TREWTH	sh	show, SHOH
f	FOOT		action, AK shuhn
	enough, ee NUHF		mission, MIH shuhn
g	GET		vicious, VIH shuhss
h	HIM	t	tie, TIGH
hw	whether, HWEH thuhr		Thomas, TAH muhss
i, ih	city, SIH tih	th	thin, THIHN, THIN
igh	sign, SIGHN	<u>th</u>	there, <u>TH</u>EHR
	eye, IGH	tw	TWIN
<u>igh</u>	lite, L<u>IGH</u>T	u, uh	tub, TUHB
ih	pin, PIHN, PIN		Joshua, JAHSH yew uh
j	jack, JAK		term TUHRM
	germ, JUHRM	v	veil, VAYL
k	KISS		of, AHV
	cow, KOW	w	WAY
ks	ox, AHKS		
kw	quail, KWAYL	wh	(whether) see *hw*
l	live, LIHV, LIGHV	y	year, YEER
m	more, MOHR	z	xerox, ZIHR ahks
n	note, NOHT		ZEE rahks
ng	ring, RING		his, HIHZ, HIZ
oh	go, GOH		zebra, ZEE bruh
	row, ROH (a boat)	zh	version, VUHR zhuhn

Taken from the book by W. Murray Severance, *That's Easy for You to Say: Your Quick Guide to Pronouncing Bible Names* (Nashville: Broadman & Holman Publishers, 1997). Used by permission.

Transliteration Guide
from Greek into English

GREEK LETTER	NAME	TRANSLITERATION INTO ENGLISH
α	alpha	a
β	beta	b
γ	gamma	g
δ	delta	d
ε	epsilon	e[1]
ζ	zeta	z
η	eta	e[1]
θ	theta	th
ι	iota	i
κ	kappa	k
λ	lambda	l
μ	mu	m
ν	nu	n
ξ	xi[2]	x
ο	omicron	o[1]
π	pi	p
ρ	rho	r
σ, ς	sigma	s[3]
τ	tau	t
υ	upsilon	u[4]
φ	phi	ph
χ	chi	ch
ψ	psi	ps
ω	omega	o[1]
'	[rough breathing mark]	h

[1] No distinction is made in transliteration between the two *e* class vowels or between the two *o* class vowels. The distinction can be seen in the pronunciation guide: *epsilon* is a short *e* ("eh"); *eta* is a long *e* ("ay"); *omicron* is a short *o* ("ah"); and *omega* is a long *o* ("oh").

[2] Pronounced *ksee*

[3] There is no difference in sound between normal *sigma* (σ) and final *sigma* (ς).

[4] The vowel *upsilon* (υ) is often transliterated into English as *y* because Greek words containing an *upsilon* often come into English as *y* (for example, English *dynamite* is a loan word from the Greek term *dunamis*). However, transliteration is primarily concerned with the proper sound, and *upsilon* never has the sound of the English *y*. *Upsilon* has the sound of a long *u* in English (as in the word *rule*), so we always use *u* to transliterate *upsilon*.

Greek Word Studies

in the Gospel of Matthew

MATTHEW

THE GENEALOGY OF JESUS CHRIST

1 The historical record[a] of Jesus Christ, the Son of David, the Son of Abraham:

FROM ABRAHAM TO DAVID

[2] Abraham fathered[b] Isaac,
Isaac fathered Jacob,
Jacob fathered Judah and his brothers,
[3] Judah fathered Perez and Zerah by Tamar,
Perez fathered Hezron,
Hezron fathered Aram,
[4] Aram fathered Amminadab,
Amminadab fathered Nahshon,
Nahshon fathered Salmon,
[5] Salmon fathered Boaz by Rahab,
Boaz fathered Obed by Ruth,
Obed fathered Jesse,
[6] and Jesse fathered King David.

FROM DAVID TO THE BABYLONIAN EXILE

Then[1] David fathered Solomon by Uriah's wife,
[7] Solomon fathered Rehoboam,
Rehoboam fathered Abijah,
Abijah fathered Asa,[2]
[8] Asa[2] fathered Jehoshaphat,
Jehoshaphat fathered Joram,
Joram fathered Uzziah,

---

[1] 1:6 Other mss add *King*
[2] 1:7,8 Other mss read *Asaph*

---

[a] 1:1 Or *The book of the genealogy*
[b] 1:2 In vv. 2–16 either a son, as here, or a later descendant, as in v. 8

^{9} Uzziah fathered Jotham,
Jotham fathered Ahaz,
Ahaz fathered Hezekiah,
^{10} Hezekiah fathered Manasseh,
Manasseh fathered Amon,[1]
Amon[1] fathered Josiah,
^{11} and Josiah fathered Jechoniah and his brothers
at the time of the exile to Babylon.

FROM THE EXILE TO THE MESSIAH

^{12} Then after the exile to Babylon
Jechoniah fathered Shealtiel,
Shealtiel fathered Zerubbabel,
^{13} Zerubbabel fathered Abiud,
Abiud fathered Eliakim,
Eliakim fathered Azor,
^{14} Azor fathered Zadok,
Zadok fathered Achim,
Achim fathered Eliud,
^{15} Eliud fathered Eleazar,
Eleazar fathered Matthan,
Matthan fathered Jacob,
^{16} and Jacob fathered Joseph the husband of Mary,
who gave birth to[a] Jesus who is called Messiah.[b]

^{17} So all the generations from Abraham to David were fourteen generations; and from David until the exile to Babylon, fourteen generations; and from the exile to Babylon until the Messiah, fourteen generations.

THE NATIVITY OF THE MESSIAH

^{18} The birth of Jesus Christ came about this way: After His mother Mary had been engaged[c] to Joseph, before they came together, she was found to be with child by the Holy Spirit. ^{19} So Joseph, her husband, being a righteous man, and not wanting to disgrace her publicly, decided to divorce her secretly.

^{20} But after he had considered these things, an angel of the Lord suddenly appeared to him in a dream, saying, "Joseph, son of David, don't be afraid to take Mary

Unusual Times Call for Uncommon Faith

When you face confusing circumstances, don't start blaming God. Don't give up following Him. Go to God. Ask Him to reveal the truth of your circumstances. Ask Him to show you His perspective. Then wait on the Lord.

But after he had considered these things, an angel of the Lord suddenly appeared to him in a dream, saying, "Joseph, son of David, don't be afraid to take Mary as your wife, because what has been conceived in her is by the Holy Spirit."

—Matthew 1:20

[1]1:10 Other mss read *Amos*

[a]1:16 Lit *Mary, from whom was born*
[b]1:16 Or *Christ* ("Anointed One")
[c]1:18 Or *betrothed* (engaged). Jewish betrothal was a binding agreement and required divorce to break it.

2

as your wife, because what has been conceived in her is by the Holy Spirit. [21] She will give birth to a son, and you are to name Him Jesus,[a] because He will save His people from their sins."

[22] Now all this took place to fulfill what was spoken by the Lord through the prophet:

[23] **See, the virgin will be with child and give birth to a son,**
and they will name Him Immanuel,[b]

which is translated "God is with us."

[24] When Joseph woke up from his sleep, he did as the Lord's angel had commanded him. He took his wife home, [25] but he did not know her intimately until she gave birth to a son.[1] And he named Him Jesus.

WISE MEN SEEK THE KING

2 After Jesus was born in Bethlehem of Judea in the days of King Herod,[c] wise men[d] from the east arrived unexpectedly in Jerusalem, [2] saying, "Where is He who has been born King of the Jews? For we saw His star in the east[e] and have come to worship Him."[f]

[3] When King Herod heard this, he was deeply disturbed, and all Jerusalem with him. [4] So he assembled all the chief priests and scribes[g] of the people and asked them where the Messiah would be born.

[5] "In Bethlehem of Judea," they told him, "because this is what was written through the prophet:

[6] **And you, Bethlehem,** in the land of Judah,
are by no means **least among the leaders of Judah:**
because out of you will come a Leader
who will shepherd My people Israel."[h]

[7] Then Herod secretly summoned the wise men and learned from them the time when the star appeared. [8] He sent them to Bethlehem and said, "Go and search

---

[1]**1:25** Other mss read *her firstborn son*

---

[a]**1:21** The name *Jesus* means *"The LORD saves" (Yahweh saves).*
[b]**1:23** Is 7:14
[c]**2:1** Idumean ruler over Palestine under Rome (37 B.C.–4 B.C.)
[d]**2:1** Gk *magoi,* "Magi," Eastern sages; observers of the heavens

[e]**2:2** Or *star at its rising*
[f]**2:2** Or *to pay Him homage*
[g]**2:4** Scholars and authorities on the law of Moses
[h]**2:6** Mc 5:2

WORD STUDY

Greek word: **parthenos**
[pahr THEHN ahss]
Translation: **virgin**
Uses in Matthew's Gospel: **4** (Lk, 2)
Uses in the NT: **15**
Key passage: **Matthew 1:23**

The Greek word *parthenos* referred to an unmarried woman who was sexually pure, though it could refer to a man as well (Rv 14:4). Matthew and Luke used the term once each in reference to Mary (Mt 1:23; Lk 1:27), but Matthew indicated that Jesus' birth through the virgin Mary was the fulfillment of a prophecy given eight centuries earlier. In Isaiah 7:14 the prophet describes a virgin (*parthenos* is used here in the Greek OT that Matthew quoted) who would give birth to a child, and He would be named Immanuel. Matthew explained that Isaiah 7:14 was referring to the birth of the Messiah, who would bear the government on His shoulders (Is 9:6), whose name would be "Prince of Peace" (Is 9:6), and who by "the Spirit of the LORD" would judge the world (Is 11:2–5).

WORD STUDY

Greek word: *magos* [MAH gahss]
Translation: **wise man**
Uses in Matthew's Gospel: **4**
Uses in the NT: **6**
Key passage: **Matthew 2:1-12**

The Greek term *magos* was not a positive one from a Christian perspective. In the Greek OT, it occurs only in Daniel 2, where it describes one group of the various practitioners of the occult arts that Nebuchadnezzar summoned to explain his dream (see vv. 2,10). Other than Matthew 2, *magos* occurs in the NT only in Acts 13 and refers both times to Elymas "the sorcerer" (vv. 6,8). The term normally refers to those who studied and interpreted formations in heavenly bodies (modern astrology). The irony in Matthew 2 is hard to miss and was probably intentional on the writer's part: King Herod in Jerusalem, a practicing Jew, the ruler of the Jewish people on behalf of Tiberius Caesar—indeed, the one who retained the title "King of the Jews"—did everything he could to find and kill Jesus when He was born just a few miles away in Bethlehem. But these sorcerers from the east (probably either Persia or Babylon) recognized a special star provided by God, traveled a great distance to find the real King of the Jews, presented valuable gifts to Him, and then even worshiped Him.

carefully for the child. When you find Him, report back to me so that I too can go and worship Him."a
[9] After hearing the king, they went on their way. And there it was—the star they had seen in the east!b It led them until it came and stopped above the place where the child was. [10] When they saw the star, they were overjoyed beyond measure. [11] Entering the house, they saw the child with Mary His mother, and falling to their knees, they worshiped Him.c Then they opened their treasures and presented Him with gifts: gold, frankincense, and myrrh. [12] And being warned in a dream not to go back to Herod, they returned to their own country by another route.

THE FLIGHT INTO EGYPT

[13] After they were gone, an angel of the Lord suddenly appeared to Joseph in a dream, saying, "Get up! Take the child and His mother, flee to Egypt, and stay there until I tell you. For Herod is about to search for the child to destroy Him." [14] So he got up, took the child and His mother during the night, and escaped to Egypt. [15] He stayed there until Herod's death, so that what was spoken by the Lord through the prophet might be fulfilled: **"Out of Egypt I called My Son."d**

THE MASSACRE OF THE INNOCENTS

[16] Then Herod, when he saw that he had been outwitted by the wise men, flew into a rage. He gave orders to massacre all the male children in and around Bethlehem who were two yearse old and under, in keeping with the time he had learned from the wise men. [17] Then what was spoken through Jeremiah the prophet was fulfilled:

> [18] **A voice was heard in Ramah,**
> **weeping,[1] and great mourning,**
> **Rachel weeping for her children;**
> **and she refused to be consoled,**
> **because they were no more.f**

[1]2:18 Other mss read *Lamentation, and weeping*

---

a2:8 Or *and pay Him homage*
b2:9 See 2:2 note
c2:11 Or *they paid Him homage*

d2:15 Hs 11:1
e2:16 Lit *were from two years*
f2:18 Jr 31:15

THE HOLY FAMILY IN NAZARETH

[19] After Herod died, an angel of the Lord suddenly appeared in a dream to Joseph in Egypt, [20] saying, "Get up! Take the child and His mother and go to the land of Israel, because those who sought the child's life are dead." [21] So he got up, took the child and His mother, and entered the land of Israel. [22] But when he heard that Archelaus[a] was ruling over Judea in place of his father Herod, he was afraid to go there. And being warned in a dream, he withdrew to the region of Galilee. [23] Then he went and settled in a town called Nazareth to fulfill what was spoken through the prophets, that He will be called a Nazarene.[b]

THE MESSIAH'S HERALD

3 In those days John the Baptist came, preaching in the wilderness of Judea [2] and saying, "Repent, because the kingdom of heaven has come near!" [3] For he is the one spoken of through the prophet Isaiah, who said:

> **A voice of one crying out in the wilderness:**
> **"Prepare the way for the Lord;**
> **make His paths straight!"**[c]

[4] John himself had a camel hair garment with a leather belt around his waist, and his food was locusts and wild honey. [5] Then Jerusalem, all Judea, and all the vicinity of the Jordan were flocking to him, [6] and they were baptized by him in the Jordan River as they confessed their sins.

[7] When he saw many of the Pharisees and Sadducees[d] coming to the place of his baptism,[e] he said to them, "Brood of vipers! Who warned you to flee from the coming wrath? [8] Therefore produce fruit consistent with[f] repentance. [9] And don't presume to say to your-

---

God's Voice Is Remarkably Clear

When God chose to speak to an individual in the Bible, the person had no doubt that it was God, and he knew what God was saying. When God speaks to you, you will be able to know He is the One speaking, and you will know clearly what He is saying to you.

After they were gone, an angel of the Lord suddenly appeared to Joseph in a dream, saying, "Get up! Take the child and His mother, flee to Egypt, and stay there until I tell you."

—Matthew 2:13a

Turn from Your Way and Walk God's Way

It is impossible to love anything else as much as you love God and still please Him.

"Therefore produce fruit consistent with repentance."

—Matthew 3:8

---

a2:22 A son of Herod the Great who ruled a portion of his father's kingdom from 4 B.C. to A.D. 6
b2:23 *Nazarene* = a person from Nazareth; growing up in Nazareth was an aspect of the Messiah's humble beginnings. See Jn 1:46 (reproach); Is 9:1 (location); or Is 11:1 ("branch").
c3:3 Is 40:3
d3:7 Pharisees and Sadducees were two of the major groups within Judaism. The Pharisees followed the whole body of written and oral law, but the Sadducees followed primarily the first five books of the OT (Torah).
e3:7 Lit *to his baptism*
f3:8 Lit *fruit worthy of*

WORD STUDY

Greek word: **baptizo**
[bap TEE zoh]

Translation: **baptize**

Uses in Matthew's Gospel: **7**
(Mk, 13; Lk, 10; Jn, 13)

Uses in the NT: **77**

Key passage: **Matthew 3:11–17**

The Greek word *baptizo* comes from the word *bapto,* which means *to immerse, dip,* or *plunge under.* *Bapto* occurs only three times in the NT ("dip" in Lk 16:24; Jn 13:26; "dye" in Rv 19:13), but *baptizo* (an intensive form of *bapto*) is quite common. *Baptizo* was rare in secular Greek, and the related noun *(baptisma)* was not used at all, indicating that Jesus and the early church may have coined the term in reference to *baptizo.* While *bapto* is always literal in the NT, *baptizo* and *baptisma* are always religious, referring either to water baptism (Mt 3:13; 28:19; Ac 8:36–38), Spirit baptism (Mk 1:8; Ac 1:5; 1 Co 12:13), or fire baptism (Mt 3:11; Lk 3:16). On one occasion *baptizo* and *baptisma* were used metaphorically by Jesus to describe His suffering on the cross (Mk 10:38).

John baptized in water those who identified with the kingdom community marked by forgiveness and confession of sins (Mt 3:5–11; Mk 1:4–5). Yet John indicated that Jesus Himself would baptize also. Jesus would baptize, not "with water" (see Jn 4:1–2), but "with the Holy Spirit" (those who repented) and "with fire" (those who did not), "with fire" being a reference to final judgment (Mt 3:11–12).

While similar to John's baptism (see Ac 19:1–5), Christian baptism identifies the believer with the Trinity (Mt 28:19) and symbolizes Jesus' death, burial, and resurrection (Rm 6:3–5).

selves, 'We have Abraham as our father.' For I tell you that God is able to raise up children for Abraham from these stones! [10] Even now the ax is ready to strike the root of the trees! Therefore, every tree that doesn't produce good fruit will be cut down and thrown into the fire.

[11] "I baptize you with[a] water for repentance.[b] But the One who is coming after me is more powerful than I; I am not worthy to take off[c] His sandals. He Himself will baptize you with[a] the Holy Spirit and fire. [12] With a winnowing shovel[d] in His hand, He will clear His threshing floor and gather His wheat into the barn, but the chaff He will burn up with fire that never goes out."

THE BAPTISM OF JESUS

[13] Then Jesus came from Galilee to John at the Jordan, to be baptized by him. [14] But John tried to stop Him, saying, "I need to be baptized by You, and yet You come to me?"

[15] Jesus answered him, "Allow it for now, because this is the way for us to fulfill all righteousness." Then he allowed Him to be baptized.[e]

[16] After Jesus was baptized, He went up immediately from the water. The heavens suddenly opened for Him,[1] and He saw the Spirit of God descending like a dove and coming down on Him. [17] And there came a voice from heaven:

> "This is My beloved Son.
> I take delight in Him!"

THE TEMPTATION OF JESUS

4 Then Jesus was led up by the Spirit into the wilderness to be tempted by the Devil. [2] And after He had fasted forty days and forty nights, He was hungry. [3] Then the tempter approached Him and said, "If You are the Son of God, tell these stones to become bread."

[4] But He answered, "It is written:

[1]3:16 Other mss omit *for Him*

---

[a]3:11 Or *in*
[b]3:11 That is, baptism was the means by which repentance was expressed publicly.
[c]3:11 Or *to carry*
[d]3:12 A wooden farm implement

used to toss threshed grain into the wind so the lighter chaff would blow away and separate from the heavier grain.
[e]3:15 *to be baptized* implied

Man must not live on bread alone,
but on every word that comes from the
mouth of God."[a]

5 Then the Devil took Him to the holy city,[b] had Him stand on the pinnacle of the temple, 6 and said to Him, "If You are the Son of God, throw Yourself down. For it is written:

He will give His angels orders concerning you, and,
in their hands they will lift you up,
so you will not strike your foot against a stone."[c]

7 Jesus told him, "It is also written:

You must not tempt the Lord your God."[d]

8 Again, the Devil took Him to a very high mountain and showed Him all the kingdoms of the world and their splendor. 9 And he said to Him, "I will give You all these things if You will fall down and worship me."[e]
10 Then Jesus told him, "Go away,[1] Satan! For it is written:

You must worship the Lord your God,
and you must serve Him only."[f]

11 Then the Devil left Him, and immediately angels came and began to serve Him.

MINISTRY IN GALILEE

12 But after He heard that John had been arrested, He withdrew into Galilee. 13 He left Nazareth behind and went to live in Capernaum by the sea, in the region of Zebulun and Naphtali. 14 This was to fulfill what was spoken through the prophet Isaiah:

15 **O land of Zebulun and land of Naphtali,**
along the sea road, beyond the Jordan,
Galilee of the Gentiles!
16 **The people who live in darkness**
have seen a great light,

[1]4:10 Other mss read *Get behind Me*

[a]4:4 Dt 8:3
[b]4:5 That is, Jerusalem
[c]4:6 Ps 91:11–12
[d]4:7 Dt 6:16
[e]4:9 Or *and pay me homage*
[f]4:10 Dt 6:13

Fear God Even When You Can't Feel Him

We usually want God to speak to us so He can give us a devotional thought to make us feel good all day. If you want the God of the universe to speak to you, you need to be ready for Him to reveal to you what He is doing where you are.

But He answered, "It is written: 'Man must not live on bread alone, but on every word that comes from the mouth of God.'"

—Matthew 4:4

— What Satan wants
kingdom of G
destroyed

Is He Your Lord, or Is He Not?

God's commands are not given so you can pick and choose the ones you want to obey and forget the rest. He expects you to obey all of His commands out of your love relationship with Him.

Then Jesus told him, "Go away, Satan! For it is written: 'You must worship the Lord your God, and you must serve Him only.'"

—Matthew 4:10

7

WORD STUDY

Greek word: **basileia**
[bah sihl IGH uh]

Translation: **kingdom**

Uses in Matthew's Gospel: **55**
(Mk, 20; Lk, 46; Jn, 5)

Uses in the NT: **162**

Key passage: **Matthew 4:17**

Jesus' first recorded proclamation when He began His ministry is "Repent, for the kingdom of heaven is near" (Mt 4:17). Matthew alone records the phrase "the kingdom of heaven" (33 times), while Mark (5 times), Luke (33 times), and John (twice) have "the kingdom of God." The two phrases are interchangeable, as seen in the similarity of teachings about them (Mt 8:5–13 & Lk 13:22–30; Mt 19:23–24) and in parallel passages recording the same event (Mt 11:11 = Lk 7:28). Often the term *basileia* alone is used with the same meaning.

God's kingdom does include His sovereign rule and authority over all things (Dn 4:34–35), but this is not the dominant NT use of the term *basileia*. Kingdom in the NT refers to God's manifested reign in human affairs. Jesus taught that the kingdom is both a present spiritual reality and a future physical reality. It began with the ministry of Jesus as He demonstrated divine power through casting out demons, healing the sick, and proclaiming the way to enter the kingdom (Mt 4:17,23; 11:2–15). Since then the kingdom has been invisible and in secret form; only the initiated (those loyal to Jesus as King) can see it (Mt 13; especially vv. 11–17). But when Jesus returns, the kingdom will be visible and universal (Mt 25:31–46; see Rv 11:15–18), at which time He will reign as King by sitting on David's throne forever (Lk 1:32–33).

and for those living in the shadowland of
    death,
light has dawned.[ab]

[17] From then on Jesus began to preach, "Repent, because the kingdom of heaven has come near!"

THE FIRST DISCIPLES

[18] As He was walking along the Sea of Galilee, He saw two brothers, Simon, who was called Peter, and his brother Andrew. They were casting a net into the sea, since they were fishermen. [19] "Follow Me," He told them, "and I will make you fishers of men!" [20] Immediately they left their nets and followed Him.

[21] Going on from there, He saw two other brothers, James the son of Zebedee, and his brother John. They were in a boat with Zebedee their father, mending their nets, and He called them. [22] Immediately they left the boat and their father and followed Him.

TEACHING, PREACHING, AND HEALING

[23] Jesus[c] was going all over Galilee, teaching in their synagogues, preaching the good news of the kingdom, and healing every disease and sickness among the people. [24] Then the news about Him spread throughout Syria. So they brought to Him all those who were afflicted, those suffering from various diseases and intense pains, the demon–possessed, the epileptics, and the paralytics. And He healed them. [25] Large crowds followed Him from Galilee, Decapolis,[d] Jerusalem, Judea, and beyond the Jordan.

THE SERMON ON THE MOUNT

5 When He saw the crowds, He went up on the mountain, and after He sat down, His disciples came to Him. [2] Then He began to teach them,[e] saying:

THE BEATITUDES

[3] "Blessed are the poor in spirit,
    because the kingdom of heaven is theirs.

---

[a] 4:16 Lit *dawned on them*
[b] 4:15,16 Is 9:1–2
[c] 4:23 Lit *He*
[d] 4:25 A region of Gentile popula-

tions originally in a federation of ten cities with Greco-Roman buildings
[e] 5:2 Lit *Opening His mouth He began to teach them*

⁴Blessed are those who mourn,
   because they will be comforted.
⁵Blessed are the gentle,
   because they will inherit the earth.
⁶Blessed are those who hunger and thirst for
      righteousness,
   because they will be filled.
⁷Blessed are the merciful,
   because they will be shown mercy.
⁸Blessed are the pure in heart,
   because they will see God.
⁹Blessed are the peacemakers,
   because they will be called sons of God.
¹⁰Blessed are those who are persecuted for
      righteousness,
   because the kingdom of heaven is theirs.

¹¹"Blessed are you when they insult you and persecute you, and say every kind of evil against you falsely because of Me. ¹²Be glad and rejoice, because your reward is great in heaven. For that is how they persecuted the prophets who were before you.

BELIEVERS ARE SALT AND LIGHT

¹³"You are the salt of the earth. But if the salt should lose its taste, how can it be made salty? It's no longer good for anything but to be thrown out and trampled on by men.

¹⁴"You are the light of the world. A city situated on a hill cannot be hidden. ¹⁵No one lights a lamp and puts it under a basket,ᵃ but rather on a lampstand, and it gives light for all who are in the house. ¹⁶In the same way, let your light shineᵇ before men, so that they may see your good works and give glory to your Father in heaven.

CHRIST FULFILLS THE LAW

¹⁷"Don't assume that I came to destroy the Law or the Prophets. I did not come to destroy but to fulfill. ¹⁸For I assure you:ᶜ Until heaven and earth pass away,

---

ᵃ**5:15** A large basket used to measure grain
ᵇ**5:16** Or *way, your light must shine*
ᶜ**5:18** "I assure you" is literally *Amen I say to you.* The term *Amen* transliterates the Hb word expressing affirmation (Dt 27:15; 1 Kg 1:36; Jr 28:6; Ps 106:48). Jesus used it to testify to the certainty and importance of His words (see Rv 3:14).

WORD STUDY

Greek word: *makarios*
[mah KAH ree ahss]
Translation: *blessed*
Uses in Matthew's Gospel: **13**
(Lk, 15; Jn, 2)
Uses in the NT: **50**
Key passage: **Matthew 5:3–12**

The term *makarios* occurs thirty times in the Gospels, all but two on the lips of Jesus (Lk 1:45; 11:27). Jesus used this word in both versions of the Beatitudes (Mt 5:3–11; Lk 6:20–22). *Makarios* is never used in the NT in the secular Greek sense of *happy* or *fortunate*. Behind NT usage is the Hebrew term *ashrey* [AHSH ray], which is common in the OT and is normally translated "blessed" also (see Ps 1:1).

There are two main uses of the term *makarios* in the NT. The dominant one is in reference to God's blessing upon His people; the secondary one is when God's people bless Him, making the term basically synonymous with *praise* (Eph 1:3). Being blessed by God refers to the status of one who is approved by God. The opposite of this state of blessing is "woe" (Gk *ouai;* see word study on page 149), the status of one who is not approved by God and thus the object of impending judgment (Mt 23:13–32; Lk 6:24–26). God's blessing today does not necessarily include material prosperity in this life (Mt 19:23–24; Lk 6:24; 16:19–31)—the contrary, in fact, is quite possible (Mt 5:3; Lk 6:20)—but it does anticipate full, uninterrupted prosperity in the future kingdom (Mt 5:4–9,11–12; 25:34).

WORD STUDY

Greek word: ***dikaiosune***
[dih kigh ah SOO nay]

Translation: ***righteousness***

Uses in Matthew's Gospel: **7**
(Lk, 1; Jn, 2)

Uses in the NT: **92**

Key passage: **Matthew 5:20**

The Greek noun *dikaiosune* is normally translated "righteousness" and the related verb *dikaioo* [dih kigh AH oh] "to justify." These terms have a specialized meaning in Paul's letters (especially in Romans). In Pauline theology these terms most often refer to a right relationship with God by faith in Christ. In the other NT books, *dikaiosune* has the basic meaning of "that which is right," especially that which is right as determined by God.

Therefore, *dikaiosune* emphasizes conformity to a divine standard, and in the Synoptic Gospels especially, the term refers to the way a true disciple provides evidence that he is qualified to enter the kingdom. This is what Jesus meant in Matthew 5:20. The scribes and Pharisees depended on their own good works to enter the kingdom, but the disciple of Jesus knows that his good works can only provide evidence that he is qualified for the kingdom. In the Sermon on the Mount (Mt 5—7) the hallmarks of a true disciple are specifically those qualities described by Jesus in verses 3–19 and in what He would say in the rest of the sermon (5:21—7:20; see especially 6:1 where Jesus said righteousness is to be practiced). But additional hallmarks can be found in Jesus' teachings elsewhere (Mt 16:24-26; Lk 9:57-62; 14:25-35; Jn 13:34-35; 15:5,8,16), and in other NT passages as well (Ac 14:22; Eph 2:10; 2 Tm 3:12).

not the smallest letter or one stroke of a letter[a] will ever pass from the law until all things are accomplished. [19] Therefore, whoever breaks one of the least of these commandments and teaches people to do so will be called least in the kingdom of heaven. But whoever practices and teaches these commandments[b] will be called great in the kingdom of heaven. [20] For I tell you, unless your righteousness surpasses that of the scribes and Pharisees, you will never enter the kingdom of heaven.

MURDER BEGINS IN THE HEART

[21] "You have heard that it was said to our ancestors,[c] **'You shall not murder,'**[d] and 'whoever murders will be subject to judgment.' [22] But I tell you, everyone who is angry with his brother[1] will be subject to judgment. And whoever says to his brother, 'Fool!'[e] will be subject to the council.[f] But whoever says, 'You moron!' will be subject to hellfire.[g] [23] So if you are offering your gift on the altar, and there you remember that your brother has something against you, [24] leave your gift there in front of the altar. First go and be reconciled with your brother, and then come and offer your gift. [25] Reach a settlement quickly with your adversary, while you're on the way with him, or your adversary will hand you over to the judge, the judge to[2] the officer, and you will be thrown into prison. [26] I assure you:[h] You will never get out of there until you have paid the last penny![i]

ADULTERY IN THE HEART

[27] "You have heard that it was said, **'You shall not commit adultery.'**[j] [28] But I tell you, everyone who looks at a woman to lust for her has already committed adultery with her in his heart. [29] If your right eye causes

[1] **5:22** Other mss add *without a cause*
[2] **5:25** Other mss read *hand you over to*

---

[a]**5:18** The smallest letter of the Gk alphabet is *iota*.
[b]**5:19** *these commandments* added for clarity
[c]**5:21** Lit *to the ancients*
[d]**5:21** Ex 20:13; Dt 5:17
[e]**5:22** Lit *Raca*. Aramaic term of abuse similar to "airhead"
[f]**5:22** Lit *Sanhedrin*
[g]**5:22** Gk *gehenna*, Aramaic for Val-

ley of Hinnom on south side of Jerusalem. It was formerly a place of human sacrifice and in NT times, a place for the burning of garbage. Therefore, it was a good illustration of hell. Lit *the gehenna of fire*
[h]**5:26** See 5:18 note
[i]**5:26** Lit *quadran*, a Roman coin worth about one and one-half cents
[j]**5:27** Ex 20:14; Dt 5:18

you to sin, gouge it out and throw it away.[a] For it is better that you lose one of your members than for your whole body to be thrown into hell.[b] [30] And if your right hand causes you to sin, cut it off and throw it away.[a] For it is better that you lose one of your members than for your whole body to go into hell!

DIVORCE PRACTICES CENSURED

[31] "It was also said, **'Whoever divorces his wife must give her a written notice of divorce.'**[c] [32] But I tell you, everyone who divorces his wife, except in a case of sexual immorality,[d] causes her to commit adultery. And whoever marries a divorced woman commits adultery.

TELL THE TRUTH

[33] "Again, you have heard that it was said to our ancestors,[e] **'You must not break your oath, but you must keep your oaths to the Lord.'**[f] [34] But I tell you, don't take an oath at all: either by heaven, because it is God's throne; [35] or by the earth, because it is His footstool; or by Jerusalem, because it is the city of the great King. [36] Neither should you swear by your head, because you cannot make a single hair white or black. [37] But let your word 'yes,' be 'yes,' and your 'no,' be 'no.'[g] Anything more than this is from the evil one.

GO THE SECOND MILE

[38] "You have heard that it was said, **'An eye for an eye'** and **'a tooth for a tooth.'**[h] [39] But I tell you, don't resist[i] an evildoer. On the contrary, if anyone slaps you on your right cheek, turn the other to him also. [40] As for the one who wants to sue you and take away your shirt,[j] let him have your coat[k] as well. [41] And if anyone

Keep Your View of God Unobstructed

If your love relationship with God is not right, nothing else will be right.

"So if you are offering your gift on the altar, and there you remember that your brother has something against you, leave your gift there in front of the altar. First go and be reconciled with your brother, and then come and offer your gift."

—Matthew 5:23–24

---

[a] **5:29,30** Lit *throw it from you*
[b] **5:29** Gk *gehenna;* see 5:22
[c] **5:31** Dt 24:1
[d] **5:32** Gk *porneia,* fornication or possibly a violation of Jewish marriage laws
[e] **5:33** Lit *to the ancients*
[f] **5:33** Lv 19:12; Nm 30:2; Dt 23:21
[g] **5:37** That is, say what you mean and mean what you say
[h] **5:38** Ex 21:24; Lv 24:20; Dt 19:21
[i] **5:39** Or *don't set yourself against* or *retaliate against*
[j] **5:40** Lit *tunic* (inner garment)
[k] **5:40** Lit *robe* or *garment* (outer garment)

forces[a] you to go one mile, go with him two. [42] Give to the one who asks you, and don't turn away from the one who wants to borrow from you.

LOVE YOUR ENEMIES

[43] "You have heard that it was said, '**You shall love your neighbor**[b] and hate your enemy.' [44] But I tell you, love your enemies,[1] and pray for those who[2] persecute you, [45] so that you may be[c] sons of your Father in heaven. For He causes His sun to rise on the evil and the good, and sends rain on the righteous and the unrighteous. [46] For if you love those who love you, what reward will you have? Don't even the tax collectors do the same? [47] And if you greet only your brothers, what are you doing out of the ordinary?[d] Don't even the Gentiles[3] do the same? [48] Be perfect, therefore, as your heavenly Father is perfect.

HOW TO GIVE

6 "Be careful not to practice your righteousness[4] in front of people, to be seen by them. Otherwise, you will have no reward from your Father in heaven. [2] So whenever you give to the poor, don't sound a trumpet before you as the hypocrites do in the synagogues and in the streets, to be applauded by people. I assure you: They've got their reward! [3] But when you give to the poor, don't let your left hand know what your right hand is doing, [4] so that your giving may be in secret. And your Father who sees in secret will reward you.[5]

HOW TO PRAY

[5] "Whenever you pray, you must not be like the hypocrites, because they love to pray standing in the synagogues and on the street corners to be seen by people. I assure you: They've got their reward! [6] But when you

God's People Must Be Praying People

The greatest untapped resource that I know of is the united prayer of God's people.

"But when you pray, go into your private room, shut your door, and pray to your Father who is in secret. And your Father who sees in secret will reward you."

—Matthew 6:6

[1] **5:44** Other mss add *bless those who curse you, do good to those who hate you,*
[2] **5:44** Other mss add *mistreat you and*
[3] **5:47** Other mss read *tax collectors*
[4] **6:1** Other mss read *charitable giving*
[5] **6:4** Other mss read *will Himself reward you openly*

[a] **5:41** Roman soldiers could require people to carry loads for them.
[b] **5:43** Lv 19:18
[c] **5:45** Or *become* or *show yourselves to be*
[d] **5:47** Lit *doing more* or *doing that is superior*

pray, go into your private room, shut your door, and pray to your Father who is in secret. And your Father who sees in secret will reward you.[1] [7] When you pray, don't babble like the idolaters,[a] since they imagine they'll be heard for their many words. [8] Don't be like them, because your Father knows the things you need before you ask Him.

THE MODEL PRAYER

[9] "Therefore, you should pray like this:

> Our Father in heaven,
> Your name be honored as holy.
> [10] Your kingdom come.
> Your will be done
> on earth as it is in heaven.
> [11] Give us today our daily bread.[b]
> [12] And forgive us our debts,
> as we also have forgiven our debtors.
> [13] And do not bring us into[c] temptation,
> but deliver us from the evil one.[d]
> ⌐For Yours is the kingdom
> and the power
> and the glory forever,
> Amen.⌐[2]

[14] "For if you forgive people their wrongdoing,[e] your heavenly Father will forgive you as well. [15] But if you don't forgive people,[3] your Father will not forgive your wrongdoing.[e]

HOW TO FAST

[16] "Whenever you fast, don't be sad-faced like the hypocrites. For they make their faces unattractive[f] so they may show their fasting to people. I assure you: They've

Don't Just Pray to Hear Yourself Talk

When you begin asking questions to God in prayer, always check to see if you have asked the right question before you pursue the answer.

"When you pray, don't babble like the idolaters, since they imagine they'll be heard for their many words. Don't be like them, because your Father knows the things you need before you ask Him."

—Matthew 6:7–8

Share the Same Mercy You Have Received

When you consider the incredible, undeserved mercy you have been granted, how can you refuse to extend the same unconditional mercy to others?

"For if you forgive people their wrongdoing, your heavenly Father will forgive you as well."

—Matthew 6:14

---

[1] 6:6 Other mss add *openly*
[2] 6:13 Other mss omit *For Yours* through *Amen.*
[3] 6:15 Other mss add *their trespasses*

---

[a] 6:7 The Gk word may also be translated: *Gentiles, nations, heathen,* or *pagans.*
[b] 6:11 Or *our necessary bread* or *our bread for tomorrow*
[c] 6:13 Or *do not cause us to come into*
[d] 6:13 Or *from evil*
[e] 6:14,15 Or *trespasses*
[f] 6:16 Or *faces unrecognizable* or *disfigured*

WORD STUDY

Greek word: **kardia**
[kahr DEE uh]

Translation: **heart**

Uses in Matthew's Gospel: **16**
(Mk, 11; Lk, 22; Jn, 7)

Uses in the NT: **156**

Key passage: **Matthew 6:21**

The English word *heart* is used literally of the vital organ that pumps blood and figuratively of the inner person. The same was true for *kardia* in ancient Greek, but in the NT the literal sense of the term never occurs. As is the case for the related Hebrew term in the OT (*leb* [layb]), *kardia* can refer to the whole person (Lk 16:15; see 1 Chr 28:9) or to various aspects of a person's inner self: physical needs or wants (Ac 14:17; Jms 5:5; see Pr 15:15), thoughts or intellect (Lk 12:45; see Gn 6:5; Pr 23:7), values (Mt 6:21; see Jb 12:24), emotions (Ac 21:13; Phl 1:7; see Pr 31:11; Sg 8:6), volition (Lk 21:14; 2 Co 9:7; see Ex 7:22-23; Ml 4:6), and affections (Mt 22:37; see Dt 6:5; 30:6,10). The heart as a reflection of the inner self shows that every person is corrupt by nature and in need of redemption, which alone allows a person to fulfill the greatest commandment, to "love the Lord your God with all your heart" (Mt 22:37). Jesus used the term *kardia* three times in the Sermon on the Mount: to describe the whole person (5:4), to describe lustful thoughts (5:28), and to describe values (6:21)—the latter indicating that a person reveals what he values most by where he puts his money.

got their reward! [17] But when you fast, brush your hair[a] and wash your face, [18] so that you don't show your fasting to people, but to your Father who is in secret. And your Father who sees in secret will reward you.[1]

GOD AND POSSESSIONS

[19] "Don't collect for yourselves treasures[b] on earth, where moth and rust destroy and where thieves break in and steal. [20] But collect for yourselves treasures in heaven, where neither moth nor rust destroys, and where thieves don't break in and steal. [21] For where your treasure is, there your heart will be also.

[22] "The eye is the lamp of the body. If your eye is generous,[c] your whole body will be full of light. [23] But if your eye is stingy,[d] your whole body will be full of darkness. So if the light within you is darkness—how deep is that darkness!

[24] "No one can be a slave of two masters, since either he will hate one and love the other, or be devoted to one and despise the other. You cannot be slaves of God and of money.[e]

THE CURE FOR ANXIETY

[25] "This is why I tell you: Don't worry about your life, what you will eat or what you will drink; or about your body, what you will wear. Isn't life more than food and the body more than clothing? [26] Look at the birds of the sky: they don't sow, or reap, or gather into barns, yet your heavenly Father feeds them. Aren't you worth more than they? [27] Can any of you add a single cubit to his height by worrying?[f] [28] And why do you worry about clothes? Learn how the wildflowers of the field grow: they don't labor or spin thread. [29] Yet I tell you that not even Solomon in all his splendor was adorned like one of these! [30] If that's how God clothes the grass of the field, which is here today and thrown into the furnace tomorrow, won't He do much more for you—you

[1]**6:18** Other mss add *openly*

[a]**6:17** Lit *anoint your head*
[b]**6:19** Or *valuables*
[c]**6:22** Lit *simple; single; clear; healthy;* or *sincere*
[d]**6:23** Lit *evil; envious;* or *bad*
[e]**6:24** Aram. *mammon* (Eng. Mammon)
[f]**6:27** A cubit is about 18 inches, so our Lord may be exaggerating for effect; He may mean adding days to one's life-span.

of little faith? [31] So don't worry, saying, 'What will we eat?' or 'What will we drink?' or 'What will we wear?' [32] For the Gentiles eagerly seek all these things, and your heavenly Father knows that you need them. [33] But seek first the kingdom of God[1] and His righteousness, and all these things will be provided for you. [34] Therefore don't worry about tomorrow, because tomorrow will worry about itself. Each day has enough trouble of its own.

DO NOT JUDGE

7 "Do not judge, so that you won't be judged. [2] For with the judgment you use,[a] you will be judged, and with the measure you use,[b] it will be measured to you. [3] Why do you look at the speck in your brother's eye, but don't notice the log in your own eye? [4] Or how can you say to your brother, 'Let me take the speck out of your eye,' and look, there's a log in your eye? [5] Hypocrite! First take the log out of your eye, and then you will see clearly to take the speck out of your brother's eye. [6] Don't give what is holy to dogs or toss your pearls before pigs, or they will trample them with their feet, turn, and tear you to pieces.

KEEP ASKING, SEARCHING, KNOCKING

[7] "Keep asking,[c] and it will be given to you. Keep searching,[d] and you will find. Keep knocking,[e] and the door[f] will be opened to you. [8] For everyone who asks receives, and the one who searches finds, and to the one who knocks, the door[f] will be opened. [9] What man among you, if his son asks him for bread, will give him a stone? [10] Or if he asks for a fish, will give him a snake? [11] If you, then, who are evil know how to give good gifts to your children, how much more will your Father in heaven give good things to those who ask Him! [12] Therefore, whatever you want others to do for you, do also the same for them—this is the Law and the Prophets.[g]

---

[1]6:33 Other mss omit *of God*

---

[a]7:2 Lit *you judge*
[b]7:2 Lit *the measure you measure*
[c]7:7 Or *Ask*
[d]7:7 Or *Search*

[e]7:7 Or *Knock*
[f]7:7,8 Lit *and it*
[g]7:12 That is, the OT

WORD STUDY

Greek word: **adelphos**
[ah dehl FAHSS]
Translation: **brother**
Uses in Matthew's Gospel: **39** (Mk, 20; Lk, 24; Jn, 14)
Uses in the NT: **343**
Key passage: **Matthew 7:3–5**

The Greek word *adelphos* comes from a root meaning *from the same womb*. Literally, this masculine term means *brother,* the feminine *adelphe* meaning *sister.* In the OT the Hebrew term for brother *(ach)* referred to a blood relative a majority of the time, but could also be used metaphorically of a close companion (2 Sm 1:26), distant neighbors (Gn 29:4), or those in Israel's covenant community (Lv 21:10; Dt 15:7,11). In the NT the situation is slightly different: *adelphos* is literal in the Gospels most of the time but elsewhere is almost always metaphorical for the Christian community. In the Sermon on the Mount Jesus set the precedent for the use of *adelphos* to refer to the Christian community, not just national blood relations. He stated that offenses must be settled between brothers before making offerings to God (Mt 5:21–24) and that we must judge ourselves rightly before attempting to judge a brother (Mt 7:3–5). On a later occasion Jesus more clearly defined *adelphos* by saying that a true brother is not just a blood relative but one who does the will of the Father (Mt 12:46–50; see Jn 20:17). Thus, in the early church *adelphos* became the common way to address or refer to other Christians (Ac 1:15–16; 21:17; Rm 1:13; Heb 3:1; Jms 1:2; 2 Pt 1:10; 1 Jn 3:13–17; Rv 1:9), both men and women (though *adelphe* was used when only Christian women were in view; Rm 16:1; 1 Co 9:5).

15

ENTERING THE KINGDOM

13 "Enter through the narrow gate; because the gate is wide and the road is broad that leads to destruction, and there are many who go through it. 14 How narrow is the gate and difficult the road that leads to life; and few find it.

15 "Beware of false prophets who come to you in sheep's clothing, but inwardly are ravaging wolves. 16 You'll recognize them by their fruit. Are grapes gathered from thornbushes or figs from thistles? 17 In the same way, every good tree produces good fruit, but a bad tree produces bad fruit. 18 A good tree can't produce bad fruit; neither can a bad tree produce good fruit. 19 Every tree that doesn't produce good fruit is cut down and thrown into the fire. 20 So you'll recognize them by their fruit.

21 "Not everyone who says to Me, 'Lord, Lord!' will enter the kingdom of heaven, but the one who does the will of My Father in heaven. 22 On that day many will say to Me, 'Lord, Lord, didn't we prophesy in Your name, drive out demons in Your name, and do many miracles in Your name?' 23 Then I will announce to them, 'I never knew you! **Depart from Me, you lawbreakers!'**ab

THE TWO FOUNDATIONS

24 "Therefore, everyone who hears these words of Mine and acts on them will be like a sensible man who built his house on the rock. 25 The rain fell, the rivers rose, and the winds blew and pounded that house. Yet it didn't collapse, because its foundation was on the rock. 26 But everyone who hears these words of Mine and doesn't act on them will be like a foolish man who built his house on the sand. 27 The rain fell, the rivers rose, the winds blew and pounded that house, and it collapsed. And its collapse was great!"

28 When Jesus had finished this sermon,c the crowds were astonished at His teaching. 29 For He was teaching them like one who had authority, and not like their scribes.

The Way Is Hard, But the Reward Is Heavenly

There are no shortcuts to spiritual maturity. Maturity only comes through hard work and obedience to what God says.

"Enter through the narrow gate; because the gate is wide and the road is broad that leads to destruction, and there are many who go through it. How narrow is the gate and difficult the road that leads to life; and few find it."

—Matthew 7:13–14

---

a**7:23** Lit *those who work lawlessness*
b**7:23** Ps 6:8
c**7:28** Lit *had ended these words*

CLEANSING A LEPER

8 When He came down from the mountain, immense crowds followed Him. [2] Right away a leper[a] came up and knelt before Him, saying, "Lord, if You are willing, You can make me clean."[b]

[3] And reaching out His hand He touched him, saying, "I am willing; be made clean." Immediately his leprosy[a] was cleansed. [4] Then Jesus told him, "See that you don't tell anyone; but go, show yourself to the priest, and offer the gift that Moses prescribed, as a testimony to them."

A CENTURION'S FAITH

[5] When He entered Capernaum, a centurion[c] came to Him, pleading with Him, [6] "Lord, my servant is lying at home paralyzed, in terrible agony!"

[7] "I will come and heal him," He told him.

[8] "Lord," the centurion replied, "I am not worthy to have You come under my roof. But only say the word, and my servant will be cured. [9] For I too am a man under authority, having soldiers under my command.[d] I say to this one, 'Go!' and he goes; and to another, 'Come!' and he comes; and to my slave, 'Do this!' and he does it."

[10] Hearing this, Jesus was amazed, and said to those following Him, "I assure you: I have not found anyone in Israel with so great a faith! [11] I tell you that many will come from east and west, and recline at the table with Abraham, Isaac, and Jacob in the kingdom of heaven. [12] But the sons of the kingdom will be thrown into the outer darkness. In that place there will be weeping and gnashing of teeth." [13] Then Jesus told the centurion, "Go. As you have believed, let it be done for you." And his servant was cured that very moment.[e]

HEALINGS AT CAPERNAUM

[14] When Jesus went into Peter's house, He saw his mother-in-law lying in bed with a fever. [15] So He touched

Your Belief Can Make a Believer Out of Others

What does God want to do in the lives of those around you that waits upon your trust in Him and the removal of your doubts?

Then Jesus told the centurion, "Go. As you have believed, let it be done for you." And his servant was cured that very moment.

—Matthew 8:13

---

[a]**8:2,3** In the Bible, *leprosy* covers many skin disorders in addition to Hansen's disease.
[b]**8:2** *Clean,* in these verses, includes healing, ceremonial purification, return to fellowship with people, and worship in the temple. See Lv 14:1-31
[c]**8:5** Roman commander of about 100 soldiers
[d]**8:9** Lit *under me*
[e]**8:13** Lit *hour*

17

WORD STUDY

Greek word: *pleroo*
[play RAH oh]

Translation: *fulfill*

Uses in Matthew's Gospel: **16**
(Mk, 2; Lk, 9; Jn, 15)

Uses in the NT: **86**

Key passage: **Matthew 8:17**

The Greek word *pleroo* means *fill* or *fulfill* and by extension *accomplish* or *complete*. One of the key functions of *pleroo* in the NT, and especially in Matthew, is to indicate the fulfillment of OT Scripture ("that it might be fulfilled," or something similar). Fulfillment passages in Matthew fall into three main categories: directly prophetic, analogically prophetic, and typologically prophetic. An OT passage is directly prophetic when it predicts an event that occurs at a later time, such as Jesus' birth to a virgin (Mt 1:22–23; see Is 7:14; see also the word study on page 3), His ministry in Galilee (Mt 4:12–16; see Is 9:1–7), and His power over sin and disease (Mt 8:17; see Is 53:4). The Bethlehem prophecy is also of this kind, though *pleroo* does not occur here (Mt 2:6; see Mc 5:2). The analogically prophetic passage sees parallels between the life of Israel and the life of Jesus, showing that God anticipated events in the life of His Son by incorporating them into the covenant life of His people. An example of this is the calling of both Israel and Jesus out of Egypt (Mt 2:15; see Hs 11:1; see also Mt 2:17–18; Jr 31:15). Finally, the typologically prophetic passage sees parallels between an OT character and a NT character when a direct prophecy is not involved, such as Judas' betrayal of Jesus for thirty pieces of silver (Mt 27:9; see Jr 19:1–13, Zch 11:12–13).

her hand, and the fever left her. Then she got up and began to serve Him. [16] When evening came, they brought to Him many who were demon-possessed. He drove out the spirits with a word and healed all who were sick, [17] so that what was spoken through the prophet Isaiah might be fulfilled:

**He Himself took our weaknesses
and carried our diseases.**[a]

FOLLOWING JESUS

[18] When Jesus saw large crowds[1] around Him, He gave the order to go to the other side of the sea.[b] [19] A scribe approached Him and said, "Teacher, I will follow You wherever You go!"

[20] Jesus told him, "Foxes have dens and birds of the sky have nests, but the Son of Man[c] has no place to lay His head."

[21] "Lord," another of His disciples said, "first let me go bury my father."[d]

[22] But Jesus told him, "Follow Me, and let the dead bury their own dead."

WIND AND WAVE OBEY THE MASTER

[23] As He got into the[2] boat, His disciples followed Him. [24] Suddenly, a violent storm arose on the sea, so that the boat was being swamped by the waves. But He was sleeping. [25] So they came and woke Him up, saying, "Lord, save us![e] We're going to die!"

[26] But He said to them, "Why are you fearful, you of little faith?" Then He got up and rebuked the winds and the sea. And there was a great calm.

[27] The men were amazed and said, "What kind of man is this?—even the winds and the sea obey Him!"

DEMONS DRIVEN OUT BY THE MASTER

[28] When He had come to the other side, to the region of the Gadarenes,[3] two demon-possessed men met Him

[1]**8:18** Other mss read *saw a crowd*
[2]**8:23** Other mss read *into a*
[3]**8:28** Other mss read *Gergesenes*

[a]**8:17** Is 53:4
[b]**8:18** *of the sea* (Galilee) is implied
[c]**8:20** Dn 7:13–14

[d]**8:21** Not necessarily meaning his father was already dead
[e]**8:25** *us* implied

as they came out of the tombs. They were so violent that no one could pass that way. [29] Suddenly they shouted, "What do You have to do with us,[1a] Son of God? Have You come here to torment us before the time?"

[30] Now a long way off from them, a large herd of pigs was feeding. [31] "If You drive us out," the demons begged Him, "send us into the herd of pigs."

[32] "Go!" He told them. So when they had come out, they entered the pigs. And suddenly the whole herd rushed down the steep bank into the sea and perished in the water. [33] Then the men who tended them fled, went into the city, and reported everything—especially what had happened to those who were demon–possessed. [34] At that, the whole town went out to meet Jesus! When they saw Him, they begged Him to leave their region.

THE SON OF MAN FORGIVES AND HEALS

9 So He got into a boat, crossed over, and came to His own town. [2] Just then some men[b] brought to Him a paralytic lying on a stretcher. Seeing their faith, Jesus told the paralytic, "Have courage, son, your sins are forgiven."

[3] At this, some of the scribes said among themselves, "He's blaspheming!"

[4] But perceiving their thoughts, Jesus said, "Why are you thinking evil things in your hearts?[c] [5] For which is easier: to say, 'Your sins are forgiven,' or to say, 'Get up and walk'? [6] But so you may know that the Son of Man has authority on earth to forgive sins"—then He told the paralytic, "Get up, pick up your stretcher, and go home." [7] And he got up and went home. [8] When the crowds saw this, they were awestruck[2d] and gave glory to God who had given such authority to men.

THE CALL OF MATTHEW

[9] As Jesus went on from there, He saw a man named Matthew sitting at the tax office, and He said to him, "Follow Me!" So he got up and followed Him.

---

[1] 8:29 Other mss add *Jesus*
[2] 9:8 Other mss read *they were amazed*

---

[a] 8:29 Lit *What to us and to you*
[b] 9:2 Lit *then they*
[c] 9:4 Or *minds*
[d] 9:8 Lit *they were afraid*

There's No Excuse for Doubting God

The moment you sense that God is moving in your life, you give Him a whole list of reasons why He has the wrong person or why the time is not right. When your focus is on yourself, you cannot see things from God's perspective.

"Lord," another of His disciples said, "first let me go bury my father." But Jesus told him, "Follow Me, and let the dead bury their own dead."
—Matthew 8:21–22

Thoughts about myself hinder my relationship w/ God.

WORD STUDY

Greek word: **eleos** [EH leh ahss]

Translation: **mercy**

Uses in Matthew's Gospel: **3**
(Lk, 6)

Uses in the NT: **27**

Key passage: **Matthew 9:13**

The Greek word *eleos* is one of several words in the NT meaning *mercy* or something similar. All three times this word occurs in Matthew, Jesus uses it to refer to the OT, twice quoting Hosea 6:6, "I desire mercy and not sacrifice" (Mt 9:13; 12:7). The Hebrew term *chesed* in Hosea 6:6 occurs 250 times in the OT and combines the ideas of love, mercy, and covenant loyalty. The Pharisees condemned Jesus for fellowshiping with the outcasts of society ("tax collectors and sinners," v. 11), but He reminded them of God's priority: mercy before sacrifice. Sacrificing to God is worthless without the willingness to show mercy to those in need. In Matthew 23 Jesus rebuked the Pharisees even more harshly, and one of His grievances was their majoring on the minors and minoring on the majors (v. 23): they neglected the more important aspects of the law ("justice, mercy [*eleos*], and faithfulness") but meticulously gave their tithes on small items ("mint, dill, and cummin").

[10] While He was reclining at the table in the house, many tax collectors and sinners came as guests[a] with Jesus and His disciples. [11] When the Pharisees saw this, they asked His disciples, "Why does your Teacher eat with tax collectors and sinners?"

[12] But when He heard this, He said, "Those who are well don't need a doctor, but the sick do. [13] Go and learn what this means: **'I desire mercy and not sacrifice.'**[b] For I didn't come to call the righteous, but sinners."[1]

A QUESTION ABOUT FASTING

[14] Then John's disciples came up to Him, saying, "Why do we and the Pharisees fast often, but Your disciples do not fast?"

[15] Jesus said to them, "Can the wedding guests[c] be sad while the groom is with them? The days will come when the groom is taken away from them, and then they will fast. [16] No one patches an old garment with unshrunk cloth, because the patch pulls away from the garment and makes the tear worse. [17] And no one puts[d] new wine into old wineskins. Otherwise, the skins burst, the wine spills out, and the skins are ruined. But they put new wine into fresh wineskins, and both are preserved."

A GIRL RESTORED AND A WOMAN HEALED

[18] As He was telling them these things, suddenly one of the leaders[e] came and knelt down before Him, saying, "My daughter is near death,[f] but come and lay Your hand on her, and she will live." [19] So Jesus and His disciples got up and followed him.

[20] Just then, a woman who had suffered from bleeding for twelve years approached from behind and touched

[1] 9:13 Other mss add *to repentance*

[a] 9:10 Lit *coming, they were reclining* (at the table). At important meals the custom was to recline on a mat at a low table and lean on the left elbow.

[b] 9:13 Hs 6:6

[c] 9:15 Lit *the sons of the bridal chamber*

[d] 9:17 Lit *And they do not put*

[e] 9:18 That is, a leader of a synagogue (Mk 5:22)

[f] 9:18 Lit *daughter has now come to the end*

research tassel

the tassel on His robe,[a] [21] for she said to herself, "If I can just touch His robe, I'll be made well!"[b]

[22] But Jesus turned and saw her. "Have courage, daughter," He said. "Your faith has made you well."[c] And the woman was made well from that moment.[d]

[23] When Jesus came to the leader's house, He saw the flute players and a crowd lamenting loudly. [24] "Leave," He said, "because the girl isn't dead, but sleeping." And they started laughing at Him. [25] But when the crowd had been put outside, He went in and took her by the hand, and the girl got up. [26] And this news spread throughout that whole area.

HEALING THE BLIND

[27] As Jesus went on from there, two blind men followed Him, shouting, "Have mercy on us, Son of David!"

[28] When He entered the house, the blind men approached Him, and Jesus said to them, "Do you believe that I can do this?"

"Yes, Lord," they answered Him.

[29] Then He touched their eyes, saying, "Let it be done for you according to your faith!" [30] And their eyes were opened. Then Jesus warned them sternly, "Be sure that no one finds out!"[e] [31] But they went out and spread the news about Him throughout that whole area.

DRIVING OUT A DEMON

[32] Just as they were going out, a demon–possessed man who was unable to speak was brought to Him. [33] When the demon had been driven out, the man[f] spoke. And the crowds were amazed, saying, "Nothing like this has ever been seen in Israel!"

[34] The Pharisees however, said, "He drives out demons by the ruler of the demons!"

THE LORD OF THE HARVEST

[35] Then Jesus went to all the towns and villages, teaching in their synagogues, preaching the good news of the

Belief Frees You to Experience God

When God lets you know what He wants to do through you, it will be something only God can do. If you have faith in the God who called you, you will obey Him, and He will bring to pass what He has purposed to do.

When He entered the house, the blind men approached Him, and Jesus said to them, "Do you believe that I can do this?" "Yes, Lord," they answered Him. Then He touched their eyes, saying, "Let it be done for you according to your faith!"

—Matthew 9:28–29

---

[a]9:20 Observant Jews wore tassels (or fringes) on their clothes to remind them to keep the law (see Nm 15:37–41).
[b]9:21 Or *be delivered*

[c]9:22 Or *has saved you*
[d]9:22 Lit *hour*
[e]9:30 Lit *no one knows*
[f]9:33 Lit *the man who was unable to speak*

kingdom, and healing every disease and every sickness.[1]
[36] When He saw the crowds, He felt compassion for
them, because they were weary and worn out, like
sheep without a shepherd. [37] Then He said to His disciples, "The harvest is abundant, but the workers are few.
[38] Therefore, pray to the Lord of the harvest to send out
workers into His harvest."

COMMISSIONING THE TWELVE

10 Summoning His twelve disciples, He gave them
authority over unclean[a] spirits, to drive them
out, and to heal every disease and every sickness.
[2] These are the names of the twelve apostles:

> First, Simon, who is called Peter, and Andrew
> his brother;
> James the son of Zebedee, and John his brother;
> [3] Philip and Bartholomew;[b]
> Thomas and Matthew the tax collector;
> James the son of Alphaeus, and Thaddaeus;[2]
> [4] Simon the Zealot,[c] and Judas Iscariot,[d] who also
> betrayed Him.

[5] Jesus sent out these twelve after giving them instructions: "Don't take the road leading to other nations, and
don't enter any Samaritan[e] town. [6] Instead, go to the lost
sheep of the house of Israel. [7] As you go, announce this:
'The kingdom of heaven has come near.' [8] Heal the sick,
raise the dead, cleanse the lepers, drive out demons.
You have received free of charge; give free of charge.
[9] Don't take along gold, silver, or copper for your
money-belts, [10] or a backpack for the road, or an extra
shirt, or sandals, or a walking stick, for the worker is
worthy of his food.
[11] "Whatever town or village you enter, find out who
is worthy, and stay there until you leave. [12] Greet a
household when you enter it, [13] and if the household is
worthy, your peace should come upon it. But if it is un-

God's Business Is Now Your Occupation

Your job as a servant is to follow Jesus' example: Do what the Father is already doing—watch to see where God is at work and join Him!

"A disciple is not above his teacher, or a slave above his master. It is enough for a disciple to become like his teacher and a slave like his master."

—Matthew 10:24–25a

When God Speaks, That's the Time to Act

Unless God allows you to see where He is working, you will not see it. When God reveals to you what He is doing around you, that is your invitation to join Him.

"What I tell you in the dark, speak in the light. What you hear in a whisper, proclaim on the housetops."

—Matthew 10:27

---

[1] **9:35** Other mss add *among the people*
[2] **10:3** Other mss read *Lebbaeus, whose surname was Thaddaeus.*

---

[a] **10:1** That is, morally or ceremonially impure
[b] **10:3** Probably the Nathanael of Jn 1:45–51
[c] **10:4** Lit *Cananaean*
[d] **10:4** Probably = *man of Kerioth* (a town in Judah)
[e] **10:5** Samaritans were a group of people with a mixed ancestry who lived between Galilee and Judea.

worthy, your peace should return to you. [14] If anyone will not welcome you or listen to your words, shake the dust off your feet when you leave that house or town. [15] I assure you: It will be more tolerable on the day of judgment for the land of Sodom and Gomorrah than for that town.

PERSECUTIONS PREDICTED

[16] "Look, I'm sending you out like sheep among wolves. Therefore be as shrewd as serpents and harmless as doves. [17] Because people will hand you over to sanhedrins[a] and flog you in their synagogues, beware of them. [18] You will even be brought before governors and kings because of Me, to bear witness to them and to the nations. [19] But when they hand you over, don't worry about how or what you should speak. For you will be given what to say at that hour, [20] because you are not speaking, but the Spirit of your Father is speaking in you. [21] "Brother will betray brother to death, and a father his child. Children will even rise up against their parents and have them put to death. [22] You will be hated by everybody because of My name. And the one who endures to the end will be delivered.[b] [23] But when they persecute you in one town, move on to another. For I assure you: You will not have covered the towns of Israel before the Son of Man comes. [24] A disciple[c] is not above his teacher, or a slave above his master. [25] It is enough for a disciple to become like his teacher and a slave like his master. If they called the head of the house 'Beelzebul,'[d] how much more the members of his household.

FEAR GOD

[26] "Therefore, don't be afraid of them, since there is nothing covered that won't be uncovered, and nothing hidden that won't be made known. [27] What I tell you in the dark, speak in the light. What you hear in a whisper,[e] proclaim on the housetops. [28] Don't fear those who kill the body but are not able to kill the soul; but rather, fear Him who is able to destroy both soul and body in

WORD STUDY

Greek word: **phobeo**
[fah BEH oh]

Translation: **fear**

Uses in Matthew's Gospel: **18**
(Mk, 12; Lk, 23; Jn, 5)

Uses in the NT: **95**

Key passage: **Matthew 10:28**

The Greek verb *phobeo* and the related noun *phobos* (English *phobia*) have two main applications in the NT: fear of God and fear of man or circumstances. Like the English term *fear*, *phobeo* can cover a broad spectrum of meanings. These meanings range from hesitatation or worry about something (Mt 1:20), to discomfort at possible physical pain or uncomfortable circumstances (2:22; 10:31; 14:5; 21:26,46), to a feeling of awe, especially in the presence of the supernatural (9:8; 14:27; 17:6-7; 27:54; 28:5,10), to sheer terror of someone with the power of life and death (10:28).

Within these parameters, fear can also be understood as a healthy understanding of who God is, His power, and what He demands from us (see Pr 1:7; 9:10). The unbeliever should tremble in terror before such a God, for He is the one who can "destroy both body and soul in hell" (Mt 10:28). But for the believer, such fear is replaced by a relationship in which perfect love can flourish (1 Jn 4:18; see Rm 8:15), though the awe or fear of God's greatness remains (2 Co 5:11; 7:1).

---

[a]**10:17** That is, local Jewish courts
[b]**10:22** Or *saved*
[c]**10:24** Or *student*
[d]**10:25** Term of slander variously interpreted, "lord of flies," "lord of dung," or "ruler of demons" (cf. 2 Kg 1:2)
[e]**10:27** Lit *in the ear*

hell.[a] [29] Aren't two sparrows sold for a penny?[b] Yet not one of them falls to the ground without your Father's consent.[c] [30] But even the hairs of your head have all been counted. [31] Don't be afraid therefore; you are worth more than many sparrows.

ACKNOWLEDGING CHRIST

[32] "Therefore, everyone who will acknowledge Me before men, I will also acknowledge Him before My Father in heaven. [33] But whoever denies Me before men, I will also deny him before My Father in heaven. [34] Don't assume that I came to bring peace on the earth. I did not come to bring peace, but a sword. [35] For I came to turn

**A man against his father,
a daughter against her mother,
a daughter-in-law against her
mother-in-law;**
[36] **and a man's enemies will be the members
of his household.**[d]

[37] The person who loves father or mother more than Me is not worthy of Me; the person who loves son or daughter more than Me is not worthy of Me. [38] And whoever doesn't take up his cross and follow[e] Me is not worthy of Me. [39] Anyone finding[f] his life will lose it, and anyone losing[g] his life because of Me will find it.

A CUP OF COLD WATER

[40] "The one who welcomes you welcomes Me, and the one who welcomes Me welcomes Him who sent Me. [41] Anyone who[h] welcomes a prophet because he is a prophet[i] will receive a prophet's reward. And anyone who[h] welcomes a righteous person because he's righteous[j] will receive a righteous person's reward. [42] And whoever gives just a cup of cold water to one of these little ones because he is a disciple[k]—I assure you: He will never lose his reward!"

Yielding Control Yields Real Results

Oh, that we would discover the difference when we let God be the Head of the church. He will accomplish more in six months through a people yielded to Him than we could do in sixty years without Him.

"Anyone finding his life will lose it, and anyone losing his life because of Me will find it."

—Matthew 10:39

---

[a] **10:28** Gk *gehenna*
[b] **10:29** Gk *assarion,* a small copper coin
[c] **10:29** Lit *ground apart from your Father*
[d] **10:35,36** Mc 7:6
[e] **10:38** Lit *follow after*
[f] **10:39** Or *The one who finds*
[g] **10:39** Or *the one who loses*
[h] **10:41** Or *the one who*
[i] **10:41** Lit *a prophet in the name of a prophet . . .*
[j] **10:41** Lit *a righteous person in the name of a righteous person*
[k] **10:42** Lit *little ones in the name of a disciple*

IN PRAISE OF JOHN THE BAPTIST

11 When Jesus had finished giving orders to His twelve disciples, He moved on from there to teach and preach in their towns. ² When John heard in prison what the Messiah[a] was doing, he sent a message[b] by his disciples ³ and asked Him, "Are You the Coming One, or should we expect someone else?"

⁴ Jesus replied to them, "Go and report to John what you hear and see: ⁵ the blind see, the lame walk, lepers are cleansed, the deaf hear, the dead are raised, and the poor are told the good news. ⁶ And if anyone is not offended because of Me, he is blessed."

⁷ As these men went away, Jesus began to speak to the crowds about John: "What did you go out into the wilderness to see? A reed swaying in the wind? ⁸ What then did you go out to see? A man dressed in soft clothes? Look, those who wear soft clothes are in kings' palaces. ⁹ But what did you go out to see? A prophet? Yes, I tell you, and far more than a prophet. ¹⁰ This is the one of whom it is written:

> **Look, I am sending My messenger ahead of You;[c]**
> **He will prepare Your way before You.[d]**

¹¹ "I assure you: Among those born of women no one greater than John the Baptist has appeared,[e] but the least in the kingdom of heaven is greater than he. ¹² From the days of John the Baptist until now, the kingdom of heaven has been suffering violence,[f] and the violent have been seizing it by force. ¹³ For all the prophets and the law prophesied until John; ¹⁴ if you're willing to accept it, he is the Elijah who is to come. ¹⁵ Anyone who has ears[1] should listen!

AN UNRESPONSIVE GENERATION

¹⁶ "To what should I compare this generation? It's like children sitting in the marketplaces who call out to each other:

[1]11:15 Other mss add *to hear*

---

[a]11:2 Or *the Christ*
[b]11:2 *a message* supplied for clarity
[c]11:10 Lit *messenger before Your face*
[d]11:10 Mal 3:1
[e]11:11 Lit *arisen*
[f]11:12 Or *has been forcefully advancing*

WORD STUDY

Greek word: **_angelos_**
[ahn geh LAHSS]
Translation: **_messenger_**
Uses in Matthew's Gospel: **20** (Mk, 6; Lk, 25; Jn, 3)
Uses in the NT: **175**
Key passage: **Matthew 11:10**

The Greek noun *angelos* is related to the verb *angello,* which means *proclaim* or *announce.* Thus an *angelos* is a *proclaimer* or *messenger,* and the term can refer to human or celestial beings. In the vast majority of cases in the NT, *angelos* refers to a celestial being, an *angel.* A few times, human beings are in view, such as John the Baptist (Mt 11:10; Mk 1:2; Lk 7:27), his disciples (Lk 7:24), and Jesus' disciples (Lk 9:52). Each reference in the Gospels to John the Baptist as an *angelos* follows the Greek OT and is a quote of Malachi 3:1, where the Hebrew word *mal'ak* is used for "messenger," a term referring to humans much more often in the OT than *angelos* does in the NT. The final example in the NT of *angelos* used of men is in James 2:25 in reference to Joshua's spies (see Jos 6:25; in the Hb text, *mal'ak* is used here also).

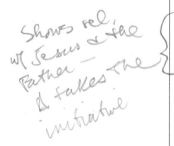

people are so fickle

[17] 'We played the flute for you,
   but you didn't dance;
   we sang a lament,
   but you didn't mourn!'[a]

[18] For John did not come eating or drinking, and they say, 'He has a demon!' [19] The Son of Man came eating and drinking, and they say, 'Look, a glutton and a drunkard, a friend of tax collectors and sinners!' Yet wisdom is vindicated[b] by her deeds."[1]

[20] Then He proceeded to denounce the towns where most of His miracles were done, because they did not repent: [21] "Woe to you, Chorazin! Woe to you, Bethsaida! For if the miracles that were done in you had been done in Tyre and Sidon, they would have repented in sackcloth and ashes long ago! [22] But I tell you, it will be more tolerable for Tyre and Sidon on the day of judgment than for you. [23] And you, Capernaum, will you be exalted to heaven? You will go down to Hades.[cd] For if the miracles that were done in you had been done in Sodom, it would have remained until today. [24] But I tell you, it will be more tolerable for the land of Sodom on the day of judgment than for you."

THE SON GIVES KNOWLEDGE AND REST

[25] At that time Jesus said, "I praise[e] You, Father, Lord of heaven and earth, because You have hidden these things from the wise and learned and revealed them to infants. [26] Yes, Father, because this was Your good pleasure.[f] [27] All things have been entrusted to Me by My Father. No one knows[g] the Son except the Father, and no one knows[g] the Father except the Son and anyone to whom the Son desires[h] to reveal Him.

[28] "Come to Me, all you who are weary and burdened, and I will give you rest. [29] Take My yoke upon you and learn from Me, because I am gentle and humble in heart, and you will find rest for your souls. [30] For My yoke is easy and My burden is light."

God Wants a Relationship with You

If we are to have any relationship with Him or His Son, God will have to take the initiative. This is exactly what He does. God draws us to Himself.

"All things have been entrusted to Me by My Father. No one knows the Son except the Father, and no one knows the Father except the Son and anyone to whom the Son desires to reveal Him."

—Matthew 11:27

Shows rel w/ Jesus & the Father — & takes the initiative

[1]11:19 Other mss read *children*

[a]11:17 Or *beat your breasts*
[b]11:19 Or *declared right*
[c]11:23 The Gk word for the place of the dead corresponding to the OT Hb word *Sheol*
[d]11:23 Is 14:13,15

[e]11:25 Or *thank*
[f]11:26 Lit *was well-pleasing in Your sight*
[g]11:27 Or *knows exactly*
[h]11:27 Or *wills* or *chooses*

LORD OF THE SABBATH

12 At that time Jesus passed through the grainfields on the Sabbath. His disciples were hungry and began to pick and eat some heads of grain. [2] But when the Pharisees saw it, they said to Him, "Look, Your disciples are doing what is not lawful to do on the Sabbath!"

[3] He said to them, "Haven't you read what David did when he was hungry, and those who were with him— [4] how he entered the house of God, and they ate[1] the sacred bread,[a] which is not lawful for him or for those with him to eat, but only for the priests? [5] Or haven't you read in the law[b] that on Sabbath days the priests in the temple violate the Sabbath and are guiltless? [6] But I tell you that something greater than the temple is here! [7] If you had known what this means: **'I desire mercy and not sacrifice,'**[c] you would not have condemned the guiltless. [8] For the Son of Man is Lord of the Sabbath."

THE MAN WITH THE PARALYZED HAND

[9] Moving on from there, He entered their synagogue. [10] There He saw a man who had a paralyzed hand. And in order to accuse Him they asked Him, "Is it lawful to heal on the Sabbath?"

[11] But He said to them, "What man among you, if he had a sheep[d] that fell into a pit on the Sabbath, wouldn't take hold of it and lift it out? [12] A man is worth far more than a sheep, so it is lawful to do good on the Sabbath."

[13] Then He told the man, "Stretch out your hand." So he stretched it out, and it was restored, as good as the other. [14] But the Pharisees went out and plotted against Him, how they might destroy Him.

THE SERVANT OF THE LORD

[15] When Jesus became aware of this, He withdrew from there. Huge crowds[2] followed Him, and He healed them all. [16] He warned them not to make Him known,

Take Your Obedience to the Next Level

God expects us to obey more than the letter of the law. When we follow the ways of God, He will take us far beyond the usual and expected.

But He said to them, "What man among you, if he had a sheep that fell into a pit on the Sabbath, wouldn't take hold of it and lift it out? A man is worth far more than a sheep, so it is lawful to do good on the Sabbath."

—Matthew 12:11–12

[1] **12:4** Other mss read *He ate*
[2] **12:15** Other mss read *Many*

[a] **12:4** These were twelve loaves, representing the twelve tribes of Israel, put on the table in the holy place in the tabernacle and later in the temple. The priests ate the previous week's loaves. See Ex 29:32; Lv 24:5.
[b] **12:5** That is, the Torah (Pentateuch)
[c] **12:7** Hs 6:6
[d] **12:11** Or *had one sheep*

WORD STUDY

Greek word: ***blasphemia***
[blahss fay MEE uh]

Translation: ***blasphemy***

Uses in Matthew's Gospel: **4**
(Mk, 3; Lk, 1; Jn, 1)

Uses in the NT: **18**

Key passage: **Matthew 12:31**

The Greek noun *blasphemia* comes from a compound verb *(blasphemeo)*, meaning *to speak evil against (blas, evil; phemi, to speak), to slander, to revile.* In the NT blasphemy is an extremely serious offense and is primarily against God (Mt 9:3; 26:65), Christ (Lk 22:65), or anything related to either Person (1 Tm 6:1; Ti 2:5; Jms 2:7). Blasphemy can also be directed against angels (2 Pt 2:10; Jd 8) and human beings (Rm 3:8; 1 Co 4:13; 10:30; Ti 3:2). Jesus told the Jewish religious leaders that the most grievous sin, one that cannot be forgiven, is blasphemy against the Holy Spirit (Mt 12:31-32). Apparently, they were in danger of committing this sin, or perhaps already had, for Jesus' warning was in response to their claim that He cast out demons through the power of Satan (Mt 12:24) and that Jesus Himself was demon-possessed (Mk 3:30).

[17] so that what was spoken through the prophet Isaiah might be fulfilled:

> [18] **Here is My Servant whom I have chosen,**
> **My beloved in whom My soul delights;**
> **I will put My Spirit on Him,**
> **and He will proclaim justice to the nations.**
> [19] **He will not argue or shout,**
> **and no one will hear His voice in the streets.**
> [20] **He will not break a bruised reed,**
> **and He will not put out a smoldering wick,**
> **until He has led justice to victory.**[a]
> [21] **The nations will hope in His name.**[b]

A HOUSE DIVIDED

[22] Then a demon-possessed man who was blind and unable to speak was brought to Him. He healed him, so that the man[c] both spoke and saw. [23] And all the crowds were astounded and said, "Perhaps this is the Son of David!"

[24] When the Pharisees heard this, they said, "The man drives out demons only by Beelzebul,[d] the ruler of the demons."

[25] Knowing their thoughts, He told them: "Every kingdom divided against itself is headed for destruction, and no city or house divided against itself will stand. [26] If Satan drives out Satan, he is divided against himself. How then will his kingdom stand? [27] And if I drive out demons by Beelzebul, by whom do your sons drive them out? For this reason they will be your judges. [28] If I drive out demons by the Spirit of God, then the kingdom of God has come to you. [29] How can someone enter a strong man's house and steal his possessions unless he first ties up the strong man? Then he can rob his house. [30] Anyone who is not with Me is against Me, and anyone who does not gather with Me scatters. [31] Because of this, I tell you, people will be forgiven every sin and blasphemy, but the blasphemy against[e] the Spirit will not

---

[a]**12:20** Or *until He has successfully put forth justice*
[b]**12:18-21** Is 42:1-4
[c]**12:22** Lit *the mute*
[d]**12:24** See 10:25 note
[e]**12:31** Or *blasphemy of*

be forgiven.[1] [32] Whoever speaks a word against the Son of Man, it will be forgiven him. But whoever speaks against the Holy Spirit, it will not be forgiven him, either in this age or in the one to come.

A TREE AND ITS FRUIT

[33] "Either make the tree good and its fruit good, or make the tree bad[a] and its fruit bad; for a tree is known by its fruit. [34] Brood of vipers! How can you speak good things when you are evil? For the mouth speaks from the overflow of the heart. [35] A good man produces good things from his storeroom of good,[2] and an evil man produces evil things from his storeroom of evil. [36] I tell you that on the day of judgment people will have to account for every careless word they speak.[b] [37] For by your words you will be acquitted, and by your words you will be condemned."

THE SIGN OF JONAH

[38] Then some of the scribes and Pharisees said to Him, "Teacher, we want to see a sign from You."

[39] But He answered them, "An evil and adulterous generation demands a sign, but no sign will be given to it except the sign of the prophet Jonah. [40] For as Jonah was in the belly of the great fish three days and three nights,[c] so the Son of Man will be in the heart of the earth three days and three nights. [41] The men of Nineveh will stand up at the judgment with this generation and condemn it, because they repented at Jonah's proclamation; and look—something greater than Jonah is here! [42] The queen of the south will rise up at the judgment with this generation and condemn it, because she came from the ends of the earth to hear the wisdom of Solomon; and look—something greater than Solomon is here!

AN UNCLEAN SPIRIT'S RETURN

[43] "When an unclean[d] spirit comes out of a man, it roams through waterless places looking for rest, but

Your Life Is a Walking Testimony

How you live your life is a testimony of what you believe about God.

"Either make the tree good and its fruit good, or make the tree bad and its fruit bad; for a tree is known by its fruit."
—Matthew 12:33

Discipline Yourself to Speak Careful Words

Think carefully about the words that come from your mouth. Christians should speak only words that uplift and bring grace to others.

"I tell you that on the day of judgment people will have to account for every careless word they speak."
—Matthew 12:36

[1]12:31 Other mss read *forgiven people*
[2]12:35 Other mss read *from the storehouse of his heart*

[a]12:33 Lit *rotten, decayed*   [c]12:40 Jnh 1:17
[b]12:36 Lit *will speak*   [d]12:43 See 10:1 note

Streams of living water?

doesn't find any. [44] Then it says, 'I'll go back to my house that I came from.' And when it arrives, it finds the house[a] vacant, swept, and put in order. [45] Then off it goes and brings with it seven other spirits more evil than itself, and they enter and settle down there. As a result, that man's last condition is worse than the first. That's how it will also be with this evil generation."

TRUE RELATIONSHIPS

[46] He was still speaking to the crowds when suddenly His mother and brothers were standing outside wanting to speak to Him. [47] And someone told Him, "Look, Your mother and Your brothers are standing outside, wanting to speak to You."[1]

[48] But He replied to the one who told Him, "Who is My mother and who are My brothers?" [49] And stretching out His hand toward His disciples, He said, "Here are My mother and My brothers! [50] For whoever does the will of My Father in heaven, that person is My brother and sister and mother."

THE PARABLE OF THE SOWER

13 On that day Jesus went out of the house and was sitting by the sea. [2] Such large crowds gathered around Him that He got into a boat and sat down, while the whole crowd stood on the shore.

[3] Then He told them many things in parables, saying: "Consider the sower who went out to sow. [4] As he was sowing, some seeds fell along the path, and the birds came and ate them up. [5] Others fell on rocky ground, where they didn't have much soil, and they sprang up quickly since they had no deep soil. [6] But when the sun came up they were scorched, and since they had no root, they withered. [7] Others fell among thorns, and the thorns came up and choked them. [8] Still others fell on good ground, and produced a crop: some a hundred, some sixty, and some thirty times what was sown.[b] [9] Anyone who has ears[2] should listen!"

[1] 12:47 Other mss omit this verse
[2] 13:9 Other mss add to hear

[a] 12:44 the house implied   [b] 13:8 what was sown is implied

---

Never Grow Tired of Walking with God

The constant presence of God is the most practical part of your life and ministry.

"'For this people's heart has grown callous; their ears are hard of hearing and they have shut their eyes; otherwise they might see with their eyes and hear with their ears, understand with their hearts and turn back—and I would cure them.' But your eyes are blessed because they do see, and your ears because they do hear!"

—Matthew 13:15–16

WHY JESUS USED PARABLES

[10] Then the disciples came up and asked Him, "Why do You speak to them in parables?"

[11] He answered them, "To know the secrets[a] of the kingdom of heaven has been granted to you, but to them it has not been granted. [12] For whoever has, more[b] will be given to him, and he will have more than enough. But whoever does not have, even what he has will be taken away from him. [13] For this reason I speak to them in parables, because looking they do not see, and hearing they do not listen or understand. [14] In them the prophecy of Isaiah is fulfilled that says:

> You will listen and listen,
> yet never understand;
> and you will look and look,
> yet never perceive.
> [15] For this people's heart has grown callous;
> their ears are hard of hearing,
> and they have shut their eyes;
> otherwise they might see with their eyes
> and hear with their ears,
> understand with their hearts
> and turn back—and I would cure them.[c]

[16] "But your eyes are blessed because they do see, and your ears because they do hear! [17] For I assure you: Many prophets and righteous people longed to see the things you see, yet didn't see them; to hear the things you hear, yet didn't hear them.

THE PARABLE OF THE SOWER EXPLAINED

[18] "You, then, listen to the parable of the sower: [19] When anyone hears the word[d] about the kingdom and doesn't understand it, the evil one comes and snatches away what was sown in his heart. This is the one sown along the path. [20] And the one sown on rocky ground— this is one who hears the word and immediately receives it with joy. [21] Yet he has no root in himself, but is short-lived. When pressure or persecution comes because of

WORD STUDY

Greek word: **parabole**
[pa rah bah LAY]

Translation: **parable**

Uses in Matthew's Gospel: **17**
(Mk, 13; Lk, 18)

Uses in the NT: **50**

Key passage: **Matthew 13:10-17**

The Greek noun *parabole* comes from the verb *paraballo*, which literally means *to throw alongside;* thus, a *parabole* is that which is figuratively placed next to something else for the purpose of illustration. A parable, then, is an extended simile ("this is like") in which a simple comparison is turned into a story (sometimes an elaborate one) with setting, characters, and significant events. The parable was Jesus' favorite method of illustrating His teachings, and only He used parables in the Gospels. With two exceptions (Heb 9:9; 11:19), *parabole* occurs only in the Synoptic Gospels. The purpose of Jesus' parables was two-fold: to reveal the truth about Jesus and the kingdom to people of faith; and to conceal the truth about Jesus and the kingdom from people without faith (see Mt 13:10-17).

he comes to steal, kill & destroy

---

[a] **13:11** The Gk word *musterion* does not mean "mystery" in the Eng sense, but things that we can know only by divine revelation, or *a secret*, as here.

[b] **13:12** *more* is added for clarity

[c] **13:15** Is 6:9–10

[d] **13:18** Gk *logos (word, message, saying, thing)*

the word, immediately he stumbles. ²²Now the one sown among the thorns—this is one who hears the word, but the worries of this age and the pleasure of wealth choke the word, and it becomes unfruitful. ²³But the one sown on the good ground—this is one who hears and understands the word, who does bear fruit and produce: some a hundred, some sixty, some thirty times what was sown.''

THE PARABLE OF THE WHEAT AND THE WEEDS

²⁴He presented another parable to them: ''The kingdom of heaven may be compared to a man who sowed good seed in his field. ²⁵But while people were sleeping, his enemy came, sowed weeds[a] among the wheat, and left. ²⁶When the plants sprouted and produced grain, then the weeds also appeared. ²⁷The landowner's slaves came to him and said, 'Master, didn't you sow good seed in your field? Then where did the weeds come from?'

²⁸ '' 'An enemy did this!' he told them.

'' 'So, do you want us to go and gather them up?' the slaves asked him.

²⁹ '' 'No,' he said. 'When you gather up the weeds, you might also uproot the wheat with them. ³⁰Let both grow together until the harvest. At harvest time I'll tell the reapers, "Gather the weeds first and tie them in bundles to burn them, but store the wheat in my barn." ' ''

THE PARABLES OF THE MUSTARD SEED AND OF THE YEAST

³¹He presented another parable to them: ''The kingdom of heaven is like a mustard seed that a man took and sowed in his field. ³²It's the smallest of all the seeds, but when grown, it's taller than the vegetables and becomes a tree, so that the birds of the sky come and nest in its branches.''[b]

³³He told them another parable: ''The kingdom of heaven is like yeast that a woman took and mixed into three measures[c] of flour until it spread through all of it.''[d]

Stay alert! The enemy prowls like a lion seeking whom he may devour

Are Your Orders Coming from God?

If you are experiencing a time of fruitlessness right now, you may be trying to do things on your own that God has not initiated.

''But the one sown on the good ground—this is one who hears and understands the word, who does bear fruit and produce: some a hundred, some sixty, some thirty times what was sown.''

—Matthew 13:23

---

[a]13:25 Or *darnel*, a weed similar in appearance to wheat in the early stages
[b]13:32 Ezk 17:23
[c]13:33 Lit *three sata*, about forty quarts
[d]13:33 Or *until all of it was leavened*

USING PARABLES FULFILLS PROPHECY

³⁴Jesus told the crowds all these things in parables, and He would not speak anything to them without a parable, ³⁵so that what was spoken through the prophet might be fulfilled:

I will open My mouth in parables;
I will declare things kept secret from the
foundation of the world.ᵃ

JESUS INTERPRETS THE WHEAT AND THE WEEDS

³⁶Then He dismissed the crowds and went into the house. And His disciples approached Him and said, "Explain the parable of the weeds in the field to us."
³⁷He replied: "The One who sows the good seed is the Son of Man; ³⁸the field is the world; and the good seed—these are the sons of the kingdom. The weeds are the sons of the evil one, and ³⁹the enemy who sowed them is the Devil. The harvest is the end of the age, and the harvesters are angels. ⁴⁰Therefore just as the weeds are gathered and burned in the fire, so it will be at the end of the age. ⁴¹The Son of Man will send out His angels, and they will gather from His kingdom everything that causes sinᵇ and those guilty of lawlessness.ᶜ ⁴²They will throw them into the blazing furnace where there will be weeping and gnashing of teeth. ⁴³Then the righteous will shine like the sun in their Father's kingdom. Anyone who has ears¹ should listen!

THE PARABLES OF THE HIDDEN TREASURE AND OF THE PRICELESS PEARL

⁴⁴"The kingdom of heaven is like treasure, buried in a field, that a man found and reburied. Then in his joy he goes and sells everything he has and buys that field.
⁴⁵"Again, the kingdom of heaven is like a merchant in search of fine pearls. ⁴⁶When he found one pricelessᵈ pearl, he went and sold everything he had, and bought it.

¹13:43 Other mss add *to hear*

ᵃ13:35 Ps 78:2
ᵇ13:41 Or *causes stumbling*
ᶜ13:41 Or *those who do lawlessness*
ᵈ13:46 Or *very precious*

He really wanted His disciples to understand

Expect a Word from the Lord

When God speaks to you by the Holy Spirit through the Bible, prayer, circumstances, and the church, you will know it is God, and you will know what He is saying.

"'I will open my mouth in parables; I will declare things kept secret from the foundation of the world.'"

—Matthew 13:35b

THE PARABLE OF THE NET

[47] "Again, the kingdom of heaven is like a large net thrown into the sea. It collected every kind of fish,[a] [48] and when it was full, they dragged it ashore, sat down, and gathered the good fish[a] into containers, but threw out the worthless ones. [49] So it will be at the end of the age. The angels will go out, separate the evil who are among the righteous, [50] and throw them into the blazing furnace. In that place there will be weeping and gnashing of teeth.

THE STOREHOUSE OF TRUTH

[51] "Have you understood all these things?" [1]

"Yes," they told Him.

[52] "Therefore," He said to them, "every student of Scripture[b] instructed in the kingdom of heaven is like a landowner who brings out of his storeroom what is new and what is old." [53] When Jesus had finished these parables, He left there.

REJECTION AT NAZARETH

[54] Having come to His hometown, He began to teach them in their synagogue, so that they were astonished and said, "How did this wisdom and these miracles come to Him? [55] Isn't this the carpenter's son? Isn't His mother called Mary, and His brothers James, Joseph,[2] Simon, and Judas? [56] And His sisters, aren't they all with us? So where does He get all these things?" [57] And they were offended by Him.

But Jesus said to them, "A prophet is not without honor except in his hometown and in his household." [58] And He did not do many miracles there because of their unbelief.

JOHN THE BAPTIST BEHEADED

14 At that time Herod the tetrarch[c] heard the report about Jesus. [2] "This is John the Baptist!" he told his servants. "He has been raised from the dead, and that's why these powers are working in him."

[1] **13:51** Other mss add *Jesus asked them*
[2] **13:55** Other mss read *Joses*. See Mk 6:3

[a] **13:47, 48** *fish* supplied
[b] **13:52** Or *every scribe*
[c] **14:1** That is, Herod Antipas, son of Herod the Great, who ruled one fourth of his father's kingdom under Rome

---

God's Voice Is Ever True, Ever Fresh

God speaks through the Holy Spirit. The Holy Spirit will teach you all things, will call to your memory the things Jesus said, will guide you into all truth, will speak what He hears from the Father, will tell you what is yet to come, and will glorify Christ as He reveals Christ to you.

"Therefore," He said to them, "every student of Scripture instructed in the kingdom of heaven is like a landowner who brings out of his storeroom what is new and what is old."

—Matthew 13:52

handwritten: 2nd building block of faith?

handwritten: Staying in the middle of the Impossible

³ For Herod had arrested John, chained[a] him, and put him in prison on account of Herodias, his brother Philip's wife, ⁴ because John had been telling him, "It's not lawful for you to have her!" ⁵ Though he wanted to kill him, he feared the crowd, since they regarded him as a prophet.

⁶ But when Herod's birthday celebration came, Herodias's daughter danced before them[b] and pleased Herod. ⁷ So he promised with an oath to give her whatever she might ask. ⁸ And prompted by her mother, she answered, "Give me John the Baptist's head here on a platter!" ⁹ Although the king regretted it, he commanded that it be granted because of his oaths and his guests. ¹⁰ So he sent orders and had John beheaded in the prison. ¹¹ His head was brought on a platter and given to the girl, who carried it to her mother. ¹² Then his disciples came, removed the corpse,[1] buried it, and went and reported to Jesus.

FEEDING FIVE THOUSAND

handwritten: again He withdrew

¹³ When Jesus heard about it, He withdrew from there by boat to a remote place to be alone. When the crowds heard this, they followed Him on foot from the towns. ¹⁴ As He stepped ashore,[c] He saw a huge crowd, felt compassion for them, and healed their sick.

¹⁵ When evening came, the disciples approached Him and said, "This place is a wilderness, and the hour is already late.[d] Send the crowds away so they can go into the villages and buy food for themselves."

¹⁶ "They don't need to go away," Jesus told them. "You give them something to eat."

¹⁷ "But we only have five loaves and two fish here," they said to Him.

¹⁸ "Bring them here to Me," He said. ¹⁹ Then He commanded the crowds to sit down[e] on the grass. He took the five loaves and the two fish, and looking up to heaven, He blessed them. He broke the loaves and gave them to the disciples, and the disciples gave them[f] to the crowds. ²⁰ Everyone ate and was filled. Then they

¹**14:12** Other mss read *body*

---

[a]**14:3** Or *bound*
[b]**14:6** Lit *danced in the middle*
[c]**14:14** Lit *Coming out* (of the boat)

[d]**14:15** Lit *the time* (for the evening meal) *has already passed*
[e]**14:19** Lit *to recline*
[f]**14:19** *gave them* implied

People Will Notice God's Work in You

When God's people and the world see something happen that only God can do, they come to know God.

They were astonished and said, "How did this wisdom and these miracles come to Him? Isn't this the carpenter's son? Isn't His mother called Mary, and His brothers James, Joseph, Simon, and Judas? And His sisters, aren't they all with us? So where does He get all these things?"
—Matthew 13:54b–56

Don't Avoid the Impossible

Christ will lead you into many situations that will seem impossible. But stay in the middle of them, for that is where you will experience God.

"But we only have five loaves and two fish here," they said to Him. "Bring them here to Me," He said.
—Matthew 14:17–18

handwritten: Jesus is resp. for breaking + distr. the bread bring Him what you have + He will multiply it.

handwritten: When Jesus is @ the center of activity, everyone is filled.

35

WORD STUDY

Greek word: **phantasma**
[FAN tahss mah]

Translation: **ghost**

Uses in Matthew's Gospel: **1**
(Mk, 1)

Uses in the NT: **2**

Key passage: **Matthew 14:26**

The Greek noun *phantasma* comes from a verb *(phantazomai)* meaning *to appear* or *make visible.* This word group normally refers to things like visions, dreams, mental images, and other phenomena that are products of the imagination. Not surprisingly, this Greek root became the basis for English words like *phantasm, phantom, fancy, fantasy,* and *fantastic.*

The word *phantasma* means *ghost* or *apparition* and occurs only twice in the NT parallel accounts of Jesus' walking on the water found in Matthew (14:26) and Mark (6:49). Luke does not record this miracle, and John only states that the disciples were frightened when they saw Jesus. The disciples' use of the term *phantasma* may indicate that they were somewhat superstitious. Watching Jesus walk on water made them decide that they were seeing a disembodied spirit—one that probably meant them harm. Jesus assured them that such was not the case, and the disciples worshiped Him when He reached the boat. A similar incident occurred after Jesus' resurrection, and this time the term *pneuma* ("spirit") is used (see Lk 24:36-40).

picked up twelve baskets full of leftover pieces! [21] Now those who ate were about five thousand men, besides women and children.

WALKING ON THE WATER

[22] Immediately He[1] made the disciples get into the boat and go ahead of Him to the other side, while He dismissed the crowds. [23] After dismissing the crowds, He went up on the mountain by Himself to pray. When evening came, He was there alone. [24] But the boat was already over a mile from land,[2] battered by the waves, because the wind was against them. [25] Around three in the morning,[a] He came toward them walking on the sea. [26] When the disciples saw Him walking on the sea, they were terrified. "It's a ghost!" they said, and cried out in fear.

[27] Immediately Jesus spoke to them. "Have courage! It is I. Don't be afraid."

[28] "Lord, if it's You," Peter answered Him, "command me to come to You on the water."

[29] "Come!" He said.

And climbing out of the boat, Peter started walking on the water and came toward Jesus. [30] But when he saw the strength of the wind,[3] he was afraid. And beginning to sink he cried out, "Lord, save me!"

[31] Immediately Jesus reached out His hand, caught hold of him, and said to him, "You of little faith, why did you doubt?" [32] When they got into the boat, the wind ceased. [33] Then those in the boat worshiped Him and said, "Truly You are the Son of God!"

MIRACULOUS HEALINGS

[34] Once they crossed over, they came to land at Gennesaret. [35] When the men of that place recognized Him, they alerted[b] the whole vicinity and brought to Him all who were sick. [36] They were begging Him that they might only touch the tassel on His robe.[c] And as many as touched it were made perfectly well.

[1]14:22 Other mss read *Jesus*
[2]14:24 Other mss read *in the middle of the sea;* lit *many stadios; stadios* = six hundred feet.
[3]14:30 Other mss read *He saw the wind*

---

[a]14:25 Lit *fourth watch of the night:* from three to six in the morning
[b]14:35 Lit *sent into*
[c]14:36 See 9:20 note

THE TRADITION OF THE ELDERS

15 Then Pharisees and scribes came from Jerusalem to Jesus and asked, [2] "Why do Your disciples break the tradition of the elders? For they don't wash their hands when they eat!"[a]

[3] He answered them, "And why do you break God's commandment because of your tradition? [4] For God said:[1]

> Honor your father and your mother;[b] and,
> The one who speaks evil of father or
>   mother must be put to death.[c]

[5] But you say, 'Whoever tells his father or mother, "Whatever benefit you might have received from me is a gift committed to the temple"[d]— [6] he does not have to honor his father.'[2] In this way, you have revoked God's word[3] because of your tradition. [7] Hypocrites! Isaiah prophesied correctly about you when he said:

> [8] This people[4] honors Me with their lips,
>   but their heart is far from Me.
> [9] They worship Me in vain,
>   teaching as doctrines the commands of
>   men."[e]

DEFILEMENT IS FROM WITHIN

[10] Summoning the crowd, He told them, "Listen and understand: [11] It's not what goes into the mouth that defiles a man, but what comes out of the mouth, this defiles a man."

[12] Then the disciples came up and told Him, "Do You know that the Pharisees took offense when they heard this statement?"

[13] He replied, "Every plant that My heavenly Father didn't plant will be uprooted. [14] Leave them alone! They

honoring the traditions of men vs. G's Word.

Obedience Is a Step Toward the Impossible

When God calls a person to join Him in a God-sized task, faith is always required. Obedience indicates faith in God.

"Lord, if it's You," Peter answered Him, "command me to come to You on the water." "Come!" He said. And climbing out of the boat, Peter started walking on the water and came toward Jesus.

—Matthew 14:28–29

Jesus' words are spirit + life.

---

[1] **15:4** Other mss read *commanded, saying*
[2] **15:6** Other mss read *then he does not have to honor his father or mother.*
[3] **15:6** Other mss read *commandment*
[4] **15:8** Other mss add *draws near to Me with their mouths, and*

---

[a] **15:2** Lit *eat bread,* that is, eat a meal
[b] **15:4** Ex 20:12; Dt 5:16
[c] **15:4** Ex 21:17; Lv 20:9
[d] **15:5** *committed to the temple* implied
[e] **15:8,9** Is 29:13, LXX

are blind guides.[1] And if the blind guide the blind, both will fall into a pit."

[15] Then Peter replied to Him, "Explain this parable to us."

[16] "Are even you still lacking in understanding?" He[2] asked. [17] "Don't you realize[3] that whatever goes into the mouth passes into the stomach and is eliminated?[a] [18] But what comes out of the mouth comes from the heart, and these defile a man. [19] For from the heart come evil thoughts, murders, adulteries, sexual immoralities, thefts, false testimonies, blasphemies. [20] These are the things that defile a man, but eating with unwashed hands does not defile a man."

A GENTILE MOTHER'S FAITH

[21] When Jesus left there, He withdrew to the area of Tyre and Sidon. [22] Just then a Canaanite woman from that region came and kept crying out,[4] "Have mercy on me, Lord, Son of David! My daughter is cruelly tormented by a demon."

[23] Yet He did not say a word to her. So His disciples approached Him and urged Him, "Send her away, because she cries out after us."[b]

[24] He replied, "I was sent only to the lost sheep of the house of Israel."

[25] But she came, knelt before Him, and said, "Lord, help me!"

[26] He answered, "It isn't right to take the children's bread and throw it to their dogs."

[27] "Yes, Lord," she said, "yet even the dogs eat the crumbs that fall from their masters' table!"

[28] Then Jesus replied to her, "Woman, your faith is great. Let it be done for you as you want." And from that moment[c] her daughter was cured.

Worry More About Worship Than Words

If you have a heart that is truly grateful for your own salvation, you will find yourself sharing the good news about Christ more often.

"But what comes out of the mouth comes from the heart . . ."

—Matthew 15:18a

Life Has Its Problems, Faith Has the Victory

Faith keeps you in a trusting relationship with God in the midst of your problems. Faith has to do with your relationship with God, not your circumstances.

Then Jesus replied to her, "Woman, your faith is great. Let it be done for you as you want." And from that moment, her daughter was cured.

—Matthew 15:28

---

[1] **15:14** Other mss add *for the blind*
[2] **15:16** Other mss read *Jesus*
[3] **15:17** Other mss add *yet*
[4] **15:22** Other mss read *cried out to Him*

---

[a] **15:17** Lit *and goes out into the toilet*

[b] **15:23** Lit *she is yelling behind us* or *after us*
[c] **15:28** Lit *hour*

HEALING MANY PEOPLE

[29] Moving on from there, Jesus passed along the Sea of Galilee. He went up on a mountain and sat there, [30] and large crowds came to Him, having with them those who were lame, blind, deformed, unable to speak, and many others. They put them at His feet, and He healed them. [31] So the crowd was amazed when they saw those unable to speak talking, the deformed restored, the lame walking, and the blind seeing. And they gave glory to the God of Israel.

FEEDING THE FOUR THOUSAND

[32] Now Jesus summoned His disciples and said, "I have compassion on the crowd, because they've already stayed with Me three days and have nothing to eat. I don't want to send them away hungry; otherwise they might collapse on the way."

[33] The disciples said to Him, "Where could we get enough bread in this desolate place to fill such a crowd?"

[34] "How many loaves do you have?" Jesus asked them.

"Seven," they said, "and a few small fish."

[35] After commanding the crowd to sit down on the ground, [36] He took the seven loaves and the fish, and He gave thanks, broke them, and kept on giving them to the disciples, and the disciples gave them[a] to the crowds. [37] They all ate and were filled. Then they collected the leftover pieces—seven large baskets full. [38] Now those who ate were four thousand men, besides women and children. [39] After dismissing the crowds, He got into the boat and went to the region of Magadan.[1]

THE YEAST OF THE PHARISEES AND THE SADDUCEES

16 The Pharisees and Sadducees approached, and as a test, asked Him to show them a sign from heaven.

[2] He answered them: "When evening comes you say, 'It will be good weather, because the sky is red.' [3] And in the morning, 'Today will be stormy because the sky is red and threatening.' You[2] know how to read the appear-

[1] 15:39 Other mss read *Magdala*
[2] 16:3 Other mss read *Hypocrites! You*

---

[a] 15:36 *gave them* is understood

WORD STUDY

Greek word: **splanchnizomai**
[splahnk NEE zah migh]

Translation: **moved with compassion**

Uses in Matthew's Gospel: **5** (Mk, 4; Lk, 3)

Uses in the NT: **12**

Key passage: **Matthew 15:32**

The Greek word *splanchnizomai* is the verb form of the noun *splanchnon,* which literally means *bowel* and always occurs in the plural *(bowels).* In the ancient world the internal organs were considered the seat of emotions and feelings, so figuratively *splanchnon* referred to that part of a person that felt compassion, mercy, and tenderness. *Splanchnon* is used literally only in Acts 1:18 (Judas' suicide). The other ten occurrences, eight of them in Paul's letters, refer to the tender affections one person may have toward another. The verb *splanchnizomai* occurs only in the Synoptic Gospels and is always related to Jesus: He was moved with compassion to provide the people with leadership (Mt 9:36; Mk 6:34), to feed people (Mt 15:32; Mk 8:2), and to heal people (Mt 14:14; 20:34; Mk 1:41; Lk 7:13); others called on Him to show them compassion (Mk 9:22); and He used this term in parables to describe the forgiving king (Mt 18:27), the Good Samaritan (Lk 10:33), and the father of the prodigal (Lk 15:20).

Desiring the signs more than Him

WORD STUDY

Greek word: **Christos**
[KRIHSS tahss]

Translation: **Messiah**

Uses in Matthew's Gospel: **16**
(Mk, 7; Lk, 12; Jn, 19)

Uses in the NT: **529**

Key passage: **Matthew 16:16**

The Greek noun *christos* comes from the verb *chrio* meaning *to anoint*. The verb was used in the Greek OT for the Hebrew verb *mashach*, an anointing that was ceremonial and was most often reserved for those in a special religious office, such as a priest or a king. This Hebrew verb was also the word for "the anointed one," *ha mashiach*. In Greek this was *ho Christos*, literally "the Christ." Therefore, one can see that behind the Greek term *Christos* was the Hebrew term *Mashiach*, that is, "Messiah." In the majority of occurrences in the Gospels and Acts, *Christos* is best understood as representing the Hebrew term *Mashiach* and should be translated "Messiah" to bring this out (as in Peter's confession; Mt 16:16). Because Jesus of Nazareth was the Messiah, *Christos* eventually became, not just a title for Jesus, but another name for Him, as can be seen in the Epistles. The fact that Jesus was the Messiah is still present but not as prominent in passages where the word *Christos* occurs as a name; thus, it is appropriate to translate *Christos* as "Christ" in these instances, which are actually the vast majority in the NT.

ance of the sky, but you can't read the signs of the times.[1] [4] An evil and adulterous generation wants a sign, but no sign will be given to it except the sign of[2] Jonah." Then He left them and went away.

[5] When the disciples reached the other shore,[a] they had forgotten to take bread. [6] Then Jesus told them, "Watch out and beware of the yeast[b] of the Pharisees and Sadducees."

[7] And they discussed among themselves, "We didn't bring any bread!"

[8] Aware of this, Jesus said, "You of little faith! Why are you discussing among yourselves that you do not have bread? Don't you understand yet? Don't you remember the five loaves for the five thousand and how many baskets you collected? [10] Or the seven loaves for the four thousand and how many large baskets you collected? [11] Why is it you don't understand that when I told you, 'Beware of the yeast of the Pharisees and Sadducees,' it wasn't about bread?" [12] Then they understood that He did not tell them to beware of the yeast in bread, but of the teaching of the Pharisees and Sadducees.

PETER'S CONFESSION OF THE MESSIAH

[13] When Jesus came to the region of Caesarea Philippi,[c] He asked His disciples, "Who do people say that the Son of Man is?"[3]

[14] And they said, "Some say John the Baptist; others, Elijah; still others, Jeremiah or one of the prophets."

[15] "But you," He asked them, "who do you say that I am?"

[16] Simon Peter answered, "You are the Messiah,[d] the Son of the living God!"

[17] And Jesus responded, "Blessed are you, Simon son of Jonah,[e] because flesh and blood did not reveal this to you, but My Father in heaven. [18] And I also say to you that you are Peter,[f] and on this rock[f] I will build My

[1] **16:2-3** Other mss omit *When* (v. 2) through end of v. 3.
[2] **16:4** Other mss add *the prophet*
[3] **16:13** Other mss read *that I, the Son of Man, am*

[a] **16:5** Lit *disciples went to the other side*
[b] **16:6** Or *leaven*
[c] **16:13** A town north of Galilee at the base of Mt. Hermon

[d] **16:16** Or *the Christ*
[e] **16:17** Or *son of John*
[f] **16:18** *Peter* (Gk *Petros*) means a specific stone or rock; *rock* (Gk *petra*) means a rocky crag or bedrock.

church, and the forces[a] of Hades will not overpower it. [19] I will give you the keys of the kingdom of heaven, and whatever you bind on earth will have been bound[b] in heaven, and whatever you loose on earth will have been loosed[b] in heaven."

[20] And He gave the disciples orders to tell no one that He was[1] the Messiah.[c]

HIS DEATH AND RESURRECTION PREDICTED

[21] From then on Jesus began to point out to His disciples that He must go to Jerusalem and suffer many things from the elders, chief priests, and scribes, be killed, and be raised the third day. [22] Then Peter took Him aside and began to rebuke Him, "Oh no,[d] Lord! This will never happen to You!"

[23] But He turned and told Peter, "Get behind Me, Satan! You are an offense to Me, because you're not thinking about God's concerns,[e] but man's." *I want to be thinking about You*

TAKE UP YOUR CROSS

[24] Then Jesus said to His disciples, "If anyone wants to come with Me, he must deny himself, take up his cross, and follow Me. [25] For whoever wants to save his life[f] will lose it, but whoever loses his life[f] because of Me will find it. [26] What will it benefit a man if he gains the whole world yet loses his life?[f] Or what will a man give in exchange for his life?[f] [27] For the Son of Man is going to come with His angels in the glory of His Father, and then He will reward each according to what he has done. [28] I assure you: There are some of those standing here who will not taste death until they see the Son of Man coming in His kingdom."

THE TRANSFIGURATION

17 After six days Jesus took Peter, James, and his brother John, and led them up on a high mountain by themselves. [2] He was transformed[g] in front of

[1]16:20 Other mss add *Jesus*

[a]16:18 Lit *gates*
[b]16:19 Or *will be bound, will be loosed*
[c]16:20 Or *the Christ*
[d]16:22 Lit *Mercy to You! That is, May God have mercy on you*

[e]16:23 Lit *about the things of God*
[f]16:25,26 The same Gk word *(psyche)* can mean *life* or *soul.*
[g]17:2 Or *transfigured*

WORD STUDY

Greek word: **metamorphoo**
[meh tah mohr FAH oh]

Translation: **transform**

Uses in Matthew's Gospel: **1** (Mk, 1)

Uses in the NT: **4**

Key passage: **Matthew 17:2**

The Greek verb *metamorphoo* is a compound word from *meta,* meaning *after* (normally signifying change), and *morphoo,* meaning *to form.* Thus the verb means *to change form.* The four occurrences of the term in the NT always refer to change originating from the inside and being manifested on the outside. Two other terms mean *conform (suschematizo* in Rm 12:2; 1 Pt 1:14; *summorphos* in Rm 8:29; Php 3:21) and refer to change originating from external pressure, whether positive or negative.

Jesus told the disciples that some of them would not die until they had seen Him in His kingdom (Mt 16:28). His words were fulfilled six days later (Mt 17:1) when Jesus was transfigured (v. 2; Mk 9:2) on the "holy mountain" (2 Pt 1:18; see Lk 9:29) while Peter, James, and John looked on—as did Moses and Elijah! Jesus' deity and glory were temporarily allowed to shine through the veil of His human flesh so that He could be seen as He will be in His kingdom.

The term *metamorphoo* was used twice by Paul. He commanded believers to be "transformed" through renewing the mind (Rm 12:2), referring to an internal change in the believer, and not to let the world "conform" us through external pressure. Similarly, Paul referred to being "transformed" to the image of Christ through the work of the Spirit (2 Co 3:18).

41

them, and His face shone like the sun. Even His clothes became as white as the light. [3] Suddenly, Moses and Elijah appeared to them, talking with Him.

[4] Then Peter said to Jesus, "Lord, it's good for us to be here! If You wish, I will make[1] three tabernacles[a] here: one for You, one for Moses, and one for Elijah."

[5] While he was still speaking, suddenly a bright cloud covered[b] them, and a voice from the cloud[c] said:

"This is My beloved Son.
I take delight in Him.
Listen to Him!"

[6] When the disciples heard it, they fell on their faces and were terrified.

[7] Then Jesus came up, touched them, and said, "Get up; don't be afraid." [8] When they looked up they saw no one, except Jesus Himself[2] alone. [9] As they were coming down from the mountain, Jesus commanded them, "Don't tell anyone about the vision until the Son of Man is raised[3] from the dead."

[10] So the disciples questioned Him, "Why then do the scribes say that Elijah must come first?"

[11] "Elijah is coming[4] and will restore everything," He replied.[5] [12] "But I tell you: Elijah has already come, and they didn't recognize him. On the contrary, they did whatever they pleased to him. In the same way the Son of Man is going to suffer at their hands."[d] [13] Then the disciples understood that He spoke to them about John the Baptist.

THE POWER OF FAITH OVER A DEMON

[14] When they reached the crowd, a man approached and knelt down before Him. [15] "Lord," he said, "have mercy on my son, because he has seizures[e] and suffers severely. He often falls into the fire and often into the

Stay Focused on What God Is Doing

Do you find yourself focusing on everything else but Christ and the work He is doing around you? Are you so eager to get to the work that you have not yet clearly heard what is on God's heart?

While he was still speaking, suddenly a bright cloud covered them, and a voice from the cloud said: "This is My beloved Son. I take delight in Him. Listen to Him!"

—Matthew 17:5

[1]17:4 Other mss read *Let's make*
[2]17:8 Other mss omit *Himself*
[3]17:9 Other mss read *Man has risen*
[4]17:11 Other mss add *first*
[5]17:11 Other mss read *Jesus said to them*

[a]17:4 Or *tents* or *shelters* used for temporary housing
[b]17:5 Or *enveloped*; see Ex 40:34–35
[c]17:5 2 Pt 1:16–18
[d]17:12 Lit *Suffer by them*
[e]17:15 Lit *he is moonstruck* (thought to be a form of epilepsy)

[Handwritten margin notes:]

I want to always be listening to Jesus, not the many other things, many other people, etc

Do this study: It seems like whenever angels, etc showed up & revealed themselves to people, the message was always the same: Don't be afraid. "Perfect love casts out fear."

water. [16] I brought him to Your disciples, but they couldn't heal him."

[17] Jesus replied, "O unbelieving and rebellious[a] generation! How long will I be with you? How long must I put up with you? Bring him here to Me." [18] Then Jesus rebuked the demon,[b] and it[c] came out of him, and from that moment[d] the boy was healed.

[19] Then the disciples approached Jesus privately and said, "Why couldn't we drive it out?"

[20] "Because of your little faith," He[1] told them. "For I assure you: If you have faith the size of[e] a mustard seed, you will tell this mountain, 'Move from here to there,' and it will move. Nothing will be impossible for you. [21] However, this kind does not come out except by prayer and fasting."[2]

THE SECOND PREDICTION OF HIS DEATH

[22] As they were meeting[3] in Galilee, Jesus told them, "The Son of Man is about to be betrayed into the hands of men. [23] They will kill Him, and on the third day He will be raised up." And they were deeply distressed.

PAYING THE TEMPLE TAX

[24] When they came to Capernaum, those who collected the double-drachma tax[f] approached Peter and said, "Doesn't your Teacher pay the double-drachma tax?"

[25] "Yes," he said.

When he went into the house, Jesus spoke to him first,[g] "What do you think, Simon? From whom do earthly kings collect tariffs or taxes? From their sons or from strangers?"[h]

[26] "From strangers,"[h] he said.[4]

---

[1]17:20 Other mss read *your unbelief, Jesus*
[2]17:21 Other mss omit v. 21 (see Mk 9:29).
[3]17:22 Other mss read *were staying*
[4]17:26 Other mss read *Peter said to Him*

---

[a]17:17 Or *corrupt, perverted, twisted;* see Dt 32:5
[b]17:18 Lit *rebuked him* or *it*
[c]17:18 Lit *the demon*
[d]17:18 Lit *hour*
[e]17:20 Lit *faith like*

[f]17:24 A tax on Jewish men to support the temple; Ex 30:11f. A double-drachma could purchase two sheep.
[g]17:25 Lit *Jesus anticipated him by saying*
[h]17:25,26 Or *foreigners*

Commit Yourself to Helping People

God ought to be able to send a hurting person to any of His children and expect that they will be helped. Be a faithful steward of every life God sends to you.

"I brought him to Your disciples, but they couldn't heal him."

—Matthew 17:16

A Little Faith Can Go a Long Way

Do you sense there may be far more that God wants to do through your life than what you have been experiencing? Ask God to show you what it is, then respond in faith.

"For I assure you: If you have faith the size of a mustard seed, you will tell this mountain, 'Move from here to there,' and it will move. Nothing will be impossible for you."

—Matthew 17:20b

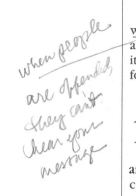

when people are offended they can't hear your message

"Then the sons are free," Jesus told him. [27] "But, so we won't offend them, go to the sea, cast in a fishhook, and catch the first fish that comes up. When you open its mouth you'll find a coin.[a] Take it and give it to them for Me and you."

WHO IS THE GREATEST?

18 At that time[b] the disciples came to Jesus and said, "Who is greatest in the kingdom of heaven?" [2] Then He called a child to Him and had him stand among them. [3] "I assure you," He said, "unless you are converted[c] and become like children, you will never enter the kingdom of heaven. [4] Therefore, whoever humbles himself like this child—this one is the greatest in the kingdom of heaven. [5] And whoever welcomes[d] one child like this in My name welcomes Me.

[6] "But whoever causes the downfall[e] of one of these little ones who believe in Me—it would be better for him if a heavy millstone[f] were hung around his neck and he were drowned in the depths of the sea! [7] Woe to the world because of offenses.[g] For offenses must come, but woe to that man by whom the offense comes. [8] If your hand or your foot causes your downfall,[h] cut it off and throw it away. It is better for you to enter life maimed or lame, than to have two hands or two feet and be thrown into the eternal fire. [9] And if your eye causes your downfall,[h] gouge it out and throw it away. It is better for you to enter life with one eye, rather than to have two eyes and be thrown into hellfire![i]

THE PARABLE OF THE LOST SHEEP

[10] "See that you don't look down on one of these little ones, because I tell you that in heaven their angels continually view the face of My Father in heaven. [11] For the Son of Man has come to save the lost.]¹ [12] What do you

Give God Room to Work Through You

You must move from doing work for God according to your abilities, your gifts, your goals, your likes, and your dislikes, to being totally dependent on God, His working, and His resources.

"I assure you," He said, "unless you are converted and become like children, you will never enter the kingdom of heaven. Therefore, whoever humbles himself like this child—this one is the greatest in the kingdom of heaven."

—Matthew 18:3–4

---

¹**18:11** Other mss omit v. 11

ª**17:27** Gk *stater,* worth two double-drachmas
ᵇ**18:1** Lit *hour*
ᶜ**18:3** Or *turned around*
ᵈ**18:5** Or *receives*
ᵉ**18:6** Or *causes to sin.* The Gk word *skandalizo* has no real Eng counterpart; "offend," "cause to sin," or

"cause the downfall of" are common translations.
ᶠ**18:6** That is, a millstone turned by a donkey
ᵍ**18:7** Or *causes of stumbling*
ʰ**18:8,9** See 18:6 note
ⁱ**18:9** Lit *gehenna of fire*

think? If a man has a hundred sheep, and one of them goes astray, won't he leave the ninety-nine on the hillside, and go and search for the stray? [13] And if he finds it, I assure you: He rejoices over that sheep[a] more than over the ninety-nine that did not go astray. [14] In the same way, it is not the will of your Father in heaven that one of these little ones perish.

RESTORING A BROTHER

[15] "If your brother sins against you,[1] go and rebuke him in private.[b] If he listens to you, you have won your brother. [16] But if he won't listen, take one or two more with you, so that **'by the testimony[c] of two or three witnesses every fact may be established.'**[d] [17] If he pays no attention to them, tell the church.[e] But if he doesn't pay attention even to the church, let him be like an unbeliever[f] and a tax collector to you. [18] I assure you: Whatever you bind on earth will have been bound in heaven,[g] and whatever you loose on earth will have been loosed in heaven.[g] [19] Again, I assure you: If two of you on earth agree about any matter that you[h] pray for, it will be done for you[i] by My Father in heaven. [20] For where two or three are gathered together in My name, I am there among them."

THE PARABLE OF THE UNFORGIVING SLAVE

[21] Then Peter came to Him and said, "Lord, how many times could my brother sin against me and I forgive him? As many as seven times?"[j]

[22] "I tell you, not as many as seven," Jesus said to him, "but seventy times seven. [23] For this reason, the kingdom of heaven can be compared to a king who wanted to settle accounts with his slaves. [24] When he began to settle accounts, one who owed ten thousand talents[k]

check cross refs & study more

God Speaks Through His Church

You can and should depend on God to speak through other believers and the church to help you know what assignment you are to carry out in the ministry of the kingdom.

"For where two or three are gathered together in My name, I am there among them."

—Matthew 18:20

---

[1] **18:15** Other mss omit *against you*

---

[a] **18:13** Lit *over it*
[b] **18:15** Lit *him between you and him alone*
[c] **18:16** Lit *mouth*
[d] **18:16** Dt 19:15
[e] **18:17** Or *congregation*
[f] **18:17** Or *a Gentile*
[g] **18:18** See 16:19 note
[h] **18:19** Lit *they*
[i] **18:19** Lit *for them*
[j] **18:21** See the opposite attitude in Gn 4:24
[k] **18:24** A huge sum of money that could never be repaid by a slave; a talent = six thousand denarii

WORD STUDY

Greek word: **aphiemi**
[ah FEE ay mee]

Translation: **forgive**

Uses in Matthew's Gospel: **33**
(Mk, 23; Lk, 48)

Uses in the NT: **129**

Key passage: **Matthew 18:27**

The basic meaning of the Greek verb *aphiemi* is *to leave*. This is the dominant use of the term in the NT, but the more important meaning is *to forgive*. In the NT the verb *aphiemi* and the related noun *aphesis* describe the cancelation of a debt. Two of Jesus' parables demonstrate this meaning: (1) the parable of the unmerciful servant (Mt 18:23–35), in response to Peter's question about how many times to forgive someone (v. 21); and (2) the parable of the moneylender who forgave both a large debt and a small debt (Lk 7:41–42). Jesus' statement "forgive us our debts" (Mt 6:12) has the same idea but carries it beyond the monetary to offensive actions that affect personal relationships, and this is how He applied the two parables. Paul used the terms to describe the cancelation of sin's infinite debt to God through the cross of Christ (Rm 3:21—4:8; Eph 1:7; Col 1:14). The resurrected Lord told the disciples that "forgiveness of sins will be preached" in His name, and the apostles were the first to do exactly that (Ac 2:38; 5:31; 10:43; 13:38; 26:18). Forgiveness of sins is available only through faith in Jesus, who paid the price of sin that we would have to pay in hell if He had not paid it for us.

was brought before him. [25] Since he had no way to pay it back, his master commanded that he, his wife, his children, and everything he had be sold to pay the debt.

[26] "At this, the slave fell down on his face before him and said, 'Be patient with me, and I will pay you everything!' [27] Then the master of that slave had compassion, released him, and forgave him the loan.

[28] "But that slave went out and found one of his fellow slaves who owed him a hundred denarii.[a] He grabbed him, started choking him, and said, 'Pay what you owe!'

[29] "At this, his fellow slave fell down[1] and began begging him, 'Be patient with me, and I will pay you back.' [30] But he wasn't willing. On the contrary, he went and threw him into prison until he could pay what was owed. [31] When the other slaves saw what had taken place, they were deeply distressed and went and reported to their master everything that had happened.

[32] "Then, after he had summoned him, his master said to him, 'You wicked slave! I forgave you all that debt because you begged me. [33] Shouldn't you also have had mercy on your fellow slave, as I had mercy on you?' [34] And his master got angry and handed him over to the jailers[b] until he could pay everything that was owed. [35] So My heavenly Father will also do to you if each of you does not forgive his brother[2] from his[c] heart."

THE QUESTION OF DIVORCE

19 When Jesus had finished this instruction, He departed from Galilee and went to the region of Judea across the Jordan. [2] Large crowds followed Him, and He healed them there. [3] Some Pharisees approached Him to test Him. They asked, "Is it lawful for a man to divorce his wife on any grounds?"

[4] "Haven't you read," He replied, "that He who created[3] them in the beginning **'made them male and female,'**[d] [5] and He also said:

[1] **18:29** Other mss add *at his feet*
[2] **18:35** Other mss add *his trespasses*
[3] **19:4** Other mss read *made*

[a] **18:28** A small sum compared to ten thousand talents
[b] **18:34** Or *torturers*
[c] **18:35** Lit *your*
[d] **19:4** Gn 1:27; 5:2

For this reason a man will leave his father
  and mother
and be joined to his wife,
and the two will become one flesh?"[a]

[6] So they are no longer two, but one flesh. Therefore what God has joined together, man must not separate."

[7] "Why then," they asked Him, "did Moses command us[b] to give divorce papers and to send her away?"

[8] He told them, "Moses permitted you to divorce your wives because of the hardness of your hearts. But it was not like that from the beginning. [9] And I tell you, whoever divorces his wife, except for sexual immorality, and marries another, commits adultery."[1]

[10] His disciples said to Him, "If the relationship of a man with his wife is like this, it's better not to marry!"

[11] But He told them, "Not everyone can accept this saying, but only those to whom it has been given. [12] For there are eunuchs who were born that way from their mother's womb, there are eunuchs who were made by men, and there are eunuchs who have made themselves that way because of the kingdom of heaven. Let anyone accept this who can."

BLESSING THE CHILDREN

[13] Then children were brought to Him so He might put His hands on them and pray. But the disciples rebuked them. [14] Then Jesus said, "Leave the children alone, and don't try to keep them from coming to Me, because the kingdom of heaven is made up of people like this."[c] [15] After putting His hands on them, He went on from there.

THE RICH YOUNG RULER

[16] Just then someone came up and asked Him, "Teacher, what good must I do to have eternal life?"

[17] "Why do you ask Me about what is good?"[2] He said to him. "There is only One who is good.[3] If you want to enter into life, keep the commandments."

---

[1] 19:9 Other mss add *Also whoever marries a divorced woman commits adultery* (see Mt 5:32).
[2] 19:17 Other mss read *Why do you call Me good?*
[3] 19:17 Other mss read *No one is good but One—God*

---

[a] 19:5 Gn 2:24
[b] 19:7 *us* implied
[c] 19:14 Lit *heaven is of such ones*

WORD STUDY

Greek word: **apoluo**
[ah pah LOOoh]
Translation: **divorce**
Uses in Matthew's Gospel: **19**
(Mk, 12; Lk 14; Jn, 5)
Uses in the NT: **66**
Key passage: **Matthew 19:3**

The Greek word *apoluo* is a compound verb from *apo*, meaning *away from*, and *luo*, meaning *to loose* or *release*. Thus, *apoluo* is a loosing or releasing of one thing away from another, and the meanings *to send away, to let go,* and *to release* are the dominant uses of the term in the NT (see Mt 14:15; 18:27; 27:15). A technical use of the term is for a husband releasing or sending away his wife in divorce (or vice versa). This use of *apoluo* occurs twelve times, all in the Synoptic Gospels. The term first occurs in the infancy narrative when Joseph decided to divorce Mary because he thought she had been unfaithful to him (Mt 1:19). The other three contexts in which *apoluo* occurs are the Sermon on the Mount (Mt 5:31–32), Jesus' dispute with the Pharisees over the divorce issue (Mt 19:1–11 = Mk 10:1–12), and a brief statement about divorce late in Jesus' ministry (Lk 16:18). Jesus condemned divorce but did allow it in cases of infidelity (Mt 19:9). This reflects His interpretation of the law of Moses (Mt 19:9; see Dt 24:1-4), which the Pharisees hoped to use against Him (Mt 19:3,7).

[18] "Which ones?" he asked Him. Jesus answered,

> **"You shall not murder; You shall not commit adultery; You shall not steal; You shall not bear false witness;** [19]**Honor your father and your mother;**[a] **And you shall love your neighbor as yourself."**[b]

[20] "I have kept all these,"[1] the young man told Him. "What do I still lack?"

[21] "If you want to be perfect,"[c] Jesus said to him, "go, sell your belongings and give to the poor, and you will have treasure in heaven. Then come, follow Me."

[22] When the young man heard that command, he went away grieving, because he had many possessions.

POSSESSIONS AND THE KINGDOM

[23] Then Jesus said to His disciples, "I assure you: It is hard for a rich person to enter the kingdom of heaven! [24] Again I tell you, it is easier for a camel to go through the eye of a needle than for a rich person to enter the kingdom of God."

[25] When the disciples heard this, they were utterly astonished and asked, "Then who can be saved?"

[26] But Jesus looked at them and said, "With men this is impossible, but with God all things are possible."

[27] Then Peter responded to Him, "Look, we have left everything and followed You. So what will there be for us?"

[28] Jesus said to them, "I assure you: In the Messianic Age,[d] when the Son of Man sits on His glorious throne, you who have followed Me will also sit on twelve thrones, judging the twelve tribes of Israel. [29] And everyone who has left houses, brothers or sisters, father or mother,[2] children, or fields because of My name will receive a hundred times more and will inherit eternal life. [30] But many who are first will be last, and the last first.

[1]**19:20** Other mss add *from my youth*
[2]**19:29** Other mss add *or wife*

[a]**19:18b-19a** Ex 20:12-16; Dt 5:16-20
[b]**19:18b** Lv 19:18
[c]**19:21** Or *complete*
[d]**19:28** Lit *in the regeneration*

Are You Willing to Give Your All to God?

When God asks you to do something that you cannot do, you will face a crisis of belief.

"If you want to be perfect," Jesus said to him, "go, sell your belongings and give to the poor, and you will have treasure in heaven. Then come, follow Me." When the young man heard that command, he went away grieving, because he had many possessions.

—Matthew 19:21

THE PARABLE OF THE
VINEYARD WORKERS

20 "For the kingdom of heaven is like a landowner who went out early in the morning to hire workers for his vineyard. [2] After agreeing with the workers on one denarius[a] for the day, he sent them into his vineyard. [3] When he went out about nine in the morning,[b] he saw others standing in the marketplace doing nothing. [4] To those men he said, 'You also go to my vineyard, and I'll give you whatever is right.' So off they went. [5] About noon and at three,[c] he went out again and did the same thing. [6] Then about five[d] he went and found others standing around,[1] and said to them, 'Why have you been standing here all day doing nothing?'

[7] " 'Because no one hired us,' they said to him.

" 'You also go to my vineyard,' he told them.[2] [8] When evening came, the owner of the vineyard told his foreman, 'Call the workers and give them their pay, starting with the last and ending with the first.'[e]

[9] "When those who were hired about five[f] came, they each received one denarius. [10] So when the first ones came, they assumed they would get more, but they also received a denarius each. [11] When they received it, they began to complain to the landowner: [12] 'These last men put in one hour, and you made them equal to us who bore the burden of the day and the burning heat!'

[13] "He replied to one of them, 'Friend, I'm doing you no wrong. Didn't you agree with me on a denarius? [14] Take what's yours and go. I want to give this last man the same as I gave you. [15] Don't I have the right to do what I want with my business?[g] Are you jealous[h] because I'm generous?'[i]

[16] "So the last will be first, and the first last."[3]

God Is in Charge, You Are in Submission

God has a right to interrupt your life. He is Lord. When you surrendered to Him as Lord, you gave Him the right to help Himself to your life anytime He wants.

"Don't I have the right to do what I want with my business?"

—Matthew 20:15a

[1] 20:6 Other mss add *doing nothing*
[2] 20:7 Other mss add *and you'll get whatever is right.*
[3] 20:16 Other mss add *For many are called, but few are chosen.*

[a] 20:2 A small silver coin equal to a day's wages
[b] 20:3 Lit *about the third hour*
[c] 20:5 Lit *About the sixth hour and the ninth hour*
[d] 20:6 Lit *about the eleventh hour*
[e] 20:8 Lit *starting from the last until the first*
[f] 20:9 Lit *about the eleventh hour*
[g] 20:15 Lit *with what is mine*
[h] 20:15 Lit *is your eye evil,* an idiom for jealousy or stinginess
[i] 20:15 Lit *good*

Greek word: **egeiro**
[eh GIGH roh]
Translation: **resurrect**
Uses in Matthew's Gospel: **36**
(Mk, 19; Lk, 18; Jn, 13)
Uses in the NT: **144**
Key passage: **Matthew 20:19**

The Greek verb *egeiro,* meaning *to rise,* was a common term in the Greek-speaking world, with numerous applications. In the Greek OT the term often occurs for rising from sleep (see Gn 41:4; 49:9; 2 Kg 4:31; Jr 51:39), and it is used this way in the NT also (Mt 8:25 = Mk 4:38; Rm 13:11; see Eph 5:14). The normal meaning *to rise* occurs several times in the NT (Mt 26:46; Lk 13:25; Jn 14:31; Ac 10:26; Rv 11:1), especially in the Gospels, but Jesus' and the early church's comparison of death to sleep (Mk 5:39; Jn 11:11; 1 Co 15:20; 1 Th 4:13–14) brought *egeiro* into the theological vocabulary of the NT as the dominant verb describing the resurrection—both believers' and Jesus'. The term was used for healing the lame and raising the dead (Mt 9:6 = Mk 2:9; Lk 7:14; 8:54; Jn 12:1), both of which anticipated the greater and permanent raising of dead believers in the resurrection at the end times (Jn 5:21–29; see 11:23–26). But it is not surprising that about half of the occurrences of *egeiro* in the NT describe Jesus' resurrection, particularly in Acts and the Epistles (Ac 3:15; 4:10; 5:30; 10:40; 13:30; Rm 6:4; 1 Co 15:4; Eph 1:20; 2 Tm 2:8; 1 Pt 1:21). For more on this subject, see the word study on *anastasis,* a similar term meaning *resurrection* (page 242).

THE THIRD PREDICTION OF HIS DEATH

[17] While going up to Jerusalem, Jesus took the twelve disciples aside privately and said to them on the way: [18] "Listen! We are going up to Jerusalem. The Son of Man will be handed over to the chief priests and scribes, and they will condemn Him to death. [19] Then they will hand Him over to the Gentiles to be mocked, flogged,[a] and crucified, and He will be resurrected on the third day."[1]

SUFFERING AND SERVICE

[20] Then the mother of Zebedee's sons approached Him with her sons. She knelt down to ask Him for something. [21] "What do you want?" He asked her.

"Promise,"[b] she said to Him, "that these two sons of mine may sit, one on Your right and the other on Your left, in Your kingdom."

[22] But Jesus answered, "You don't know what you're asking. Are you able to drink the cup[c] that I am about to drink?"[2]

"We are able," they said to Him.

[23] He told them, "You will indeed drink My cup.[3] But to sit at My right and left is not Mine to give; instead, it belongs to those for whom it has been prepared by My Father." [24] When the ten disciples[d] heard this, they became indignant with the two brothers. [25] But Jesus called them over and said, "You know that the rulers of the Gentiles dominate them, and the men of high position exercise power over them. [26] It must not be like that among you. On the contrary, whoever wants to become great among you must be your servant, [27] and whoever wants to be first among you must be your slave. [28] Just as the Son of Man did not come to be served, but to serve, and to give His life—a ransom for many."

[1] **20:19** Other mss read *will rise again*
[2] **20:22** Other mss add *and (or) to be baptized with the baptism that I am baptized with.*
[3] **20:23** Other mss add *and be baptized with the baptism that I am baptized with.*

[a] **20:19** Or *scourged*
[b] **20:21** Lit *Say*
[c] **20:22** Figurative language referring to His coming suffering. See Mt 26:39; Jn 18:11.
[d] **20:24** *disciples* supplied for clarity

TWO BLIND MEN HEALED

29 As they were leaving Jericho, a large crowd followed Him. 30 There were two blind men sitting by the road. When they heard that Jesus was passing by, they cried out, "Lord, have mercy on us, Son of David!" 31 The crowd told them to keep quiet, but they cried out all the more, "Lord, have mercy on us, Son of David!"

32 Jesus stopped, called them, and said, "What do you want Me to do for you?"

33 "Lord," they said to Him, "open our eyes!" 34 Moved with compassion, Jesus touched their eyes. Immediately they could see, and followed Him.

THE TRIUMPHAL ENTRY

When they approached Jerusalem and came to Bethphage at the Mount of Olives, Jesus then sent two disciples, 2 telling them, "Go into the village ahead of you. At once you will find a donkey tied there, and a colt with her. Untie them and bring them to Me. 3 If anyone says anything to you, you should say that the Lord needs them, and immediately he will send them."

4 This took place so that what was spoken through the prophet might be fulfilled:

5 Tell the Daughter of Zion,
   "See, your King is coming to you,
   gentle, and mounted on a donkey,
   even on a colt, the foal of a beast of
      burden."a

6 The disciples went and did just as Jesus directed them. 7 They brought the donkey and the colt, laid their robes on them, and He sat on them. 8 A very large crowd spread their robes on the road; others were cutting branches from the trees and spreading them on the road. 9 Then the crowds who went before Him and those who followed kept shouting:

   "Hosannab to the Son of David!
   Blessed is He who comes in the name of
      the Lord!c
   Hosanna in the highest heaven!"

Be Ready—God Could Call at Any Time

The next time you are in a crowd, listen to what the Holy Spirit is saying. You may discover that God has much on His heart for those people—and is waiting for one of His disciples to respond to His prompting.

Moved with compassion, Jesus touched their eyes. Immediately they could see and followed Him.

—Matthew 20:34

You Will Get All the Directions You Need

Your relationship with God is far more important to Him than any planning you can do. We cannot know the when, or where, or how of God's will until He tells us.

The disciples went and did just as Jesus directed them.

—Matthew 21:6

---

a21:5 Is 62:11; Zch 9:9
b21:9 A term of praise derived from the Hb word for *save;* it occurs in the OT original of this quotation.
c21:9 Ps 118:26

WORD STUDY

Greek word: **hosanna**
[hoh sahn NAH]

Translation: **Hosanna**

Uses in Matthew's Gospel: **3**
(Mk, 2; Jn, 1)

Uses in the NT: **6**

Key passage: **Matthew 21:9,15**

The word *hosanna* is actually a combination of two Hebrew words transliterated into Greek as one word all six times it occurs in the NT. The two words are *yasha'*, meaning *to deliver* or *save* (the root behind the name Jesus), and *na,* meaning *now!* or *please!* The words occur together in Psalm 118:25 ("Lord, *save us now!*"), but by the time of Jesus the two words had formed a standard expression or exclamation of praise and thanksgiving to God. Five of the six uses of the term occur in connection with Jesus' triumphal entry (Mt 21:1–11 = Mk 11:1–11 = Jn 12:12–19); the other is related to Jesus' subsequent ministry in the temple complex (Mt 21:12–16).

[10] When He entered Jerusalem, the whole city was shaken, saying, "Who is this?" [11] And the crowds kept saying, "This is the prophet Jesus from Nazareth in Galilee!"

CLEANSING THE TEMPLE COMPLEX

[12] Jesus went into the temple complex[1] and drove out all those buying and selling in the temple. He overturned the money changers' tables and the chairs of those selling doves. [13] And He said to them, "It is written, **'My house will be called a house of prayer.'**[a] But you are making it **'a den of thieves'**!"[b]

CHILDREN CHEER JESUS

[14] The blind and the lame came to Him in the temple complex, and He healed them. [15] When the chief priests and the scribes saw the wonders that He did, and the children in the temple complex cheering, "*Hosanna* to the Son of David!" they were indignant [16] and said to Him, "Do You hear what these children[c] are saying?"

"Yes," Jesus told them. "Have you never read:

> **From the mouths of children and nursing infants**
> **You have prepared[d] praise?"[e]**

[17] Then He left them, went out of the city to Bethany, and spent the night there.

THE BARREN FIG TREE

[18] Early in the morning, as He was returning to the city, He was hungry. [19] Seeing a lone fig tree by the road, He went up to it and found nothing on it except leaves. And He said to it, "May no fruit ever come from you again!" At once the fig tree withered.

[20] When the disciples saw it, they were amazed and said, "How did the fig tree wither so quickly?"

[21] Jesus answered them, "I assure you: If you have faith and do not doubt, you will not only do what was done to the fig tree, but even if you tell this mountain,

[1] 21:12 Other mss add *of God*

[a] 21:13 Is 56:7
[b] 21:13 Jr 7:11
[c] 21:16 *children* understood
[d] 21:16 Or *restored*
[e] 21:16 Ps 8:3, LXX

'Be lifted up and thrown into the sea,' it will be done. [22] And everything—whatever you ask in prayer, believing—you will receive."

MESSIAH'S AUTHORITY CHALLENGED

[23] When He entered the temple complex, the chief priests and the elders of the people came up to Him as He was teaching and said, "By what authority are You doing these things? Who gave You this authority?"

[24] Jesus answered them, "I will also ask you one question, and if you answer it for Me, then I will tell you by what authority I do these things. [25] Where did John's baptism come from? From heaven or from men?"

They began to argue among themselves, "If we say, 'From heaven,' He will say to us, 'Then why didn't you believe him?' [26] But if we say, 'From men,' we're afraid of the crowd, because everyone thought that John was a prophet." [27] So they answered Jesus, "We don't know."

And He said to them, "Neither will I tell you by what authority I do these things.

THE PARABLE OF THE TWO SONS

[28] "But what do you think? A man had two sons. He went to the first and said, 'My son, go, work in the vineyard today.'

[29] "He answered, 'I don't want to!' Yet later he changed his mind and went. [30] Then the man went to the other and said the same thing.

"'I will, sir,' he answered. But he didn't go.

[31] "Which of the two did his father's will?"

"The first," they said.

Jesus said to them, "I assure you: Tax collectors and prostitutes are entering the kingdom of God before you! [32] For John came to you in the way of righteousness,[a] and you didn't believe him. Tax collectors and prostitutes did believe him, but you, when you saw it, didn't change your mind later to believe him.

THE PARABLE OF THE VINEYARD OWNER

[33] "Listen to another parable: There was a man, a landowner, who planted a vineyard, put a fence around it, dug a winepress in it, and built a watchtower.[b] He leased

---

[a]**21:32** That is, John came preaching and practicing righteousness   [b]**21:33** Is 5:1–2

If It Seems Too Hard, It's Probably God

If you or your church are not responding to God by attempting things that only He can accomplish, then you are not exercising faith.

Jesus answered them, "I assure you: If you have faith and do not doubt, you will not only do what was done to the fig tree, but even if you tell this mountain, 'Be lifted up and thrown into the sea,' it will be done."

—Matthew 21:21

it to tenant farmers and went away. [34] When the grape harvest[a] drew near, he sent his slaves to the farmers to collect his fruit. [35] But the farmers took his slaves, beat one, killed another, and stoned a third. [36] Again, he sent other slaves, more than the first group, and they did the same to them. [37] Finally, he sent his son to them. 'They will respect my son,' he said.

[38] "But when the tenant farmers saw the son, they said among themselves, 'This is the heir. Come, let's kill him and seize[b] his inheritance!' [39] So they seized him and threw him out of the vineyard, and killed him. [40] Therefore, when the owner of the vineyard comes, what will he do to those farmers?"

[41] "He will destroy those terrible men in a terrible way," they told Him, "and lease his vineyard to other farmers who will give him his produce at the harvest."[c]

[42] Jesus said to them, "Have you never read in the Scriptures:

> **The stone that the builders rejected,**
> **this has become the cornerstone.[d]**
> **This cornerstone[e] came from the Lord**
> **and is wonderful in our eyes?[f]**

[43] Therefore I tell you, the kingdom of God will be taken away from you and given to a nation producing its[g] fruit. [44] Whoever falls on this stone will be broken to pieces; but on whomever it falls, it will grind him to powder!"[1h]

[45] When the chief priests and the Pharisees heard His parables, they knew He was speaking about them. [46] Although they were looking for a way to arrest Him, they feared the crowds, because they[i] regarded Him as a prophet.

THE PARABLE OF THE WEDDING BANQUET

22 Once more Jesus spoke to them in parables: [2] "The kingdom of heaven may be compared to a

He Is the Potter, You Are the Clay

If your tendency is to tell the Father what you can and cannot do for Him, submit to His agenda and allow Him to shape you into the person He wants you to be. Like clay.

"Whoever falls on this stone will be broken to pieces; but on whomever it falls, it will grind him to powder!"

—Matthew 21:44

[1] 21:44 Other mss omit this verse.

[a] 21:34 Lit *the season of fruits*
[b] 21:38 Lit *have*
[c] 21:41 Lit *him the fruits in their seasons*
[d] 21:42 Lit *head of the corner*
[e] 21:42 The word *cornerstone* is supplied for clarity.
[f] 21:42 Ps 118:22,23
[g] 21:43 The word *its* refers back to *kingdom.*
[h] 21:44 Dn 2:34-35,44
[i] 21:46 That is, *the crowds*

king who gave a wedding banquet for his son. [3] He sent out his slaves to summon those invited to the banquet, but they didn't want to come. [4] Again, he sent out other slaves, and said, 'Tell those who are invited, "Look, I've prepared my dinner; my oxen and fatted cattle have been slaughtered, and everything is ready. Come to the wedding banquet." '

[5] "But they paid no attention and went away, one to his own farm, another to his business. [6] And the others seized his slaves and killed them. [7] The king[1] was enraged, so he sent out his troops, destroyed those murderers, and burned down their city.

[8] "Then he told his slaves, 'The banquet is ready, but those who were invited were not worthy. [9] Therefore, go to where the roads exit the city and invite everyone you find to the banquet.' [10] So those slaves went out on the roads and gathered everyone they found, both evil and good. The wedding banquet was filled with guests.[a] [11] But when the king came in to view the guests,[a] he saw a man there who was not dressed for a wedding. [12] So he said to him, 'Friend, how did you get in here without wedding clothes?' The man was speechless.

[13] "Then the king told the attendants, 'Tie him up hand and foot,[2] and throw him into the outer darkness, where there will be weeping and gnashing of teeth.'

[14] "For many are invited, but few are chosen."

GOD AND CAESAR

[15] Then the Pharisees went and plotted how to trap Him by what He said.[b] [16] They sent their disciples to Him, with the Herodians.[c] "Teacher," they said, "we know that You are truthful and teach the way of God in truth. You defer to no one, for You don't show partiality.[d] [17] Tell us, therefore, what You think. Is it lawful to pay taxes to Caesar or not?"

[18] But perceiving their malice, Jesus said, "Why are you testing Me, hypocrites? [19] Show Me the coin used for

---

[1]22:7 Other mss read *But when the (that) king heard about it he*
[2]22:13 Other mss add *take him away*

---

[a]22:10,11 Lit *those reclining* (to eat)
[b]22:15 Lit *trap Him in* (a) *word*
[c]22:16 Political supporters of Herod the Great and his family

[d]22:16 Lit *don't look on the face of men* (that is, outward appearance)

Don't Expect Everyone to Want Your Jesus

Many people are simply too busy to stop and too self-assured to realize that they have a need for a Savior. Don't take their rejection personally. They may be closer to responding than you think.

"He sent out his slaves to summon those invited to the banquet, but they didn't want to come."

—Matthew 22:3

the tax." So they brought Him a denarius.[a] 20 "Whose image and inscription is this?" He asked them.

21 "Caesar's," they said to Him.

Then He said to them, "Therefore, give back to Caesar the things that are Caesar's, and to God the things that are God's." 22 When they heard this, they were amazed. So they left Him and went away.

THE SADDUCEES AND THE RESURRECTION

23 The same day some Sadducees, who say there is no resurrection, came up to Him and questioned Him: 24 "Teacher, Moses said, **'if a man dies, having no children, his brother is to marry his wife and raise up offspring[b] for his brother.'**[c] 25 Now there were seven brothers among us. The first got married and died. Having no offspring,[b] he left his wife to his brother. 26 The same happened to the second also, and the third, and so to all seven.[d] 27 Then last of all the woman died. 28 Therefore, in the resurrection, whose wife will she be of the seven? For they all had married her."[e]

29 Jesus answered them, "You are deceived, because you don't know the Scriptures or the power of God. 30 For in the resurrection they neither marry nor are given in marriage, but are like[1] angels in heaven. 31 Now concerning the resurrection of the dead, haven't you read what was spoken to you by God: 32 **'I am the God of Abraham and the God of Isaac and the God of Jacob'?**[f] He[2] is not the God of the dead, but of the living."

33 And when the crowds heard this, they were astonished at His teaching.

THE PRIMARY COMMANDMENTS

34 When the Pharisees heard that He had silenced the Sadducees, they came together in the same place. 35 And one of them, an expert in the law, asked a question to

Loving God Is a Choice, Not a Feeling

More than anything else, God wants us to love Him with our total being.

He said to him, " 'You shall love the Lord your God with all your heart, with all your soul, and with all your mind.' This is the greatest and most important commandment."

—Matthew 22:37-38

[handwritten note:] What makes someone deceived?
- not knowing the Scriptures
- not knowing the power of God

1 22:30 Other mss add *God's*
2 22:32 Other mss read *God*

a 22:19 See 20:2 note
b 22:24,25 Lit *seed*
c 22:24 Dt 25:5

d 22:26 Lit *so until the seven*
e 22:28 Lit *all had her*
f 22:32 Ex 3:6,15,16

56

test Him: [36] "Teacher, which commandment in the law is the greatest?"[a]

[37] He said to him, "'You shall love the Lord your God with all your heart, with all your soul, and with all your mind.'[b] [38] This is the greatest and most important[c] commandment. [39] The second is like it: 'You shall love your neighbor as yourself.'[d] [40] All the Law and the Prophets depend[e] on these two commandments."

THE QUESTION ABOUT THE MESSIAH

[41] While the Pharisees were together, Jesus questioned them, [42] "What do you think about the Messiah?[f] Whose Son is He?"

"David's," they told Him.

[43] He asked them, "How is it then that David, inspired by the Spirit,[g] calls Him 'Lord':

[44] The Lord said to my Lord,
'Sit at My right hand
until I put Your enemies under Your feet'?[1h]

[45] "If, then, David calls Him 'Lord,' how is He his Son?" [46] No one was able to answer Him at all,[i] and from that day no one dared to question Him any more.

RELIGIOUS HYPOCRITES DENOUNCED

23 Then Jesus spoke to the crowds and to His disciples: [2] "The scribes and the Pharisees are seated in the chair of Moses.[j] [3] Therefore do and observe whatever they tell you. But don't do what they do,[k] because they don't do what they say. [4] They tie up heavy loads that are hard to carry[2] and put them on people's shoulders, but they themselves aren't willing to lift a finger[l] to move them. [5] They do everything[m] to be observed by

---

[1]22:44 Other mss read *Until I make Your enemies Your footstool.*
[2]23:4 Other mss omit *that are hard to carry.*

---

[a]22:36 Lit *great*
[b]22:37 Dt 6:5
[c]22:38 Lit *and first*
[d]22:39 Lv 19:18
[e]22:40 Or *hang*
[f]22:42 Or *the Christ*
[g]22:43 Lit *David in Spirit*
[h]22:44 Ps 110:1
[i]22:46 Lit *answer Him a word*

[j]23:2 Perhaps a special chair for teaching in synagogues or metaphorical for teaching with Moses' authority
[k]23:3 Lit *do according to their works*
[l]23:4 Lit *lift with their finger*
[m]23:5 Lit *all their works*

WORD STUDY

Greek word: **entole**
[ehn tah LAY]

Translation: **commandment**

Uses in Matthew's Gospel: **6** (Mk, 6; Lk, 4; Jn, 10)

Uses in the NT: **67**

Key passage: **Matthew 22:35–40**

The Greek noun *entole* usually refers to specific demands from God to mankind, either those given in the OT (like one of the Ten Commandments), OT teaching in general, or some other aspect of divine instruction (especially true in John's writings). Despite the numerous commandments in the OT (over 600), Jesus stated that they all are contained in the one command to love God (Mt 22:37), a truth already proclaimed in the OT (see Dt 6:4–5). The number two command is to love our neighbors (Mt 22:38; see Lv 19:18). Every other commandment God has given directly relates to these two: we must first love God our Creator and Redeemer, and then we must love everyone whom He created in His image and for whom He has provided redemption in Christ.

WORD STUDY

Greek word: **hupokrites**
[hoo pah kree TAYSS]

Translation: **hypocrite**

Uses in Matthew's Gospel: **14**
(Mk, 1; Lk, 3)

Uses in the NT: **18**

Key passage: **Matthew 23:13-36**

The Greek noun *hupokrites* comes from the verb *hupokrinomai,* meaning *to pretend* (see Lk 20:20, its only occurrence in the NT). The verb was often used to describe what actors did on the stage. Thus, it is not surprising that the noun *hupokrites* was not originally a negative term in the Greek world. It was, in fact, the term used in classical times as the word for *actor,* one who plays a role by pretending to be someone else.

The word *hupokrites* eventually developed into the negative concept of one involved in play acting, that is, one who pretends in real life to be something he is not. All seventeen NT uses of the term are in the Synoptic Gospels and from the lips of Jesus when He denounced on several occasions the fraudulent claims of spirituality by the Jewish religious leaders—the most scorching one being Jesus' repetitive use of *ouai* ("woe"; see word study on page 149) and *hupokrites* in Matthew 23:13-36. Two other related words are the noun *hupokrisis,* meaning *hypocrisy* (see Mt 23:28; Gl 2:13), and the adjective *anupokritos* meaning *genuine* (literally, *without hypocrisy;* see Rm 12:9; Jms 3:17). Each term is used six times in the NT.

others: They enlarge their phylacteries[a] and lengthen their tassels.[1] [6] They love the place of honor at banquets, the front seats in the synagogues, [7] greetings in the marketplaces, and to be called 'Rabbi' by people.

[8] "But as for you, do not be called 'Rabbi,' because you have one Teacher,[2] and you are all brothers. [9] Do not call anyone on earth your father, because you have one Father, who is in heaven. [10] And do not be called masters either, because you have one Master,[b] the Messiah.[c] [11] The greatest among you will be your servant. [12] Whoever exalts himself will be humbled, and whoever humbles himself will be exalted.

[13] "But woe to you, scribes and Pharisees, hypocrites! You lock up the kingdom of heaven from people. For you don't go in, and you don't allow those entering to go in.

⌈[14] "Woe to you, scribes and Pharisees, hypocrites! You devour widows' houses, and make long prayers just for show.[d] This is why you will receive a harsher punishment.⌋[3]

[15] "Woe to you, scribes and Pharisees, hypocrites! You travel over land and sea to make one convert,[e] and when he becomes one, you make him twice as fit for hell[f] as you are!

[16] "Woe to you, blind guides, who say, 'Whoever takes an oath by the sanctuary, it is nothing. But whoever takes an oath by the gold of the sanctuary is bound by his oath.'[g] [17] Blind fools![h] For which is greater, the gold or the sanctuary that sanctified the gold? [18] Also, 'Whoever takes an oath by the altar, it is nothing. But whoever takes an oath by the gift that is on it is bound by his oath.'[g] [19] Blind people![4] For which is greater, the gift or the altar that sanctifies the gift? [20] Therefore the one who takes an oath by the altar takes an oath by it and by everything on it. [21] The one who takes an oath by the

[1] 23:5 Other mss add *on their robes*
[2] 23:8 Other mss add *the Messiah*
[3] 23:14 Other mss omit v. 14
[4] 23:19 Other mss read *Fools and blind*

---

[a] 23:5 Small leather boxes containing OT texts, worn by Jews on their arms and foreheads during prayers
[b] 23:10 Or *Teacher*
[c] 23:10 Or *the Christ*

[d] 23:14 Or *prayers with false motivation*
[e] 23:15 Lit *proselyte,* that is, one who has "come over" to Judaism
[f] 23:15 Lit *twice the son of gehenna*
[g] 23:16,18 Lit *is obligated*
[h] 23:17 Lit *Fools and blind*

sanctuary takes an oath by it and by Him who dwells in it. [22] And the one who takes an oath by heaven takes an oath by God's throne and by Him who sits on it.

[23] "Woe to you, scribes and Pharisees, hypocrites! You pay a tenth of[a] mint, dill and cumin,[b] yet you have neglected the more important matters of the law—justice, mercy and faith. These things should have been done without neglecting the others. [24] Blind guides! You strain out a gnat, yet gulp down a camel!

[25] "Woe to you, scribes and Pharisees, hypocrites! You clean the outside of the cup and dish, but inside they are full of greed[c] and self-indulgence! [26] Blind Pharisee! First clean the inside of the cup,[1] so the outside of it[2] may also become clean.

[27] "Woe to you, scribes and Pharisees, hypocrites! You are like whitewashed tombs, which appear beautiful on the outside, but inside are full of dead men's bones and every impurity. [28] In the same way, on the outside you seem righteous to people, but inside you are full of hypocrisy and lawlessness.

[29] "Woe to you, scribes and Pharisees, hypocrites! You build the tombs of the prophets and decorate the monuments of the righteous, [30] and you say, 'If we had lived in the days of our fathers, we wouldn't have taken part with them in shedding the prophets' blood.'[d] [31] You therefore testify against yourselves that you are sons of those who murdered the prophets. [32] Fill up, then, the measure of your fathers' sins![e]

[33] "Snakes! Brood of vipers! How can you escape being condemned to hell?[f] [34] This is why I am sending you prophets, sages, and scribes. Some of them you will kill and crucify, and some of them you will flog in your synagogues and hound from town to town. [35] So all the righteous blood shed on the earth will be charged to you,[g] from the blood of righteous Abel to the blood of

Does Your Faith Have Form, But No Power?

Religious activity apart from fellowship with God is empty ritual. Don't settle for a religious life that lacks a vital relationship with Jesus Christ.

"Blind fools! For which is greater, the gold or the sanctuary that sanctified the gold?"

—Matthew 23:17

[1]**23:26** Other mss add *and dish*
[2]**23:26** Other mss read *them*

[a]**23:23** Or *You tithe*
[b]**23:23** A plant whose seeds are used as a seasoning
[c]**23:25** Or *full of violence*
[d]**23:30** Lit *have been partakers with them in the blood of the prophets*
[e]**23:32** Lit *the measure of your fathers*
[f]**23:33** Lit *escape from the judgment of gehenna;* see 5:22 note
[g]**23:35** Lit *will come on you*

Zechariah, son of Berechiah, whom you murdered between the sanctuary and the altar. [36] I assure you: All these things will come on this generation!

JESUS' LAMENTATION OVER JERUSALEM

[37] "O Jerusalem! Jerusalem that kills the prophets and stones those who are sent to her! How often I wanted to gather your children together, as a hen gathers her chicks[a] under her wings, yet you were not willing! [38] See! Your house is left to you desolate. [39] For I tell you, you will never see Me again until you say, **'Blessed is He who comes in the name of the Lord!'** "[b]

DESTRUCTION OF THE TEMPLE PREDICTED

24 As Jesus left and was going out of the temple complex, His disciples came up and called His attention to the temple buildings. [2] Then He replied to them, "Do you not see all these things? I assure you: Not one stone will be left here on another that will not be thrown down!"

SIGNS OF THE END OF THE AGE

[3] While He was sitting on the Mount of Olives,[c] the disciples approached Him privately and said, "Tell us, when will these things happen? And what is the sign of Your coming and of the end of the age?"

[4] Then Jesus replied to them: "Watch out that no one deceives you. [5] For many will come in My name, saying, 'I am the Messiah,'[d] and they will deceive many. [6] You are going to hear of wars and rumors of wars. See that you are not alarmed, because these things must take place, but the end is not yet. [7] For nation will rise up against nation, and kingdom against kingdom. There will be famines[1] and earthquakes in various places. [8] All these events are the beginning of birth pains.

[1] 24:7 Other mss add *epidemics*

---

[a] 23:37 Or *as a mother bird gathers her young*
[b] 23:39 Ps 118:26
[c] 24:3 A mountain east of Jerusalem across the Kidron Valley
[d] 24:4 Or *the Christ*

You Don't Know How Much God Loves You

God loves you, not because you deserve His love, but because His nature is love. His love for you gives you an inherent worth that nothing can diminish.

"O Jerusalem! Jerusalem that kills the prophets and stones those who are sent to her! How often I wanted to gather your children together, as a hen gathers her chicks under her wings, yet you were not willing!"

—Matthew 23:37

PERSECUTIONS PREDICTED

9 "Then they will hand you over to persecution,[a] and they will kill you. You will be hated by all nations because of My name. 10 Then many will take offense, betray one another and hate one another. 11 Many false prophets will rise up and deceive many. 12 And because lawlessness will multiply, the love of many will grow cold. 13 But the one who endures to the end, this one will be delivered.[b] 14 This good news of the kingdom will be proclaimed in all the world[c] as a testimony to all nations. And then the end will come.

THE GREAT TRIBULATION

15 "So when you see **'the abomination that causes desolation,'**[de] spoken of by the prophet Daniel, standing in the holy place" (let the reader understand[f]), 16 "then those in Judea must flee to the mountains! 17 A man on the housetop[g] must not come down to get things out of his house. 18 And a man in the field must not go back to get his clothes. 19 Woe to pregnant women and nursing mothers in those days! 20 Pray that your escape may not be in winter or on a Sabbath. 21 For at that time there will be great tribulation, the kind that hasn't taken place since the beginning of the world until now, and never will again! 22 Unless those days were cut short, no one[h] would survive.[i] But because of the elect those days will be cut short.

23 "If anyone tells you then, 'Look, here is the Messiah!'[j] or, 'Over here!' do not believe it! 24 False messiahs[j] and false prophets will arise and perform great signs and wonders to lead astray, if possible, even the elect. 25 Take note: I have told you in advance. 26 So if they tell you, 'Look, He's in the wilderness!' don't go out; 'Look, he's in the inner rooms!' do not believe it. 27 For as the lightning comes from the east and flashes as

WORD STUDY

Greek word: **thlipsis**
[THLIHP sihss]
Translation: **tribulation**
Uses in Matthew's Gospel: **4**
(Mk, 3; Jn, 2)
Uses in the NT: **45**
Key passage: **Matthew 24:21**

The Greek noun *thlipsis* comes from the verb *thlibo* (ten occurrences in the NT), which means *to press* or *to crush*. The picture is one of being between a rock and a hard place, but the literal concept is rarely used in the NT. Instead, figurative kinds of crushing that cause difficulties in life are in view most of the time. Both terms are used for persevering through *afflictions* (as *thlipsis* is often translated, especially in Paul's letters) in the Christian life (Rm 5:3; 8:35; 12:12; 2 Co 1:4; see also Ac 14:22), though unbelievers can be afflicted by God's judgment (Rm 2:9). On four occasions *thlipsis* is used in the expression "great tribulation"; two are in an end times context (Mt 24:21; Rv 7:14), and two are related to difficulties in the present age (Ac 7:11; Rv 2:22). Despite the incredibly difficult times the world had already experienced—and is still experiencing—Jesus warned that the worst is yet to come (Mt 24:15–28); yet Revelation 7:9–17 indicates that great multitudes will be saved around the globe in the face of the evil permeating the world.

---

a24:9 Or *tribulation, distress*
b24:13 Or *be saved*
c24:14 Or *inhabited earth*
d24:15 Or *abomination of desolation* or *desolating sacrilege*
e24:15 Dn 9:27

f24:15 These are, most likely, Matthew's words to his readers.
g24:17 Or *roof*
h24:22 Lit *all flesh*
i24:22 Or *be saved/delivered*
j24:23,24 Or *the Christ . . . False christs*

far as the west, so will be the coming of the Son of Man.[a] [28] Wherever the carcass is, there the vultures[b] will gather.

THE COMING OF THE SON OF MAN

[29] "Immediately after the tribulation of those days,

The sun will be darkened,
and the moon will not shed her light;
the stars will fall from the sky,
and the celestial powers will be shaken.[c]

[30] "Then the sign of the Son of Man will appear in the sky, and then all the tribes of the land[d] will mourn;[e] and they will see the Son of Man coming on the clouds of heaven with power and great glory. [31] He will send out His angels with a loud trumpet, and they will gather His elect from the four winds, from one end of the sky to the other.

THE PARABLE OF THE FIG TREE

[32] "Now from the fig tree learn this parable: As soon as its branch becomes tender and sprouts leaves, you know that summer is near. [33] In the same way, when you see all these things, know[f] that He[g] is near—at the door! [34] I assure you: This generation will certainly not pass away until all these things take place. [35] Heaven and earth will pass away, but My words will never pass away.

NO ONE KNOWS THE DAY OR HOUR

[36] "Now concerning that day and hour no one knows—neither the angels in heaven, nor the Son[1]—except the Father only. [37] As the days of Noah were, so the coming of the Son of Man will be. [38] For in those days before the Flood they were eating and drinking, marrying and giving in marriage, until the day Noah boarded the ark. [39] They didn't know[h] until the flood came and swept them all away. So this is the way the

God's Way Is the Only Way

He did not say, "I will show you the way." He said, "I AM the way." Jesus knows the way; He is your way.

"Heaven and earth will pass away, but My words will never pass away."

—Matthew 24:35

Obey Every Day

If you were to do everything that Jesus tells you one day at a time, you would always be right in the center of His will.

"Who then is a faithful and sensible slave, whom his master has put in charge of his household, to give them food at the proper time? Blessed is that slave whom his master, when he comes, will find working."

—Matthew 24:45-46

[1]24:36 Other mss omit *nor the Son*

[a]24:27 Zch 9:14
[b]24:28 Or *eagles*
[c]24:29 Is 13:10; 34:4; cf. Jl 2:10; 2:31; 3:15
[d]24:30 Or *earth*
[e]24:30 Lit *beat (their breasts)*

[f]24:33 Or *you know*
[g]24:33 Or *it,* that is, summer
[h]24:39 That is, *they didn't know* the day and hour of the coming judgment

coming of the Son of Man will be: [40] Then two men will be in the field: one will be taken and one left. [41] Two women will be grinding at the mill: one will be taken and one left. [42] Therefore be alert, since you don't know what day[1] your Lord is coming. [43] But know this: If the homeowner had known what time[a] the thief was coming, he would have stayed alert and not let his house be broken into. [44] This is why you also should get ready, because the Son of Man is coming at an hour you do not expect.

FAITHFUL SERVICE TO THE MESSIAH

[45] "Who then is a faithful and sensible slave, whom his master has put in charge of his household, to give them food at the proper time? [46] Blessed is that slave whom his master, when he comes, will find working.[b] [47] I assure you: He will put him in charge of all his possessions. [48] But if that wicked slave says in his heart, 'My master is delayed,' [49] and starts to beat his fellow slaves, and eats and drinks with drunkards, [50] that slave's master will come on a day he does not expect and at a time[c] he does not know. [51] He will cut him to pieces[d] and assign him a place with the hypocrites. In that place there will be weeping and gnashing of teeth.

THE PARABLE OF THE TEN VIRGINS

25 "Then the kingdom of heaven will be like ten virgins[e] who took their lamps and went out to meet the groom. [2] Five of them were foolish and five were sensible. [3] When the foolish took their lamps, they didn't take oil with them. [4] But the sensible ones took oil in their flasks with their lamps. [5] Since the groom was delayed, they all became drowsy and fell asleep.

[6] "In the middle of the night there was a shout: 'Here's the groom! Come out to meet him.'

[7] "Then all those virgins got up and trimmed their lamps. [8] But the foolish ones said to the sensible ones, 'Give us some of your oil, because our lamps are going out.'

Stay Close, Very Close

Christians lose many opportunities to experience God's activity because they have not devoted enough time to their relationship with God.

"But the foolish ones said to the sensible ones, 'Give us some of your oil, because our lamps are going out.' . . . When they had gone to buy some, the groom arrived. Then those who were ready went in with him to the wedding banquet, and the door was shut."

—Matthew 25:8,10

---

[1]24:42 Other mss read *hour* (time)

[a]24:43 Lit *watch,* a division of the night in ancient times
[b]24:46 Lit *doing thus*
[c]24:50 Lit *hour*
[d]24:51 Lit *him in two*
[e]25:1 Or *bridesmaids*

WORD STUDY

Greek word: ***talanton***
[TAL ahn tahn]
Translation: ***talent***
Uses in Matthew's Gospel: **14**
Uses in the NT: **14**
Key passage: **Matthew 25:14–30**

Despite the fact that the English word *talent* comes from the Greek noun *talanton,* the Greek term in NT times had nothing to do with natural or acquired abilities. A *talanton* was a balance and in the plural referred to a pair of scales, so weight was the primary concern of this term. Eventually, a *talanton* could refer to a specific weight and then the sum of money represented by that weight. In coinage, a *talanton* of silver became 6,000 *drachmas* (Latin *denarii*), one *drachma* being a day's wage for a common laborer.

The term *talanton* occurs once in Jesus' parable about forgiveness as an illustration of the greatness of human debt to God because of sin (Mt 18:22–35; see v. 24). The 10,000 talents (60 million drachmas!) the slave owed represents millions of dollars in modern currency, well beyond the slave's ability to pay back to his master. The other thirteen occurrences of the term occur in Jesus' parable about the judgment in the end times (Mt 25:14–30). The talents represent the responsibilities that the Lord has given each of us to invest in His kingdom. When the kingdom arrives, more talents are given to those who have faithfully done so, but judgment awaits those who have not.

[9] "The sensible ones answered, 'No, there won't be enough for us and for you. Go instead to those who sell, and buy oil for yourselves.'

[10] "When they had gone to buy some, the groom arrived. Then those who were ready went in with him to the wedding banquet, and the door was shut.

[11] "Later the rest of the virgins also came and said, 'Master, master, open up for us!'

[12] "But he replied, 'I assure you: I do not know you!'

[13] "Therefore be alert, because you don't know either the day or the hour.[1]

THE PARABLE OF THE TALENTS

[14] "For it is just like a man going on a journey. He called his own slaves and turned over his possessions to them. [15] To one he gave five talents;[a] to another, two; and to another, one—to each according to his own ability. Then he went on a journey. Immediately [16] the man who had received five talents went, put them to work, and earned five more. [17] In the same way the man with two earned two more. [18] But the man who had received one talent went off, dug a hole in the ground, and hid his master's money.

[19] "After a long time the master of those slaves came and settled accounts with them. [20] The man who had received five talents approached, presented five more talents, and said, 'Master, you gave me five talents. Look, I've earned five more talents.'

[21] "His master said to him, 'Well done, good and faithful slave! You were faithful over a few things; I will put you in charge of many things. Enter your master's joy!'

[22] "Then the man with two talents also approached. He said, 'Master, you gave me two talents. Look, I've earned two more talents.'

[23] "His master said to him, 'Well done, good and faithful slave! You were faithful over a few things; I will put you in charge of many things. Enter your master's joy!'

[24] "Then the man who had received one talent also approached and said, 'Master, I know you. You're a difficult[b] man, reaping where you haven't sown and gather-

[1]25:13 Other mss add *in which the Son of Man is coming.*

[a]25:15 Worth a very large sum of money, equaling 6,000 denarii per talent

[b]25:24 Or *hard*

ing where you haven't scattered seed. [25] So I was afraid and went off and hid your talent in the ground. Look, you have what is yours.'

[26] "But his master replied to him, 'You evil, lazy slave! If you knew that I reap where I haven't sown and gather where I haven't scattered,[a] [27] then you should have deposited my money with the bankers. And when I returned I would have received my money[b] back with interest.

[28] "'So take the talent from him and give it to the one who has ten talents. [29] For to everyone who has, more will be given, and he will have more than enough. But from the one who does not have, even what he has will be taken away from him. [30] And throw this good-for-nothing slave into the outer darkness. In that place there will be weeping and gnashing of teeth.'

THE SHEEP AND THE GOATS

[31] "When the Son of Man comes in His glory, and all the angels[1] with Him, then He will sit on the throne of His glory. [32] All the nations[c] will be gathered before Him, and He will separate them one from another, just as a shepherd separates the sheep from the goats. [33] He will put the sheep on His right, and the goats on the left. [34] Then the King will say to those on His right, 'Come, you who are blessed by My Father, inherit the kingdom prepared for you from the foundation of the world:

[35] For I was hungry and you gave Me something to eat;
I was thirsty and you gave Me something to drink;
I was a stranger and you took Me in;
[36] I was naked and you clothed Me;
I was sick and you took care of Me;
I was in prison and you visited Me.'

[37] "Then the righteous will answer Him, 'Lord, when did we see You hungry and feed You, or thirsty and give You something to drink? [38] When did we see You a stranger and take You in, or without clothes and clothe

Be Faithful in the Small Things

Any assignment that comes from the Maker of the universe is an important assignment. Don't use human standards to measure the importance or value of an assignment.

"His master said to him, 'Well done, good and faithful slave! You were faithful over a few things; I will put you in charge of many things. Enter your master's joy!'"
—Matthew 25:21

[1]**25:31** Other mss read *holy angels*

[a]**25:26** This clause can also be taken as a statement.

[b]**25:27** Lit *received what is mine*
[c]**25:32** Or *Gentiles*

You? [39] When did we see You sick, or in prison, and visit You?'

[40] "And the King will answer them, 'I assure you: Whatever you did for one of the least of these brothers of Mine, you did for Me.' [41] Then He will also say to those on the left, 'Depart from Me, you who are cursed, into the eternal fire prepared for the Devil and his angels!

[42] For I was hungry and you gave Me nothing to eat;
I was thirsty and you gave Me nothing to drink;
[43] I was a stranger and you didn't take Me in;
I was naked and you didn't clothe Me,
sick and in prison and you didn't take care of Me.'

[44] "Then they too will answer, 'Lord, when did we see You hungry, or thirsty, or a stranger, or without clothes, or sick, or in prison, and not help You?'

[45] "Then He will answer them, 'I assure you: Whatever you did not do for one of the least of these, you did not do for Me either.'

[46] "And they will go away into eternal punishment, but the righteous into eternal life."

THE PLOT TO KILL JESUS

26 When Jesus had finished saying all this, He told His disciples, [2] "You know[a] that the Passover takes place after two days, and the Son of Man will be handed over to be crucified."

[3] Then the chief priests[1] and the elders of the people assembled in the palace of the high priest, who was called Caiaphas, [4] and they conspired to arrest Jesus by deceit and kill Him. [5] "Not during the festival," they said, "so there won't be rioting among the people."

THE ANOINTING AT BETHANY

[6] While Jesus was in Bethany at the house of Simon the leper, [7] a woman approached Him with an alabaster jar of very expensive fragrant oil. She poured it on His head as He was reclining at the table. [8] When the disci-

[1] 26:3 Other mss add *and the scribes*

[a] 26:2 Or *Know* as a command

Are You Ready to Go Where God Says?

Is your heart so filled with love for God that you are watching for the first opportunity to say, as Isaiah did, "Here am I. Send me!"?

"And the King will answer them, 'I assure you: Whatever you did for one of the least of these brothers of Mine, you did for Me.'"

—Matthew 25:40

all according to God's divine plan

ples saw it, they were indignant. "Why this waste?" they asked. [9] "This might have been sold for a great deal and given to the poor."

[10] But Jesus, aware of this, said to them, "Why are you bothering this woman? She has done a noble thing for Me. [11] You always have the poor with you, but you do not always have Me. [12] By pouring this fragrant oil on My body, she has prepared Me for burial. [13] I assure you: Wherever this gospel is proclaimed in the whole world, what this woman has done will also be told in memory of her."

[14] Then one of the Twelve—the man called Judas Iscariot—went to the chief priests [15] and said, "What are you willing to give me if I hand Him over to you?" So they weighed out thirty pieces of silver for him. [16] And from that time he started looking for a good opportunity to betray Him.

BETRAYAL AT THE PASSOVER

[17] On the first day of Unleavened Bread[a] the disciples came to Jesus and asked, "Where do You want us to prepare the Passover[b] so You may eat it?"

[18] "Go into the city to a certain man," He said, "and tell him, 'The Teacher says, "My time is near; I am celebrating the Passover at your place[c] with My disciples."'"

[19] So the disciples did as Jesus had directed them and prepared the Passover. [20] When evening came, He was reclining at the table with the Twelve. [21] While they were eating, He said, "I assure you: One of you will betray Me."

[22] Deeply distressed, each one began to say to Him, "Surely not I, Lord?"

[23] He replied, "The one who dipped his hand with Me in the bowl—he will betray Me. [24] The Son of Man will go just as it is written about Him, but woe to that man by whom the Son of Man is betrayed! It would have been better for that man if he had not been born."

[25] Then Judas, His betrayer, replied, "Surely not I, Rabbi?"

"You have said it yourself," He told him.

created to worship

Worship Is Not a Waste of Time

Jesus taught that our highest priority must be our relationship with Him. Have you been serving God so diligently that you have not had time to spend with Him?

"Why this waste?" they asked. "This might have been sold for a great deal and given to the poor." But Jesus, aware of this, said to them, "Why are you bothering this woman? She has done a noble thing for Me."

—Matthew 26:8b–10

---

[a]**26:17** A seven-day festival celebrated in conjunction with the Passover (Ex 12:1–20)
[b]**26:17** The Jewish ritual meal celebrating Israel's deliverance from slavery in Egypt
[c]**26:18** Lit *Passover with you*

THE FIRST LORD'S SUPPER

[26] As they were eating, Jesus took bread, blessed and broke it, gave it to the disciples, and said, "Take, eat; this is My body." [27] Then He took a cup, and after giving thanks, He gave it to them and said, "Drink from it, all of you. [28] For this is My blood of the covenant,[1] which is shed for many for the forgiveness of sins. [29] But I tell you, from this moment I will not drink of this fruit of the vine until that day when I drink it new[a] in My Father's kingdom with you." [30] After singing psalms,[b] they went out to the Mount of Olives.

PETER'S DENIAL PREDICTED

[31] Then Jesus said to them, "Tonight all of you will fall[c] because of Me, for it is written:

> **I will strike the shepherd,**
> **and the sheep of the flock will be**
> **scattered.[d]**

[32] But after I have been resurrected, I will go ahead of you to Galilee."

[33] Peter told Him, "Even if everyone falls because of You, I will never fall!"[e]

[34] "I assure you," Jesus said to him, "tonight—before the rooster crows, you will deny Me three times!"

[35] "Even if I have to die with You," Peter told Him, "I will never deny You!" And all the disciples said the same thing.

THE PRAYER IN THE GARDEN

[36] Then Jesus came with them to a place called Gethsemane,[f] and He told the disciples, "Sit here while I go over there and pray." [37] Taking along Peter and the two sons of Zebedee, He began to be sorrowful and deeply distressed. [38] Then He said to them, "My soul is swallowed up in sorrow[g]—to the point of death.[h] Remain

---

God Wants to Use You—Warts and All

If you feel weak, limited, ordinary, you are the best material through which God can work!

Then Jesus said to them, "Tonight all of you will fall because of Me, for it is written: 'I will strike the shepherd, and the sheep of the flock will be scattered.' But after I have been resurrected, I will go ahead of you to Galilee."

—Matthew 26:31–32

Not My Will, But Yours Be Done

God's ways and thoughts are so different from yours and mine, they will often sound wrong, crazy, or impossible. When you recognize that the task is humanly impossible, you need to be ready to believe God and trust Him completely.

Going a little farther, He fell on His face, praying, "My Father! If it is possible, let this cup pass from Me. Yet not as I will, but as You will."

—Matthew 26:39

---

[1] **26:28** Other mss read *new covenant*

---

[a] **26:29** Or *drink new wine* or *drink in a new way*
[b] **26:30** Pss 113–118 were sung during and after the Passover meal.
[c] **26:31** Or *stumble*
[d] **26:31** Zch 13:7
[e] **26:33** See 26:31 note

[f] **26:36** A garden east of Jerusalem at the base of the Mt. of Olives; *Gethsemane* means "Olive oil press"
[g] **26:38** Or *I am deeply grieved,* or *overwhelmed, by sorrow;* see Ps 42:6,11; 43:5
[h] **26:38** Lit *unto death*

here and stay awake with Me." [39] Going a little farther,[1] He fell on His face, praying, "My Father! If it is possible, let this cup pass from Me. Yet not as I will, but as You will."

[40] Then He came to the disciples and found them sleeping. "What?" [a] He asked Peter. "Couldn't you[b] stay awake with Me one hour? [41] Stay awake and pray, so that you won't enter into temptation. The spirit is willing, but the flesh is weak."

[42] Again, a second time, He went away and prayed, "My Father, if this[2] cannot pass[3] unless I drink it, Your will be done." [43] And He came again and found them sleeping, because they could not keep their eyes open.[c]

[44] After leaving them, He went away again and prayed a third time, saying the same thing once more. [45] Then He came to the disciples and said to them, "Are you still sleeping and resting?[d] Look, the time[e] is near. The Son of Man is being betrayed into the hands of sinners. [46] Get up; let's go! See—My betrayer is near."

THE JUDAS KISS

[47] While He was still speaking, Judas, one of the Twelve, suddenly arrived. With him was a large mob, with swords and clubs, who were sent by[f] the chief priests and elders of the people. [48] His betrayer had given them a sign: "The one I kiss, He's the one; arrest Him!" [49] So he went right up to Jesus and said, "Greetings, Rabbi!"—and kissed[g] Him.

[50] "Friend," Jesus asked him, "why have you come?"[h]

Then they came up, took hold of Jesus, and arrested Him. [51] At that moment one of those with Jesus reached out his hand and drew his sword. He struck the high priest's slave and cut off his ear.

[52] Then Jesus told him, "Put your sword back in place because all who take up a sword will perish by a sword.

---

[1] **26:39** Other mss read *Drawing nearer*
[2] **26:42** Other mss add *cup*
[3] **26:42** Other mss add *from Me*

---

[a] **26:40** Or *So*
[b] **26:40** The plural verb in Gk refers to all three disciples.
[c] **26:43** Lit *because their eyes were weighted down*
[d] **26:45** Or *Sleep on now and take your rest.*
[e] **26:45** Lit *hour*
[f] **26:47** Lit *clubs, from*
[g] **26:49** Perhaps suggesting repetition or affection
[h] **26:50** Or *do what you have come for*

WORD STUDY

Greek word: ***paradidomi***
[pah rah DIHD oh mee]
Translation: ***betray***
Uses in Matthew's Gospel: **31**
(Mk, 20; Lk, 17; Jn, 15)
Uses in the NT: **119**
Key passage: **Matthew 26:46**

The Greek verb *paradidomi* is an extremely flexible word. The term is a compound from two words meaning *to give alongside* though in usage *paradidomi* actually means *give over.*

Positively, *paradidomi* is used to describe commendation for service (Ac 14:26; 15:26); the passing on of traditions (Lk 1:2; Ac 6:14; Rm 6:17; 1 Co 11:2,23; 15:3; Jd 3; 2 Pt 2:21; the related noun *paradosis* is the word for *tradition,* and can be used negatively as well); the Father delivering all things to the Son (Mt 11:27; Lk 10:22; see Mt 25:14,20,22) and the Son in turn delivering all things to the Father (1 Co 15:24); Jesus being delivered to death by the Father (Rm 8:32); Jesus giving His own life for us (Gl 2:20; Eph 5:2,25); and the very moment of Jesus' death (Jn 19:30).

Negatively, *paradidomi* is used to describe arrest and/or imprisonment (Mt 4:12; 10:19; 18:34; Ac 8:3; 22:4; 2 Pt 2:4); the passing on of traditions (Mk 7:13); Jesus being delivered to death by His enemies (Mt 26:2; 27:2,26; Ac 3:13); believers being persecuted (Mt 10:21; 24:9; Ac 21:11); professing believers being turned over to Satan (1 Co 5:5; 1 Tm 1:20); and God's progressively harsher judgment on sin (Rm 1:24,26,28). Not surprisingly, the dominant use of the term *paradidomi* is to describe one of the most notorious acts in history, Judas's betrayal of Jesus (forty times, as in Mt 26:46).

⁵³Or do you think that I cannot call on My Father, and He will provide Me at once with more than twelve legions[a] of angels? ⁵⁴How, then, would the Scriptures be fulfilled that say it must happen this way?"

⁵⁵At that time[b] Jesus said to the crowds, "Have you come out with swords and clubs, as if I were a criminal,[c] to capture Me? Every day I used to sit, teaching in the temple complex, and you didn't arrest Me. ⁵⁶But all this has happened so that the prophetic Scriptures[d] would be fulfilled." Then all the disciples deserted Him and ran away.

JESUS FACES THE SANHEDRIN

⁵⁷Those who had arrested Jesus led Him away to Caiaphas the high priest, where the scribes and the elders had convened. ⁵⁸Meanwhile, Peter was following Him at a distance right to the high priest's courtyard.[e] He went in and was sitting with the temple police[f] to see the outcome.[g]

⁵⁹The chief priests and the whole Sanhedrin[h] were looking for false testimony against Jesus so they could put Him to death. ⁶⁰But they could not find any, even though many false witnesses came forward.[1] Finally, two[2] who came forward ⁶¹stated, "This man said, 'I can demolish God's sanctuary and rebuild it in three days.'"

⁶²The high priest then stood up and said to Him, "Don't You have an answer to what these men are testifying against You?" ⁶³But Jesus kept silent. Then the high priest said to Him, "By the living God I place You under oath: tell us if You are the Messiah,[i] the Son of God!"

⁶⁴"You have said it yourself,"[j] Jesus told him. "But I tell you, in the future[k] you will see 'the Son of Man seated at the right hand' of the Power, and 'coming on the clouds of heaven.'"[l]

Everything Must Square with the Scripture

Throughout your life, you will have times when you want to respond based on your experiences or your wisdom. This should be your guideline: Always go back to the Bible for truth.

"Or do you think that I cannot call on My Father, and He will provide Me at once with more than twelve legions of angels? How, then, would the Scriptures be fulfilled that say it must happen this way?"

—Matthew 26:53-54

Obedience Is Faith Without Words

What you do in response to His Word reveals what you believe about God regardless of what you say.

Then all the disciples deserted Him and ran away.

—Matthew 26:56b

---

¹26:60 Other mss add *they found none*
²26:60 Other mss add *false witnesses*

[a]26:53 A Roman legion contained up to six thousand soldiers
[b]26:55 Lit *hour*
[c]26:55 Lit *as against a criminal*
[d]26:56 Or *the Scriptures of the prophets*
[e]26:58 Or *palace*
[f]26:58 Or *officers*, or *servants*
[g]26:58 Lit *end*
[h]26:59 The seventy-member supreme council of Judaism patterned after Moses' seventy elders
[i]26:63 Or *the Christ*
[j]26:64 Or *That is true*
[k]26:64 Lit *you, from now*
[l]26:64 Ps 110:1; Dn 7:13

65 Then the high priest tore his robes and said, "He has blasphemed! Why do we still need witnesses? Look, now you've heard the blasphemy! 66 What is your decision?"a

They answered, "He deserves death!" 67 Then they spit in His face and beat Him; and others slapped Him 68 and said, "Prophesy to us, you Messiah!b Who hit You?"

PETER DENIES HIS LORD

69 Now Peter was sitting outside in the courtyard. A servant approached him and she said, "You were with Jesus the Galilean too."

70 But he denied it in front of everyone: "I don't know what you're talking about!"

71 When he had gone out to the gateway, another woman saw him and told those who were there, "This man was with Jesus the Nazarene!"

72 And again he denied it with an oath, "I don't know the man!"

73 After a little while those standing there approached and said to Peter, "You certainly are one of them, since even your accentc gives you away."

74 Then he started to curse d and to swear with an oath, "I do not know the man!" Immediately a rooster crowed. 75 And Peter remembered the words Jesus had spoken, "Before the rooster crows, you will deny Me three times." And he went outside and wept bitterly.

JESUS HANDED OVER TO PILATE

27 When daybreak came, all the chief priests and the elders of the people plotted against Jesus to put Him to death. 2 After tying Him up, they led Him away and handed Him over to Pilate,1e the governor.

1 27:2 Other mss read *Pontius Pilate*

a 26:66 Lit *What does it seem to you?*
b 26:68 Or *Christ*
c 26:73 Or *speech*
d 26:74 That is, to call down curses on himself if what he said wasn't true

c 27:2 Pontius Pilate was appointed by Caesar Tiberius as the fifth governor of the province of Judea in A.D. 26. His jurisdiction included Samaria to the north, Gaza and the Dead Sea area to the south. He remained at this post until A.D. 36.

Never Be Ashamed to Be Called One of His

If we want to enjoy the blessings of God's presence, we must be willing to endure the costs and responsibilities of being known by His name.

Now Peter was sitting outside in the courtyard. A servant approached him and she said, "You were with Jesus the Galilean too." But he denied it in front of everyone: "I don't know what you're talking about!"

—Matthew 26:69–70

JUDAS HANGS HIMSELF

[3] Then Judas, His betrayer, seeing that He had been condemned, was full of remorse and returned the thirty pieces of silver to the chief priests and to the elders. [4] "I have sinned by betraying innocent blood," he said.

"What's that to us?" they said. "See to it yourself!"

[5] So he threw the silver into the sanctuary and departed. Then he went and hanged himself.

[6] The chief priests took the silver and said, "It's not lawful to put it into the temple treasury,[a] since it is blood money."[b] [7] So they conferred together and bought the potter's field with it as a burial place for foreigners. [8] Therefore that field has been called "Blood Field" to this day. [9] Then what was spoken through the prophet Jeremiah was fulfilled:

> **They took the thirty pieces of silver, the price of Him whose price was set by the sons of Israel, [10] and they gave them for the potter's field, as the Lord directed me.**[c]

JESUS FACES THE GOVERNOR

[11] Now Jesus stood before the governor. "Are You the King of the Jews?" the governor asked Him.

Jesus answered, "You have said it yourself."[d] [12] And while He was being accused by the chief priests and elders, He didn't answer.

[13] Then Pilate said to Him, "Don't You hear how much they are testifying against You?" [14] But He didn't answer him on even one charge, so that the governor was greatly amazed.

JESUS OR BARABBAS

[15] At the festival it was the governor's custom to release to the crowd one prisoner whom they wanted. [16] At that time they had a notorious prisoner called Barabbas.[1] [17] So when they had gathered together, Pilate said to them, "Whom do you want me to release for

You Can Witness Without Saying a Word

The most compelling evidence that Christ is alive and triumphant is His activity in the lives of His people. Everywhere we go, our lives should demonstrate to others that Christ is victorious.

But He didn't answer him on even one charge, so that the governor was greatly amazed.

—Matthew 27:14

---

[1]27:16 Other mss read *Jesus Barabbas*

---

[a]27:6 See Mk 7:11 where the same Heb word used here *(Korban)* means a gift (pledged to the temple).
[b]27:6 Lit *is the price of blood*

[c]27:10 Jr 32:6–9; Zch 11:12–13
[d]27:11 Or *That is true:* an affirmative oath (see also at 26:64)

you—Barabbas,[1] or Jesus who is called Messiah?"[a] [18] For he knew they had handed Him over because of envy.

[19] While he was sitting on the judge's bench,[b] his wife sent word to him, "Have nothing to do with that righteous man, for today I've suffered terribly in a dream because of Him!"

[20] The chief priests and the elders, however, persuaded the crowds to ask for Barabbas and to execute Jesus. [21] The governor asked them, "Which of the two do you want me to release for you?"

"Barabbas!" they answered.

[22] Pilate asked them, "What should I do then with Jesus, who is called Messiah?"[c]

They all answered, "Crucify Him!"[d]

[23] Then he said, "Why? What has He done wrong?"

But they kept shouting, "Crucify Him!" all the more.

[24] When Pilate saw that he was getting nowhere,[e] but that a riot was starting instead, he took some water, washed his hands in front of the crowd, and said, "I am innocent of this man's[2] blood. See to it yourselves!"

[25] All the people answered, "His blood be on us and on our children!" [26] Then he released Barabbas to them. But after having Jesus flogged, he handed Him over to be crucified.

MOCKED BY THE MILITARY

[27] Then the governor's soldiers took Jesus into headquarters[f] and gathered the whole company around Him. [28] They stripped Him and dressed Him in a scarlet robe. [29] They twisted a crown out of thorns, put it on His head, and placed a reed in His right hand. And they knelt down before Him and mocked Him: "Hail, King of the Jews!" [30] Then they spit at Him, took the reed, and kept hitting Him on the head. [31] When they had mocked Him, they stripped Him of the robe, put His clothes on Him, and led Him away to crucify Him.

[1]27:17 Other mss read *Jesus Barabbas*
[2]27:24 Other mss read *this righteous man's blood*

[a]27:17 Or *Christ*
[b]27:19 Gk *bema,* same word as *judgment seat* in 2 Co 5:10
[c]27:22 Or *Christ*
[d]27:22 Lit *Him—be crucified*
[e]27:24 Lit *that it availed nothing*
[f]27:27 Lit *the Praetorium,* a Latin word meaning military headquarters (or the governor's palace)

WORD STUDY

Greek word: **stauroo**
[stow RAH oh]
Translation: **crucify**
Uses in Matthew's Gospel: **10**
(Mk, 8; Lk, 6; Jn, 11)
Uses in the NT: **46**
Key passage: **Matthew 27:31**

The Greek verb *stauroo* originally referred to building a fence by driving stakes into the ground, and the related noun *(stauros)* was the term for an upright stake or pale. Such a stake could easily be used as an instrument of death (impaling someone on a stake), and impalement was an early form of crucifixion (running a stake through someone and then thrusting the stake into a tree). Roman influence eventually caused *stauroo* and *stauros* to refer mainly to the common form of execution of non-Roman citizens—tying or nailing someone to a *stauros* and leaving him hanging on it until he died. The vast majority of the occurrences of both terms, of course, refer to the manner of Jesus' death, though the NT mentions other people who died the same way (Mt 23:34; 27:38). The shameful death signified by dying on a cross became a subject to boast about regarding the death of Christ (Gl 6:14), since believers proclaim a crucified and risen Savior as Lord and Messiah (Ac 2:36; 4:10; 1 Co 1:23; 2:2; 2 Co 13:4).

Both *stauroo* and *stauros* were used metaphorically of the Christian life on occasion (Mt 16:24; Gl 5:24; 6:14; see Rm 6:6; Gl 2:20, where the compound *sustauroo,* meaning "crucify with," is used the same way). This metaphor emphasizes the importance of the believers' identity with Christ and His death for godly living.

CRUCIFIED BETWEEN TWO CRIMINALS

[32] As they were going out, they found a Cyrenian man named Simon. They forced this man to carry His cross. [33] When they came to a place called *Golgotha* (which means Skull Place), [34] they gave Him wine[1] mixed with gall[a] to drink. But when He tasted it, He would not drink it. [35] After crucifying Him they divided His clothes by casting lots.[2] [36] Then they sat down and were guarding Him there. [37] Above His head they put up the charge against Him in writing:

> **THIS IS JESUS**
> **THE KING OF THE JEWS**

[38] Then two criminals[b] were crucified with Him, one on the right and one on the left. [39] Those who passed by were yelling insults at[c] Him, shaking their heads [40] and saying, "The One who would demolish the sanctuary and rebuild it in three days, save Yourself! If You are the Son of God, come down from the cross!" [41] In the same way the chief priests, with the scribes and elders,[3] mocked Him and said, [42] "He saved others, but He cannot save Himself! He[4] is the King of Israel! Let Him come down now from the cross, and we will believe in Him. [43] He has put His trust in God; let God rescue Him now—if He wants Him![d] For He said, 'I am God's Son.'" [44] In the same way even the criminals who were crucified with Him kept taunting Him.

YOUR SERVICE SHOULD BE FREE, NOT BY FORCE

Your Service Should Be Free, Not by Force

God will often call us out of our comfort zones and use us to do things we would never undertake on our own. Our task is to follow Him willingly and to trust Him to know what is best.

As they were going out, they found a Cyrenian man named Simon. They forced this man to carry His cross.

—Matthew 27:32

THE DEATH OF JESUS

[45] From noon until three in the afternoon[e] darkness came over the whole land.[f] [46] At about three in the afternoon Jesus cried out with a loud voice, *"Elí, Elí, lemá*

[1] 27:34 Other mss read *sour wine*
[2] 27:35 Other mss add *that what was spoken by the prophet might be fulfilled: They divided My clothes among them, and for My clothing they cast lots* (Ps 22:18); see Jn 19:24.
[3] 27:41 Other mss add *and Pharisees*
[4] 27:42 Other mss read *If He*

[a] 27:34 Ps 69:21
[b] 27:38 Or perhaps political *revolutionaries*
[c] 27:39 Lit *passed by blasphemed* (or *were blaspheming*)
[d] 27:43 Ps 22:8; or *if He takes pleasure in Him*
[e] 27:45 Lit *From the sixth hour to the ninth hour*
[f] 27:45 Or *earth*

sabachtháni?" that is, "My God, My God, why have You forsaken[a] Me?"[b]

[47] When some of those standing there heard this, they said, "He's calling for Elijah!"

[48] Immediately one of them ran and got a sponge, filled it with sour wine, fixed it on a reed, and offered Him a drink. [49] But the rest said, "Let us see if Elijah comes to save Him!"

[50] Jesus shouted again with a loud voice and gave up His spirit. [51] Suddenly, the curtain of the sanctuary was split in two from top to bottom; the earth quaked and the rocks were split. [52] The tombs also were opened and many bodies of the saints who had gone to their rest[c] were raised. [53] And they came out of the tombs after His resurrection, entered the holy city, and appeared to many.

[54] When the centurion and those with him, who were guarding Jesus, saw the earthquake and the things that had happened, they were terrified and said, "This man really was God's Son!"[d]

[55] Many women were there, looking on from a distance, who had followed Jesus from Galilee and ministered to Him. [56] Among them were Mary Magdalene, Mary the mother of James and Joseph, and the mother of Zebedee's sons.

THE BURIAL OF JESUS

[57] When it was evening, a rich man from Arimathea named Joseph came, who himself had also become a disciple of Jesus. [58] He approached Pilate and asked for Jesus' body. Then Pilate ordered that it[1] be released. [59] So Joseph took the body, wrapped it in clean, fine linen, [60] and placed it in his new tomb, which he had cut into the rock. He left after rolling a great stone against the entrance of the tomb. [61] Mary Magdalene and the other Mary were seated there, facing the tomb.

[1]27:58 Other mss read *the body*

There's Power in the Blood

Never forget the power of the cross. When you face challenging times in life, remember God's power, and let Him be your strength.

Jesus shouted again with a loud voice and gave up His spirit. Suddenly, the curtain of the sanctuary was split in two from top to bottom; the earth quaked and the rocks were split.

—Matthew 27:50–51

---

[a]27:46 Or *abandoned*
[b]27:45 Ps 22:1
[c]27:52 That is, *had died;* lit *saints having fallen asleep*
[d]27:54 Or *the Son of God*

THE CLOSELY GUARDED TOMB

⁶² The next day, which followed the Preparation Day, the chief priests and the Pharisees gathered before Pilate ⁶³ and said, "Sir, we remember that while this deceiver was still alive, He said, 'After three days I will rise again.' ⁶⁴ Therefore give orders that the tomb be made secure until the third day. Otherwise, His disciples may come, steal Him, and tell the people, 'He has been raised from the dead.' Then the last deception will be worse than the first."

⁶⁵ "You have a guard of soldiers,"ᵃ Pilate told them. "Go and make it as secure as you know how." ⁶⁶ Then they went and made the tomb secure by sealing the stone and settingᵇ the guard.

RESURRECTION MORNING

28 After the Sabbath, as the first day of the week was dawning, Mary Magdalene and the other Mary went to view the tomb. ² Suddenly there was a violent earthquake, because an angel of the Lord descended from heaven and approached the tomb.ᶜ He rolled back the stone and was sitting on it. ³ His appearance was like lightning, and his robe was as white as snow. ⁴ The guards were so shaken from fear of him that they became like dead men.

⁵ But the angel told the women, "Don't be afraid, because I know you are looking for Jesus who was crucified. ⁶ He is not here! For He has been resurrected, just as He said. Come and see the place where He lay. ⁷ Then go quickly and tell His disciples, 'He has been raised from the dead. In fact, He is going ahead of you to Galilee; you will see Him there.' Listen, I have told you."

⁸ So, departing quickly from the tomb with fear and great joy, they ran to tell His disciples the news. ⁹ Just then¹ Jesus met them and said, "Rejoice!" They came up, took hold of His feet, and worshiped Him. ¹⁰ Then

¹**28:9** Other mss add *as they were on their way to tell the news to His disciples*

ᵃ**27:65** *soldiers* is supplied; it is uncertain whether this guard consisted of temple police or Roman soldiers. The verb *You have* can also be translated *Take.*

ᵇ**27:66** Lit *with the guard*
ᶜ**28:2** *the tomb* supplied from v. 1

[handwritten:] First word out of His mouth after death

Have You Decided to Follow Jesus?

Jesus never excused those who struggled to follow Him. He made it clear that to follow Him meant that He set the direction and they were to follow.

"Go, therefore, and make disciples of all nations, baptizing them in the name of the Father and of the Son and of the Holy Spirit, teaching them to observe everything I have commanded you. And remember, I am with you always, to the end of the age."

—Matthew 28:19–20

Jesus told them, "Do not be afraid. Go and tell My brothers to leave for Galilee, and they will see Me there."

THE SOLDIERS ARE BRIBED TO LIE

[11] As they were on their way, some of the guard came into the city and reported to the chief priests everything that had happened. [12] After the priests[a] had assembled with the elders and agreed on a plan, they gave the soldiers a large sum of money [13] and told them, "Say this, 'His disciples came during the night and stole Him while we were sleeping.' [14] If this reaches the governor's ears,[b] we will deal with[c] him and keep you out of trouble." [15] So they took the money and did as they were instructed. And this story has been spread among Jewish people to this day.

THE GREAT COMMISSION

[16] The eleven disciples traveled to Galilee, to the mountain where Jesus had directed them. [17] When they saw Him, they worshiped,[1] but some doubted. [18] Then Jesus came near and said to them, "All authority has been given to Me in heaven and on earth. [19] Go, therefore, and make disciples[d] of all nations, baptizing them in the name of the Father and of the Son and of the Holy Spirit, [20] teaching them to observe everything I have commanded you. And remember,[e] I am with you always,[f] to the end of the age."

WORD STUDY

Greek word: **matheteuo**
[mah they TYOO oh]
Translation: **make disciples**
Uses in Matthew's Gospel: **3**
Uses in the NT: **4**
Key passage: **Matthew 28:19**

The Greek word *matheteuo* is the verb form of the noun *mathetes,* meaning *disciple* (see word study on page 251). On two occasions, *matheteuo* means become a disciple (Mt 13:52; 27:57), and in the other two occurrences it means make disciples (Mt 28:19; Ac 14:21). In the Great Commission (Mt 28:18–20), the word translated "Go" is a participle, but the word *matheteuo* is in the imperative or command mode. This is a common construction in the writings of Matthew and Luke (a participle followed by an imperative). The significance of this construction is that the action expressed by the participle is necessary but is not the main idea. The participle expresses that which must be done to accomplish the main task, which is expressed by the imperative form of the verb. This is instructive for missionary efforts: Jesus' only command in the Great Commission is to make disciples— which makes this our main task— but in order to do this we must go.

[1] **28:17** Other mss add *Him*

[a] **28:12** Lit *After they*
[b] **28:13** Lit *this is heard by the governor*
[c] **28:14** Lit *will persuade*
[d] **28:19** Lit *and instruct* or *disciple* (verb)
[e] **28:20** Lit *look*
[f] **28:20** Lit *all the days*

Greek Word Studies

in the Gospel of Mark

THE GOSPEL OF

MARK

THE MESSIAH'S HERALD

1 The beginning of the gospel of Jesus Christ the Son of God. [2] As it is written in Isaiah the prophet:[1]

> Look, I am sending My messenger ahead of You,
> who will prepare Your way.[2]
> [3] A voice of one crying out in the wilderness:
> "Prepare the way for the Lord;
> make His paths straight!"[a]

[4] John came baptizing[b] in the wilderness and preaching a baptism of repentance[c] for the forgiveness of sins. [5] The whole Judean countryside and all the people of Jerusalem were flocking to him, and they were baptized by him in the Jordan River as they confessed their sins. [6] John wore a camel hair garment with a leather belt around his waist, and ate locusts and wild honey. [7] He was preaching: "Someone more powerful than I will come after me. I am not worthy to stoop down and untie the strap of His sandals. [8] I have baptized you with[d] water, but He will baptize you with[d] the Holy Spirit."

THE BAPTISM OF JESUS

[9] In those days Jesus came from Nazareth in Galilee and was baptized in the Jordan by John. [10] As soon as he came up out of the water, He saw the heavens being torn

[1] 1:2 Other mss read *in the prophets*
[2] 1:2 Other mss add *before You*

---

[a] 1:3 Is 40:3; Ml 3:1
[b] 1:4 Or *John the Baptist came* or *John the Baptizer came*

[c] 1:4 Or *a baptism based on repentance*
[d] 1:8 Or *in*

WORD STUDY

Greek word: *Iesous*
[ee ay S<u>OO</u>SS]
Translation: *Jesus*
Uses in Mark's Gospel: **82**
(Mt, 152; Lk, 88; Jn, 244)
Uses in the NT: **917**
Key passage: **Mark 1:1**

The proper name *Iesous* is the Greek form of the Hebrew name *Yeshua,* which in turn is a shortened form of the name *Yehoshua,* meaning *Yahweh saves.* This name and variations of it were common in Old and New Testament times (see Col 4:11). *Iesous* is the name used for Joshua in the Greek OT and also refers to him three times in the NT (Lk 3:29; Ac 7:45; Heb 4:8). Jesus was specifically given the name *Yeshua* by the angel of the Lord because He would "save His people from their sins" (Mt 1:21), which emphasizes His purpose for coming into the world. Mark identified Him at the beginning of his Gospel as "Jesus Christ, the Son of God" (1:1), which stresses both His Messiahship (see Mt 16:16; 26:63; Lk 4:41; Jn 1:49; 11:27; 20:31; Ac 9:20) and His deity (see Mt 4:3,6; 14:33; Mk 15:39; Jn 3:18; 5:25).

open and the Spirit descending to Him like a dove. [11] And a voice came from heaven:

"You are My beloved Son;[a]
In You I take delight!"[bc]

THE TEMPTATION OF JESUS

[12] Immediately the Spirit drove Him into the wilderness. [13] He was in the wilderness forty days, being tempted by Satan. He was with the wild animals, and the angels began to serve Him.

MINISTRY IN GALILEE

[14] But after John was arrested, Jesus went to Galilee, preaching the good news[1d] of God:[e] [15] "The time is fulfilled, and the kingdom of God has come near. Repent and believe in the good news!"[d]

THE FIRST DISCIPLES

[16] As He was passing along by the Sea of Galilee, He saw Simon and Andrew, Simon's brother. They were casting a net into the sea, since they were fishermen. [17] "Follow Me," Jesus told them, "and I will make you into fishers of men!" [18] Immediately they left their nets and followed Him. [19] Going on a little farther, He saw James the son of Zebedee and his brother John. They were in their boat mending their nets. [20] Immediately He called them, and they left their father Zebedee in the boat with the hired men and followed Him.

DRIVING OUT AN UNCLEAN SPIRIT

[21] Then they went into Capernaum, and right away He entered the synagogue[f] on the Sabbath and began to teach. [22] They were astonished at His teaching because, unlike the scribes, He was teaching them as one having authority.

[23] Just then a man with an unclean spirit was in their

---

[1]1:14 Other mss add *of the kingdom*

---

[a]1:11 Ps 2:7
[b]1:11 Or *In You I am well pleased*
[c]1:11 Is 42:1
[d]1:14,15 Or *gospel*

[e]1:14 That is, either *from God* or *about God*
[f]1:21 A place where the Jewish people met for prayer, worship and teaching of the Scriptures

synagogue. He cried out,[1] [24] "What do You have to do with us,[a] Jesus—Nazarene? Have You come to destroy us? I know who You are—the Holy One of God!"

[25] But Jesus rebuked him and said, "Be quiet,[b] and come out of him!" [26] And the unclean spirit convulsed him, shouted with a loud voice, and came out of him.

[27] Then they were all amazed, so they began to argue with one another, saying, "What is this? A new teaching with authority![2] He commands even the unclean spirits, and they obey Him." [28] His fame then spread throughout the entire vicinity of Galilee.

HEALINGS AT CAPERNAUM

[29] As soon as they left the synagogue, they went into Simon and Andrew's house with James and John. [30] Simon's mother-in-law was lying in bed with a fever, and they told Him about her at once. [31] So He went to her, took her by the hand, and raised her up. The fever left her,[3] and she began to serve them.

[32] When evening came, after the sun had set, they began bringing to Him all those who were sick and those who were demon-possessed. [33] The whole town was assembled at the door, [34] and He healed many who were sick with various diseases, and drove out many demons. But He would not permit the demons to speak, because they knew Him.

PREACHING IN GALILEE

[35] Very early in the morning, while it was still dark, He got up, went out, and made His way to a deserted place. And He was praying there. [36] Simon and his companions went searching for Him. [37] They found Him and said, "Everyone's looking for You!"

[38] And He said to them, "Let's go on to the neighboring villages, so that I may preach there too. This is why I have come." [39] So He went into all of Galilee, preaching in their synagogues and driving out demons.

[1] **1:23** Other mss add to the beginning of v. 24 *Leave us alone!*
[2] **1:27** Other mss read *What is this? What is this new teaching? For with authority*
[3] **1:31** Other mss add *at once*

[a] **1:24** Lit *What to us and to you*   [b] **1:25** Or *Be muzzled*

He Doesn't Expect You to Know It All

He does not ask us to dream our dreams for Him and then ask Him to bless our plans. He is already at work when He comes to us. His desire is to get us from where we are to where He is working.

"Follow Me," He told them, "and I will make you into fishers of men!" Immediately they left their nets and followed Him.

—Mark 1:17-18

Do People See You Seeking Jesus?

Whenever we see Peter coming to Jesus, he is always accompanied by others. Because Peter was seeking Jesus, others sought Him too.

Simon and his companions went searching for Him.

—Mark 1:36

CLEANSING A LEPER

[40] Then a leper[a] came to Him, and begged on his knees before[1] Him, saying, "If You are willing, You can make me clean."[b]
[41] Moved with compassion, Jesus[c] reached out His hand and touched him. "I am willing," He told him. "Be made clean." [42] Immediately the leprosy left him, and he was made clean. [43] Then He sternly warned him and sent him away at once, [44] telling him, "See that you say nothing to anyone; but go and show yourself to the priest, and offer what Moses prescribed for your cleansing, as a testimony to them." [45] Yet he went out and began to proclaim it widely and to spread the news, with the result that Jesus[d] could no longer enter a town openly. But He was out in deserted places, and they would come to Him from everywhere.

THE SON OF MAN FORGIVES AND HEALS

2 When He entered Capernaum again after some days, it was reported that He was at home. [2] So many people gathered together that there was no more room, even near the door, and He was speaking the message to them. [3] Then they came to Him bringing a paralytic, carried by four men. [4] Since they were not able to bring[2] him to Jesus[e] because of the crowd, they removed the roof above where He was. And when they had broken through, they lowered the stretcher on which the paralytic was lying.

[5] Seeing their faith, Jesus told the paralytic, "Son, your sins are forgiven."

[6] But some of the scribes were sitting there, reasoning in their hearts:[f] [7] "Why does He speak like this? He's blaspheming! Who can forgive sins but God alone?"

[8] Right away Jesus understood in His spirit that they were reasoning like this within themselves, and said to

Just Show People Jesus

Our job is not to transform people into Christians nor to convict them of their sin. Our task is to bring them to Jesus, and He will perform His divine work in their lives.

Yet he went out and began to proclaim it widely and to spread the news, with the result that Jesus could no longer enter a town openly. But He was out in deserted places, and they would come to Him from everywhere.

—Mark 1:45

---

[1] 1:40 Other mss omit *on his knees before*
[2] 2:4 Other mss read *able to get near*

---

[a] 1:40 In the Bible, *leprosy* covers many skin disorders in addition to Hansen's disease.
[b] 1:40 *Clean,* in these verses, includes healing, ceremonial purification, return to fellowship with people, and worship in the temple. See Lv 14:1–31
[c] 1:41 Lit *He*
[d] 1:45 Lit *He*
[e] 2:4 Lit *bring to Him*
[f] 2:6 Or *minds*

them, "Why are you reasoning these things in your hearts?[a] [9] Which is easier: to say to the paralytic, 'Your sins are forgiven,' or to say, 'Get up, pick up your stretcher, and walk'? [10] But so you may know that the Son of Man has authority on earth to forgive sins," He told the paralytic, [11] "I tell you: get up, pick up your stretcher, and go home."

[12] Immediately he got up, picked up the stretcher, and went out in front of everyone. As a result, they were all astounded and gave glory to God, saying, "We have never seen anything like this!"

THE CALL OF MATTHEW

[13] Then Jesus[b] went out again beside the sea. The whole crowd was coming to Him, and He taught them. [14] Then, moving on, He saw Levi the son of Alphaeus sitting at the tax office, and He said to him, "Follow Me!" So he got up and followed Him.

DINING WITH SINNERS

[15] While He was reclining at the table in Levi's[c] house, many tax collectors and sinners were also guests[d] with Jesus and His disciples, because there were many who were following Him. [16] When the scribes of the Pharisees[1e] saw that He was eating with sinners and tax collectors, they asked His disciples, "Why does He eat[2] with tax collectors and sinners?"

[17] When Jesus heard this, He told them, "Those who are well don't need a doctor, but the sick do need one.[f] I didn't come to call the righteous, but sinners."

A QUESTION ABOUT FASTING

[18] Now John's disciples and the Pharisees[3] were fasting. People[g] came and asked Him, "Why do John's disciples and the Pharisees' disciples fast, but Your disciples do not fast?"

[1]2:16 Other mss read scribes and Pharisees
[2]2:16 Other mss add and drink
[3]2:18 Other mss read the disciples of John and of the Pharisees

[a]2:8 Or minds
[b]2:13 Lit He
[c]2:15 Lit his
[d]2:15 Lit reclining (at the table). At important meals the custom was to recline on a mat at a low table and lean on the left elbow.
[e]2:16 See Mt 3:7 note
[f]2:17 do need one implied
[g]2:18 Gk they

WORD STUDY

Greek word: **nesteuo**
[nay STYOO oh]
Translation: **fast**
Uses in Mark's Gospel: **6** (Mt, 8; Lk, 4)
Uses in the NT: **20**
Key passage: **Mark 2:18**

The Greek verb nesteuo can mean to be hungry or without food, but most often it means to fast (that is, to purposely abstain from food). The related noun nesteia can mean a fast (Lk 2:37; Ac 14:23; 27:9) or simply hunger (2 Co 6:5; 11:27), which is also the meaning of another related term in both of its NT occurrences (nestis; Mt 15:32 = Mk 8:3).

In the law of Moses fasting was commanded only for the Day of Atonement (Lv 16:29, using the idiom "humble your souls"), but the OT records several other occasions of fasting by certain Israelites, particularly in times of physical or spiritual need (Dt 9:9,18; 1 Sm 1:7; 20:34; 2 Sm 12:21; Est 4:16; Ps 35:13; Dn 9:3; 10:2). The purpose of fasting was to set aside everyday and even necessary activities so that matters of great spiritual significance could receive a person's full attention, a pattern followed on occasion in the NT also (Mt 4:2; Lk 2:37; Ac 9:9; 13:2).

By Jesus' time the Pharisees normally fasted twice a week, and His parable about the Pharisee and the tax collector includes a not-so-veiled reference to their surface spirituality in fasting this often (Lk 18:9-14). Every other occurrence of nesteuo in the Gospels refers either to Jesus' fasting (Mt 4:2), His warnings about hypocritical fasting (Mt 6:17-18), or His discussion about fasting with various disciples (Mt 9:14-15 = Mk 2:18-19 = Lk 5:33-35).

[19] Jesus said to them, "The wedding guests[a] cannot fast while the groom is with them, can they? As long as they have the groom with them, they cannot fast. [20] But the time[b] will come when the groom is taken away from them, and then they will fast in that day. [21] No one sews a patch of unshrunk cloth on an old garment. Otherwise, the new patch pulls away from the old cloth, and a worse tear is made. [22] And no one puts new wine into old wineskins. Otherwise, the wine will burst the skins, and the wine is lost as well as the skins.[1] But new wine is for fresh wineskins."

LORD OF THE SABBATH

[23] On the Sabbath He was going through the grainfields, and His disciples began to make their way picking some heads of grain. [24] The Pharisees said to Him, "Look, why are they doing what is not lawful on the Sabbath?"

[25] And He said to them, "Have you never read what David did when he was in need and hungry, he and his companions: [26] how he entered the house of God in the time of Abiathar[c] the high priest and ate the sacred bread[d]—which is not lawful for anyone to eat except the priests—and also gave some to his companions?"

[27] Then He told them, "The Sabbath was made for[e] man, and not man for[e] the Sabbath. [28] Therefore the Son of Man is Lord even of the Sabbath."

THE MAN WITH THE PARALYZED HAND

3 Now He entered the synagogue again, and a man was there who had a paralyzed hand. [2] In order to accuse Him, they were watching Him closely to see whether He would heal him on the Sabbath. [3] He told the man with the paralyzed hand, "Stand before us."[f] [4] Then He said to them, "Is it lawful on the Sabbath to do good or to do evil, to save life or to kill?" But they

Never Put Limits on What God Can Do

Many people get an assignment from God and say, "That couldn't possibly be from God. That is not the area of my gifts." If it is an assignment from God, you obey Him and you will see the manifestation of the Holy Spirit in new ways you may have never experienced before.

"And no one puts new wine into old wineskins. Otherwise, the wine will burst the skins, and the wine is lost as well as the skins. But new wine is for fresh wineskins."

—Mark 2:22

[1] **2:22** Other mss read *the wine spills out and the skins will be ruined*

[a] **2:19** Lit *The sons of the bridal chamber*
[b] **2:20** Lit *days*
[c] **2:26** 1 Sm 21:1–16
[d] **2:26** These were twelve loaves, representing the twelve tribes of Israel, put each week on the table in the holy place in the tabernacle and later in the temple. The priests ate the previous week's loaves. Ex 29:32; Lv 24:5–9; Mt 12:4
[e] **2:27** Or *because of*
[f] **3:3** Lit *Rise up in the middle*

were silent. [5] After looking around at them with anger and sorrow at the hardness of their hearts, He told the man, "Stretch out your hand." So he stretched it out, and his hand was restored. [6] Immediately the Pharisees went out and started plotting with the Herodians[a] against Him, how they might destroy Him.

MINISTERING TO THE MULTITUDE

[7] Jesus departed with His disciples to the sea, and a great multitude followed from Galilee, Judea, [8] Jerusalem, Idumea, beyond the Jordan, and around Tyre and Sidon. The great multitude came to Him because they heard everything He was doing. [9] Then He told His disciples to have a small boat ready for Him, so the crowd would not crush Him. [10] Since He had healed many, all who had diseases were pressing toward Him to touch Him. [11] Whenever the unclean spirits saw Him, they would fall down before Him and cry out, "You are the Son of God!" [12] And He would strongly warn them not to make Him known.

THE TWELVE APOSTLES

[13] Then He went up the mountain and summoned those He wanted, and they came to Him. [14] He appointed twelve, whom He also named apostles,[1] that they might be with Him and that He might send them out to preach [15] and to have authority to[2] drive out demons.

[16] He appointed the Twelve:[3]

To Simon, He gave the name Peter,
[17] and to James the son of Zebedee, and to his brother John,
He gave the name "Boanerges" (that is, "Sons of Thunder"),
[18] Andrew,
Philip and Bartholomew,
Matthew and Thomas,

[1]**3:14** Other mss omit *whom He also named apostles*
[2]**3:15** Other mss add *heal diseases, and*
[3]**3:16** Other mss omit *He appointed the Twelve*

[a]**3:6** See Mt 22:16 note

WORD STUDY

Greek word: **apostolos**
[ah PAHSS tah lahss]
Translation: **apostle**
Uses in Mark's Gospel: **2** (Mt, 1; Lk, 6; Jn, 1)
Uses in the NT: **80**
Key passage: **Mark 3:14**

The Greek noun *apostolos* comes from the common verb *apostello* and literally means *one sent forth with a message*. The noun did not attain the significance of being sent with authority, as the verb already had in the Greek speaking world, until its adoption by Jesus and the NT writers. The original twelve disciples were chosen and named *apostles* by Jesus (Mt 10:2; Mk 3:14; Lk 6:13); they were trained by Him (see Ac 1:15–26) and invested with His authority to lead the church to accomplish the ongoing task He had given it (Mt 28:18–20). Apostles are referred to 28 times in Acts (most in the NT), which describes the growth and expansion of the church. Apostles had to be eyewitnesses of Jesus' resurrection (Ac 1:22; 1 Co 9:1; 15:8–9). Together with prophets, apostles were foundational for the early church (Eph 2:20), particularly in being responsible for giving divine revelation to God's people (Eph 3:5). Only fifteen people are *clearly* referred to as apostles in the NT: the original twelve (numerous times), Matthias (Ac 1:26), Paul (numerous times), and Barnabas (Ac 14:14).

James the son of Alphaeus, and Thaddaeus, Simon the Zealot,[a] [19] and Judas Iscariot,[b] who also betrayed Him.

A HOUSE DIVIDED

[20] Then He went into a house, and the crowd gathered again so that they were not even able to eat.[c] [21] When His family heard this, they set out to restrain Him, because they said, "He's out of His mind."[d]

[22] And the scribes who had come down from Jerusalem said, "He has Beelzebul[e] in Him!" and, "He drives out demons by the ruler of the demons!"

[23] So He summoned them and spoke to them in parables: "How can Satan drive out Satan? [24] If a kingdom is divided against itself, that kingdom cannot stand. [25] If a house is divided against itself, that house cannot stand. [26] And if Satan rebels against himself and is divided, he cannot stand but is finished![f]

[27] "On the other hand, no one can enter a strong man's house and rob his possessions unless he first ties up the strong man. Then he will rob his house. [28] I assure you: People will be forgiven for all sins[g] and whatever blasphemies they may blaspheme. [29] But whoever blasphemes against the Holy Spirit never has forgiveness, but is guilty of an eternal sin"[1]— [30] because they were saying, "He has an unclean spirit."

TRUE RELATIONSHIPS

[31] Then His mother and His brothers came, and standing outside, they sent word to Him[h] and called Him. [32] A crowd was sitting around Him, and told Him, "Look, Your mother, Your brothers, and Your sisters[2] are outside asking for You."

[33] He replied to them, "Who are My mother and My brothers?" [34] And looking about at those who were sit-

Obedience Travels a One-Way Street

Sin robs you of the good things God has given. Diligently abstain from every form of evil, and you will be free to enjoy every good thing God has for you.

"If a kingdom is divided against itself, that kingdom cannot stand. If a house is divided against itself, that house cannot stand."

—Mark 3:24–25

Being His—What Else Could You Want?

A love relationship with God is more important than any other single factor in your life.

"Whoever does the will of God is My brother and sister and mother."

—Mark 3:35

---

[1]3:29 Other mss read *is subject to eternal judgment*
[2]3:32 Other mss omit *and Your sisters*

---

[a]3:18 Lit *Cananaean*
[b]3:19 Probably means *a man of Kerioth* (a town in Judea)
[c]3:20 Lit *eat bread,* or *eat a meal*
[d]3:21 Jn 7:5
[e]3:22 Term of slander, variously interpreted, "lord of flies," "lord of dung," or "ruler of demons" (2 Kg 1:2; Mt 12:24)
[f]3:26 Lit *but he has an end*
[g]3:28 Lit *All things will be forgiven the sons of men*
[h]3:31 Lit *they sent to Him*

ting in a circle around Him, He said, "Here are My mother and My brothers! [35] Whoever does the will of God is My brother and sister and mother."

THE PARABLE OF THE SOWER

4 Again He began to teach by the sea, and a very large crowd gathered around Him. So He got into a boat on the sea and sat down, while the whole crowd was on the shore facing the sea. [2] He taught them many things in parables, and in His teaching He said to them: [3] "Listen! Consider the sower who went out to sow. [4] As he sowed, this occurred: Some seed fell along the path, and the birds came and ate it up. [5] Other seed fell on rocky ground where it didn't have much soil, and it sprang up right away, since it didn't have deep soil. [6] When the sun came up, it was scorched, and since it didn't have a root, it withered. [7] Other seed fell among thorns, and the thorns came up and choked it, and it didn't produce a crop. [8] Still others fell on good ground and produced a crop that increased thirty, sixty, and a hundred times what was sown."[a] [9] Then He said, "Anyone who has ears to hear should listen!"

WHY JESUS USED PARABLES

[10] When He was in private, those who were around Him, along with the Twelve, asked Him about the parables. [11] He answered them, "The secret[b] of the kingdom of God has been granted to you, but to those outside, everything comes in parables [12] so that

> They may look and look, yet not
>   perceive;
> they may listen and listen, yet not
>   understand;
> otherwise, they might turn back—
>   and be forgiven."[1c]

[1]4:12 Other mss read *And their sins be forgiven them*

---

[a]4:8 *what was sown* is implied
[b]4:11 The Gk word *musterion* does not mean "mystery" in the Eng sense, but things that we can know only by divine revelation, or *a secret*, as here.
[c]4:12 Is 6:9–10

WORD STUDY

Greek word: **musterion**
[moo STAY ree ahn]
Translation: **secret**
Uses in Mark's Gospel: **1**
(Mt, 1; Lk, 1)
Uses in the NT: **28**
Key passage: **Mark 4:11**

The English word *mystery* comes from the Greek noun *musterion,* though our English word does not do it justice. A *musterion* in the ancient world was any religious cult that demanded secrecy from its participants, who had to undergo sacred rites for membership. An element of this may lie behind *musterion* in the NT, but the word normally translated "mystery" in Daniel is more likely the background for NT usage. In Daniel a mystery (Aramaic *raz*) was a revealed secret, something that could not be understood apart from divine revelation or explanation (Dan 2:17–47; 4:9); this is certainly the force of the numerous instances of *musterion* in the NT. Jesus used *musterion* only once, and this was in reference to the mysteries or secrets about the kingdom that He revealed and explained to His disciples (Mt 13:11 = Mk 4:11 = Lk 8:10). Paul used *musterion* 21 times, and on each occasion the secret is already known from previous revelation (see Rm 16:25; Eph 1:9; 6:19; Col 2:2; 4:3; 1 Tm 3:16), or it is explained in the context (see Rm 11:25; 1 Co 15:51; Eph 3:1–13; 5:32; Col 1:25–27)—that is, it is no longer a secret! The final four uses of *musterion* in the NT occur in Revelation, where the secret is a symbol that needs to be decoded (1:20; 10:7; 17:5,7).

THE PARABLE OF THE SOWER EXPLAINED

[13] Then He said to them: "Do you not understand this parable? How then will you understand all[a] the parables? [14] The sower sows the word. [15] These[b] are the ones along the path where the word is sown: when they hear, immediately Satan comes and takes away the word sown in them.[1] [16] And these are[2] the ones sown on rocky ground: when they hear the word, immediately they receive it with joy. [17] But they have no root in themselves; they are short-lived. And when affliction or persecution comes because of the word, they stumble immediately. [18] Others are sown among thorns; these are the ones who hear the word, [19] but the worries of this age, the pleasure[c] of wealth, and the desires for other things enter in and choke the word, and it becomes unfruitful. [20] But the ones sown on good ground are those who hear the word, welcome it, and produce a crop: thirty, sixty, and a hundred times what was sown."

USING YOUR LIGHT

[21] He also said to them, "Is a lamp brought in to be put under a basket or under a bed? Isn't it to be put on a lampstand? [22] For nothing is concealed except to be revealed, and nothing hidden except to come to light. [23] If anyone has ears to hear, he should listen!" [24] Then He said to them, "Pay attention to what you hear. By the measure you use,[d] it will be measured and added to you. [25] For to the one who has, it will be given, and from the one who does not have, even what he has will be taken away."

THE PARABLE OF THE GROWING SEED

[26] "The kingdom of God is like this," He said. "A man scatters seed on the ground; [27] night and day he sleeps and gets up, and the seed sprouts and grows—he doesn't know how. [28] The soil produces a crop by

Keep Your Ears Open, Your Calendar Clear

A tender and sensitive heart will be ready to respond to God at the slightest prompting. Then when God opens your spiritual eyes, you will know it is Him at work.

"If anyone has ears to hear, he should listen!"

—Mark 4:23

[1]4:15 Other mss read *their hearts*
[2]4:16 Other mss read *are like*

---

[a]4:13 Or *any of*
[b]4:15 That is, some people

[c]4:19 Or *deceitfulness*
[d]4:24 Lit *the measure you measure*

itself—first the blade, then the head, and then the ripe grain on the head. [29] But as soon as the crop is ready, he sends for the sickle,[a] because harvest has come."

THE PARABLE OF THE MUSTARD SEED

[30] And He said: "How can we illustrate the kingdom of God, or with what parable should we describe it? [31] It's like a mustard seed that, when sown in the soil, is smaller than all the seeds on the ground. [32] But when sown, it comes up and grows taller than all the vegetables, and produces large branches, so that the birds of the sky can nest in its shade."

USING PARABLES

[33] He would speak the word to them with many parables like these, as they were able to hear. [34] And He did not speak to them without a parable. Privately, however, He would explain everything to His own disciples.

WIND AND WAVE OBEY THE MASTER

[35] On that day, when evening had come, He told them, "Let's cross over to the other side of the lake."[b] [36] So they left the crowd and took Him along since He was[c] in the boat. And there were other boats with Him. [37] A fierce windstorm arose, and the waves were breaking over the boat, so that the boat was already being swamped. [38] But He was in the stern, sleeping on the cushion. So they woke Him up and said to Him, "Teacher! Don't you care that we're going to die?"[d]

[39] He got up, rebuked the wind, and said to the sea, "Silence! Be still!" The wind ceased, and there was a great calm. [40] Then He said to them, "Why are you fearful? Do you still have no faith?"

[41] And they were terrified and said to one another, "Who then is this? Even the wind and the sea obey Him!"

DEMONS DRIVEN OUT BY THE MASTER

5 Then they came to the other side of the sea, to the region of the Gerasenes.[1] [2] As soon as He got out of the boat, a man with an unclean spirit came out of the tombs and met Him. [3] He lived in the tombs; and no one

[1]5:1 Other mss read *Gadarenes* and some *Gergesenes*

[a]4:29 Jl 3:13; Rv 14:14–19
[b]4:35 *of the lake* supplied for clarity
[c]4:36 Lit *Him as He was*
[d]4:38 Lit *we're perishing*

Don't Believe Everything You Hear

God speaks by the Holy Spirit through the Bible, prayer, circumstances, and the church to reveal Himself, His purposes, and His ways.

And He did not speak to them without a parable. Privately, however, He would explain everything to His own disciples.

—Mark 4:34

You Must Trust God, No Doubt About It

The fact that you have doubts indicates that you do not know God as you should.

Then He said to them, "Why are you fearful? Do you still have no faith?" And they were terrified and said to one another, "Who then is this? Even the wind and the sea obey Him!"

—Mark 4:40–41

WORD STUDY

Greek word: **daimonizomai**
[digh mah NEE zah migh]
Translation: **be demon-possessed**
Uses in Mark's Gospel: **4**
(Mt, 7; Lk, 1; Jn, 1)
Uses in the NT: **13**
Key passage: **Mark 5:1-20**

The Greek verb *daimonizomai* comes from the noun *daimonion,* meaning *demon,* an evil spirit. The verb literally means *to be demonized* and refers to the activities of demons in harassing, oppressing, and even possessing people. The phrase "to have a demon" occurs a few times in the NT with the same meaning. Though possession is not always in view when the NT mentions demonic activity, this is clearly the case in Mark 5 where a man is described with a "Legion" (v. 9) of demons that Jesus cast into a herd of pigs. A legion in the Roman army was 6,000 soldiers, and the loss of 2,000 pigs (v. 13) strongly implies an incredibly high multiple possession in this instance, which explains the man's bizarre behavior and astounding strength. The word *daimonion* (and *daimonizomai* to a lesser extent) was used in the ancient world to refer to pagan gods and lesser deities (such as stars), but the NT reveals that they are actually Satan's followers. The verb is rare in the NT and occurs only in the Gospels; the noun *daimonion* occurs sixty-three times with fifty-three occurrences in the Gospels. The concentration of these terms in the Gospels demonstrates both the reality of the unseen world of spirit beings and Jesus' absolute power over demons, regardless of the evil they cause.

was able to restrain him any more—even with chains, [4] because he often had been bound with shackles and chains, but had snapped off the chains and smashed the shackles. No one was strong enough to subdue him. [5] And always, night and day, among the tombs and in the mountains, he was crying out and cutting himself with stones.

[6] When he saw Jesus from a distance, he ran and knelt down before Him. [7] And he cried out with a loud voice, "What do You have to do with me,[a] Jesus, Son of the Most High God? I beg[b] You before God, don't torment me!" [8] For He had told him, "Come out of the man, you unclean spirit!"

[9] "What is your name?" He asked him.

"My name is Legion,"[c] he answered Him, "because we are many." [10] And he kept begging Him not to send them out of the region.

[11] Now a large herd of pigs was there, feeding on the hillside. [12] The demons[1] begged Him, "Send us to the pigs, so we may enter them." [13] And He gave them permission. Then unclean spirits came out and entered the pigs, and the herd of about two thousand rushed down the steep bank into the sea and drowned there. [14] The men who tended them[2] ran off and reported it in the town and the countryside, and people[d] went to see what had happened. [15] They came to Jesus and saw the man who had been demon-possessed by the legion sitting there, dressed and in his right mind; and they were afraid. [16] The eyewitnesses described to them what had happened to the demon-possessed man and told[e] about the pigs. [17] Then they began to beg Him to leave their region.

[18] As He was getting into the boat, the man who had been demon-possessed kept begging Him to be with Him. [19] But He would not let him; instead, He told him, "Go back home to your own people, and report to them how much the Lord has done for you and how He has

[1] **5:12** Lit *they;* other mss read *all the demons*
[2] **5:14** Other mss read *the pigs*

[a] **5:7** Lit *What to me and to You*
[b] **5:7** Or *adjure*
[c] **5:9** See Mt 26:53 note; here of a large number

[d] **5:14** Lit *they*
[e] **5:16** *told* supplied for clarity

When Jesus comes into a place, He changes things & messes w/ the status quo. Do I welcome Jesus?

had mercy on you." ²⁰And off he went and began to proclaim in the Decapolis^a how much Jesus had done for him; and they were all amazed.

A GIRL RESTORED AND A WOMAN HEALED

²¹When Jesus had crossed over again by boat to the other side, a large crowd gathered around Him while He was by the sea. ²²One of the synagogue leaders, named Jairus, came, and when he saw Jesus^b he fell at His feet ²³and kept begging Him, "My little daughter is at death's door.^c Come and lay Your hands on her, so that she may get well and live."

²⁴So Jesus^d went with him, and a large crowd was following and pressing against Him. ²⁵A woman suffering from bleeding for twelve years ²⁶had endured much under many doctors. She had spent everything she had, and was not helped at all. On the contrary, she became worse. ²⁷Having heard about Jesus, she came behind Him in the crowd and touched His robe. ²⁸For she said, "If I can just touch His robes, I'll be made well!" ²⁹Instantly her flow of blood ceased, and she sensed in her body that she was cured of her affliction.

³⁰At once Jesus realized in Himself that power had gone out from Him. He turned around in the crowd and said, "Who touched My robes?"

³¹His disciples said to Him, "You see the crowd pressing against You, and You say, 'Who touched Me?'"

³²So He was looking around to see who had done this. ³³Then the woman, knowing what had happened to her, came with fear and trembling, fell down before Him, and told Him the whole truth. ³⁴"Daughter," He said to her, "your faith has made you well.^e Go in peace and be free^f from your affliction."

³⁵While He was still speaking, people came from the synagogue leader's house and said, "Your daughter is dead. Why bother the Teacher any more?"

³⁶But when Jesus overheard what was said, He told the synagogue leader, "Don't be afraid. Only believe." ³⁷He did not let anyone accompany Him except Peter,

Trust God to Do What You Cannot

We don't have to be able to accomplish the task within our limited ability or resources. With faith, we can proceed confidently, because we know that He is going to bring to pass what He purposes.

For she said, "If I can just touch His robes, I'll be made well!"

—Mark 5:28

Watch for People Who Are Open to God

When Jesus passed through a crowd, He always looked for where the Father was at work. The crowd was not the harvest field. The harvest field was within the crowd.

His disciples said to Him, "You see the crowd pressing against You, and You say, 'Who touched Me?'" So He was looking around to see who had done this. Then the woman, knowing what had happened to her, came with fear and trembling, fell down before Him, and told Him the whole truth.

—Mark 5:31–33

---

^a**5:20** A region of Gentile populations originally in a federation of ten cities with Greco-Roman buildings
^b**5:22** Lit *Him*
^c**5:23** Lit *She has it finally,* that is, to be at the end of life
^d**5:24** Lit *He*
^e**5:34** Or *has saved you*
^f**5:34** Lit *healthy*

James, and John, James's brother. [38] They came to the synagogue leader's house, and He saw a commotion—people weeping and wailing loudly. [39] He went in and said to them, "Why are you making a commotion and weeping? The child is not dead but asleep."

[40] They started laughing at Him, but He put them all outside. He took the child's father, mother, and those who were with Him, and entered the place where the child was. [41] Then He took the child by the hand and said to her, *"Talitha koum!"*[a] (which is translated, "Little girl, I say to you, get up!"). [42] Immediately the girl got up and began to walk. (She was twelve years old.) At this they were utterly astounded. [43] Then He gave them strict orders that no one should know about this, and said that she should be given something to eat.

REJECTION AT NAZARETH

6 He went away from there and came to His hometown, and His disciples followed Him. [2] When the Sabbath came, He began to teach in the synagogue, and many who heard Him were astonished. "Where did this man get these things?" they said. "What is this wisdom given to Him, and these miracles performed by His hands? [3] Isn't this the carpenter, the son of Mary, and the brother of James, Joses, Judas, and Simon? And aren't His sisters here with us?" So they were offended by Him.

[4] Then Jesus said to them, "A prophet is not without honor except in his hometown, among his relatives, and in his household." [5] So He was not able to do any miracles[b] there, except that He laid His hands on a few sick people and healed them. [6] And He was amazed at their unbelief.

COMMISSIONING THE TWELVE

Now He was going around the villages in a circuit, teaching. [7] He summoned the Twelve and began to send them out in pairs, and gave them authority over unclean spirits. [8] He instructed them to take nothing for the road except a walking stick: no bread, no backpack, no money in their belts, [9] but to wear sandals, and not to put on an extra shirt. [10] Then He said to them, "When-

---

Maybe You're Not Dreaming Big Enough

The reason much of the world is not being attracted to Christ and His church is that God's people lack the faith to attempt those things that only God can do.

So He was not able to do any miracles there, except that He laid His hands on a few sick people and healed them. And He was amazed at their unbelief.

—Mark 6:5–6

---

[a] 5:41 An Aramaic expression   [b] 6:5 Lit *miracle*

ever you enter a house, stay there until you leave that place. [11] Whatever place will not welcome you, and people refuse to listen to you, when you leave there, shake the dust off your feet as a testimony against them."[1]

[12] So they went out and preached that people should repent.[a] [13] And they were driving out many demons, anointing many sick people with oil, and healing.

JOHN THE BAPTIST BEHEADED

[14] King Herod[b] heard of this, because Jesus'[c] name had become well known. Some[2] said, "John the Baptist has been raised from the dead, and that's why these powers are working in him." [15] But others said, "He's Elijah." Still others said, "He's a prophet[d]—like one of the prophets."

[16] When Herod heard of it, he said, "John, the one I beheaded, has been raised!" [17] For Herod himself had given orders to arrest John and to chain him in prison on account of Herodias, his brother Philip's wife, whom he had married. [18] John had been telling Herod, "It is not lawful for you to have your brother's wife!" [19] So Herodias held a grudge against him and wanted to kill him. But she could not, [20] because Herod was in awe of[e] John and was protecting him, knowing he was a righteous and holy man. When Herod[f] heard him he would be very disturbed,[3] yet would hear him gladly.

[21] Now an opportune day came on his birthday, when Herod gave a banquet for his nobles, military commanders, and the leading men of Galilee. [22] When Herodias's own daughter[4] came in and danced, she pleased Herod and his guests. The king said to the girl, "Ask me whatever you want, and I'll give it to you." [23] So he swore oaths to her: "Whatever you ask me I will give you, up to half my kingdom."

[24] Then she went out and said to her mother, "What should I ask for?"

WORD STUDY

Greek word: **kerusso**
[kay ROO soh]
Translation: **preach**
Uses in Mark's Gospel: **14**
(Mt, 9; Lk, 9)
Uses in the NT: **61**
Key passage: **Mark 6:12**

The Greek verb *kerusso* is one of the three main words in the NT that refers to proclamation. The other two are *euangelizo* (the verb form of *euangelion,* which means *gospel* or *good news*), meaning *to evangelize* or *proclaim good news;* and *martureo,* which means *to witness or testify* (see word study on page 225). The noun *kerux,* meaning *herald* or *preacher,* was very important in the Greek world, for a herald often proclaimed important news and decrees from ruling authorities to the common people. Significantly, *kerux* occurs only three times in the NT (1 Tm 2:7; 2 Tm 1:11; 2 Pt 2:5), as opposed to sixty-one for the verb *kerusso,* for in preaching the gospel the emphasis is on the act of proclaiming the message or on the message itself and not on the person. The message proclaimed is called the *kerugma* in Greek (eight uses in the NT; see Mt 12:41 = Lk 11:32; Rm 16:25; 1 Co 1:21; 2:4; 15:4; 2 Tm 4:17; Ti 1:3), which in all six uses by Paul is a reference to the only message worth proclaiming to the world—the *euangelion,* that is, the gospel.

---

[1]6:11 Other mss add *I assure you, it will be more tolerable for Sodom or Gomorrah on judgment day than for that town*
[2]6:14 Other mss read *he*
[3]6:20 Other mss read *when he heard him, he did many things*
[4]6:22 Other mss read *When his daughter Herodias*

---

[a]6:12 Lit *that they should repent*
[b]6:14 Herod Antipas, son of Herod the Great, was the ruler of Galilee and Perea from 4 B.C. to A.D. 39.
[c]6:14 Lit *His*
[d]6:15 Lit *Others said, A prophet*
[e]6:20 Or *Herod feared*
[f]6:20 Lit *he*

"John the Baptist's head!" she said.

25 Immediately she hurried to the king and said, "I want you to give me John the Baptist's head on a platter—right now!"

26 Though the king was deeply distressed, because of his oaths and the guests[a] he did not want to refuse her. 27 The king immediately sent for an executioner and commanded him to bring John's[b] head. So he went and beheaded him in prison, 28 brought his head on a platter, and gave it to the girl. Then the girl gave it to her mother. 29 When his disciples[c] heard about it, they came and removed his corpse and placed it in a tomb.

FEEDING FIVE THOUSAND

30 The apostles gathered around Jesus and reported to Him all that they had done and taught. 31 He said to them, "Come away by yourselves to a remote place and rest a little." For many people were coming and going, and they did not even have time to eat. 32 So they went away in the boat by themselves to a remote place, 33 but many saw them leaving and recognized them. Then they ran there on foot from all the towns and arrived ahead of them.[1] 34 So as He stepped ashore, He saw a huge crowd and had compassion on them, because they were like sheep without a shepherd. Then He began to teach them many things.

35 When it was already late, His disciples approached Him and said, "This place is a wilderness, and the hour is already late! 36 Send them away, so they can go into the surrounding countryside and villages to buy themselves something to eat."

37 "You give them something to eat," He responded.

They said to Him, "Should we go and buy two hundred denarii[d] worth of bread and give them something to eat?"

38 And He asked them, "How many loaves do you have? Go look."

When they found out they said, "Five, and two fish."

His Timing Is Always Right and Best

Depend on God's timing. Don't get in a hurry. He may be withholding directions to cause you to seek Him more intently. Don't try to skip over the relationship to get on with the doing.

He said to them, "Come away by yourselves to a remote place and rest a little." For many people were coming and going, and they did not even have time to eat.

—Mark 6:31

People Are Needing You to Notice Them

As long as you focus on yourself, you will be oblivious to the needs of others. Ask God to free you from selfishness so that your life is free to bless others.

So as He stepped ashore, He saw a huge crowd and had compassion on them, because they were like sheep without a shepherd. Then He began to teach them many things.

—Mark 6:34

1 6:33 Other mss add *and gathered around Him*

a 6:26 Lit *and those reclining with Him at the table*
b 6:27 Lit *his*
c 6:29 That is, John's disciples

d 6:37 *Denarius,* a Latin word for a silver coin that was the common pay for a workman's daily wage.

39 Then He instructed them to have all the people sit down[a] in groups on the green grass. 40 So they sat down in ranks of hundreds and fifties. 41 Then He took the five loaves and the two fish, and looking up to heaven, He blessed and broke the loaves. And He kept giving them to His disciples to set before the people. He also divided the two fish among them all. 42 Everyone ate and was filled. 43 Then they picked up twelve baskets full of pieces of bread and fish. 44 Now those who ate the loaves were five thousand men.

WALKING ON THE WATER

45 Immediately He made His disciples get into the boat and go ahead of Him to the other side, to Bethsaida, while He dismissed the crowd. 46 Having said goodbye to them, He went away to the mountain to pray. 47 When evening came, the boat was in the middle of the sea, and He was alone on the land. 48 He saw them being battered as they rowed,[b] because the wind was against them. Around three in the morning[c] He came toward them walking on the sea, and wanted to pass by them. 49 When they saw Him walking on the sea, they thought it was a ghost and cried out; 50 for they all saw Him and were terrified. Immediately He spoke with them and said, "Have courage! It is I. Don't be afraid." 51 Then He got into the boat with them, and the wind ceased. They were completely astounded,[d] 52 because they did not understand about the loaves. Instead, their hearts were hardened.

MIRACULOUS HEALINGS

53 When they had crossed over, they came to land at Gennesaret and beached the boat. 54 As they got out of the boat, immediately people recognized Him. 55 They hurried throughout that vicinity and began to carry the sick on stretchers to wherever they heard He was. 56 Wherever He would go, into villages, towns, or the country, they laid the sick in the marketplaces and begged Him that they might touch just the tassel of His robe. And everyone who touched it was made well.

The Mountaintop Is for Praying

It is tempting to relax after a spiritual victory, but a crisis could follow at any time. You must stand your guard over your high points.

Having said goodbye to them, He went away to the mountain to pray.

—Mark 6:46

---

[a]6:39 Lit *people recline*
[b]6:48 Or *them struggling as they rowed*
[c]6:48 Lit *Around the fourth watch of the night;* from three to six in the morning
[d]6:51 Lit *astounded in themselves*

WORD STUDY

Greek word: **_grammateus_**
[grahm mah T<u>OO</u>SS]

Translation: **_scribe_**

Uses in Mark's Gospel: **21**
(Mt, 22; Lk, 14; Jn, 1)

Uses in the NT: **63**

Key passage: **Mark 7:5**

The Greek noun *grammateus* means *a secretary,* and the related noun *gramma* can mean *a letter of the alphabet* or *a letter* (that is, *an epistle* or *a document*). Both terms are derived from the verb *grapho,* meaning *to write* (see the word study on page 138). In Jewish culture in NT times the *grammateus* was more than just a secretary. He was *a scribe* or *scholar,* a recognized expert in the law of Moses and the authoritative traditions related to it. Scribes could be Sadducees or Pharisees, and they are often mentioned in the same context as chief priests, elders, or Pharisees. These four influential groups of men made up the Sanhedrin, the ruling body of political and religious life for the Jewish people. All but six references to the scribes occur in the Synoptic Gospels, and the vast majority of the time they are antagonistic to Jesus. They questioned whom Jesus ate with (Mk 2:16) and how He ate (Mk 7:1–5), charged Jesus with being in league with Satan (Mk 3:22), challenged Jesus' views on the greatest commandment (Mk 12:28), and participated in Jesus' trial and death (Mk 14:1, 43,53; 15:1,31). Jesus in turn warned them about committing an unforgivable sin (Mk 3:23–30), rebuked them for hypocrisy (Mk 7:6–23; see Mt 23), and questioned their understanding of the Messiah, the Son of David (Mk 12:35–37)—a question that they could not answer despite their learning.

THE TRADITIONS OF THE ELDERS

7 The Pharisees and some of the scribes who had come from Jerusalem gathered around Him. [2] They observed that some of His disciples were eating their bread with unclean—that is, unwashed—hands. [3] (For the Pharisees, in fact all the Jews, will not eat unless they wash their hands ritually, keeping the tradition of the elders. [4] When they come from the marketplace, they do not eat unless they have washed. And there are many other customs they have received and keep, like the washing of cups, jugs, copper utensils, and dining couches.[1]) [5] Then the Pharisees and the scribes asked Him, "Why don't Your disciples live according to the tradition of the elders, instead of eating bread with ritually unclean[2] hands?"

[6] But He said to them, "Isaiah prophesied correctly about you hypocrites, as it is written:

'This people honors Me with their lips,
but their heart is far from Me.
[7] They worship Me in vain,
teaching as doctrines the commands of men.'[a]

[8] Disregarding the commandment of God, you keep the tradition of men."[3] [9] He also said to them, "You splendidly disregard God's commandment, so that you may maintain[4] your tradition! [10] For Moses said:

'Honor your father and your mother;'[b] and,
'Whoever speaks evil of father or mother must be put to death.'[c]

[11] But you say, 'If a man tells his father or mother, "Whatever benefit you might have received from me is *Corban*"' (that is, a gift committed to the temple[d]), [12] "you no longer let him do anything for his father or mother. [13] You revoke God's word by your tradition that you

[1] 7:4 Other mss omit *and dining couches*
[2] 7:5 Other mss read *with unwashed*
[3] 7:8 Other mss add *the washing of jugs, and cups, and many other similar things you practice*
[4] 7:9 A few mss read *establish*

[a] 7:6b–7 Is 29:13
[b] 7:10 Ex 20:12; Dt 5:16
[c] 7:10 Ex 21:17; Lv 20:9

[d] 7:11 *committed to the temple* implied

have handed down. And you do many other similar things." [14] Summoning the crowd again, He told them, "Listen to Me, all of you, and understand: [15] Nothing that goes into a man from outside can defile him, but the things that come out of a man are what defile a man. [16] If anyone has ears to hear, he should listen!"[1]

[17] When He went into the house away from the crowd, the disciples asked Him about the parable. [18] And He said to them, "Are you also as lacking in understanding? Don't you realize that nothing going into a man from the outside can defile him? [19] For it doesn't go into his heart but into the stomach, and is eliminated."[a] (As a result, He made all foods clean.)[2] [20] Then He said, "What comes out of a man—that defiles a man. [21] For from within, out of people's hearts, come evil thoughts, sexual immoralities, thefts, murders, [22] adulteries, greed, evil actions, deceit, lewdness, stinginess,[b] blasphemy, pride, and foolishness. [23] All these evil things come from within and defile a man."

A GENTILE MOTHER'S FAITH

[24] From there He got up and departed to the region of Tyre and Sidon.[3] He entered a house and did not want anyone to know it, but He could not escape notice. [25] Instead, immediately after hearing about Him, a woman whose little daughter had an unclean spirit came and fell at His feet. [26] Now the woman was Greek, a Syrophoenician by birth, and she kept asking Him to drive the demon out of her daughter. [27] And He said to her, "Allow the children to be satisfied first, because it isn't right to take the children's bread and throw it to the dogs."

[28] But she replied to Him, "Lord, even the dogs under the table eat the children's crumbs."

[29] Then He told her, "Because of this reply, you may go. The demon has gone out of your daughter." [30] When she went back to her home, she found her child lying on the bed, and the demon was gone.

Obedience Is More Than Skin-Deep

If you have an obedience problem, you have a love problem.

But He said to them, "Isaiah prophesied correctly about you hypocrites, as it is written: 'This people honors Me with their lips, but their heart is far from Me.'"

—Mark 7:6

[1]7:16 Other mss omit this verse
[2]7:19 Other mss read *is eliminated, making all foods clean*
[3]7:24 Other mss omit *and Sidon*

---

[a]7:19 Lit *goes out into the toilet*   [b]7:22 Lit *evil eye*

97

JESUS DOES EVERYTHING WELL

³¹ Again, leaving the region of Tyre, He went by way of Sidon to the Sea of Galilee, through the region of the Decapolis.ᵃ ³² And they brought to Him a deaf man who also had a speech difficulty, and begged Him to lay His hand on him. ³³ So He took him away from the crowd privately. After putting His fingers in the man's ears and spitting, He touched his tongue. ³⁴ Then, looking up to heaven, He sighed deeply and said to him, *"Ephpha-tha!"*ᵇ (that is, "Be opened!"). ³⁵ Immediately his ears were opened, his speech difficulty was removed,ᶜ and he began to speak clearly. ³⁶ Then He ordered them to tell no one, but the more He would order them, the more they would proclaim it.

³⁷ They were extremely astonished and said, "He has done everything well! He even makes deaf people hear, and people unable to speak, talk!"

FEEDING FOUR THOUSAND

8 In those days there was again a large crowd, and they had nothing to eat. He summoned the disciples and said to them, ² "I have compassion on the crowd, because they've already stayed with Me three days and have nothing to eat. ³ If I send them home famished,ᵈ they will collapse on the way, and some of them have come a long distance."

⁴ His disciples answered Him, "Where can anyone get enough bread here in this desolate place to fill these people?"

⁵ "How many loaves do you have?" He asked them.

"Seven," they said. ⁶ Then He commanded the crowd to sit down on the ground. Taking the seven loaves, He gave thanks, broke the loaves,ᵉ and kept on giving them to His disciples to set before them. So they served the loavesᵉ to the crowd. ⁷ They also had a few small fish, and when He had blessed them, He said these were to be served as well. ⁸ They ate and were filled. Then they collected seven large baskets of leftover pieces. ⁹ About

---

Do You Need a Miracle—Or a Master?

There are times when we prefer the miracle over the miracle worker.

But sighing deeply in His spirit, He said, "Why does this generation demand a sign? I assure you: No sign will be given to this generation!"

—Mark 8:12

ᵃ**7:31** See 5:20 note
ᵇ**7:34** An Aramaic expression
ᶜ**7:35** Lit *opened, the chain of his tongue was untied*

ᵈ**8:3** Or *fasting*
ᵉ**8:6** *loaves* implied

four thousand were there. He dismissed them, [10] and immediately got into the boat with His disciples and went to the district of Dalmanutha.[a]

THE YEAST OF THE PHARISEES AND HEROD

[11] The Pharisees came out and began to argue with Him, demanding of Him a sign from heaven to test Him. [12] But sighing deeply in His spirit, He said, "Why does this generation demand a sign? I assure you: No sign will be given to this generation!" [13] Then He left them, got on board the boat[b] again, and went to the other side.

[14] They had forgotten to take bread and had only one loaf with them in the boat. [15] Then He began to give them strict orders: "Watch out! Beware of the yeast[c] of the Pharisees and the yeast of Herod."

[16] They were discussing among themselves that they did not have any bread. [17] Aware of this, He said to them, "Why are you discussing that you don't have any bread? Do you not yet understand or comprehend? Is your heart hardened?[d] [18] **Do you Have eyes, and not see, and do you have ears, and not hear?**[e] And do you not remember? [19] When I broke the five loaves for the five thousand, how many baskets full of pieces of bread did you collect?"

"Twelve," they told Him.

[20] "When I broke the seven loaves for the four thousand, how many large baskets full of pieces of bread did you collect?"

"Seven," they said.

[21] And He said to them, "Don't you understand yet?"

HEALING A BLIND MAN

[22] Then they came to Bethsaida. They brought a blind man to Him and begged Him to touch him. [23] He took the blind man by the hand and brought him out of the village. Spitting on his eyes and laying His hands on him, He asked him, "Do you see anything?"

[24] He looked up and said, "I see people—they look to me like trees walking."

God's Word Shouldn't Freeze Us, But Free Us

If you serve the Lord out of duty and habit, but not out of joy and gratitude, you will envy those who are experiencing joy in the Lord and miss the abundant life the Father has planned for you.

Then He began to give them strict orders: "Watch out! Beware of the yeast of the Pharisees and the yeast of Herod."

—Mark 8:15

---

[a]**8:10** Probably on the western shore of the Sea of Galilee
[b]**8:13** *the boat* added for clarity
[c]**8:15** Or *leaven*
[d]**8:17** 6:52
[e]**8:18** Jr 5:21; Ezk 12:2

WORD STUDY

Greek word: **psuche** [ps<u>oo</u> KAY]

Translation: *life*

Uses in Mark's Gospel: **8**
(Mt, 16; Lk, 14; Jn, 10)

Uses in the NT: **103**

Key passage: **Mark 8:35**

The Greek noun *psuche* comes from the verb *psucho,* meaning *to blow,* and then by extension *to become cold* (Mt 24:12). This is similar to the synonym *pneuma,* meaning *wind, breath, spirit* (or *Spirit*), which comes from the verb *pneo,* also meaning *to blow* (both *pneuma* and *pneo* are used in Jn 3:8). Overlap occurs between *psuche* and *soma* since both can refer to physical life or existence (Mt 2:20, *psuche;* Mt 27:52, *soma*), and both *psuche* and *pneuma* can refer to spiritual life or the inner self (Mk 8:36, *psuche;* Mk 14:38, *pneuma*). But no such overlap exists between *pneuma* and *soma* since the spirit and the body are distinguished in the NT. Sometimes both the physical and spiritual aspects of *psuche* are combined so that the whole person is in view, not just one aspect of his existence (Mk 8:35, used twice). An important synonym for *psuche* is *zoe,* another word meaning *life* (see word study on page 220).

[25] Again He placed His hands on his eyes, and he saw distinctly. He was cured and could see everything clearly. [26] Then He sent him home, saying, "Don't even go into the village."[1]

PETER'S CONFESSION OF THE MESSIAH

[27] Jesus went out with His disciples to the villages of Caesarea Philippi. And on the road He asked His disciples, "Who do people say that I am?"

[28] And they answered Him, "John the Baptist; others, Elijah; still others, one of the prophets."

[29] "But you," He asked them again, "who do you say that I am?"

Peter answered Him, "You are the Messiah!"[a]

[30] And He strictly warned them to tell no one about Him.

HIS DEATH AND
RESURRECTION PREDICTED

[31] Then He began to teach them that the Son of Man must suffer many things, and be rejected by the elders, the chief priests, and the scribes, be killed, and rise after three days. [32] And He was openly talking about this. So Peter took Him aside and began to rebuke Him.

[33] But turning around and looking at His disciples, He rebuked Peter and said, "Get behind Me, Satan, because you're not thinking about God's concerns,[b] but man's!"

TAKE UP YOUR CROSS

[34] Summoning the crowd along with His disciples, He said to them, "If anyone wants to be My follower, he must deny himself, take up his cross, and follow Me. [35] For whoever wants to save his life[c] will lose it, but whoever loses his life[c] because of Me and the gospel will save it. [36] For what does it benefit a man to gain the whole world yet lose his life?[c] [37] What can a man give in exchange for his life?[c] [38] For whoever is ashamed of Me and of My words in this adulterous and sinful generation, the Son of Man will also be ashamed of him when

[1]8:26 Other mss add *or tell anyone in the village*

[a]8:29 Gk *Christos,* which can be translated as *Christ* or *Messiah*

[b]8:33 Lit *about the things of God*

[c]8:35 Or *soul* (see Mt 16:25,26 note)

He comes in the glory of His Father with the holy angels."

9 Then He said to them, "I assure you: There are some of those standing here who will not taste death until they see the kingdom of God come[a] in power."

THE TRANSFIGURATION

[2] After six days Jesus took Peter, James, and John, and led them up on a high mountain by themselves to be alone. He was transformed[b] in front of them, [3] and His clothes became dazzling, extremely white, as no launderer on earth could whiten them. [4] Elijah appeared to them with Moses, and they were talking with Jesus.

[5] Then Peter said to Jesus, "Rabbi, it is good for us to be here! Let us make three tabernacles:[c] one for You, one for Moses, and one for Elijah"— [6] because he did not know what he should say, since they were terrified.

[7] A cloud appeared, overshadowing them, and a voice came from the cloud:[d]

> "This is My beloved Son;
> Listen to Him!"

[8] Then suddenly, looking around, they no longer saw anyone with them except Jesus alone.

[9] As they were coming down from the mountain, He ordered them to tell no one what they had seen until the Son of Man had risen from the dead. [10] They kept this word to themselves, discussing what "rising from the dead" meant.

[11] Then they began to question Him, "Why do the scribes say that Elijah must come first?"[e]

[12] "Elijah does come first and restores everything," He replied. "How then is it written about the Son of Man that He must suffer many things and be treated with contempt? [13] But I tell you that Elijah really has come, and they did to him whatever they wanted, just as it is written about him."

Dying to Self Is the Only Way to Live

Self-centeredness is a subtle trap. God-centeredness requires a daily death to self and submission to God.

Summoning the crowd along with His disciples, He said to them, "If anyone wants to be My follower, he must deny himself, take up his cross, and follow Me."

—Mark 8:34

---

[a]9:1 Or *having come*
[b]9:2 Or *transfigured*
[c]9:5 Or *tents* or *shelters* used for temporary housing

[d]9:7 2 Pt 1:16–18
[e]9:11 Mal 4:5

THE POWER OF FAITH OVER A DEMON

[14] When they came to the disciples, they saw a large crowd around them and scribes disputing with them. [15] All of a sudden, when the whole crowd saw Him, they were amazed[a] and ran to greet Him. [16] Then He asked them, "What are you arguing with them about?"

[17] Out of the crowd, one man answered Him, "Teacher, I brought my son to You. He has a spirit that makes him unable to speak. [18] Wherever it seizes him, it throws him down, and he foams at the mouth, grinds his teeth, and becomes rigid. So I asked Your disciples to drive it out, but they couldn't."

[19] He replied to them, "O, unbelieving generation![b] How long will I be with you? How long must I put up with you? Bring him to Me." [20] So they brought him to Him. When the spirit saw Him, it immediately convulsed the boy. He fell to the ground and rolled around, foaming at the mouth. [21] "How long has this been happening to him?" Jesus asked his father.

"From childhood," he said. [22] "And many times it has thrown him into fire or water to destroy him. But if You can do anything, have compassion on us and help us."

[23] Then Jesus said to him, " 'If You can?'[1c] Everything is possible to the one who believes."

[24] Immediately the father of the boy cried out, "I do believe! Help my unbelief."

[25] When Jesus saw that a crowd was rapidly coming together, He rebuked the unclean spirit, saying to it, "You mute and deaf spirit,[d] I command you: come out of him and never enter him again!"

[26] Then it came out, shrieking and convulsing him[e] violently. The boy became like a corpse, so that many said, "He's dead." [27] But Jesus, taking him by the hand, raised him, and he stood up.

[28] After He went into a house, His disciples asked Him privately, "Why couldn't we drive it out?"

Faith Isn't Something You Figure Out

Faith is confidence that what God has promised or said will come to pass. If you can see clearly how something can be accomplished, then you are not living by faith.

"But if You can do anything, have compassion on us and help us." Then Jesus said to him, " 'If You can?' Everything is possible to the one who believes." Immediately the father of the boy cried out, "I do believe! Help my unbelief."

—Mark 9:22b–24

---

[1]9:23 Other mss add *believe*

---

[a]9:15 Or *surprised*
[b]9:19 Dt 32:5; Mk 6:6; Php 2:15
[c]9:23 Jesus appears to quote the father's words in v. 22 and then comment on them.

[d]9:25 That is, a spirit that caused the boy to be deaf and unable to speak
[e]9:26 *him* inferred by context and found in many mss

[29] And He told them, "This kind can come out by nothing but prayer ⌜and fasting."⌝[1]

THE SECOND PREDICTION OF HIS DEATH

[30] Then they left that place and made their way through Galilee, but He did not want anyone to know it. [31] For He was teaching His disciples and telling them, "The Son of Man is being betrayed[a] into the hands of men. They will kill Him, and after He is killed, He will rise three days later." [32] But they did not understand this statement, and they were afraid to ask Him.

WHO IS THE GREATEST?

[33] Then they came to Capernaum. When He was in the house, He asked them, "What were you arguing about on the way?" [34] But they were silent, because on the way they had been arguing with one another about who was the greatest. [35] Sitting down, He called the Twelve and said to them, "If anyone wants to be first, he must be last of all and servant of all." [36] Then He took a child, had him stand among them, and taking him in His arms, He said to them, [37] "Whoever welcomes[b] one little child such as this in My name welcomes Me. And whoever welcomes Me does not welcome Me, but Him who sent Me."

IN HIS NAME

[38] John said to Him, "Teacher, we saw someone[2] driving out demons in Your name, and we tried to stop him because he wasn't following us."
[39] "Don't stop him," said Jesus, "because there is no one who will perform a miracle in My name who can soon afterward speak evil of Me. [40] For whoever is not against us is for us. [41] And whoever gives you a cup of water to drink because of My name,[c] since you belong to the Messiah—I assure you: He will never lose his reward.

[1]9:29 Other mss omit *and fasting*
[2]9:38 Other mss add *who didn't go along with us*

[a]9:31 Or *handed over*
[b]9:37 Or *Whoever receives*
[c]9:41 Lit *drink in (the) name* (that is, of Messiah)

One Life, One Lord, No Two Ways About It

Your plans and purposes must be God's plans and purposes or you will not experience God working through you.

"The Son of Man is being betrayed into the hands of men. They will kill Him, and after He is killed, He will rise three days later." But they did not understand this statement, and they were afraid to ask Him.

—Mark 9:31b–32

Give Others Room to Serve God Their Way

Are you able to rejoice in the spiritual victories of others? Are you encouraging those who serve the Lord in a different way or who belong to a different group than you do?

John said to Him, "Teacher, we saw someone driving out demons in Your name, and we tried to stop him because he wasn't following us."

—Mark 9:38

WORD STUDY

Greek word: **skandalizo**
[skahn dah LEE zoh]

Translation: **cause the downfall of**

Uses in Mark's Gospel: **8**
(Mt, 14; Lk, 2; Jn, 2)

Uses in the NT: **29**

Key passage: **Mark 9:42–50**

The Greek verb *skandalizo* means *to entrap* and comes from the noun *skandalon,* meaning *trap* or *snare.* Metaphorically, *skandalizo* can mean *to cause [someone] to stumble* or (passively) *to take offense.* Similarly, the noun *skandalon* can mean *offense* or *stumblingblock.* In the NT both *skandalizo* and *skandalon* always refer to offenses either given or taken in spiritual matters. Paul used *skandalizo* three times (1 Co 8:13 [twice]; 2 Co 11:29) and *skandalon* once (Rm 14:13), all in connection with a Christian's responsibility to other Christians. Every other use of *skandalizo* occurs in the Gospels. Jesus often warns about offending people, that is, doing spiritual harm to others (Mk 9:42–50; see Jn 16:1). Incredibly, Jesus Himself is often the cause of offense, for those who did not believe in Him often misunderstood His words and actions (see Mt 11:6; 13:57; 15:12; 17:27; Mk 6:3; 14:27; Jn 6:61).

WARNINGS FROM JESUS

[42] "But whoever causes the downfall[a] of one of these little ones who believe in Me—it would be better for him if a heavy millstone[b] were hung around his neck and he were thrown into the sea. [43] And if your hand causes your downfall,[a] cut it off. It is better for you to enter life maimed than to have two hands and go to hell[c]—the unquenchable fire, [44] where

**Their worm does not die,
and the fire is not quenched.**[1d]

[45] And if your foot causes your downfall,[e] cut it off. It is better for you to enter life lame than to have two feet and be thrown into hell—the unquenchable fire, [46] where

**Their worm does not die,
and the fire is not quenched.**[2d]

[47] And if your eye causes your downfall,[e] gouge it out. It is better for you to enter the kingdom of God with one eye than to have two eyes and be thrown into hell, [48] where

**Their worm does not die,
and the fire is not quenched.**[d]

[49] For everyone will be salted with fire.[3f] [50] Salt is good, but if the salt should lose its flavor, how can you make it salty? Have salt among yourselves and be at peace with one another."

THE QUESTION OF DIVORCE

10 He set out from there and went to the region of Judea and across the Jordan. Then crowds converged on Him again and, as He usually did, He began teaching them once more. [2] Some Pharisees approached

[1]9:44 Other mss omit this verse
[2]9:45, 46 Other mss omit bracketed text
[3]9:49 Other mss add *and every sacrifice will be salted with salt*

[a]9:42–43 The Gk word *skandalizo* has no real Eng counterpart; "offend," "cause to sin," or "cause to fall" are common translations.
[b]9:42 That is, a millstone turned by a donkey
[c]9:43 Gk *gehenna,* Aramaic for Valley of Hinnom on the south side of Jerusalem. It was formerly a place of human sacrifice, and in NT times, a place for the burning of garbage. Therefore, it was a good illustration of hell.
[d]9:44,46,48 Is 66:24
[e]9:45,47 See 9:42 note
[f]9:49 Lv 2:16; Ezk 43:24

Him to test Him. They asked, "Is it lawful for a man to divorce his[a] wife?"

[3] He replied to them, "What did Moses command you?"

[4] They said, "Moses permitted us to write divorce papers and send her away."[b]

[5] But Jesus told them, "He wrote this commandment for you because of the hardness of your hearts. [6] But from the beginning of creation God[1] 'made them male and female':[c]

> [7] For this reason a man will leave his father
>   and mother
> ⌈and be joined to his wife,⌉[2]
> [8] and the two will become one flesh.[d]

So they are no longer two, but one flesh. [9] Therefore what God has joined together, man must not separate."

[10] Now in the house the disciples questioned Him again about this matter. [11] And He said to them, "Whoever divorces his wife and marries another commits adultery against her. [12] Also, if she divorces her husband and marries another, she commits adultery."

BLESSING THE CHILDREN

[13] Some people[e] were bringing little children to Him so He might touch them. But His disciples rebuked them. [14] When Jesus saw it, He was indignant and said to them, "Let the little children come to Me; don't stop them, for the kingdom of God belongs to such as these. [15] I assure you: Whoever does not welcome[f] the kingdom of God like a little child will never enter it." [16] After taking them in His arms, He laid His hands on them and blessed them.

THE RICH YOUNG RULER

[17] As He was going out on the road, a man ran up, knelt down before Him, and asked Him, "Good Teacher, what must I do to inherit eternal life?"

[1] 10:6 Other mss omit *God*
[2] 10:7 Other mss omit bracketed text

---

[a] 10:2 *his* implied
[b] 10:4 Dt 24:1,3
[c] 10:6 Gn 1:27; 5:2
[d] 10:7–8 Gn 2:24
[e] 10:13 Lit *They*
[f] 10:15 Or *not receive*

Invest Your Life in Things That Last

The world will entice you to adopt its goals and to invest in temporal things. Rather, deny yourself and join the activity of God as He reveals it to you.

When Jesus saw it, He was indignant and said to them, "Let the little children come to Me; don't stop them, for the kingdom of God belongs to such as these."

—Mark 10:14

[handwritten margin note: The Word became flesh & dwelt among us]

[handwritten margin note: Oh, Lord, that I would welcome the Kingdom of G — as a little child — awe & wonder]

[18] But Jesus asked him, "Why do you call Me good? No one is good but One—God. [19] You know the commandments:

> **Do not murder; do not commit adultery; do not steal; do not bear false witness; do not defraud; honor your father and mother."[a]**

[20] He said to Him, "Teacher, I have kept all these from my youth."

[21] Then, looking at him, Jesus loved him and said to him, "You lack one thing: Go, sell all you have and give to the poor, and you will have treasure in heaven. Then come,[1] follow Me." [22] But he was stunned[b] at this demand, and he went away grieving, because he had many possessions.

POSSESSIONS AND THE KINGDOM

[23] Jesus looked around and said to His disciples, "How hard it is for those who have wealth to enter the kingdom of God!" [24] But the disciples were astonished at His words. Again Jesus said to them, "Children, how hard it is[2] to enter the kingdom of God! [25] It is easier for a camel to go through the eye of a needle than for a rich person to enter the kingdom of God."

[26] But they were even more astonished, saying to one another, "Then who can be saved?"

[27] Looking at them, Jesus said, "With men it is impossible, but not with God, because all things are possible with God."

[28] Peter began to tell Him, "Look, we have left everything and followed You."

[29] "I assure you," Jesus said, "there is no one who has left house, brothers or sisters, mother or father,[3] children, or fields because of Me and the gospel, [30] who will not receive a hundred times more, now at this time— houses, brothers and sisters, mothers and children, and

---

Make Sure His Will Is Your Sole Desire

If you want to know God's will, you must respond to His invitation to love Him wholeheartedly. God works through those He loves to carry out His kingdom purposes in the world.

Jesus looked around and said to His disciples, "How hard it is for those who have wealth to enter the kingdom of God!"

—Mark 10:23

God Is Not Bound by Your Limitations

The Christ who lived His life in complete obedience to the Father is fully present in you to enable you to know His will and accomplish it.

Looking at them, Jesus said, "With men it is impossible, but not with God, because all things are possible with God."

—Mark 10:27

---

[1] **10:21** Other mss add *taking up the cross*
[2] **10:24** Other mss add *for those trusting in wealth*
[3] **10:29** Other mss add *or wife*

---

[a] **10:19** Ex 20:12–17; Dt 5:16–21   [b] **10:22** Or *he became gloomy*

fields, with persecutions—and eternal life in the age to come. ³¹ But many who are first will be last, and the last first."

THE THIRD PREDICTION OF HIS DEATH

³² They were on the road, going up to Jerusalem, and Jesus was walking ahead of them. They were astonished, but those who followed Him were afraid. And taking the Twelve aside again, He began to tell them the things that would happen to Him.

³³ "Listen! We are going up to Jerusalem. The Son of Man will be handed over to the chief priests and the scribes, and they will condemn Him to death. Then they will hand Him over to the Gentiles, ³⁴ and they will mock Him, spit on Him, flogᵃ Him, and kill Him, and He will rise after three days."

SUFFERING AND SERVICE

³⁵ Then James and John, the sons of Zebedee, approached Him and said, "Teacher, we want You to do something for us if we ask You."

³⁶ "What do you want Me to do for you?" He asked them.

³⁷ "Grant us," they answered Him, "that we may sit at Your right and at Your left in Your glory."

³⁸ But Jesus said to them, "You don't know what you're asking. Are you able to drink the cup I drink, or to be baptized with the baptism I am baptized with?"

³⁹ "We are able," they told Him.

But Jesus said to them, "You will drink the cup I drink, and you will be baptized with the baptism I am baptized with. ⁴⁰ But to sit at My right or left is not Mine to give, but it is for those for whom it has been prepared." ⁴¹ When the other ten disciplesᵇ heard this, they began to be indignant with James and John.

⁴² And Jesus called them over and said to them, "You know that those who are regarded as rulers of the Gentiles dominate them, and their men of high positions exercise power over them. ⁴³ But it must not be like that among you. On the contrary, whoever wants to become great among you must be your servant, ⁴⁴ and whoever

God's Way Can Be Trusted

You might like to wait until God tells you all the details before you start to follow Him. But that is not the pattern we see in Christ's life or in the Scriptures.

"I assure you," Jesus said, "there is no one who has left house, brothers or sisters, mother or father, children, or fields because of Me and the gospel, who will not receive a hundred times more, now at this time . . . and eternal life in the age to come."

—Mark 10:29–30

Rev 3

ᵃ**10:34** Or *scourge*   ᵇ**10:41** *other disciples* added for clarity

WORD STUDY

Greek word: **doulos** [DOO lahss]

Translation: **slave**

Uses in Mark's Gospel: **5**
(Mt, 30; Lk, 26; Jn, 11)

Uses in the NT: **126**

Key passage: **Mark 10:44**

Several Greek words in the NT convey the idea of one person being the servant of another. By far the most common is *doulos,* which is also the term of lowest rank and is best conveyed by the English word *slave.* Other types of servants had various responsibilities, privileges, and rights, but under Roman law the *doulos* had no rights. The slave was bought by the master from a slave auction or another slave owner (see 1 Co 7:21–23). He belonged completely to his master, and had only those responsibilities and privileges granted by his master. In the NT *doulos* is normally used literally (Mt 8:9; Mk 14:47; Lk 17:7–10; Jn 13:16; Eph 6:5–8; Phm 16), but a figurative meaning describing someone who serves God and His people is also common (Mk 10:44; Ac 2:18; 4:29; Rm 1:1; 2 Co 4:5; 1 Pt 2:16; Rv 2:20). Paul has two very significant uses of *doulos,* one about Christ and the other about Christians. Philippians 2:6 refers to Jesus' condescension in the Incarnation, and Romans 6:16–18 refers to being slaves of righteousness instead of slaves of sin (see Jn 8:34).

wants to be first among you must be a slave to all. [45] For even the Son of Man did not come to be served, but to serve, and to give His life—a ransom for many."[a]

A BLIND MAN HEALED

[46] They came to Jericho. And as He was leaving Jericho, and along with His disciples and a large crowd, Bartimaeus (the son of Timaeus), a blind beggar, was sitting by the road. [47] When he heard that it was Jesus the Nazarene, he began to cry out, "Son of David, Jesus, have mercy on me!" [48] Many people told him to keep quiet, but he was crying out all the more, "Have mercy on me, Son of David!"

[49] Jesus stopped and said, "Call him."

So they called the blind man and said to him, "Have courage! Get up; He's calling for you." [50] He threw off his coat, jumped up, and came to Jesus.

[51] Then Jesus answered him, "What do you want Me to do for you?"

"*Rabbouni,*"[b] the blind man told Him, "I want to see!"

[52] "Go your way," Jesus told him. "Your faith has healed you." Immediately he could see, and began to follow Him on the road.

THE TRIUMPHAL ENTRY

11 When they approached Jerusalem, at Bethphage and Bethany, near the Mount of Olives, He sent two of His disciples [2] and told them, "Go into the village ahead of you. As soon as you enter it, you will find a young donkey tied there, on which nobody has ever sat. Untie it and bring it here. [3] If anyone says to you, 'Why are you doing this?' say, 'The Lord needs it and will send it back here right away.'"

[4] So they went and found a young donkey outside in the street, tied by a door. They untied it, [5] and some of those standing there said to them, "What are you doing, untying the donkey?" [6] Then they answered them just as Jesus had said, so they let them go. [7] And they brought the donkey to Jesus and threw their robes on it, and He sat on it.

[a] **10:45** Or *in the place of many;* see Is 53:10–12

[b] **10:51** Hebrew for *my teacher;* see Jn 20:16

[8] Many people spread their robes on the road, and others spread leafy branches cut from the fields.[1]

[9] Then those who went before and those who followed kept shouting:

> "Hosanna![a]
> **Blessed is He who comes in the name of the Lord!**[b]
> [10] Blessed is the coming kingdom of our father David!
> Hosanna in the highest heaven!"

[11] And He went into Jerusalem and into the temple complex. After looking around at everything, since the hour was already late, He went out to Bethany with the Twelve.

THE BARREN FIG TREE IS CURSED

[12] The next day, when they came out from Bethany, He was hungry. [13] After seeing in the distance a fig tree with leaves, He went to find out if there was anything on it. When He came to it, He found nothing but leaves, because it was not the season for figs. [14] And He said to it, "May no one ever eat fruit from you again!"[c] And His disciples heard it.

CLEANSING THE TEMPLE COMPLEX

[15] They came to Jerusalem, and He went into the temple complex and began to throw out those buying and selling in the temple. He overturned the money changers' tables and the seats of those who were selling doves, [16] and would not permit anyone to carry goods through the temple complex.

[17] Then He began to teach them: "Is it not written, **'My house will be called a house of prayer for all nations'**?[d] But you have made it **'a den of thieves'!**"[e] [18] Then the chief priests and the scribes heard it and started looking for a way to destroy Him. For they were

---

[1] 11:8 Other mss read *were cutting leafy branches from the trees and spreading them on the road*

---

[a] 11:9 A term of praise derived from the Hb word for *save;* it occurs in the OT original of this quotation.
[b] 11:9 Ps 118:26
[c] 11:14 Jr 8:13
[d] 11:17 Is 56:7
[e] 11:17 Jr 7:11

Obedience—Just Do It

When the Lord gives you instructions, obey immediately. Don't wait until you have figured it all out and everything makes perfect sense to you.

He sent two of His disciples and told them, "Go into the village ahead of you. As soon as you enter it, you will find a young donkey tied there, on which nobody has ever sat. Untie it and bring it here."

—Mark 11:1b–2

the religious leaders didn't want to just silence Him, they wanted to destroy Him

WORD STUDY

Greek word: **exousia**
[ehx <u>oo</u> SEE uh]
Translation: **authority**
Uses in Mark's Gospel: **10**
(Mt, 10; Lk, 16; Jn, 8)
Uses in the NT: **102**
Key passage: **Mark 11:27-33**

The Greek word *exousia* comes from the verb *exesti,* meaning *it is permissible, possible,* or *in one's power.* Thus, *exousia* can mean *authority* or *power.* The close synonym *dunamis* is normally translated *power.* (*Dynamite* comes from this term, though this is quite removed from the meaning of *dunamis.*) Ordinarily, *exousia* is used of authority or power derived from an external source, while *dunamis* is inherent to the one who possesses it, although this distinction can be pressed too far. In Matthew 7:29—the first instance of the word in Matthew's Gospel—*exousia* seems to refer to an inherent power that Jesus demonstrated by what He said. He did not rely on previous teachers to authenticate His message, a striking departure from the method of the rabbis. In Mark 11:27–33 *exousia* is used in its more normal sense of derived authority: the *exousia* of John the Baptist and Jesus came "from heaven," that is, from God the Father (although Jesus' enemies refused to admit this; Mt 21:23–27). Similarly, all *exousia* was given (by the Father) to the resurrected Lord, who then commissioned His disciples with the *exousia* to make disciples of all nations (Mt 28:18–20).

afraid of Him, because the whole crowd was astonished by His teaching.

[19] And whenever evening came, they would go out of the city.

THE BARREN FIG TREE IS WITHERED

[20] Early in the morning, as they were passing by, they saw the fig tree withered from the roots up. [21] Then Peter remembered and said to Him, "Rabbi, look! The fig tree that You cursed is withered."

[22] Jesus replied to them, "Have faith in God. [23] I assure you: If anyone says to this mountain, 'Be lifted up and thrown into the sea,' and does not doubt in his heart, but believes that what he says will happen, it will be done for him. [24] Therefore, I tell you, all the things you pray and ask for—believe that you have received[1] them, and you will have them. [25] And whenever you stand praying, if you have anything against anyone, forgive him, so that your Father in heaven may also forgive you your wrongdoing.[a] [26] But if you don't forgive, neither will your Father in heaven forgive your wrongdoing."[2a]

MESSIAH'S AUTHORITY CHALLENGED

[27] They came again to Jerusalem. As He was walking in the temple complex, the chief priests, the scribes, and the elders came and asked Him, [28] "By what authority are You doing these things? Who gave You this authority to do these things?"

[29] Jesus said to them, "I will ask you one question; then answer Me, and I will tell you by what authority I am doing these things. [30] Was John's baptism from heaven or from men? Answer Me."

[31] They began to argue among themselves: "If we say, 'From heaven,' He will say, 'Then why didn't you believe him?' [32] But if we say, 'From men'"—they were afraid of the crowd, because everyone thought that John was a

[1]11:24 Other mss read *you receive;* other mss read *you will receive*
[2]11:26 Other mss omit this verse

[a]11:25,26 These are the only uses of this word in Mark. It means "the violation of the Law" or "stepping over a boundary" or "departing from the path" or "trespass."

genuine prophet. [33] So they answered Jesus, "We don't know."

And Jesus said to them, "Neither will I tell you by what authority I do these things."

THE PARABLE OF THE VINEYARD OWNER

12 Then He began to speak to them in parables: "A man planted a vineyard, put a fence around it, dug out a pit for a winepress, and built a watchtower. Then he leased it to tenant farmers and went away. [2] At harvest time he sent a slave to the farmers so that he might collect some of the fruit of the vineyard from the farmers. [3] But they took him, beat him, and sent him away empty-handed. [4] And again he sent another slave to them, and they[1] hit him on the head and treated him shamefully.[2] [5] Then he sent another, and that one they killed. He also sent[a] many others; they beat some and they killed some.

[6] "He still had one to send, a beloved son. Finally he sent him to them, saying, 'They will respect my son.'

[7] "But those tenant farmers said among themselves, 'This is the heir. Come, let's kill him, and the inheritance will be ours!' [8] So they seized him and killed him, and threw him out of the vineyard.

[9] "Therefore, what will the owner[b] of the vineyard do? He will come and destroy the farmers and give the vineyard to others. [10] Haven't you read this Scripture:

The stone that the builders rejected,
this has become the cornerstone.[c]
[11] **This cornerstone[d] came from the Lord**
and is wonderful in our eyes?"[e]

[12] Because they knew He had said this parable against them, they were looking for a way to arrest Him, but they were afraid of the crowd. So they left Him and went away.

---

[1]12:4 Other mss add *threw stones and*
[2]12:4 Other mss add *and sent him off*

---

[a]12:5 *He . . . sent* supplied for clarity
[b]12:9 Or *lord*
[c]12:10 Lit *head of the corner;* interpreted as a cornerstone of a foun-

dation or capstone/keystone of a building or arch
[d]12:11 *cornerstone* implied
[e]12:11 Ps 118:22–23

Pray and Believe, and Watch for the Answer

Believe that He Himself will bring to pass what He has led you to pray. Then continue praying in faith and watching for it to come to pass.

"Therefore, I tell you, all the things you pray and ask for—believe that you have received them, and you will have them."
—Mark 11:24

GOD AND CAESAR

[13] Then they[a] sent some of the Pharisees and the Herodians[b] to Him in order to trap Him by what He said.[c] [14] When they came, they said to Him, "Teacher, we know You are truthful and defer to no one, for You don't show partiality,[d] but teach the way of God in truth. Is it lawful to pay taxes to Caesar or not? [15] Should we pay, or should we not pay?"

But knowing their hypocrisy, He said to them, "Why are you testing Me? Bring Me a denarius[e] to look at." [16] So they brought one. "Whose image and inscription is this?" He asked them.

"Caesar's," they said.

[17] Then Jesus told them, "Give back to Caesar the things that are Caesar's, and to God the things that are God's." And they were amazed at Him.

THE SADDUCEES AND THE RESURRECTION

[18] Some Sadducees,[f] who say there is no resurrection, came to Him and questioned Him: [19] "Teacher, Moses wrote for us that **'if a man's brother dies,'** leaves his wife behind, and **'leaves no child, his brother should take the wife and produce offspring[g] for his brother.'** [20] There were seven brothers. The first took a wife, and dying, left no offspring.[gh] [21] Also, the second took her, and he died, leaving no offspring. And the third likewise. [22] The seven also[1] left no offspring. Last of all, the woman died too. [23] In the resurrection, when they rise,[2] whose wife will she be, since the seven had married her?"[i]

[24] Jesus told them, "Are you not deceived because you don't know the Scriptures or the power of God? [25] For when they rise from the dead, they neither marry nor

Obedience and Belief Go Hand in Hand

When you come to a moment of truth, you must choose whether to obey God. You cannot obey Him unless you believe and trust Him. You cannot believe and trust Him unless you love Him. You cannot love Him unless you know Him.

Jesus told them, "Are you not deceived because you don't know the Scriptures or the power of God?"

—Mark 12:24

---

[1] **12:22** Other mss add *had taken her and*
[2] **12:23** Other mss omit *when they rise*

---

[a]**12:13** 11:27
[b]**12:13** See Mt 22:16 note
[c]**12:13** Lit *trap Him in (a) word*
[d]**12:14** Lit *don't look on the face of men* (that is, outward appearance)
[e]**12:15** See 6:37 note
[f]**12:18** Pharisees and Sadducees were two of the sects of Judaism. The Pharisees followed the whole body of written and oral law, but the Sadducees followed primarily the first five books of the OT (Torah).
[g]**12:19,20** Lit *seed.* So also in vv. 21–23
[h]**12:20** Gn 38:8; Dt 25:5
[i]**12:23** Lit *the seven had her as a wife*

are given in marriage, but are like angels in heaven. [26] Now concerning the dead being raised—haven't you read in the book of Moses, in the passage about the burning bush, how God spoke to him: '**I am the God of Abraham and the God of Isaac and the God of Jacob**'?[a] [27] He is not God of the dead, but of the living. You are badly deceived."

THE PRIMARY COMMANDMENTS

[28] One of the scribes approached. When he heard them debating and saw that Jesus[b] answered them well, he asked Him, "Which commandment is the most important of all?"[c]

[29] "This is the most important,"[1] Jesus answered:

> "'**Hear, O Israel! The Lord our God is one Lord. [30] And you shall love the Lord your God with all your heart, with all your soul, with all your mind, and with all your strength.**'[d2]

[31] "The second is: '**You shall love your neighbor as yourself.**'[e] There is no other commandment greater than these."

[32] Then the scribe said to Him, "Well said, Teacher! You have spoken in truth that He is one, and there is no one else except Him. [33] And to love Him with all the heart, with all the understanding,[3] and with all the strength, and to love one's neighbor as oneself, is far more important[f] than all the burnt offerings and sacrifices."

[34] When Jesus saw that he answered intelligently, He said to him, "You are not far from the kingdom of God." And no one dared to question Him any longer.

THE QUESTION ABOUT THE MESSIAH

[35] So Jesus asked this question as He taught in the temple complex, "How can the scribes say that the Messiah[g]

God Wants to Relate to You in Real Ways

A love relationship with God takes place between two real beings. A relationship with God is real and personal. He is a Person pouring His life into yours.

"He is not God of the dead, but of the living."

—Mark 12:27a

Loving God Is Where Your Usefulness Starts

Focus your attention on your love relationship with God. He may be waiting until you respond to His loving invitation before entrusting an assignment to you.

"And to love Him with all the heart, with all the understanding, and with all the strength, and to love one's neighbor as oneself, is far more important than all the burnt offerings and sacrifices."

—Mark 12:33

---

[1]**12:29** Other mss add *of all the commandments*
[2]**12:30** Other mss add *This is the first commandment*
[3]**12:33** Other mss add *with all the soul*

---

[a]**12:26** Ex 3:6,15,16
[b]**12:28** Lit *He*
[c]**12:28** Lit *Which commandment is first of all*
[d]**12:30** Dt 6:4-5; Jos 22:5
[e]**12:31** Lv 19:18
[f]**12:33** *important* implied
[g]**12:35** Gk *Christos;* or *Christ*

WORD STUDY

Greek word: **sunagoge**
[soon ah goh GAY]
Translation: **synagogue**
Uses in Mark's Gospel: **8**
(Mt, 9; Lk, 15; Jn, 2)
Uses in the NT: **56**
Key passage: **Mark 12:39**

The Greek noun *sunagoge* comes from the verb *sunago,* meaning *to bring* or *gather together;* thus, a *sunagoge* is *a gathering,* referring either to the place or the people (that is, an assembly or congregation). Among Greek speaking Jews, *sunagoge* was used for the Hebrew term *qahal* and the Aramaic *keneset,* both meaning *a gathering* and referring to either the place or the people.

The synagogue developed in Jewish life after the Babylonian exile and the destruction of Jerusalem and the temple (586 B.C.). After the exile ended, the temple was rebuilt and the sacrificial system resumed (515 B.C.), but by then synagogues were emerging as centralized places of worship emphasizing the study of the law of Moses. Synagogues eventually replaced the temple as focal points of Jewish worship since they were more accessible to those not living near Jerusalem. Such a shift in worship patterns gave rise to rabbis and synagogue elders who challenged the established authority of the priesthood. By the time of Jesus, the lines of spiritual authority were drawn between the Sadducees, who controlled the priesthood and temple worship, and the Pharisees, who exercised influence over the synagogues, the rabbis and elders, and thus the common people.

is the Son of David? [36] David himself says by the Holy Spirit:

> 'The Lord said to my Lord,
> "Sit at My right hand
> Until I put Your enemies under Your feet." ' [a]

[37] David himself calls Him 'Lord'; so how is He his Son?" And the large crowd was listening to Him with delight.

WARNING AGAINST THE SCRIBES

[38] He also said in His teaching, "Beware of the scribes, who want to go around in long robes, and who want greetings in the marketplaces, [39] the front seats in the synagogues, and the places of honor at banquets. [40] They devour widows' houses and say long prayers just for show. These will receive harsher punishment."

THE WIDOW'S GIFT

[41] Sitting across from the temple treasury, He watched how the crowd dropped money into the treasury. Many rich people were putting in large sums. [42] And a poor widow came and dropped in two tiny coins worth very little.[b] [43] Summoning His disciples, He said to them, "I assure you: This poor widow has put in more than all those giving to the temple treasury. [44] For they all gave out of their surplus, but she out of her poverty has put in everything she possessed—all she had to live on."

DESTRUCTION OF THE TEMPLE PREDICTED

13 As He was going out of the temple complex, one of His disciples said to Him, "Teacher, look! What massive stones! What impressive buildings!"

[2] Jesus said to him, "You see these great buildings? Not one stone will be left here on another that will not be thrown down!"

---

[a]12:36 Ps 110:1
[b]12:42 Lit two *lepta, which is a quadrans.* The *lepton* was the smallest and least valuable copper coin in use. The *quadrans* was one sixty-fourth of a daily wage.

SIGNS OF THE END OF THE AGE

[3] While He was sitting on the Mount of Olives across from the temple complex, Peter, James, John, and Andrew asked Him privately, [4] "Tell us, when will these things happen? And what will be the sign when all these things are about to take place?"

[5] Then Jesus began by telling them: "Watch out that no one deceives you. [6] Many will come in My name, saying, 'I am He,' and they will deceive many. [7] When you hear of wars and rumors of wars, don't be alarmed; these things must take place, but the end is not yet. [8] For nation will rise up against nation, and kingdom against kingdom. There will be earthquakes in various places, and famines.[1] These are the beginning of birth pains.

PERSECUTIONS PREDICTED

[9] "But you, be on your guard! They will hand you over to sanhedrins,[a] and you will be flogged in the synagogues. You will stand before governors and kings because of Me, as a witness to them. [10] And the good news[b] must first be proclaimed to all nations. [11] So when they arrest you and hand you over, don't worry beforehand what you will say. On the contrary, whatever is given to you in that hour—say it. For it isn't you who are speaking, but the Holy Spirit. [12] Then brother will betray brother to death, and a father his child. Children will rise up against parents and put them to death. [13] And you will be hated by all because of My name. But the one who endures to the end, this one will be delivered.[c]

THE GREAT TRIBULATION

[14] "When you see the **'abomination that causes desolation'**[d] standing where it should not," (let the reader understand,)[e] "then those in Judea must flee to the mountains! [15] A man on the housetop must not come down, or go in to get anything out of his house. [16] And a man in the field must not go back to get his clothes. [17] Woe to pregnant women and nursing mothers in those

[1]13:8 Other mss add *and disturbances*

[a]13:9 That is, local Jewish courts
[b]13:10 Or *gospel*
[c]13:13 Or *be saved*
[d]13:14 Dn 9:27
[e]13:14 These are, most likely, Mark's words to his readers.

WORD STUDY

Greek word: **sozo** [SOH zoh]
Translation: **deliver**
Uses in Mark's Gospel: **15**
(Mt, 15; Lk, 17; Jn, 6)
Uses in the NT: **106**
Key passage: **Mark 13:13**

The Greek verb *sozo* literally means *to preserve* or *keep safe* with an underlying idea of *making whole*. The term can refer to saving someone from physical harm (Mt 8:25) or death (Mt 14:30; 15:30-31; Ac 27:20,31), healing (Mk 5:23,28,34; 6:56; Jms 5:15), exorcism (Lk 8:36), or deliverance from a severe ordeal (Jn 12:27; Heb 5:7; Jd 5). Of course, the most common use of *sozo* in the NT, especially in Acts and the Epistles, is to describe the various aspects of salvation.

Two important nouns are derived from *sozo*: (1) *soteria,* which means *salvation* (in the redemptive sense) or *deliverance* (from physical death or danger; see Ac 7:25; 27:34), the former being by far the more common; and (2) *soter,* which means *Savior* and is always a reference to either the Father or Jesus Christ in the work of redemption. A comparison of the NT uses of *sozo* and *soteria* indicates that salvation has three aspects. First, a person is saved from sin by faith in Christ (Jn 3:17; Eph 2:5,8-9). Second, a believer is being saved as he matures in the Christian life (Rm 13:11; Php 2:12-13; 1 Tm 2:15; 4:16; Jms 1:21). Third, a believer will be saved from experiencing God's wrath in the end times (Mk 13:13; Rm 5:9-10; 1 Th 5:9-10). The first happens at a specific moment in a person's life; the second is an ongoing process throughout a Christian's life; the third will not occur until Christ's return.

days! [18] Pray that it[1] may not be in winter. [19] For those days will be a tribulation, the kind that hasn't been since the beginning of the world,[a] which God created, until now, and never will be again! [20] Unless the Lord cut short those days, no one would survive.[b] But because of the elect, whom He chose, He cut short those days.

[21] "Then if anyone tells you, 'Look, here is the Messiah!'[c] Look—there!' do not believe it! [22] For false messiahs[c] and false prophets will rise up and will perform signs and wonders to lead astray, if possible, the elect. [23] And you must watch! I have told you everything in advance.

THE COMING OF THE SON OF MAN

[24] "But in those days, after that tribulation,

The sun will be darkened,
and the moon will not shed her light;
[25] the stars will be falling from the sky,
and the celestial powers will be shaken.[d]

[26] Then they will see the Son of Man coming in clouds[e] with great power and glory. [27] Then He will send out the angels and gather His elect from the four winds, from the end of the earth to the end of the sky.

THE PARABLE OF THE FIG TREE

[28] "Learn this parable from the fig tree: As soon as its branch becomes tender and sprouts leaves, you know that summer is near. [29] In the same way, when you see these things happening, know[f] that He[g] is near—at the door! [30] I assure you: This generation will certainly not pass away until all these things take place. [31] Heaven and earth will pass away, but My words will never pass away.

Watch for Things to Begin Lining Up

When God speaks and what He is saying through the Bible, prayer, circumstances, and the church begin to line up to say the same thing, you can proceed with confidence to follow God's direction.

"In the same way, when you see these things happening, know that He is near—at the door!"

—Mark 13:29

---

[1]13:18 Other mss read *your escape*

---

[a]13:19 Lit *creation*
[b]13:20 Lit *days, all flesh would not survive*
[c]13:21,22 Or *Christ . . . false christs*

[d]13:25 Is 13:10; Jl 2:10,31; 3:15; Is 34:4
[e]13:26 Dan 7:13
[f]13:29 Or *you know*
[g]13:29 Or *it,* that is, summer

NO ONE KNOWS THE DAY OR HOUR

[32] "Now concerning that day or hour no one knows— neither the angels in heaven, nor the Son—except the Father. [33] Watch! Be alert![1] For you don't know when the time is coming.[a] [34] It is like a man on a journey, who left his house, gave authority to his slaves, gave each one his work, and commanded the doorkeeper to be alert. [35] Therefore be alert, since you don't know when the master of the house is coming—whether in the evening, or at midnight, or at the crowing of the rooster, or early in the morning. [36] Otherwise, he might come suddenly and find you sleeping. [37] And what I say to you, I say to everyone: Be alert!"

THE PLOT TO KILL JESUS

14 After two days it was the Passover[b] and the Festival of Unleavened Bread.[c] The chief priests and the scribes were looking for a way to arrest Him by deceit and kill Him. [2] "Not during the festival," they said, "or there may be rioting among the people."

THE ANOINTING AT BETHANY

[3] While He was in Bethany at the house of Simon the leper, as He was reclining at the table, a woman came with an alabaster jar of pure and expensive fragrant oil of nard. She broke the jar and poured it on His head. [4] But some were expressing indignation to one another: "Why has this fragrant oil been wasted? [5] For this oil might have been sold for more than three hundred denarii[d] and given to the poor." And they began to scold her.

[6] Then Jesus said, "Leave her alone. Why are you bothering her? She has done a noble thing for Me. [7] You always have the poor with you, and you can do good for them whenever you want, but you do not always have Me. [8] She has done what she could; she has anointed My body in advance for burial. [9] I assure you:

Wait with Your Eyes Wide Open

Waiting on the Lord is anything but inactive. While you wait on Him, you will be praying with a passion to know Him, His purposes, and His ways. You will be watching circumstances and asking God to interpret them by revealing to you His perspective. You will be sharing with other believers to find out what God is saying to them.

"Watch! Be alert! For you don't know when the time is coming."
—Mark 13:33

---

[1] 13:33 Other mss add *and pray*

---

[a] 13:33 *coming* supplied for clarity
[b] 14:1 The Jewish ritual meal celebrating Israel's deliverance from slavery in Egypt
[c] 14:1 A seven-day festival celebrated in conjunction with the Passover (Ex 12:1–20)
[d] 14:5 This amount was about a year's wages for a common worker.

Wherever the gospel is proclaimed in the whole world, what this woman has done will also be told in memory of her."

[10] Then Judas Iscariot, one of the Twelve, went to the chief priests to hand Him over to them. [11] And when they heard this, they were glad and promised to give him silver.[a] So he started looking for a good opportunity to betray Him.

PREPARATION FOR PASSOVER

[12] On the first day of Unleavened Bread, when they sacrifice the Passover lamb, His disciples asked Him, "Where do You want us to go and prepare the Passover so You may eat it?"

[13] So He sent two of His disciples and told them, "Go into the city, and a man carrying a water jug will meet you. Follow him. [14] Wherever he enters, tell the owner of the house, 'The Teacher says, "Where is the guest room for Me to eat the Passover with My disciples?"' [15] He will show you a large room upstairs, furnished and ready. Make the preparations for us there." [16] So the disciples went out, entered the city, and found it just as He had told them, and they prepared the Passover.

BETRAYAL AT THE PASSOVER

[17] When evening came, He arrived with the Twelve. [18] While they were reclining and eating, Jesus said, "I assure you: One of you will betray Me—one who is eating with Me!"

[19] They began to be distressed and to say to Him one by one, "Surely not I?"

[20] He said to them, "It is[b] one of the Twelve—the one who is dipping bread[c] with Me in the bowl. [21] For the Son of Man will go just as it is written about Him, but woe to that man by whom the Son of Man is betrayed! It would have been better for that man if he had not been born."

Experience Comes from Obedience

To experience Him at work in and through you, you must obey Him. When you obey Him, He will accomplish His work through you, and you will come to know Him by experience.

So the disciples went out, entered the city, and found it just as He had told them, and they prepared the Passover.

—Mark 14:16

---

[a]**14:11** Or *money;* in Mt 26:15 it is specified as 30 pieces of silver. See Zch 11:12–13

[b]**14:20** *It is* supplied
[c]**14:20** *bread* supplied for clarity

[22] As they were eating, He took bread, blessed and broke it, gave it to them, and said, "Take it;[1a] this is My body."

[23] Then He took a cup, and after giving thanks, He gave it to them, and so they all drank from it. [24] He said to them, "This is My blood of the covenant,[2] which is shed for many. [25] I assure you: I will no longer drink of the fruit of the vine until that day when I drink it new in the kingdom of God." [26] After singing psalms,[b] they went out to the Mount of Olives.

PETER'S DENIAL PREDICTED

[27] Then Jesus said to them, "All of you will fall,[3c] because it is written:

**I will strike the shepherd,
and the sheep will be scattered.[d]**

[28] But after I have been resurrected, I will go ahead of you to Galilee."

[29] Peter told Him, "Even if everyone falls, yet I will not!"

[30] "I assure you," Jesus said to him, "today, this very night, before the rooster crows twice, you will deny Me three times!"

[31] But he kept insisting, "If I have to die with You, I will never deny You!" And they all said the same thing.

THE PRAYER IN THE GARDEN

[32] Then they came to a place named Gethsemane, and He told His disciples, "Sit here while I pray." [33] He took Peter, James, and John with Him, and He began to be horrified and deeply distressed. [34] Then He said to them, "My soul is swallowed up in sorrow—[e] to the point of death. Remain here and stay awake." [35] Then He went a little farther, fell to the ground, and began to pray that if it were possible, the hour might pass from Him. [36] And

When in Doubt, Do What You Know

Whenever a silence comes, continue doing the last thing God told you and watch and wait for a fresh encounter with Him.

"But after I have been resurrected, I will go ahead of you to Galilee."
—Mark 14:28

Is Your Faith Bigger Than Your Questions?

Even when His will doesn't make sense from your human perspective, your obedience will reveal that His will was right.

Then He went a little farther, fell to the ground, and began to pray that if it were possible, the hour might pass from Him.
—Mark 14:35

[1] 14:22 Other mss add *eat*
[2] 14:24 Other mss read *new covenant*
[3] 14:27 Other mss add *because of Me this night*

[a] 14:22 *it* supplied for clarity
[b] 14:26 Pss 113–118 were sung during and after the Passover meal.
[c] 14:27 Or *stumble*
[d] 14:27 Zch 13:7
[e] 14:34 Or *I am deeply grieved*

Greek word: **abba** [ab bah]
Translation: **Abba**
Uses in Mark's Gospel: **1**
Uses in the NT: **3**
Key passage: **Mark 14:36**

The word *abba* is the Aramaic term for *father,* equivalent to *ab* in Hebrew and *pater* in Greek. Other than Mark 14:36, *abba* occurs only in Roman 8:15 and Galatians 4:6. All three occurrences of *abba* are followed by *pater* ("Abba Father"). In Mark 14:36 Jesus used the common Aramaic term for *father* that was used by Jewish people of all ages to address their fathers. Jesus used *pater* in the Gospels numerous times in reference to the Father, but many of them are probably translations of Jesus' original Aramaic expression *abba.* It is possible that Mark supplied the Greek *pater* by way of explanation to those in his audience not familiar with Aramaic, but it is equally possible that Jesus also said *pater* for emphasis. The Jews in Jesus' day did not normally use *abba* (or *pater*) in reference to God because it seemed too intimate an expression, but Jesus did, and He taught us to do the same.

He said, "*Abba,*[a] Father! All things are possible for You. Take this cup away from Me. Nevertheless, not what I will, but what You will."

37 Then He came and found them sleeping. "Simon, are you sleeping?" He asked Peter. "Couldn't you stay awake one hour? 38 Stay awake and pray, so that you won't enter into temptation. The spirit is willing, but the flesh is weak."[b]

39 Once again He went away and prayed, saying the same thing. 40 And He came again and found them sleeping, because they could not keep their eyes open.[c] They did not know what to say to Him. 41 Then He came a third time and said to them, "Are you still sleeping and resting? Enough! The time[d] has come. Look, the Son of Man is being betrayed into the hands of sinners. 42 Get up; let's go! See—My betrayer is near."

THE JUDAS KISS

43 While He was still speaking, Judas, one of the Twelve, suddenly arrived. With him was a mob, with swords and clubs, from the chief priests, the scribes, and the elders. 44 His betrayer had given them a signal. "The one I kiss," he said, "He's the one; arrest Him and get Him securely away." 45 So when he came, he went right up to Him and said, "Rabbi!"—and kissed[e] Him. 46 Then they laid hands on Him and arrested Him. 47 And one of those who stood by drew his sword, struck the high priest's slave, and cut off his ear.

48 But Jesus said to them, "Have you come out with swords and clubs, as though I were a criminal,[f] to capture Me? 49 Every day I was among you, teaching in the temple complex, and you didn't arrest Me. But the Scriptures must be fulfilled." 50 Then they all deserted Him and ran away.

51 Now a certain young man,[g] having a linen cloth wrapped around his naked body, was following Him. And they caught hold of him. 52 But he left the linen cloth behind and ran away naked.

---

[a]14:36 Aramaic word for father. See also Rm 8:15; Gl 4:6
[b]14:38 That is, human frailty often overcomes our best intentions
[c]14:40 Lit *because their eyes were weighed down*
[d]14:41 Lit *hour*
[e]14:45 The verb is a strengthened form of *kiss,* perhaps suggesting repetition or affection.
[f]14:48 Lit *as against a criminal*
[g]14:51 It is possible that this was young John Mark, who later wrote this Gospel.

JESUS FACES THE SANHEDRIN

53 They led Jesus away to the high priest, and all the chief priests, the elders, and the scribes convened. 54 Peter followed Him at a distance, right into the high priest's courtyard. And he was sitting with the temple police,ᵃ warming himself by the fire.ᵇ

55 The chief priests and the whole Sanhedrin were looking for testimony against Jesus to put Him to death. But they could find none. 56 For many were giving false testimony against Him, but the testimonies did not agree. 57 Some stood up and were giving false testimony against Him, stating, 58 "We heard Him say, 'I will demolish this sanctuary made by hands, and in three days I will build another not made by hands.'" 59 But not even on this did their testimony agree.

60 Then the high priest stood up before them all and questioned Jesus, "Don't You have an answer to what these men are testifying against You?" 61 But He kept silent and did not answer anything. Again the high priest questioned Him, "Are You the Messiah,ᶜ the Son of the Blessed One?"

62 "I am," said Jesus, "and all of youᵈ will see 'the Son of Man seated at the right hand' of the Power and 'coming with the clouds of heaven.'"ᵉ

63 Then the high priest tore his robes and said, "Why do we still need witnesses? 64 You have heard the blasphemy! What is your decision?"ᶠ

And they all condemned Him to be deserving of death. 65 Then some began to spit on Him, to blindfold Him, and to beat Him, saying, "Prophesy!" Even the temple policeᵍ took Him and slapped Him.

PETER DENIES HIS LORD

66 Now as Peter was in the courtyard below, one of the high priest's servants came. 67 When she saw Peter warming himself, she looked at him and said, "You also were with that Nazarene, Jesus."

68 But he denied it: "I don't know or understand what

Flesh vs. Spirit— Who's Going to Win?

Seek to bring every physical desire under the control of the Holy Spirit so that nothing will impede your accomplishing what Jesus asks of you.

Then He came and found them sleeping. "Simon, are you sleeping?" He asked Peter. "Couldn't you stay awake one hour?"

—Mark 14:37

ᵃ14:54 Lit *officers;* or *servants*
ᵇ14:54 Lit *light*
ᶜ14:61 Or *the Christ*
ᵈ14:62 Lit *and you,* plural in Gk
ᵉ14:62 Ps 110:1; Dn 7:13
ᶠ14:64 Lit *How does it appear to you*
ᵍ14:65 Or *officers;* lit *servants;*

you're talking about!" Then he went out to the entryway, and a rooster crowed.[1]

⁶⁹ When the servant saw him again she began to tell those standing nearby, "This man is one of them!"

⁷⁰ But again he denied it. After a little while those standing there said to Peter again, "You certainly are one of them, since you're a Galilean also!"[2]

⁷¹ Then he started to curse[a] and to swear with an oath, "I don't know this man you're talking about!"

⁷² Immediately a rooster crowed a second time. So Peter remembered when Jesus had spoken the word to him, "Before the rooster crows twice, you will deny Me three times." When he thought about it, he began to weep.[b]

JESUS FACES PILATE

15 As soon as it was morning, the chief priests had a meeting with the elders, scribes, and the whole Sanhedrin.[c] After tying Jesus up, they led Him away and handed Him over to Pilate.[d]

² So Pilate asked Him, "Are You the King of the Jews?"

He answered him, "You have said it."[e]

³ And the chief priests began to accuse Him of many things. ⁴ Then Pilate questioned Him again, "Are You not answering anything? Look how many things they are accusing You of!" ⁵ But Jesus still did not answer anything, so Pilate was amazed.

JESUS OR BARABBAS

⁶ At the festival it was Pilate's[f] custom to release for them one prisoner whom they requested. ⁷ There was one named Barabbas, who was in prison with rebels who had committed murder in the rebellion. ⁸ The

Don't Be Surprised to Be Misunderstood

You will fail to follow Christ as you should if you let others' reaction determine your faithfulness.

So Pilate asked Him, "Are You the King of the Jews?" He answered him, "You have said it." And the chief priests began to accuse Him of many things.

—Mark 15:2-3

---

[1] 14:68 Other mss omit *and a rooster crowed*
[2] 14:70 Other mss read *and your speech shows it*

[a] 14:71 That is, to call down curses on himself if what he said wasn't true
[b] 14:72 Or *he burst into tears;* or *he broke down*
[c] 15:1 The seventy-member supreme council of Judaism, patterned after Moses' seventy elders
[d] 15:1 Pontius Pilate was appointed by Caesar Tiberius as the fifth governor of the province of Judea in A.D. 26. His jurisdiction included Samaria to the north, Gaza and the Dead Sea area to the south. He remained at this post until A.D. 36.
[e] 15:2 Or *That is true:* an affirmative oath (see also at Mt 26:64)
[f] 15:6 Lit *his*

crowd came up and began to ask Pilate[a] to do for them as was his custom. [9] So Pilate answered them, "Do you want me to release the King of the Jews for you?" [10] For he knew it was because of envy that the chief priests had handed Him over. [11] But the chief priests stirred up the crowd so that he would release Barabbas to them instead.

[12] Pilate asked them again, "Then what do you want me to do with the One you call the King of the Jews?"

[13] And again they shouted, "Crucify Him!"

[14] Then Pilate said to them, "Why? What has He done wrong?"

But they shouted, "Crucify Him!" all the more.

[15] Then, willing to gratify the crowd, Pilate released Barabbas to them. And after having Jesus flogged,[b] he handed Him over to be crucified.

MOCKED BY THE MILITARY

[16] Then the soldiers led Him away into the courtyard (that is, headquarters[c]) and called the whole company[d] together. [17] They dressed Him in a purple robe, twisted a crown out of thorns, and put it on Him. [18] And they began to salute Him, "Hail, King of the Jews!" [19] They kept hitting Him on the head with a reed and spitting on Him. And getting down on their knees, they were paying Him homage. [20] When they had mocked Him, they stripped Him of the purple robe, put His clothes on Him, and led Him out to crucify Him.

CRUCIFIED BETWEEN TWO CRIMINALS

[21] They forced a passer-by coming in from the country to carry His cross—Simon, a Cyrenian, the father of Alexander and Rufus. [22] And they brought Him to the place called *Golgotha* (which means Skull Place). [23] They tried to give Him wine mixed with myrrh, but He did not take it. [24] Then they crucified Him and divided His clothes, by casting lots[e] for them, to decide what each would get. [25] Now it was nine in the morn-

See God's Love in the Suffering Christ

If you have lost your wonder at the incredible gift of salvation that has been given to you, you need to revisit the cross and witness your Savior suffering for you.

They dressed Him in a purple robe, twisted a crown out of thorns, and put it on Him. And they began to salute Him, "Hail, King of the Jews."

—Mark 15:17–18

[a]**15:8** *Pilate* inferred
[b]**15:15** Roman flogging was done with a whip made of leather strips embedded with pieces of bone or metal that brutally tore the flesh.
[c]**15:16** Lit *the Praetorium,* a Latin word meaning military headquarters (or the governor's palace)
[d]**15:16** Or *cohort,* a Roman military unit that numbered as many as six hundred infantry
[e]**15:24** Ps 22:18

WORD STUDY

Greek word: *enkataleipo*
[en kah tah LIGH poh]

Translation: *forsake*

Uses in Mark's Gospel: **1**
(Mt, 1)

Uses in the NT: **10**

Key passage: **Mark 15:34**

The Greek verb *enkataleipo* is a double compound that produces an intensive form of a verb meaning *to lack* or *leave (leipo)*. With one exception (Rm 9:29), each occurrence of the term in the NT means *forsake* or *abandon*. In Mark 15:34 and Matthew 27:46 *enkataleipo* is used to translate the Aramaic word *sabach*, which in turn translates the original Hebrew *'azab* in Psalm 22:1. Jesus' quote of this verse occurred toward the end of three hours of darkness (Mk 15:33) during which He endured God's wrath by being separated from the Father as payment for the sins of mankind. The word *enkataleipo* also occurs in Hebrews 13:5, "I will never forsake you." Since this promise is addressed to believers, it indicates that while God was willing to forsake Jesus on the cross in order to redeem us, He is not now willing to forsake those whom He has redeemed.

ing[a] when they crucified Him. 26 The inscription of the charge written against Him was:

> ### THE KING OF THE JEWS

27 They crucified two criminals[b] with Him, one on the right and one on His left. ⌐28 So the Scripture was fulfilled that says: **"And He was counted among outlaws."**⌐[1c] 29 Those who passed by were yelling insults at[d] Him, shaking their heads, and saying, "Ha! The One who would demolish the sanctuary and build it in three days, 30 save Yourself by coming down from the cross!" 31 In the same way, the chief priests with the scribes were mocking Him to one another and saying, "He saved others; He cannot save Himself! 32 Let the Messiah,[e] the King of Israel, come down now from the cross, so that we may see and believe." Even those who were crucified with Him were taunting Him.

THE DEATH OF JESUS

33 When it was noon,[f] darkness came over the whole land[g] until three in the afternoon.[h] 34 And at three[h] Jesus cried out with a loud voice, *"Eloi, Eloi, lemá[2] sabachtháni?"* which is translated, "My God, My God, why have You forsaken Me?"[i]

35 When some of those standing there heard this, they said, "Look, He's calling for Elijah!" 36 Someone ran and filled a sponge with sour wine, fixed it on a reed, offered Him a drink, and said, "Let us see if Elijah comes to take Him down!"

37 But Jesus let out a loud cry and breathed His last. 38 Then the curtain of the sanctuary[j] was split in two from top to bottom. 39 When the centurion,[k] who was

---

[1]15:28 Other mss omit v. 28
[2]15:34 Other mss read *lama;* or *lima*

---

[a]15:25 Lit *was the third hour*
[b]15:27 Or *revolutionaries*
[c]15:28 Is 53:12
[d]15:29 Gk *passed by blasphemed*
[e]15:32 Or *the Christ*
[f]15:33 Lit *sixth hour*
[g]15:33 Or *earth*

[h]15:33 Lit *ninth hour*
[i]15:34 Ps 22:1
[j]15:37 A heavy curtain separated the inner room of the temple from the outer.
[k]15:39 A Roman officer who commanded about one hundred men

standing opposite Him, saw the way He[1] breathed His last, he said, "This man really was God's Son!"[a] [40] There were also women looking on from a distance. Among them were Mary Magdalene,[b] Mary the mother of James the younger and of Joses, and Salome. [41] When He was in Galilee, they would follow Him and minister to Him. Many other women had come up with Him to Jerusalem.

THE BURIAL OF JESUS

[42] When it was already evening, because it was Preparation Day (that is, the day before the Sabbath), [43] Joseph of Arimathea, a prominent member of the Sanhedrin who was himself looking forward to the kingdom of God, came and boldly went in to Pilate and asked for Jesus' body. [44] Pilate was surprised that He was already dead. Summoning the centurion, he asked him whether He had already died. [45] When he found out from the centurion, he granted the corpse to Joseph. [46] After he bought some fine linen, he took Him down and wrapped Him in the linen. Then he placed Him in a tomb cut out of the rock, and rolled a stone against the entrance to the tomb. [47] Now Mary Magdalene and Mary the mother of Joses were watching where He was placed.

RESURRECTION MORNING

16 When the Sabbath was over, Mary Magdalene,[c] Mary the mother of James, and Salome bought spices, so that they might go and anoint Him. [2] Very early in the morning, on the first day of the week, they went to the tomb at sunrise. [3] And they were saying to one another, "Who will roll away the stone from the entrance to the tomb for us?" [4] Looking up, they observed that the stone—which was very large—had been rolled away. [5] When they entered the tomb, they saw a

---

[1]15:39 Other mss read *saw that He cried out like this and*

---

[a]15:39 Or *the Son of God* (See Mk 1:1)
[b]15:40 Or *Mary of Magdala;* Magdala apparently was a town on the western shore of the Sea of Galilee and north of Tiberias.
[c]16:1 See 15:40 note

WORD STUDY

Greek word: **sabbaton**
[SAHB bah than]
Translation: **sabbath**
Uses in Mark's Gospel: **12**
(Mt, 11; Lk, 20; Jn, 13)
Uses in the NT: **68**
Key passage: **Mark 16:1**

The Greek word *sabbaton* represents the Hebrew term *shabbath,* which comes from the Hebrew word for the number seven *(shabua).* The Fourth Commandment prohibited working on the Sabbath since it was a celebration of God's six days of work as Creator being finished (Ex 20:8–11; see Gn 2:1–3).

By NT times Jewish tradition had attempted to explain in detail exactly what constituted *work,* and in so doing the religious laws about keeping the Sabbath had enslaved the people instead of giving them rest. Jesus often addressed this problem, which was a constant source of antagonism between Him and the Jewish leaders (Mk 2:23–28; 3:1–5; Lk 13:10–17; 14:1–6; Jn 5:1–18; 7:22–23; 9:1–41).

One of the most signficant aspects of Sabbath celebration in the NT involves establishing a chronology for Jesus' death and resurrection. The crucifixion of Jesus occurred on a Friday, the day before the weekly Sabbath (Lk 23:54, 56; Jn 19:31). This was also the Sabbath of the week of Unleavened Bread (Lv 23:6–8; see vv. 4–5). Jesus arose from the dead on Sunday, the first day of the week, the day following the weekly Sabbath on Saturday (Mt 28:1; Mk 16:1; see Lk 24:1; Jn 20:1), which was also the day the Feast of Firstfruits was celebrated (Lv 23:9–14; see 1 Co 15:20).

young man[a] dressed in a long white robe sitting on the right side; they were amazed and alarmed.[b]

⁶ "Don't be alarmed," he told them. "You are looking for Jesus the Nazarene, who was crucified. He has been resurrected! He is not here! See the place where they put Him. ⁷ But go, tell His disciples and Peter, 'He is going ahead of you to Galilee; you will see Him there just as He told you.'"

⁸ So they went out and started running from the tomb, because trembling and astonishment had gripped them. And they said nothing to anyone, since they were afraid.

APPEARANCES OF THE RISEN LORD

¹⁹ Early on the first day of the week, after He had risen, He appeared first to Mary Magdalene, out of whom He had driven seven demons. ¹⁰ She went and reported to those who had been with Him, as they were mourning and weeping. ¹¹ Yet, when they heard that He was alive and had been seen by her, they did not believe it. ¹² Then after this, He appeared in a different form to two of them walking on their way into the country. ¹³ And they went and reported it to the rest, who did not believe them either.

THE GREAT COMMISSION

¹⁴ Later, He appeared to the Eleven themselves as they were reclining at the table. And He rebuked their unbelief and hardness of heart, because they did not believe those who saw Him after He had been resurrected. ¹⁵ Then He said to them, "Go into all the world and preach the gospel to the whole creation. ¹⁶ Whoever believes and is baptized will be saved, but whoever does not believe will be condemned. ¹⁷ And these signs will accompany those who believe: In My name they will drive out demons; they will speak with new tongues; ¹⁸ they will pick up snakes;[2] if they should drink anything deadly, it will never harm them; they will lay hands on the sick, and they will get well."

[1]**16:9-20** Other mss omit these verses.
[2]**16:18** Other mss add *with their hands*

---

[a]**16:5** See Mt 28:2, where the young man is identified as an angel.

[b]**16:5** *amazed* and *alarmed* translate the idea of one Gk word.

God Does Give Second Chances

Don't give up if you've failed the Lord. Remember what happened to Peter. God has not yet finished developing you as a disciple.

"But go, tell His disciples and Peter, 'He is going ahead of you to Galilee; you will see Him there just as He told you.'"

—Mark 16:7

THE ASCENSION

[19] Then after speaking to them, the Lord Jesus was taken up into heaven and sat down at the right hand of God. [20] And they went out and preached everywhere, the Lord working with them and confirming the word by the accompanying signs.⌐

Greek Word Studies

in the Gospel of Luke

THE GOSPEL OF

LUKE

THE DEDICATION TO THEOPHILUS

1 Since many have undertaken to compile a narrative about the events that have been fulfilled[a] among us, [2] just as the original eyewitnesses and servants of the word handed them down to us, [3] it also seemed good to me, having carefully investigated everything from the very first, to write to you in orderly sequence, most honorable Theophilus, [4] so that you may know the certainty of the things about which you have been instructed.[b]

GABRIEL PREDICTS JOHN'S BIRTH

[5] In the days of King Herod[c] of Judea, there was a priest of Abijah's division[d] named Zachariah. His wife was from the daughters of Aaron, and her name was Elizabeth. [6] Both were righteous in God's sight, living without blame according to all the commandments and requirements of the Lord. [7] But they had no children[e] because Elizabeth could not conceive,[f] and both of them were well along in years.[g]

[8] When his division was on duty, and he was serving as priest before God, [9] it happened that he was chosen by lot, according to the custom of the priesthood, to enter the sanctuary of the Lord and burn incense. [10] At the hour of incense the whole assembly of the people was praying outside. [11] An angel of the Lord appeared to him, standing to the right of the altar of incense.

---

[a]1:1 Or *accomplished* or *events most surely believed*
[b]1:4 Or *informed*
[c]1:5 Idumean ruler over Palestine under Rome (37 B.C.—4 B.C.)
[d]1:5 One of the twenty-four divisions of priests appointed by David for temple service (see 1 Ch 24:10)
[e]1:7 Lit *child*
[f]1:7 Lit *Elizabeth was sterile* or *barren*
[g]1:7 Lit *in their days*

WORD STUDY

Greek word: *horao*
[horh RAH oh]

Translation: *appeared*

Uses in Luke's Gospel: **81**
(Mt, 108; Mk, 50; Jn, 67)

Uses in Luke's Writings: **147**

Uses in the NT: **454**

Key passage: **Luke 1:11**

The Greek verb *horao* is one of several NT words meaning *to see, look, watch,* or the like. Most occurrences of *horao* mean *to see, beware,* or *watch out.* A special use of *horao* is in reference to appearances of supernatural beings or entities that enter the physical realm. In such cases *horao* means *appeared.* Examples include Moses' and Elijah's appearance at Jesus' transfiguration (Mt 17:3; Mk 9:4); God's appearance to Abraham (Ac 7:2) and then to Moses (Ac 7:30); angelic appearances to Zechariah (Lk 1:11) and Jesus (Lk 22:43); and Paul's Macedonian vision (Acts 16:9). This special meaning of *horao* is also used for Jesus' resurrection appearances, both during the forty days on earth (Lk 24:34; Ac 13:31; 1 Co 15:5,6,7) and after the ascension (Ac 26:16; 1 Co 15:8). Three apocalyptic appearances are recorded in Revelation: the ark in heaven (11:19), and the woman (12:1) pursued by the dragon (12:3).

^{12} When Zachariah saw him, he was startled and overcome with fear.^{a} ^{13} But the angel said to him:

> "Do not be afraid, Zachariah,
> because your prayer has been heard.
> Your wife Elizabeth will bear you a son,
> and you will name him John.
> ^{14} There will be joy and delight for you,
> and many will rejoice at his birth.
> ^{15} For he will be great in the sight of the Lord,
> and will never drink wine or beer.^{b}
> And he will be filled with the Holy Spirit
> while still in his mother's womb.^{c}
> ^{16} He will turn many of the sons of Israel
> to the Lord their God.
> ^{17} And he will go before Him
> in the spirit and power of Elijah,
> to turn the hearts of fathers to their children,^{d}
> and the disobedient to the understanding of the righteous,
> to make ready for the Lord a prepared people."

^{18} "How can I know this?" Zachariah asked the angel. "For I am an old man, and my wife is well along in years."^{e}

^{19} The angel answered him, "I am Gabriel, who stands in the presence of God, and I was sent to speak to you and tell you this good news. ^{20} Now listen! You will become silent and unable to speak until the day these things take place, because you did not believe my words, which will be fulfilled in their proper time."

^{21} Meanwhile, the people were waiting for Zachariah, amazed that he stayed so long in the sanctuary. ^{22} When he did come out, he could not speak to them. Then they realized that he had seen a vision in the sanctuary. He kept making signs to them and remained speechless. ^{23} And when the days of his ministry were completed, he went back home.

^{24} After these days his wife Elizabeth conceived, and kept herself in seclusion for five months. She said,

---

^{a}**1:12** Lit *and fear fell on him*
^{b}**1:15** Nm 6:3
^{c}**1:15** See 1:41,44; Jdg 13:3–5; 16:17;
  Is 44:2
^{d}**1:17** Mal 4:5–6
^{e}**1:18** Lit *in her days*

25 "The Lord has done this for me. He has looked with favor in these days to take away my disgrace among the people."

GABRIEL PREDICTS JESUS' BIRTH

26 In the sixth month, the angel Gabriel was sent by God to a town in Galilee called Nazareth, 27 to a virgin engaged[a] to a man named Joseph, of the house of David. The virgin's name was Mary. 28 And he[1] came to her and said, "Rejoice, favored woman! The Lord is with you."[2] 29 But she was deeply troubled by this statement and was wondering what kind of greeting this could be. 30 Then the angel told her:

> "Do not be afraid, Mary, for you have found favor with God.
> 31 Now listen: You will conceive and give birth to a son,
> and you will call His name JESUS.
> 32 He will be great
> and will be called the Son of the Most High,
> and the Lord God will give Him the throne of His father David.[b]
> 33 He will reign over the house of Jacob forever,
> and His kingdom will have no end."[c]

34 Mary asked the angel, "How can this be, since I have not been intimate with a man?"[d]

35 The angel replied to her:

> "The Holy Spirit will come upon you,
> and the power of the Most High will overshadow you.
> Therefore the holy child to be born[e]
> will be called the Son of God.

36 And consider Elizabeth your relative—even she has conceived a son in her old age, and this is the sixth

To Second-Guess Is Your First Mistake

You need to believe that He will enable you to do everything He asks of you. Don't try to second-guess Him. Just let Him be God. Turn to Him for the needed power, insight, skill, and resources. He will provide you with all that you need.

"How can I know this?" Zachariah asked the angel. "For I am an old man, and my wife is well along in years."

—Luke 1:18

---

[1] 1:28 Other mss read *the angel*
[2] 1:28 Other mss add *blessed are you among women*

---

[a] 1:27 Or *betrothed.* Jewish engagement was a binding agreement and required divorce to break it.
[b] 1:32 2 Sm 7:12-13
[c] 1:33 Is 9:6 (LXX); Dn 7:14
[d] 1:34 Lit *since I do not know a man*
[e] 1:35 Or *the child to be born will be holy; He*

month for her who was called barren. [37] For nothing will be impossible with God."[a]

[38] "Consider me the Lord's slave,"[b] said Mary. "May it be done to me according to your word." Then the angel left her.

MARY'S VISIT TO ELIZABETH

[39] In those days Mary set out and hurried to a town in the hill country of Judah, [40] where she entered Zachariah's house and greeted Elizabeth. [41] When Elizabeth heard Mary's greeting, the baby leaped inside her,[c] and Elizabeth was filled with the Holy Spirit. [42] Then she exclaimed with a loud cry:

> "Blessed are you among women,
> and blessed is your offspring![d]

[43] How could this happen to me, that the mother of my Lord should come to me? [44] For you see, when the sound of your greeting reached my ears, the baby leaped for joy inside me![e] [45] Blessed is she who has believed that what was spoken to her by the Lord will be fulfilled!"

MARY'S PRAISE

[46] And Mary said:

> "My soul proclaims the greatness[f] of the Lord,[g]
> [47] and my spirit has rejoiced in God my Savior,
> [48] because He has looked with favor
> on the humble condition of His slave.
> Surely, from now on all generations will call me blessed,
> [49] because the Mighty One[h] has done great things for me,
> and holy is His name.
> [50] His mercy is from generation to generation
> on those who fear Him.
> [51] He has done a mighty deed with His arm;
> He has scattered the proud because of the thoughts of their hearts;

Nothing Is Impossible with God

When God speaks of doing the impossible, it is no longer absurd. The miraculous should be a part of the Christian's experience.

"For nothing will be impossible with God."

—Luke 1:37

If God Says It, He Can Do It

No matter how big the assignment He gives you, He is able to accomplish His purposes through you.

"Blessed is she who has believed that what was spoken to her by the Lord will be fulfilled!"

—Luke 1:45

---

[a]**1:37** Gn 18:14
[b]**1:38** Or *I am the Lord's slave;* lit *Look, the Lord's slave*
[c]**1:41** Lit *leaped in her abdomen* or *womb*
[d]**1:42** Lit *is the fruit of your womb*
[e]**1:44** Lit *in my abdomen* or *womb*
[f]**1:46** Or *soul magnifies*
[g]**1:46** 1 Sm 2:1–10
[h]**1:49** Zph 3:17; Ps 89:9

52 He has toppled the mighty from their thrones
    and exalted the lowly.
53 He has satisfied the hungry with good things
    and sent the rich away empty.
54 He has helped His servant Israel,
    mindful of His mercy,[a]
55 just as He spoke to our forefathers,
    to Abraham and his descendants[b] forever."

56 And Mary stayed with her about three months; then she returned to her home.

THE BIRTH AND NAMING OF JOHN

57 Now the time for Elizabeth to give birth was completed, and she bore a son. 58 Then her neighbors and relatives heard that the Lord had shown her His great mercy,[c] and they rejoiced with her.

59 When they came to circumcise the child on the eighth day, they were going to name him Zachariah, after his father. 60 But his mother responded, "No! He will be called John."

61 Then they said to her, "None of your relatives has that name." 62 So they motioned to his father to find out what he wanted him to be called. 63 He asked for a writing tablet, and wrote:

> **His name is John.**

And they were all amazed. 64 Immediately his mouth was opened and his tongue freed,[d] and he began to speak, praising God. 65 Fear came upon all those who lived around them, and all these things were being talked about throughout the hill country of Judea. 66 All who heard took them[e] to heart, saying, "What then will this child become?" For, indeed, the Lord's hand was with him.

ZACHARIAH'S PROPHECY

67 Then his father Zachariah was filled with the Holy Spirit and prophesied:

Godly Thinking Is a Deliberate Decision

When God invites you to join Him, the first action will involve the adjustment of your life to God. The second action will be obedience to what God asks you to do. You cannot go on to obedience without first making the adjustments.

He asked for a writing tablet, and wrote: His name is John. And they were all amazed.

—Luke 1:63

---

a1:54 That is, because He remembered His mercy; see Ps 98:3
b1:55 Or *offspring;* lit *seed*
c1:58 Lit *the Lord magnified His mercy with her*
d1:64 *freed* supplied for clarity
e1:66 *them* supplied for clarity

68 "Blessed is the Lord, the God of Israel,[a]
because He has visited and provided redemption
for His people,
69 and has raised up a horn[b] of salvation[c] for us
in the house of His servant David,
70 just as He spoke by the mouth of His holy
prophets of old:
71 salvation from our enemies and from the
clutches[d] of those who hate us.
72 He has dealt mercifully with our fathers
and remembered His holy covenant—
73 the oath that He swore to our father Abraham.
He has granted us that,
74 having been rescued from our enemies'
clutches,[d]
we might serve Him without fear
75 in holiness and righteousness
in His presence all our days.
76 And you, child, will be called a prophet of the
Most High,
for you will go before the Lord to prepare His
ways,[e]
77 to give His people knowledge of salvation
through the forgiveness of their sins,
78 because of our God's merciful compassion
by which the Dawn[f] from on high[g] will visit us,
79 to shine on those who live in darkness and the
shadow of death,
to guide our feet into the way of peace."[h]

80 The child grew up and became strong in spirit, and
he was in the wilderness until the day of His public
appearance to Israel.

THE BIRTH OF JESUS

2 In those days a decree went out from Caesar Augustus[i] that the whole empire[j] should be registered.

Obedience Will Draw You Closer to God

The reward for obedience and love is that He will show Himself to you.

When the angels had left them and returned to heaven, the shepherds said to one another, "Let's go straight to Bethlehem and see this thing that has taken place, which the Lord has made known to us."

—Luke 2:15

---

[a] **1:68** Ps 41:13
[b] **1:69** The horn of an animal is a symbol for power in the OT. See 1 Sm 2:1,10; 2 Sm 22:3; Dn 7–8; Zch 2:1–4
[c] **1:69** That is, a strong Savior
[d] **1:71** Lit *from the hand*
[e] **1:76** Mal 3:1
[f] **1:78** Jr 23:5; Zch 3:8; 6:12
[g] **1:78** See 24:49; Eph 3:18; 4:8; Is 58:8
[h] **1:79** Is 9:2; 60:2
[i] **2:1** Emperor who ruled the Roman Empire from 27 B.C.—A.D. 14. Also known as Octavian, he established the peaceful era known as the *Pax Romana*. Caesar was a title for Roman emperors.
[j] **2:1** Or *the whole inhabited world*

2 This first registration took place while[a] Quirinius was governing Syria. 3 So everyone went to be registered, each to his own town.

4 And Joseph also went up from the town of Nazareth in Galilee, to Judea, to the city of David, which is called Bethlehem, because he was of the house and family line of David, 5 to be registered along with Mary, who was engaged[b] to him[1] and was pregnant. 6 While they were there, it happened that the days were completed for her to give birth. 7 Then she gave birth to her firstborn Son, and she wrapped Him snugly in cloth and laid Him in a manger—because there was no room for them at the inn.

THE SHEPHERDS AND THE ANGELS

8 In the same region, shepherds were living out in the fields and keeping watch at night over their flock. 9 Then an angel of the Lord stood before[c] them, and the glory of the Lord shone around them, and they were terrified.[d] 10 But the angel said to them, "Do not be afraid, for you see, I announce to you good news of great joy, which will be for all the people: 11 because today in the city of David was born for you a Savior, who is Christ the Lord.[e] 12 This will be the sign for you: you will find a baby wrapped snugly in cloth and lying in a manger."

13 Suddenly there was a multitude of the heavenly host with the angel, praising God and saying:

14 "Glory to God in the highest heaven,
and peace on earth to people He favors!"[2fg]

15 When the angels had left them and returned to heaven, the shepherds said to one another, "Let's go straight to Bethlehem and see this thing that has taken place, which the Lord has made known to us."

16 And they hurried off and found both Mary and Joseph, and the baby who was lying in the manger. 17 After seeing them,[h] they reported the message they

---

[1]2:5 Other mss read *was his engaged wife*
[2]2:14 Other mss read *earth good will to people*

---

[a]2:2 Or *This registration was the first while;* or *This registration was before*
[b]2:5 See 1:27 note
[c]2:9 Or *Lord appeared to*

[d]2:9 Lit *they feared a great fear*
[e]2:11 Or *is Messiah the Lord*
[f]2:14 Lit *earth to men of good will*
[g]2:14 12:51
[h]2:17 *them* supplied for clarity

WORD STUDY

Greek word: **mnesteuo**
[mnay STYOO oh]
Translation: **engaged**
Uses in Luke's Gospel: **2**
Uses in the NT: **3**
Key passage: **Luke 2:5**

The Greek verb *mnesteuo* is used only three times in the NT (Mt 1:18; Lk 1:27; 2:5), and each time it describes Mary who was "engaged" to Joseph. The word *mnesteuo* is roughly equivalent to the American concept of engagement, but the Jewish custom described by the term was much stronger. In Jewish culture in NT times, *mnesteuo* referred to a contractual arrangement that could only be broken by divorce. Joseph and Mary were legally considered husband and wife (Mt 1:19-20), although no wedding ceremony had been performed and they were neither living together nor having sexual relations (Mt 1:18; Lk 1:27). In obedience to the angel of the Lord, Joseph took Mary into his home as his wife (Mt 1:24). During this time Joseph and Mary made the trip together to Bethlehem (Lk 2:4-5). Both Matthew and Luke use the word *mnesteuo* to refer to this time period in light of the fact that Joseph and Mary refrained from sexual relations until after Jesus' birth (Mt 1:25; Lk 2:5).

were told about this child, [18] and all who heard it were amazed at what the shepherds said to them. [19] But Mary was treasuring up all these things[a] in her heart and meditating on them. [20] The shepherds returned, glorifying and praising God for all they had seen and heard, just as they had been told.

THE CIRCUMCISION AND PRESENTATION OF JESUS

[21] When the eight days were completed for His circumcision, He was named JESUS—the name given by the angel before He was conceived.[b] [22] And when the days of their purification according to the law of Moses were completed, they brought Him up to Jerusalem to present Him to the Lord [23] (just as it is written in the law of the Lord: **"Every firstborn male[c] will be called holy to the Lord"**)[d] [24] and to offer a sacrifice (according to what is stated in the law of the Lord: **"a pair of turtledoves or two young pigeons"**).[e]

SIMEON'S PROPHETIC PRAISE

[25] There was a man in Jerusalem whose name was Simeon. This man was righteous and devout, looking forward to Israel's consolation,[f] and the Holy Spirit was upon him. [26] It had been revealed to him by the Holy Spirit that he would not see death before he saw the Lord's Messiah.[g] [27] Guided by the Spirit, he entered[h] the temple complex. When the parents brought in the child Jesus to perform for Him what was customary under the law, [28] Simeon[i] took Him up in his arms, praised God, and said:

> [29] "Now, Master, You can dismiss Your slave in peace,
> according to Your word.
> [30] For my eyes have seen Your salvation,
> [31] which You have prepared in the presence of all peoples;

Stay on Task and You'll Be on Target

If you do everything He says, you will be in the center of His will when He wants to use you for a special assignment.

"Now, Master, You can dismiss Your slave in peace, according to Your word. For my eyes have seen Your salvation, which You have prepared in the presence of all peoples."

—Luke 2:29–31

---

[a]2:19 Lit *these words*
[b]2:21 Or *conceived in the womb*
[c]2:23 Lit *Every male that opens a womb*
[d]2:23 Ex 13:2,12
[e]2:24 Lv 5:11; 12:8
[f]2:25 That is, the coming of the Messiah with His salvation for the nations; see 2:26,30; Is 40:1; 61:2
[g]2:26 Or *Christ* (= "the Anointed One")
[h]2:27 Lit *And in the Spirit, he came*
[i]2:28 Lit *he*

[32] a light for revelation to the Gentiles[ab]
and glory to Your people Israel."[c]

[33] His father and mother[1] were amazed at what was being said about Him. [34] Then Simeon blessed them and told His mother Mary: "Indeed, this child is destined to cause the fall and rise of many in Israel, and to be a sign that will be opposed[d]— [35] and a sword will pierce your own soul—that the thoughts[e] of many hearts may be revealed."

ANNA'S TESTIMONY

[36] There was also a prophetess, Anna, a daughter of Phanuel, of the tribe of Asher. She was well along in years,[f] having lived with a husband seven years after her marriage,[g] [37] and was a widow for eighty-four years.[h] She did not leave the temple complex, serving God night and day with fastings and prayers. [38] At that very moment,[i] she came up and began to thank God and to speak about Him to all who were looking forward to the redemption of Jerusalem.[2j]

THE FAMILY'S RETURN TO NAZARETH

[39] When they had completed everything according to the law of the Lord, they returned to Galilee, to their own town of Nazareth. [40] The boy grew up and became strong, filled with wisdom, and God's grace was on Him.

IN HIS FATHER'S HOUSE

[41] Every year His parents traveled to Jerusalem for the Passover Festival. [42] When He was twelve years old, they went up according to the custom of the festival.[k] [43] After those days were over, as they were returning, the boy Jesus stayed behind in Jerusalem, but His parents[3] did

---

[1]**2:33** Other mss read *Joseph and His mother*
[2]**2:38** Other mss read *in Jerusalem*
[3]**2:43** Other mss read *but Joseph and His mother*

---

[a]**2:32** Or *the nations*
[b]**2:32** Is 49:6; 49:9
[c]**2:32** LXX Is 46:13
[d]**2:34** Or *spoken against*
[e]**2:35** Or *schemes*
[f]**2:36** Lit *in many days*

[g]**2:36** Lit *years from her virginity*
[h]**2:37** Or *she was a widow until the age of eighty-four*
[i]**2:38** Lit *hour*
[j]**2:38** Is 52:9
[k]**2:42** Dt 16:16–17

Loving God Is a Lifelong Habit

The key to knowing God's voice is not a formula. It is not a method you can follow. Knowing God's voice comes from an intimate love relationship with God.

There was also a prophetess, Anna, a daughter of Phanuel, of the tribe of Asher. She was well along in years, having lived with a husband seven years after her marriage, and was a widow for eighty-four years. She did not leave the temple complex, serving God night and day with fastings and prayers.

—Luke 2:36–37

WORD STUDY

Greek word: **grapho** [grah FOH]
Translation: **write**
Uses in Luke's Gospel: **20**
(Mt, 10; Mk, 10; Jn, 22)
Uses in Luke's Writings: **32**
Uses in the NT: **191**
Key passage: **Luke 3:4**

It is not surprising that *grapho* is a common word in the NT, since the written word receives such high priority in the Bible. The word *grapho* was the basic Greek verb meaning *to write.* The corresponding noun *graphe* [grah PHAY], which literally means *a writing,* almost always refers to the OT (but see 2 Pt 3:16) and should be translated *Scripture.* (Another related noun, *grammateus,* means *scribe;* see the word study on page 96.) Similarly, the verb *grapho* normally refers to an OT Scripture (Lk 3:4), a NT Scripture already written (2 Co 7:12; 2 Pt 3:15; 3 Jn 9), or a NT Scripture in the process of being written (Lk 1:3; Jn 20:30–31; 21:24–25; Rm 15:15; 16:22; 2 Co 13:10; Gl 1:20; 6:11; 2 Th 3:17; 1 Tm 3:14; Phm 19,21; 1 Pt 5:12; 2 Pt 3:1; 1 Jn 1:4; 5:13; 2 Jn 5; Jd 3; Rv 1:11). The most common use of the term *grapho* is as an introductory formula for OT quotations (over sixty times). The Greek verb tense that is normally used in this formula ("it is written" or perhaps "it stands written") emphasizes the permanence of God's written revelation.

not know it. [44] Assuming He was in the traveling party, they went a day's journey. Then they began looking for Him among their relatives and friends. [45] When they did not find Him, they returned to Jerusalem to search for Him. [46] After three days, they found Him in the temple complex sitting among the teachers, listening to them and asking them questions. [47] And all those who heard Him were astounded at His understanding and His answers. [48] When his parents[a] saw Him, they were astonished, and His mother said to Him, "Son, why have You treated us like this? Here Your father and I have been anxiously searching for You."

[49] "Why were you searching for Me?" He asked them. "Didn't you know that I must be involved in my Father's interests?"[b] [50] But they did not understand what He said to them.

IN FAVOR WITH GOD AND WITH PEOPLE

[51] Then He went down with them and came to Nazareth, and was obedient to them. His mother kept all these things in her heart. [52] And Jesus increased in wisdom and stature and in favor with God and with people.

THE MESSIAH'S HERALD

3 In the fifteenth year of the reign of Tiberius Caesar,[c] while Pontius Pilate[d] was governor of Judea, Herod[e] was tetrarch[f] of Galilee, his brother Philip tetrarch of the region of Iturea[g] and Trachonitis,[g] and Lysanias tetrarch of Abilene,[h] [2] during the high priesthood of Annas and Caiaphas, God's word came to John the son of Zachariah in the wilderness. [3] He went into all the vicinity of the Jordan, preaching a baptism of repentance[i] for

[a] **2:48** Lit *When they*
[b] **2:49** Or *house* or *things*
[c] **3:1** Emperor who ruled the Roman Empire from A.D. 14–37
[d] **3:1** Pontius Pilate was appointed by Caesar Tiberius as the fifth governor of the province of Judea in A.D. 26. His jurisdiction included Samaria to the north, Gaza and the Dead Sea area to the south. He remained at this post until A.D. 36.
[e] **3:1** That is, Herod Antipas, son of Herod the Great, who ruled one quarter of his father's kingdom under Rome
[f] **3:1** Or *ruler*
[g] **3:1** Small provinces northeast of Galilee
[h] **3:1** A small Syrian province
[i] **3:3** Or *a baptism based on repentance*

the forgiveness of sins, [4] as it is written in the book of the words of the prophet Isaiah:

> A voice of one crying out in the
>   wilderness:
> "Prepare the way for the Lord;
> make His paths straight!
> [5] Every valley will be filled,
>   and every mountain and hill will be made
>   low;[a]
> the crooked will become straight,
> the rough ways smooth,
> [6] and everyone[b] will see the salvation of
>   God."[c]

[7] He then said to the crowds who came out to be baptized by him, "Brood of vipers! Who warned you to flee from the coming wrath? [8] Therefore produce fruit consistent with repentance. And don't start saying to yourselves, 'We have Abraham as our father,' for I tell you that God is able to raise up children for Abraham from these stones! [9] Even now the ax is ready to strike[d] the root of the trees! Therefore every tree that doesn't produce good fruit will be cut down and thrown into the fire."

[10] "What then should we do?" the crowds were asking him.

[11] He replied to them, "The one who has two shirts[e] must share with someone who has none, and the one who has food must do the same."

[12] Tax collectors also came to be baptized, and they asked him, "Teacher, what should we do?"

[13] He told them, "Don't collect any more than what you have been authorized."

[14] Some soldiers also questioned him: "What should we do?"

He said to them, "Don't take money from anyone by force or false accusation; be satisfied with your wages."

[15] Now the people were waiting expectantly, and all of them were debating in their minds[f] whether John might be the Messiah. [16] John answered them all, "I baptize you with[g] water. But One is coming who is more power-

Keep Your Heart Tender, Pure, Open

Religious activity can never substitute for a heart that is pure and open before God.

As it is written in the book of the words of the prophet Isaiah: "A voice of one crying out in the wilderness: 'Prepare the way for the Lord; make His paths straight!'"

—Luke 3:4

---

[a]**3:5** Lit *be humbled*
[b]**3:6** Lk 3:6; lit *all flesh*
[c]**3:6** Is 40:3–5
[d]**3:9** Lit *the ax lies at*
[e]**3:11** Lit *tunics*
[f]**3:15** Or *hearts*
[g]**3:16** Or *in*

ful than I. I am not worthy to untie the strap of His sandals. He will baptize you with[a] the Holy Spirit and fire. [17] His winnowing shovel[b] is in His hand to clear His threshing floor and gather the wheat into His barn, but the chaff He will burn up with a fire that never goes out." [18] Then, along with many other exhortations, he announced good news to the people. [19] But Herod the tetrarch, being rebuked by him about Herodias, his brother's wife, and about all the evil things Herod had done, [20] added this to everything else—he locked John up in prison.

THE BAPTISM OF JESUS

[21] When all the people were baptized, Jesus also was baptized. As He was praying, heaven opened, [22] and the Holy Spirit descended on Him in a physical appearance like a dove. And a voice came from heaven:

> "You are My beloved Son.
> I take delight in You!"

THE GENEALOGY OF JESUS CHRIST

[23] As He began His ministry,[c] Jesus was about thirty years old and was thought to be[d] the son of Joseph, son[e] of Heli, [24] son of Matthat, son of Levi, son of Melchi, son of Jannai, son of Joseph, [25] son of Mattathias, son of Amos, son of Nahum, son of Esli, son of Naggai, [26] son of Maath, son of Mattathias, son of Semein, son of Josech, son of Joda, [27] son of Joanan, son of Rhesa, son of Zerubbabel, son of Shealtiel, son of Neri, [28] son of Melchi, son of Addi, son of Cosam, son of Elmadam, son of Er, [29] son of Joshua, son of Eliezer, son of Jorim, son of Matthat, son of Levi, [30] son of Simeon, son of Judah, son of Joseph, son of Jonan, son of Eliakim,

---

Seek God in Prayer

Prayer is not a substitute for hard work—prayer is the work! God does things in and through our lives by prayer that He does in no other way.

As He was praying, heaven opened.

—Luke 3:21b

There's Strength in the Scriptures

Jesus relied on God's Word to see Him through the temptations that could have destroyed Him and thwarted God's plan. He has modeled the way for you to meet every temptation.

And Jesus answered him, "It is written: 'You shall worship the Lord your God, and Him alone you shall serve.'"

—Luke 4:8

---

[a]3:16 Or *in*
[b]3:17 A wooden farm implement used to toss threshed grain into the wind so the lighter chaff would blow away and separate from the heavier grain
[c]3:23 *His ministry* supplied for clarity
[d]3:23 That is, people did not know about His virgin birth (see 1:26–38; Mt 1:18–25)
[e]3:23 *son* implied throughout genealogy. The relationship in some cases may be more distant than a son.

³¹ son of Melea, son of Menna, son of Mattatha,
son of Nathan, son of David, ³² son of Jesse,
son of Obed, son of Boaz, son of Salmon,¹
son of Nahshon, ³³ son of Amminadab, son of Ram,²
son of Hezron, son of Perez, son of Judah,
³⁴ son of Jacob, son of Isaac, son of Abraham,
son of Terah, son of Nahor, ³⁵ son of Serug,
son of Reu, son of Peleg, son of Eber,
son of Shelah, ³⁶ son of Cainan, son of Arphaxad,
son of Shem, son of Noah, son of Lamech,
³⁷ son of Methuselah, son of Enoch, son of Jared,
son of Mahalaleel, son of Cainan, ³⁸ son of Enos,
son of Seth, son of Adam, son of God.

THE TEMPTATION OF JESUS

Then Jesus returned from the Jordan, full of the Holy
Spirit, and was led by the Spirit in the wilderness
² for forty days to be tempted by the Devil. He ate nothing during those days, and when they were over,ᵃ He
was hungry. ³ The Devil said to Him, "If You are the Son
of God, tell this stone to become bread."

⁴ But Jesus answered him, "It is written: 'Man must
not live on bread alone.'"³ᵇ

⁵ So he took Him up⁴ and showed Him all the kingdoms of the world in a moment of time. ⁶ The Devil said
to Him, "I will give You their splendor and all this
authority, because it has been given over to me, and I
can give it to anyone I want. ⁷ If You, then, will worship
me,ᶜ all will be Yours."

⁸ And Jesus answered him,⁵ "It is written:

**You shall worship the Lord your God,
and Him alone you shall serve.**"ᵈ

⁹ So he took Him to Jerusalem, had Him stand on the
pinnacle of the temple, and said to Him, "If You are the

---

¹ 3:32 Other mss read *Sala*
² 3:33 Other mss read *Aram son of Joram;* others read *Admin son of Arni*
³ 4:4 Other mss add *But on every word of God*
⁴ 4:5 Other mss read *So the Devil took Him up on a high mountain*
⁵ 4:8 Other mss add *Get behind Me, Satan*

ᵃ 4:2 Lit *were completed*
ᵇ 4:4 Dt 8:3
ᶜ 4:7 Lit *will fall down before me*
ᵈ 4:8 Dt 6:13

WORD STUDY

Greek word: **proskuneo**
[prahss koo NEH oh]
Translation: **worship**
Uses in Luke's Gospel: **3**
(Mt, 13; Mk, 2; Jn, 11)
Uses in Luke's Writings: **7**
Uses in the NT: **60**
Key passage: **Luke 4:7–8**

The Greek verb *proskuneo* is built
from the words *pros,* meaning *toward,* and *kuneo,* meaning *kiss.*
The term suggests the custom of
falling to one's knees out of respect to someone superior in
rank—normally rulers, royalty, or
those considered divine. A few
times in the NT *proskuneo* is used
with the general meaning *bow
down* (Mt 8:2; 9:18; Mk 15:19; Rv
3:9), and such homage to persons
of great rank or power was common in the ancient world. But *proskuneo* in the sense of *worship*
(that is, *show honor and rever-
ence*) is reserved for God alone, as
the term's use in the Greek OT (Ex
20:5; Dt 11:16; 26:10) and in the
NT indicates (Jn 4:21,23–24; Rv
4:10; 7:11; 15:4; 19:10; 22:9).
One of the strongest evidences in
the NT for the deity of Christ is
that *proskuneo* often refers to
worshiping Him. If Christ is not
God, this would violate the teachings of both Testaments to worship God alone (Dt 6:13–14; see
Jesus' quote of this verse in response to one of Satan's temptations in Lk 4:7–8). Compare the
reaction of Paul and Barnabas to
being deified (Ac 14:11–18). People worshiped Christ when He
was an infant (Mt 2:2,11), during
His ministry (Mt 14:33; Jn 9:38),
and after His resurrection (Mt
28:9,17; Lk 24:52).

Son of God, throw Yourself down from here. [10] For it is written:

> **He will give His angels orders concerning you,**
> **to protect you,**[a]
>
> [11] and
>
> **In their hands they will lift you up,**
> **so you will not strike your foot against a stone.**"[b]

[12] And Jesus answered him, "It is said: 'You must not tempt the Lord your God.'"[c]

[13] After the Devil had finished every temptation, he departed from Him for a time.

MINISTRY IN GALILEE

[14] Then Jesus returned to Galilee in the power of the Spirit, and news about Him spread throughout the entire vicinity. [15] He was teaching in their synagogues, being acclaimed[d] by everyone.

REJECTION AT NAZARETH

[16] He came to Nazareth, where He had been brought up. As usual, He entered the synagogue on the Sabbath day and stood up to read. [17] The scroll of the prophet Isaiah was given to Him, and unrolling the scroll, He found the place where it was written:

> [18] **The Spirit of the Lord is upon Me,**
> **because He has anointed Me**
> **to preach good news to the poor.**
> **He has sent Me**[1] **to proclaim freedom**[e] **to the captives**
> **and recovery of sight to the blind,**
> **to set free the oppressed,**
> [19] **to proclaim the year of the Lord's favor.**[fg]

[20] He then rolled up the scroll, gave it back to the attendant, and sat down. And the eyes of everyone in

---

[1] **4:18** Other mss add *to heal the brokenhearted*

---

[a] **4:10** Ps 91:11
[b] **4:11** Ps 91:12
[c] **4:12** Dt 6:16
[d] **4:15** Or *glorified*

[e] **4:18** Or *proclaim release* or *forgiveness*
[f] **4:18–19** Is 61:1–2
[g] **4:19** That is, the time of Messianic grace

God Will Use You to Meet Others' Needs

His whole plan for the advance of the kingdom depends on His working in real and practical ways through His relationship to His people.

"The Spirit of the Lord is upon Me, because He has anointed Me to preach good news to the poor. He has sent Me to proclaim freedom to the captives and recovery of sight to the blind, to set free the oppressed, to proclaim the year of the Lord's favor."

—Luke 4:18–19

the synagogue were fixed on Him. [21] He began by saying to them, "Today this Scripture has been fulfilled in your hearing."

[22] They were all speaking well[a] of Him and were amazed by the gracious words that came from His mouth, yet they said, "Isn't this Joseph's son?"

[23] Then He said to them, "No doubt you will quote this proverb[b] to Me: 'Doctor, heal Yourself.' 'All we've heard that took place in Capernaum, do here in Your hometown also.'"

[24] He also said, "I assure you: No prophet is accepted in his hometown. [25] But I say to you, there were certainly many widows in Israel in Elijah's days, when the sky was shut up for three years and six months while a great famine came over all the land. [26] Yet Elijah was not sent to any of them, except to a widow at Zarephath in Sidon. [27] And there were many lepers in Israel in the prophet Elisha's time, yet not one of them was cleansed except Naaman the Syrian."

[28] When they heard this, all who were in the synagogue were enraged. [29] They got up, drove Him out of town, and brought Him to the edge[c] of the hill on which their town was built, intending to hurl Him over the cliff. [30] But He passed right through the crowd[d] and went on His way.

DRIVING OUT AN UNCLEAN SPIRIT

[31] Then He went down to Capernaum, a town in Galilee, and was teaching them on the Sabbath. [32] And they were astonished at His teaching because His message had authority. [33] In the synagogue there was a man with an unclean demonic spirit who cried out with a loud voice, [34] "Leave us alone![e] What do You have to do with us,[f] Jesus—Nazarene? Have You come to destroy us? I know who You are—the Holy One of God!"

[35] But Jesus rebuked him and said, "Be quiet and come out of him!"

And throwing him down before them, the demon came out of him without hurting him at all. [36] They were all struck with amazement and kept saying to one

**Hear His Voice
in the Scriptures**

Do you sense, as you read the Scripture, that God became real and personal to people? Your life also can reflect that kind of real, personal, and practical relationship as you respond to God's working in your life.

And they were astonished at His teaching because His message had authority.

—Luke 4:32

---

[a] 4:22 Or *they were testifying against Him*
[b] 4:23 Or *parable*
[c] 4:29 Lit *brow*
[d] 4:30 Lit *through them*
[e] 4:34 Or *Ha!* or *Ah!*
[f] 4:34 Lit *What to us and to you*

another, "What is this message? For with authority and power He commands the unclean spirits, and they come out!" [37] And news about Him began to go out to every place in the vicinity.

HEALINGS AT CAPERNAUM

[38] After He left the synagogue, He entered Simon's house. Simon's mother-in-law was suffering from a high fever, and they asked Him about her. [39] So He stood over her and rebuked the fever, and it left her. She got up immediately and began to serve them.

[40] When the sun was setting, all those who had anyone sick with various diseases brought them to Him. As He laid His hands on each one of them, He would heal them. [41] Also, demons were coming out of many, shouting and saying, "You are the Son of God!" But He rebuked them and would not allow them to speak, because they knew He was the Messiah.

PREACHING IN GALILEE

[42] When it was day, He went out and made His way to a deserted place. But the crowds were searching for Him. They came to Him and tried to keep Him from leaving them. [43] But He said to them, "I must proclaim the good news about the kingdom of God to the other towns also, because I was sent for this purpose." [44] And He was preaching in the synagogues of Galilee.[1]

THE FIRST DISCIPLES

As the crowd was pressing in on Jesus[a] to hear God's word, He was standing by Lake Gennesaret.[b] [2] He saw two boats at the edge of the lake;[c] the fishermen had left them and were washing their nets. [3] He got into one of the boats, which belonged to Simon, and asked him to put out a little from the land. Then He sat down and was teaching the crowds from the boat.

[4] When He had finished speaking, He said to Simon, "Put out into deep water and let down[d] your nets for a catch."

[1]4:44 Other mss read *Judea*

[a]5:1 Lit *Him*
[b]5:1 Another name for the Sea of Galilee
[c]5:2 Lit *boats standing by the lake*
[d]5:4 Lit *and you* (plur.) *let down your nets*

Leave All the Results and Rewards to God

The working of God in you will bring a blessing. The blessing is a by-product of your obedience and the experience of God working in your midst.

And news about Him began to go out to every place in the vicinity.

—Luke 4:37

Walk by Faith, Not by Sight

Many people miss out on experiencing God's mighty power working through them. If they cannot see exactly how everything can be done, they will not proceed. They want to walk with God by sight. To follow God, you will have to walk by faith, and faith always requires action.

"Master," Simon replied, "we've worked hard all night long and caught nothing! But at Your word, I'll let down the nets."

—Luke 5:5

5 "Master," Simon replied, "we've worked hard all night long and caught nothing! But at Your word, I'll let down the nets."[1]

6 When they did this, they caught a great number of fish, and their nets[1] began to tear. 7 So they signaled to their partners in the other boat to come and help them; they came and filled both boats so full that they began to sink.

8 When Simon Peter saw this, he fell at Jesus' knees and said, "Depart from me, because I'm a sinful man, Lord!" 9 For he and all those with him were amazed[a] at the catch of fish they took, 10 and so also James and John, Zebedee's sons, who were Simon's partners.

"Don't be afraid," Jesus told Simon. "From now on you will be catching people!" 11 Then they brought the boats to land, left everything, and followed Him.

CLEANSING A LEPER

12 While He was in one of the towns, a man covered with leprosy[b] was there. He saw Jesus, fell on his face, and begged Him: "Lord, if You are willing, You can make me clean."[c]

13 Reaching out His hand, He touched him, saying, "I am willing; be made clean," and immediately the leprosy left him. 14 Then He ordered him to tell no one: "But go and show yourself to the priest, and offer what Moses prescribed for your cleansing as a testimony to them."

15 But the news[d] about Him spread even more, and large crowds would come together to hear Him and to be healed of their sicknesses. 16 Yet He often withdrew to deserted places and prayed.

THE SON OF MAN FORGIVES AND HEALS

17 On one of those days while He was teaching, Pharisees and teachers of the law were sitting there who had

[1]5:5, 6 Other mss read *net*

[a]5:9 Or *for amazement had seized him and all those with him*
[b]5:12 In the Bible, *leprosy* is used for many skin disorders in addition to Hansen's disease.
[c]5:12 *Clean,* in these verses, includes healing, ceremonial purification, return to fellowship with people, and worship in the temple. See Lv 14:1–31
[d]5:15 Lit *the word*

WORD STUDY

Greek word: *epistates*
[eh pee STAH tayss]
Translation: **Master**
Uses in Luke's Gospel: **7**
Uses in the NT: **7**
Key passage: **Luke 5:5**

The Greek noun *epistates* is related to a verb meaning *to place over* and refers to an *overseer* or *superintendent.* This word, a title of respect for someone in authority, occurs only in Luke's Gospel and was used only as a term of respect for Jesus by His disciples (5:5; 8:24,45; 9:33,49; 17:13). Luke may have used the term *epistates* since He does not use *rabbi* (see Jn 1:38 note) and since in his Gospel only strangers address Jesus with the more common "Teacher" (*didaskalos;* see the word study on page 249).

In Luke 5 Jesus' request that Simon Peter and the others let the nets down once again seemed quite unreasonable to the experienced fishermen in light of their hard but unproductive day at sea (vv. 4–5). But because Peter recognized Jesus' authority as *Master* (*epistates* in v. 5), he agreed to try again and caught more fish than the nets and boats could handle— little wonder that Peter then called Him "Lord" (v. 8). With this remarkable miracle, Peter's understanding of Jesus progressed from "Master" to "Lord" (*kurios,* see the word study on page 189), and he and his partners became Jesus' disciples from that time forward (vv. 9–11).

come from every village of Galilee and Judea, and also from Jerusalem. And the Lord's power to heal was in Him. [18] Just then some men came, carrying on a stretcher a man who was paralyzed. They tried to bring him in and set him down before Him. [19] Since they could not find a way to bring him in because of the crowd, they went up on the roof and lowered him on the stretcher through the roof tiles into the middle of the crowd before Jesus.

[20] Seeing their faith He said, "Friend,[a] your sins are forgiven you."

[21] Then the scribes and the Pharisees[b] began to reason: "Who is this man who speaks blasphemies? Who can forgive sins but God alone?"

[22] But perceiving their thoughts, Jesus replied to them, "Why are you reasoning this in your hearts?[c] [23] Which is easier: to say, 'Your sins are forgiven you,' or to say, 'Get up and walk'? [24] But so you may know that the Son of Man has authority on earth to forgive sins" —He told the paralyzed man, "I tell you: get up, pick up your stretcher, and go home."

[25] Immediately he got up before them, picked up what he had been lying on, and went home glorifying God. [26] Then everyone was astounded, and they were giving glory to God. And they were filled with awe and said, "We have seen incredible things today!"

THE CALL OF LEVI

[27] After this, Jesus[d] went out and saw a tax collector named Levi sitting at the tax office, and He said to him, "Follow Me!" [28] So, leaving everything behind, he got up and began to follow Him.

DINING WITH SINNERS

[29] Then Levi hosted a grand banquet for Him at his house. Now there was a large crowd of tax collectors and others who were guests[e] with them. [30] But the Pharisees and their scribes were complaining to His disciples,

God Makes You More Than You Can Be

All of the persons that you see in the Scriptures were ordinary people. Their relationship with God and the activity of God made them extraordinary.

Then everyone was astounded, and they were giving glory to God. And they were filled with awe and said, "We have seen incredible things today!"

—Luke 5:26

---

[a]5:20 Lit *Man*
[b]5:21 Pharisees and Sadducees were two of the sects of Judaism. The Pharisees followed the whole body of written and oral law, but the Sadducees followed primarily the first five books of the OT (Torah).

[c]5:22 Or *minds*
[d]5:27 Lit *He*
[e]5:29 Lit *were reclining* (at the table). At important meals the custom was to recline on a mat at a low table and lean on the left elbow.

"Why do you eat and drink with tax collectors and sinners?"

[31] Jesus replied to them, "The healthy don't need a doctor, but the sick do. [32] I have not come to call the righteous, but sinners to repentance."

A QUESTION ABOUT FASTING

[33] Then they said to Him, "John's[1] disciples fast often and say prayers, and those of the Pharisees do the same, but Yours eat and drink."

[34] Jesus said to them, "You can't make the wedding guests[a] fast while the groom is with them, can you? [35] But the days will come when the groom will be taken away from them—then they will fast in those days."

[36] He also told them a parable: "No one tears a patch from a new garment and puts it on an old garment. Otherwise, not only will he tear the new, but also the piece from the new garment will not match the old. [37] And no one puts new wine into old wineskins. Otherwise, the new wine will burst the skins, it will spill, and the skins will be ruined. [38] But new wine should be put into fresh wineskins.[2] [39] And no one, after drinking old wine, wants new, because he says, 'The old is better.'"[3]

LORD OF THE SABBATH

[6] On a[4] Sabbath, He passed through the grainfields. His disciples were picking heads of grain, rubbing them in their hands, and eating them. [2] But some of the Pharisees said, "Why are you doing what is not lawful on the Sabbath?"

[3] And Jesus answered them, "Haven't you read what David did when he was hungry, he and those who were with him— [4] how he entered the house of God, and took and ate the sacred bread,[b] which is not lawful for

---

Be One Who Cares for Those Who Hurt

The world abounds with people whose sin has alienated them from God. And only Christ has the remedy. As His ambassadors, we are to take the message of reconciliation to a broken, divided world.

Jesus replied to them, "The healthy don't need a doctor, but the sick do. I have not come to call the righteous, but sinners to repentance."

—Luke 5:31–32

---

[1] **5:33** Other mss add *Why do John's*
[2] **5:38** Other mss add *and so both are preserved*
[3] **5:39** Other mss read *is good*
[4] **6:1** Other mss read *deuteroproto;* lit *second-first,* perhaps a special Sabbath

---

[a] **5:34** Or *the friends of the groom;* lit *sons of the bridal chamber*
[b] **6:4** Lit *bread of presentation.* These were twelve loaves, representing the twelve tribes of Israel, put on the table in the holy place in the tabernacle, and later in the temple. The priests ate the previous week's loaves. See Ex 25:30; 29:32; Lv 24:5–9; Mt 12:4

any but the priests to eat? He even gave some to those who were with him." [5] Then He told them, "The Son of Man is Lord of the Sabbath."

THE MAN WITH THE PARALYZED HAND

[6] On another Sabbath He entered the synagogue and was teaching. A man was there whose right hand was paralyzed. [7] The scribes and Pharisees were watching Him closely, to see if He would heal on the Sabbath, so that they might find a charge against Him. [8] But He knew their thoughts and told the man with the paralyzed hand, "Get up and stand here."[a] So he got up and stood there. [9] Then Jesus said to them, "I ask you: is it lawful on the Sabbath to do good or to do evil, to save life or to destroy it?" [10] After looking around at them all, He told him, "Stretch out your hand." He did so, and his hand was restored.[1] [11] They, however, were filled with rage, and started discussing with one another what they might do to Jesus.

THE TWELVE APOSTLES

[12] During those days He went out to the mountain to pray and spent all night in prayer to God. [13] When daylight came, He summoned His disciples, and from them He chose twelve, whom He also named apostles:

[14] Simon, whom He also named Peter, and Andrew his brother;
James and John;
Philip and Bartholomew;
[15] Matthew and Thomas;
James the son of Alphaeus, and Simon called the Zealot;
[16] Judas the son of James, and Judas Iscariot, who became a traitor.

TEACHING AND HEALING

[17] After coming down with them, He stood on a level place with a large crowd of His disciples and a great multitude of people from all Judea and Jerusalem and from the seacoast of Tyre and Sidon. [18] They came to

[1] 6:10 Other mss add *as sound as the other*

[a] 6:8 Lit *stand in the middle*

Even Jesus Depended on Prayer—Do You?

Becoming a person of prayer will require a major adjustment of your life to God. Prayer will always be a part of the obedience. It is in a prayer relationship that God gives further direction.

During those days He went out to the mountain to pray and spent all night in prayer to God.

—Luke 6:12

hear Him and to be healed of their diseases; and those tormented by unclean spirits were made well. [19] The whole crowd was trying to touch Him, because power was coming out from Him and healing them all.

THE BEATITUDES

[20] Then looking up[a] at His disciples, He said:

"Blessed are you who are poor,
because the kingdom of God is yours.
[21] Blessed are you who are hungry now,
because you will be filled.
Blessed are you who weep now,
because you will laugh.
[22] Blessed are you when people hate you,
when they exclude you, insult you,
and slander your name as evil,
because of the Son of Man.

[23] "Rejoice in that day and leap for joy! Take note— your reward is great in heaven, because this is the way their forefathers used to treat the prophets.

WOE TO THE SELF-SATISFIED

[24] "But woe to you who are rich,
because you have received your comfort.
[25] Woe to you who are full now,
because you will be hungry.
Woe to you[1] who are laughing now,
because you will mourn and weep.
[26] Woe to you[1] when all people speak well of you,
because this is the way their forefathers
used to treat the false prophets.

LOVE YOUR ENEMIES

[27] "But I say to you who listen: Love your enemies, do good to those who hate you, [28] bless those who curse you, pray for those who mistreat you. [29] If anyone hits you on the cheek, offer the other also. And if anyone takes away your coat, don't hold back your shirt either. [30] Give to everyone who asks from you, and from one

[1] 6:25,26 Other mss omit *to you*

[a] 6:20 Lit *Then lifting up His eyes*

WORD STUDY

Greek word: ***ouai*** [oo IGH]
Translation: ***woe***
Uses in Luke's Gospel: **15**
(Mt, 13; Mk, 2)
Uses in the NT: **46**
Key passage: **Luke 6:24–26**

The Greek interjection *ouai* serves as a warning of impending disaster, pain, or suffering. All thirty uses of *ouai* in the Gospels are by Jesus, and His warnings often denounced the Jewish religious leaders for their hypocrisy (see Mt 23:13–36; Lk 11:42–52). In Luke 6 Jesus contrasted the blessings (*makarios;* see word study on page 9) of suffering for the kingdom of God with the disasters *(ouai)* that befall those who live in comfort now but do not care about the kingdom (vv. 20–26). Jesus warned about unbelief (Mt 11:21 = Lk 10:13; see Jd 11), stumbling blocks to faith (Mt 18:7 = Lk 17:1), and disasters associated with the end times (Mt 24:19 = Mk 13:17 = Lk 21:23), which is the context of the 14 uses of *ouai* in Revelation (8:13; 9:12; 11:14; 12:12; 18:10,16,19). All three Synoptic Gospels record Jesus' *ouai* against Judas (Mt 26:24 = Mk 14:21 = Lk 22:22). The only place the term occurs in a positive context is Paul's "Woe am I—if I do not proclaim the gospel!" (1 Co 9:16).

who takes away your things, don't ask for them back. [31] Just as you want others to do for you, do the same for them. [32] If you love those who love you, what credit is that to you? Even sinners love those who love them. [33] If you do good to those who do good to you, what credit is that to you? Even sinners do that. [34] And if you lend to those from whom you expect to receive, what credit is that to you? Even sinners lend to sinners to be repaid in full. [35] But love your enemies, do good, and lend, expecting nothing in return. Then your reward will be great, and you will be sons of the Most High. For He is gracious to the ungrateful and evil. [36] Be merciful, just as your Father also is merciful.

DO NOT JUDGE

[37] "Do not judge, and you will not be judged. Do not condemn, and you will not be condemned. Forgive, and you will be forgiven. [38] Give, and it will be given to you; a good measure, pressed down, shaken together, and running over will be poured into your lap. For with the measure that you use,[a] it will be measured back to you."

[39] He also told them a parable: "Can the blind guide the blind? Won't they both fall into a pit? [40] A disciple is not above his teacher, but everyone who is fully trained will be like his teacher.

[41] "Why do you look at the speck in your brother's eye, but don't notice the log in your own eye? [42] Or how can you say to your brother, 'Brother, let me take out the speck that is in your eye,' when you yourself don't see the log in your eye? Hypocrite! First take the log out of your eye, and then you will see clearly to take out the speck in your brother's eye.

A TREE AND ITS FRUIT

[43] "A good tree doesn't produce bad fruit, nor again does a bad tree produce good fruit. [44] For each tree is known by its own fruit. Figs aren't gathered from thorn bushes, or grapes picked from a bramble bush. [45] A good man produces good out of the good storeroom of his heart, and an evil man produces evil out of the evil storeroom. For his mouth speaks from the overflow of the heart.

[a] 6:38 Lit the measure you measure

Love People, and You Will Win Their Hearts

You will be helpful to others only if you see them as God does. It is difficult to pray sincerely for someone while you are judging them.

"Do not judge, and you will not be judged. Do not condemn, and you will not be condemned. Forgive, and you will be forgiven."
—Luke 6:37

Write God's Love All Over Your Life

It is impossible to carry a message of love and yet be filled with hatred. In each of your relationships, make sure that your actions share the love and forgiveness that reflect what you have received from God.

"Why do you look at the speck in your brother's eye, but don't notice the log in your own eye?"
—Luke 6:41

THE TWO FOUNDATIONS

⁴⁶"Why do you call Me 'Lord, Lord,' and don't do the things I say? ⁴⁷I will show you what someone is like who comes to Me, hears My words, and acts on them: ⁴⁸He is like a man building a house, who dug deepᵃ and laid the foundation on the rock. When the flood rose, the river crashed against that house and couldn't shake it, because it was well built. ⁴⁹But the one who hears and does not act is like a man who built a house on the ground without a foundation. The river crashed against it, and immediately it collapsed. And the destruction of that house was great!"

A CENTURION'S FAITH

7 When He had concluded all His sayings in the hearing of the people, He entered Capernaum. ²A centurion'sᵇ slave, who was highly valued by him, was sick and about to die. ³Having heard about Jesus, he sent some Jewish elders to Him, requesting Him to come and save his slave's life. ⁴When they reached Jesus, they pleaded with Him earnestly, saying, "He is worthy for You to grant this, ⁵because he loves our nation, and has built us a synagogue." ⁶Jesus went with them, and when He was not far fromᶜ the house, the centurion sent friends to tell Him, "Lord, don't trouble Yourself, since I am not worthy to have You come under my roof. ⁷That is why I didn't even consider myself worthy to come to You. But say the word, and my servant will be cured.¹ ⁸For I too am a man placed under authority, having soldiers under my command.ᵈ I say to this one, 'Go!' and he goes; and to another, 'Come!' and he comes; and to my slave, 'Do this!' and he does it." ⁹Hearing this, Jesus was amazed at him, and turning to the crowd following Him, said, "I tell you, I have not found so great a faith even in Israel!" ¹⁰When those who had been sent returned to the house, they found the slave in good health.

¹7:7 Other mss read *and let my servant be cured*

ᵃ6:48 Lit *dug and went deep*
ᵇ7:2 Roman commander of about 100 soldiers
ᶜ7:6 Lit *He already was not far from*
ᵈ7:8 Lit *under me*

Repentance Is a Big Part of Obedience

The Bible does not speak of rededicating oneself, but of repentance. Repentance indicates a decisive change, not merely a wishful resolution.

"Why do you call Me 'Lord, Lord,' and don't do the things I say?"

—Luke 6:46

WORD STUDY

Greek word: **lepros**
[leh PRAHSS]
Translation: **leper**
Uses in Luke's Gospel: **3**
(Mt, 4; Mk, 2)
Uses in the NT: **9**
Key passage: **Luke 7:22**

The Greek word *lepros* comes from a root meaning *scaly* or *rough,* such as the scales of a fish. Leprosy referred to various skin diseases that gave the skin a scaly texture and often included discoloring, most often white. The references to Jesus' healing of lepers in Luke 7:22 and elsewhere must be seen in the light of the law of Moses. Leviticus 13—14 is concerned with identifying, containing, and purifying leprosy and other skin diseases on someone in the covenant community. A leper was unclean (unfit to participate in worship rituals and ceremonies), and anyone or anything that came into contact with a leper became unclean also. Some cases of leprosy were mild (white patches or running sores on the skin), but others involved the loss of fingers and toes and could even result in death. If a leper were healed, he was to be examined by a priest and to offer the prescribed sacrifice. The priest would then pronounce the leper clean so that he could once again join community life. The healing of lepers is one of three instances of Jesus' overcoming something that the law pronounced unclean; healing the bleeding woman (Lk 8:43-44; see Lv 15:25-30) and raising the dead (Lk 8:54-55; see Nm 19:11) are the other two.

A WIDOW'S SON RAISED TO LIFE

[11] Soon afterward He was on His way to a town called Nain. His disciples and a large crowd were traveling with Him. [12] Just as He neared the gate of the town, a dead man was being carried out. He was his mother's only son, and she was a widow. A large crowd from the city was also with her. [13] When the Lord saw her, He had compassion on her and said, "Don't cry." [14] Then He came up and touched the open coffin,[a] and the pallbearers stopped. And He said, "Young man, I tell you, get up!"

[15] The dead man sat up and began to speak, and Jesus[b] gave him to his mother.[c] [16] Then fear[d] came over everyone, and they glorified God, saying, "A great prophet has risen among us," and "God has visited[e] His people." [17] This report about Him went throughout Judea and all the vicinity.

IN PRAISE OF JOHN THE BAPTIST

[18] Then John's disciples told him about all these things. So John summoned two of his disciples [19] and sent them to the Lord, asking, "Are You the Coming One, or should we look for someone else?"

[20] When the men reached Him, they said, "John the Baptist sent us to ask You, 'Are You the Coming One, or should we look for someone else?'"

[21] At that time Jesus[f] healed many people of diseases, plagues, and evil spirits, and He granted sight to many blind people. [22] He replied to them, "Go and report to John the things you have seen and heard: The blind receive their sight, the lame walk, lepers are cleansed, the deaf hear, the dead are raised, and the poor have the good news preached to them. [23] And blessed is anyone who is not offended because of Me." [24] After John's messengers left, He began to speak to the crowds about John: "What did you go out into the wilderness to see? A reed swaying in the wind? [25] But what did you go out to see? A man dressed in soft robes? Look, those who are splendidly dressed[g] and live in luxury are in royal palaces. [26] But what did you go out to see? A prophet?

---

a[7:14] Or *bier*
b[7:15] Lit *He*
c[7:15] See 1 Kg 17:23
d[7:16] Or *awe*

e[7:16] Or *come to help*
f[7:21] Lit *He*
g[7:25] Or *who have glorious robes*

Yes, I tell you, and far more than a prophet. [27] This is the one of whom it is written:

> **Look, I am sending My messenger ahead of You;**[a]
> **he will prepare Your way before You.**[b]

[28] I tell you, among those born of women no one is greater than John,[1] but the least in the kingdom of God is greater than he."

[29] (And when all the people, including the tax collectors, heard this, they acknowledged God's way of righteousness,[c] because they had been baptized with John's baptism. [30] But since the Pharisees and experts in the law had not been baptized by him, they rejected the plan of God for themselves.)

AN UNRESPONSIVE GENERATION

[31] "To what then should I compare the people of this generation, and what are they like? [32] They are like children sitting in the marketplace and calling to each other:

> 'We played the flute for you,
>   but you didn't dance;
> we sang a lament,
>   but you didn't weep!'

[33] For John the Baptist did not come eating bread or drinking wine, and you say, 'He has a demon!' [34] The Son of Man has come eating and drinking, and you say, 'Look, a glutton and a drunkard, a friend of tax collectors and sinners!' [35] Yet wisdom is vindicated[d] by all her children."

MUCH FORGIVENESS, MUCH LOVE

[36] Then one of the Pharisees invited Him to eat with him. He entered the Pharisee's house and reclined at the table. [37] And a woman in the town who was a sinner found out that Jesus was reclining at the table in the Pharisee's house. She brought an alabaster flask of fragrant oil [38] and stood behind Him at His feet, weeping,

---

Concern Yourself with Kingdom Matters

His desire is for you to become involved in what He is doing. Finding out what He is doing helps you know what He will want to do through you.

He replied to them, "Go and report to John the things you have seen and heard: The blind receive their sight, the lame walk, lepers are cleansed, the deaf hear, the dead are raised, and the poor have the good news preached to them. And blessed is anyone who is not offended because of Me."

—Luke 7:22–23

---

[1] 7:28 Other mss read *women is not a greater prophet than John the Baptist*

---

[a] 7:27 Lit *messenger before Your face*   [c] 7:29 Lit *they justified God*
[b] 7:27 Mal 3:1   [d] 7:35 Or *wisdom is declared right*

and began to wash His feet with her tears. She wiped His feet with the hair of her head, kissing them and anointing them with the fragrant oil.

39 When the Pharisee who had invited Him saw this, he said to himself, "This man, if He were a prophet, would know who and what kind of woman this is who is touching Him—that she's a sinner!"

40 Jesus replied to him, "Simon, I have something to say to you."

"Teacher," he said, "say it."

41 "A creditor had two debtors. One owed five hundred denarii,[a] and the other fifty. 42 Since they could not pay it back, he graciously forgave them both. So, which of them will love him more?"

43 Simon answered, "I suppose the one he forgave more."

"You have judged correctly," He told him. 44 Turning to the woman, He said to Simon, "Do you see this woman? I entered your house; you gave Me no water for My feet, but she, with her tears, has washed My feet and wiped them with her hair. 45 You gave Me no kiss, but she hasn't stopped kissing My feet since I came in. 46 You didn't anoint My head with oil, but she has anointed My feet with fragrant oil. 47 Therefore I tell you, her many sins have been forgiven; that's why[b] she loved much. But the one who is forgiven little, loves little." 48 Then He said to her, "Your sins are forgiven."

49 Those who were at the table with Him began to say among themselves, "Who is this man who even forgives sins?"

50 And He said to the woman, "Your faith has saved you. Go in peace."

MANY WOMEN SUPPORT CHRIST'S WORK

8 Soon afterward He was traveling from one town and village to another, preaching and telling the good news of the kingdom of God. The Twelve were with Him, 2 and also some women who had been healed of evil spirits and sicknesses: Mary, called Magdalene, from

To Love Him Is to Know Him

An intimate love relationship with God is the key to knowing God's voice, to hearing when God speaks.

Turning to the woman, He said to Simon, "Do you see this woman? I entered your house; you gave Me no water for My feet, but she, with her tears, has washed My feet and wiped them with her hair."

—Luke 7:44

---

[a]7:41 A small silver coin equal to a day's wages

[b]7:47 That is, her love shows that she has been forgiven

whom seven demons had come out; [3] Joanna the wife of Chuza, Herod's steward; Susanna; and many others who were supporting them from their possessions.

THE PARABLE OF THE SOWER

[4] As a large crowd was gathering, and people were flocking to Him from every town, He said in a parable: [5] "A sower went out to sow his seed. As he was sowing, some fell along the path; it was trampled on, and the birds of the sky ate it up. [6] Other seed fell on the rock; when it sprang up, it withered, since it lacked moisture. [7] Other seed fell among thorns; the thorns sprang up with it and choked it. [8] Still other seed fell on good ground; when it sprang up, it produced a crop: a hundred times what was sown." As He said this, He called out, "Anyone who has ears to hear should listen!"

WHY JESUS USED PARABLES

[9] Then His disciples asked Him what this parable might mean.[a] [10] So He said, "To know the secrets[b] of the kingdom of God has been granted to you, but to the rest it is in parables, so that

Looking they may not see,
and hearing they may not understand.[c]

THE PARABLE OF THE SOWER EXPLAINED

[11] "This is the meaning of the parable:[d] The seed is the word of God. [12] The seeds along the path are those who have heard. Then the Devil comes and takes away the word from their hearts, so that they may not believe and be saved. [13] And the seeds on the rock are those who, when they hear, welcome the word with joy. Having no root, these believe for a while and depart in a time of testing. [14] As for the seed that fell among thorns, these are the ones who, when they have heard, go on their way and are choked with worries, riches, and pleasures of life, and produce no mature fruit. [15] But the

Going Our Way Is a Sure Way to Miss God

If we will not submit, God will let us follow our own devices. In following them, however, we will never experience what God is wanting to do for us and through us.

"As for the seed that fell among thorns, these are the ones who, when they have heard, go on their way and are choked with worries, riches, and pleasures of life, and produce no mature fruit."

—Luke 8:14

1) hear — unbelieving hearts
2) hear — joy — rootless hearts
3) hear — worried & preoccupied hearts
4) hear — honest & good hearts — fruitful & enduring

---

[a] **8:9** Or *What is the meaning of this parable?*
[b] **8:10** The Gk word *mysteria* does not mean "mysteries" in the Eng sense; it means what we can know only by divine revelation, or *a secret* as here.
[c] **8:10** Is 6:9
[d] **8:11** Lit *But this is the parable:*

seed in the good ground—these are the ones who,[a] having heard the word with an honest and good heart, hold on to it and bear fruit with endurance.

USING YOUR LIGHT

[16] "No one, after lighting a lamp, covers it with a basket or puts it under a bed, but puts it on a lampstand, so that those who come in may see the light. [17] For nothing is concealed that won't be revealed, and nothing hidden that won't be made known and come to light. [18] Therefore, take care how you listen. For whoever has, more will be given to him; and whoever does not have, even what he thinks he has will be taken away from him."

TRUE RELATIONSHIPS

[19] Then His mother and brothers came to Him, but they could not meet with Him because of the crowd. [20] He was told, "Your mother and Your brothers are standing outside, wanting to see You."

[21] But He replied to them, "My mother and My brothers are those who hear and do the word of God."

WIND AND WAVE OBEY THE MASTER

[22] One day He and His disciples got into a boat, and He told them, "Let's cross over to the other side of the lake." So they set out, [23] and as they were sailing He fell asleep. Then a fierce windstorm came down on the lake; they were being swamped and were in danger. [24] They came and woke Him up, saying, "Master, Master, we're going to die!"[b] Then He got up and rebuked the wind and the raging waves. So they ceased, and there was a calm. [25] He said to them, "Where is your faith?"

They were fearful and amazed, saying to one another, "Who can this be?[c] He commands even the winds and the waves, and they obey Him!"

DEMONS DRIVEN OUT BY THE MASTER

[26] Then they sailed to the region of the Gerasenes,[1] which is opposite Galilee. [27] When He got out on land, a

[1] 8:26 Other mss read *Gadarenes*

---

[a] 8:15 Or *these are the kind who*   [c] 8:25 Lit *Who then is this?*
[b] 8:24 Lit *we're perishing*

Obedience Starts in the Heart

Obedience is the outward expression of your love for God.

"But the seed in the good ground—these are the ones who, having heard the word with an honest and good heart, hold on to it and bear fruit with endurance."

—Luke 8:15

Stop, Look, and Listen

As you pray, watch to see how God uses His Word to confirm in your heart a word from Him. Watch what He is doing around you in circumstances. The God who is speaking to you as you pray and the God who is speaking to you in the Scriptures is the God who is working around you.

"Therefore, take care how you listen. For whoever has, more will be given to him; and whoever does not have, even what he thinks he has will be taken away from him."

—Luke 8:18

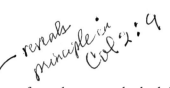

reveals principle in Col 2:9

Recognized Jesus His authority + place + power & who was really in charge JC

man from the town who had demons met Him. For a long time he had worn no clothes and did not stay in a house but in the tombs. [28] When he saw Jesus, he cried out, fell down before Him, and said in a loud voice, "What do You have to do with me, Jesus,[a] You Son of the Most High God? I beg You, don't torment me!" [29] For He had commanded the unclean spirit to come out of the man. Many times it had seized him, and although he was guarded, bound by chains and shackles, he would snap the restraints and be driven by the demon into deserted places.

[30] "What is your name?" Jesus asked him.

"Legion," he said—because many demons had entered him. [31] And they begged Him not to banish them to the abyss.[b]

[32] A large herd of pigs was there, feeding on the hillside. The demons begged Him to permit them to enter the pigs,[c] and He gave them permission. [33] The demons[d] came out of the man and entered the pigs, and the herd rushed down the steep bank into the lake and drowned. [34] When the men who tended them saw what had happened, they ran off and reported it in the town and in the countryside. [35] Then people[e] went out to see what had happened. They came to Jesus and found the man from whom the demons had departed, sitting at Jesus' feet, dressed and in his right mind. And they were afraid. [36] Meanwhile the eyewitnesses reported to them how the demon–possessed man was delivered. [37] Then all the people of the Gerasene region[f] asked Him to leave them, because they were gripped by great fear. So getting into the boat, He returned.

[38] The man from whom the demons had departed kept begging Him to be with Him. But He sent him away and said, [39] "Go back to your home, and tell all that God has done for you." And off he went, proclaiming throughout the town all that Jesus had done for him.

---

[a]8:28 Lit *What to me and to You*
[b]8:31 Or *the bottomless pit;* the prison for Satan and the demons. See Rm 10:7; Rv 9:1-2; 11; 11:7; 17:8; 20:1-3
[c]8:32 Lit *enter those*
[d]8:33 Lit *They*
[e]8:35 Lit *they*
[f]8:37 See 8:26 note

Jesus upset the status quo

WORD STUDY

Greek word: **basanizo**
[bah sah NEE zoh]
Translation: **torment**
Uses in Luke's Gospel: **1** (Mt, 3; Mk, 2)
Uses in the NT: **12**
Key passage: **Luke 8:28**

The Greek verb *basanizo* basically means *to torment* but has a wide range of uses in the NT. *Basinizo* is used literally in reference to the "terrible agony" caused by a disease (Mt 8:6; see 4:24 for the noun *basanos,* "intense pains") and the scorpion-like locusts that will torment the ungodly (Rv 9:5; see 11:10). The term also describes childbirth (Rv 12:2) and Lot's tormented soul regarding the evil he saw in Sodom and Gomorrah (2 Pt 2:8). *Basanizo* is used figuratively in Matthew's account of Jesus' walking on the water, where it refers to a boat being "battered" by waves from the sea (14:24; see Mk 6:48, where the disciples themselves are battered). *Basinizo* is also used in the account of numerous demons begging Jesus not to torment them (Mt 8:29 = Mk 5:7 = Lk 8:28—Luke explains this torment as the demons' fear of being sent into the abyss; v. 31); and of the torment of eternal punishment (Rv 14:10-11; 20:10). Related to the latter is the use of the word "torment" *(basanos)* by the rich man who was suffering in the flames to such a degree that he requested some relief from Abraham (Lk 16:23,28). Two other related nouns are *basanistes,* "jailers" who tortured prisoners (used only in Mt 18:34), and *basanismos,* which describes the torment of God's judgment and occurs only in Revelation (9:5 twice; 14:11; 18:7,10,15).

157

A GIRL RESTORED AND A WOMAN HEALED

⁴⁰ When Jesus returned, the crowd welcomed Him, for they were all expecting Him. ⁴¹ Just then, a man named Jairus came. He was a leader of the synagogue. He fell down at Jesus' feet and pleaded with Him to come to his house, ⁴² because he had an only daughter about twelve years old, and she was at death's door.ᵃ

While He was going, the crowds were nearly crushing Him. ⁴³ A woman suffering from bleeding for twelve years, who had spent all she had on doctors[1] yet could not be healed by any, ⁴⁴ approached from behind and touched the tassel of His robe.ᵇ Instantly her bleeding stopped.

⁴⁵ "Who touched Me?" Jesus asked.

When they all denied it, Peter[2] said, "Master, the crowds are hemming You in and pressing against You."[3]

⁴⁶ "Somebody did touch Me," said Jesus. "I know that power has gone out from Me." ⁴⁷ When the woman saw that she was discovered,ᶜ she came trembling and fell down before Him. In the presence of all the people, she declared the reason she had touched Him and how she was instantly cured. ⁴⁸ "Daughter," He said to her, "your faith has made you well.ᵈ Go in peace."

⁴⁹ While He was still speaking, someone came from the synagogue leader's house,ᵉ saying, "Your daughter is dead. Don't bother the Teacher anymore."

⁵⁰ But when Jesus heard it, He answered him, "Don't be afraid. Only believe, and she will be made well."

⁵¹ When He came to the house, He let no one enter with Him except Peter, John, James, and the child's father and mother. ⁵² And all were weeping and mourning for her. But He said, "Stop weeping; for she is not dead but asleep."

⁵³ They started laughing at Him, because they knew she was dead. ⁵⁴ But He[4] took her by the hand and called

Are You Too Humble for God's Good?

When you believe that nothing significant can happen through you, you have said more about your belief in God than you have said about yourself. He is able to do anything He pleases with one ordinary person fully consecrated to Him.

"Daughter," He said to her, "your faith has made you well. Go in peace."

—Luke 8:48

---

[1] **8:43** Other mss omit *who had spent all she had on doctors*
[2] **8:45** Other mss add *and those with him*
[3] **8:45** Other mss add *and You say, Who touched Me?*
[4] **8:54** Other mss add *having put them all outside*

ᵃ**8:42** Lit *she was dying*
ᵇ**8:44** Observant Jews wore tassels (or fringes) on their clothes to remind them to keep the law (see Nm 15:37–41).

ᶜ**8:47** Lit *she had not escaped notice*
ᵈ**8:48** Or *has saved you*
ᵉ**8:49** *house* or *family* implied

out, "Child, get up!" [55] Her spirit returned, and she got up at once. Then He gave orders that she be given something to eat. [56] Her parents were astounded, but He instructed them to tell no one what had happened.

COMMISSIONING THE TWELVE

9 Summoning the Twelve, He gave them power and authority over all the demons, and to heal[a] diseases. [2] Then He sent them to proclaim the kingdom of God and to heal[a] the sick.[b]

[3] "Take nothing for the road," He told them, "no walking stick, no backpack, no bread, no money; and don't have an extra shirt. [4] Whatever house you enter, stay there and leave from there. [5] Wherever they do not welcome you, when you leave that town, shake off the dust from your feet as a testimony against them." [6] So they went out and traveled from village to village, proclaiming the good news and healing everywhere.

JOHN THE BAPTIST BEHEADED

[7] Herod the tetrarch[c] heard about everything that was going on. He was perplexed, because some said that John had been raised from the dead, [8] some that Elijah had appeared, and others that one of the ancient prophets had risen. [9] "I beheaded John," Herod said. "But who is this I hear such things about?" And he wanted to see Him.

FEEDING FIVE THOUSAND

[10] When the apostles returned, they reported to Jesus[d] all that they had done. He took them along and withdrew privately to a[1] town called Bethsaida. [11] When the crowds found out, they followed Him. He welcomed them, spoke to them about the kingdom of God, and cured[e] those who needed healing.

Experience Soon Becomes Understanding

When you make the adjustments and start to obey Him, you come to know Him by experience. This is the goal of God's activity in your life—that you come to know Him.

When the apostles returned, they reported to Jesus all that they had done. He took them along and withdrew privately to a town called Bethsaida.

—Luke 9:10

---

[1]9:10 Other mss read *a deserted place near a*

---

[a]9:1,2 Different Gk words are translated as *heal*. In Eng, "to heal" or "to cure" are synonyms with little distinction in meaning. Technically, we do not *heal* or *cure* diseases. People are healed or cured from diseases.

[b]9:2 Other mss omit *the sick*
[c]9:7 That is, Herod Antipas, son of Herod the Great, who ruled one-fourth of his father's kingdom under Rome
[d]9:10 Lit *Him*
[e]9:11 Or *healed.* See 9:1,2 note

[12] Late in the day,[a] the Twelve approached and said to Him, "Send the crowd away, so they can go into the surrounding villages and countryside to find food and lodging, because we are in a deserted place here."

[13] "You give them something to eat," He told them.

"We have no more than five loaves and two fish," they said, "unless we go and buy food for all these people." [14] (For about five thousand men were there.)

Then He told His disciples, "Have them sit down[b] in groups of about fifty each." [15] They did so, and had them all sit down. [16] Then He took the five loaves and the two fish, and looking up to heaven, He blessed and broke them. He kept giving them to the disciples to set before the crowd. [17] Everyone ate and was filled. Then they picked up[c] twelve baskets of leftover pieces.

PETER'S CONFESSION OF THE MESSIAH

[18] Once when He was praying in private, and His disciples were with Him, He asked them, "Who do the crowds say that I am?"

[19] And they answered, "John the Baptist; others, Elijah; still others, that one of the ancient prophets has come back."[d]

[20] "But you," He asked them, "who do you say that I am?"

Peter answered, "God's Messiah!"[e]

HIS DEATH AND RESURRECTION PREDICTED

[21] But He strictly warned and instructed them to tell this to no one, [22] saying, "The Son of Man must suffer many things and be rejected by the elders, chief priests, and scribes, be killed, and be raised the third day."

TAKE UP YOUR CROSS

[23] Then He said to them[f] all, "If anyone wants to come with[g] Me, he must deny himself, take up his cross

---

Talk Up and Listen Up

Prayer is two-way fellowship and communication with God, not a one-way conversation. In fact, what God says in prayer is far more important than what you say. Prayer is designed more to adjust you to God than to adjust God to you.

Once when He was praying in private, and His disciples were with Him, He asked them, "Who do the crowds say that I am?"

—Luke 9:18

---

[a] 9:12 Lit *When the day began to decline*
[b] 9:14 Lit *them recline*
[c] 9:17 Lit *Then were picked up by them*
[d] 9:19 Lit *has risen*
[e] 9:20 See 2:26 note
[f] 9:23 *them* supplied
[g] 9:23 Lit *come after*

daily,[1] and follow Me. [24] For whoever wants to save his life[a] will lose it, but whoever loses his life[a] because of Me will save it. [25] What is a man benefited if he gains the whole world, yet loses or forfeits himself? [26] For whoever is ashamed of Me and My words, the Son of Man will be ashamed of him when He comes with His glory, and with the glory of the[b] Father, and of the holy angels. [27] I tell you the truth: there are some standing here who will not taste death until they see the kingdom of God."

THE TRANSFIGURATION

[28] About eight days after these words, He took along Peter, John, and James, and went up on the mountain to pray. [29] As He was praying, the appearance of His face changed, and His clothes became dazzling white. [30] Suddenly, two men were talking with Him—none other than Moses and Elijah. [31] They appeared in glory and were speaking of His death,[c] which He was about to accomplish in Jerusalem.

[32] Peter and those with him were in a deep sleep,[d] and when they became fully awake, they saw His glory and the two men who were standing with Him. [33] As the two men[e] were departing from Him, Peter said to Jesus, "Master, it's good for us to be here! Let us make three tabernacles:[f] one for You, one for Moses, and one for Elijah"—not knowing what he said.

[34] While he was saying this, a cloud appeared and overshadowed them. They became afraid as they entered the cloud. [35] Then a voice came from the cloud,[g] saying:

"This is My Son, the Chosen One;[2]
listen to Him!"

[36] After the voice had spoken, only Jesus was found. They kept silent, and in those days told no one what they had seen.

[1]9:23 Other mss omit *daily*
[2]9:35 Other mss read *the Beloved*

[a]9:24 The same Gk word (*psyche*) can mean *life* or *soul.*
[b]9:26 *glory of the* implied
[c]9:31 Or *departure;* Gk *exodus*
[d]9:32 Lit *were weighed down with sleep*
[e]9:33 Lit *As they*
[f]9:33 Or *tents* or *shelters* used for temporary housing
[g]9:35 2 Pt 1:16–18

WORD STUDY

Greek word: *dei* [DIGH]
Translation: *must*
Uses in Luke's Gospel: **18** (Mt, 8; Mk, 6; Jn, 10)
Uses in Luke's Writings: **40**
Uses in the NT: **101**
Key passage: **Luke 9:22**

The Greek word *dei* is a special form of the verb *deo,* meaning *to bind,* and refers to something that is a binding obligation upon someone. In the Gospels the term *dei* normally occurs in contexts related to some aspect of salvation, and the binding obligation comes from the decree of God, though this is not stated but is clearly implied. Thus, in Luke's Gospel *dei* indicates that Jesus must do the Father's will (2:49); preach (4:43); keep a divine appointment with a tax collector (19:5); suffer, die, and rise again (9:22; 17:25; 24:7,26; see Mt 16:21; Mk 8:31; Ac 17:3); and that the Scriptures must be fulfilled (Lk 24:44; see Jn 20:9; Ac 1:16). Luke continued the theme of divine necessity in Acts: Jesus must remain in heaven until the appointed time (Ac 3:21), everyone must believe in Jesus for salvation (Ac 4:12; 16:30–31), and believers must suffer for Jesus' sake (Ac 9:16; 14:22). Similarly, in John's Gospel *dei* refers to the necessity of the new birth (3:7), Jesus' appointment with the woman of Samaria (4:4), the obligation to worship God "in spirit and truth" (4:24), and Jesus' bringing all sheep into "one flock" (10:16). The term *dei* also describes the divine necessity of certain events in the end times that relate to final salvation (Mt 24:6 = Mk 13:7 = Lk 21:9; see 1 Co 15:25,53; 2 Co 5:10; Rv 1:1; 4:1; 11:5; 17:10; 20:3; 22:6).

THE POWER OF FAITH OVER A DEMON

37 The next day, when they came down from the mountain, a large crowd met Him. 38 Just then a man from the crowd cried out, "Teacher, I beg You to look at my son, because he's my only child.[a] 39 Often a spirit seizes him; suddenly he shrieks, and it throws him into convulsions until he foams at the mouth;[b] wounding[c] him, it hardly ever leaves him. 40 I begged Your disciples to drive it out, but they couldn't."

41 Jesus replied, "O unbelieving and rebellious[d] generation! How long will I be with you and put up with you? Bring your son here."

42 As the boy[e] was still approaching, the demon knocked him down and threw him into severe convulsions. But Jesus rebuked the unclean spirit, cured the boy, and gave him back to his father. 43 And they were all astonished at the greatness of God.

Maintain a Teachable Spirit

Don't allow the limited knowledge you have now to blind you to the great truths God still wants to reveal to you.

"Let these words sink in: the Son of Man is about to be betrayed into the hands of men."

—Luke 9:44

THE SECOND PREDICTION OF HIS DEATH

While everyone was amazed at all the things He was doing, He told His disciples, 44 "Let these words sink in:[f] the Son of Man is about to be betrayed into the hands of men."

45 But they did not understand this statement; it was concealed from them so that they could not grasp it, and they were afraid to ask Him about it.[g]

WHO IS THE GREATEST?

46 Then an argument started among them about who would be the greatest of them. 47 But Jesus, knowing the thoughts of their hearts, took a little child and had him stand next to Him. 48 He told them, "Whoever welcomes[h] this little child in My name welcomes Me. And whoever welcomes Me welcomes Him who sent Me. For whoever is least among you all—this one is great."

---

[a] 9:38 *child* implied
[b] 9:39 Lit *convulsions with foam*
[c] 9:39 Or *bruising* or *mauling*
[d] 9:41 Or *corrupt, perverted, twisted;* see Dt 32:15
[e] 9:42 Lit *As he*

[f] 9:44 Lit *Put these words in your ears*
[g] 9:45 Lit *about this statement*
[h] 9:48 Or *receives* throughout the verse

IN HIS NAME

⁴⁹ John responded, "Master, we saw someone driving out demons in Your name, and we tried to stop him because he does not follow with us."

⁵⁰ "Don't stop him," Jesus told him, "because whoever is not against you¹ is for you."¹

THE JOURNEY TO JERUSALEM

⁵¹ When the days were coming to a close for Him to be taken up,ᵃ He was determinedᵇ to journey to Jerusalem. ⁵² He sent messengers ahead of Him, and on the way they entered a village of the Samaritansᶜ to make preparations for Him. ⁵³ But they did not welcome Him, because He was determined to journey to Jerusalem. ⁵⁴ When the disciples James and John saw this, they said, "Lord, do You want us to call down fire from heaven to consume them?"²

⁵⁵ But He turned and rebuked them,³ ⁵⁶ and they went to another village.

FOLLOWING JESUS

⁵⁷ As they were traveling on the road someone said to Him, "I will follow You wherever You go!"

⁵⁸ Jesus told him, "Foxes have dens, and birds of the skyᵈ have nests, but the Son of Man has no place to lay His head." ⁵⁹ Then He said to another, "Follow Me."

"Lord," he said, "first let me go to bury my father."ᵉ

⁶⁰ But He told him, "Let the dead bury their own dead, but you go and spread the news of the kingdom of God."

⁶¹ Another also said, "I will follow You, Lord, but first let me go and say goodbye to those at my house."

God Can Give You the Strength to Obey

As you obey Him, God will prepare you for the next assignment.

When the days were coming to a close for Him to be taken up, He was determined to journey to Jerusalem.

—Luke 9:51

Be Prepared for God to Change You

Adjustments prepare you for obedience. You cannot continue life as usual or stay where you are, and go with God at the same time.

Another also said, "I will follow You, Lord, but first let me go and say goodbye to those at my house."

—Luke 9:61

---

¹9:50 Other mss read *us . . . us*
²9:54 Other mss add *as Elijah also did*
³9:55 Other mss add *and said, "You don't know what kind of spirit you belong to. 56 For the Son of Man did not come to destroy people's lives but to save them."*

ᵃ9:51 That is, *His ascension*
ᵇ9:51 Lit *He stiffened His face to go* (see Is 50:7)
ᶜ9:52 Samaritans were people of mixed ancestry (partly Jewish) who lived between Galilee and Judea.

ᵈ9:58 That is, wild birds, as opposed to domestic birds
ᵉ9:59 Not necessarily meaning his father was already dead

[62] But Jesus said to him, "No one who puts his hand to the plow and looks back is fit for the kingdom of God."

SENDING OUT THE SEVENTY

10 After this the Lord appointed seventy[1] others, and He sent them ahead of Him in pairs to every town and place where He Himself was about to go. [2] He told them: "The harvest is abundant, but the workers are few. Therefore, pray to the Lord of the harvest to send out workers into His harvest. [3] Now go; I'm sending you out like lambs among wolves. [4] Don't carry a money-bag, backpack, or sandals; don't greet anyone along the road. [5] Whatever house you enter, first say, 'Peace to this household.' [6] If a son of peace[a] is there, your peace will rest on him; but if not, it will return to you. [7] Remain in the same house, eating and drinking what they offer, for the worker is worthy of his wages. Don't be moving from house to house. [8] Whatever town you enter, and they welcome you, eat the things set before you. [9] Heal the sick who are there, and tell them, 'The kingdom of God has come near you.' [10] But whatever town you enter, and they don't welcome you, go out into its streets and say, [11] 'Even the dust of your town that clings to our feet we wipe off against you. But know this: the kingdom of God has come near.' [12] I tell you, on that day it will be more tolerable for Sodom than for that town.

UNREPENTANT TOWNS

[13] "Woe to you, Chorazin! Woe to you, Bethsaida! For if the miracles that were done in you had been done in Tyre and Sidon, they would have repented long ago, sitting in sackcloth and ashes! [14] But it will be more tolerable for Tyre and Sidon at the judgment than for you. [15] And you, Capernaum, will you be exalted to heaven? No, you will go down to Hades![bc] [16] Whoever listens to you listens to Me. Whoever rejects you rejects Me. And whoever rejects Me rejects the One who sent Me."

[1] 10:1 Other mss read *seventy-two* here and in v. 17

[a] 10:6 That is, *a peaceful person;* one open to the message of the kingdom
[b] 10:15 The Gk word for the place of the dead corresponding to the OT Hb word *Sheol*
[c] 10:15 Is 14:13,15

Are You Committed to God's Business?

Frequently, the reason we do not join Him is because we are not committed to Him. We are wanting God to bless us, not to work through us.

He told them: "The harvest is abundant, but the workers are few. Therefore, pray to the Lord of the harvest to send out workers into His harvest."

—Luke 10:2

THE RETURN OF THE SEVENTY

[17] The seventy[a] returned with joy, saying, "Lord, even the demons submit to us in Your name."

[18] He said to them, "I watched Satan fall from heaven like a lightning flash. [19] Look, I have given you the authority to trample on snakes and scorpions[b] and over all the power of the enemy; nothing will ever harm you. [20] However, don't rejoice that[c] the spirits submit to you, but rejoice that your names are written in heaven."

THE SON REVEALS THE FATHER

[21] In that same hour He[1] rejoiced in the Holy[2] Spirit and said, "I praise[d] You, Father, Lord of heaven and earth, because You have hidden these things from the wise and the learned and have revealed them to infants. Yes, Father, because this was Your good pleasure.[e] [22] All things have[3] been entrusted to Me by My Father. No one knows who the Son is except the Father, and who the Father is except the Son, and anyone to whom the Son desires[f] to reveal Him."

[23] Then turning to His disciples He said privately, "Blessed are the eyes that see the things you see! [24] For I tell you that many prophets and kings wanted to see the things you see, yet didn't see them; to hear the things you hear, yet didn't hear them."

THE PARABLE OF THE GOOD SAMARITAN[g]

[25] Just then an expert in the law stood up to test Him, saying, "Teacher, what must I do to inherit eternal life?"

[26] "What is written in the law?" He asked him. "How do you read it?"

[27] He answered:

**"You shall love the Lord your God
with all your heart, with all your soul,**

WORD STUDY

Greek word: **agapao**
[ah gah PAH oh]
Translation: **love**
Uses in Luke's Gospel: **13**
(Mt, 8; Mk, 5; Jn, 37)
Uses in the NT: **143**
Key passage: **Luke 10:27**

The most common Greek words for love in the NT are *agapao* (verb) and *agape* (noun). These two words are used to describe the purest and highest form of love, although they have other uses that are not as noble (see Lk 11:43). The synonymous verb *phileo* was also used in the noblest of senses on occasion (see word study on page 271), which reflects common Greek usage in the first century. However, *agapao* is used in the Greek OT regarding the two greatest commandments, which is what the expert in the Mosaic law quoted (Lk 10:27; see Dt 6:5; Lv 19:18). God demands that we love Him with our entire being—heart, soul, mind, strength—and loving God means that we must also love those created in His image, even our enemies (Lk 6:27). Jesus' explanation of the two greatest commandments indicates that every sin violates one or both of the commands to love God and to love others (Mt 22:40).

---

[1] 10:21 Other mss read *Jesus*
[2] 10:21 Other mss omit *Holy*
[3] 10:22 Other mss read *And turning to the disciples, He said, Everything has*

---

[a] 10:17 See 10:1 note
[b] 10:19 Dt 8:15; Ps 91:13
[c] 10:20 Lit *don't rejoice in this, that*
[d] 10:21 Or *thank*
[e] 10:21 Lit *was well-pleasing in Your sight*
[f] 10:22 Or *wills* or *chooses*
[g] 10:25 See 9:52 note

with all your strength, and with all your mind;
and your neighbor as yourself."ᵃ

²⁸ "You've answered correctly," He told him. "Do this and you will live."

²⁹ But wanting to justify himself, he asked Jesus, "And who is my neighbor?"

³⁰ Jesus took up the questionᵇ and said: "A man was going down from Jerusalem to Jericho and fell into the hands of robbers. They stripped him, beat him up, and fled, leaving him half dead. ³¹ A priest happened to be going down that road. When he saw him, he passed by on the other side. ³² In the same way, a Levite, when he arrived at the place and saw him, passed by on the other side. ³³ But a Samaritan,ᶜ while traveling, came up to him; and when he saw the man,ᵈ he had compassion. ³⁴ He went over to him and bandaged his wounds, pouring on oil and wine. Then he put him on his own animal, brought him to an inn, and took care of him. ³⁵ The next day¹ he took out two denarii,ᵉ gave them to the innkeeper, and said, 'Take care of him; and when I come back I'll reimburse you for whatever extra you spend.'

³⁶ "Which of these three do you think proved to be a neighbor to the man who fell into the hands of the robbers?"

³⁷ "The one who showed mercy to him," he said. Then Jesus told him, "Go and do the same."

A Message from God Always Has Meaning

When God speaks to you through the Bible, prayer, circumstances, the church, or in some other way, He has a purpose in mind for your life.

"Which of these three do you think proved to be a neighbor to the man who fell into the hands of the robbers?" "The one who showed mercy to him," he said. Then Jesus told him, "Go and do the same."

—Luke 10:36-37

MARTHA AND MARY

³⁸ While they were traveling, He entered a village, and a woman named Martha welcomed Him into her home.² ³⁹ She had a sister named Mary, who also sat at the Lord's³ feet and was listening to what He said.ᶠ ⁴⁰ But Martha was distracted by her many tasks, and she came up and asked, "Lord, don't You care that my sister has left me to serve alone? So tell her to give me a hand."ᵍ

¹10:35 Other mss read *day as he was leaving*
²10:38 Other mss omit *into her home*
³10:39 Other mss read *Jesus'*

ᵃ10:27 Dt 6:5; Lv 19:18
ᵇ10:30 *the question* supplied for clarity
ᶜ10:33 See 9:52 note

ᵈ10:33 *the man* supplied
ᵉ10:35 See 7:41 note
ᶠ10:39 Lit *to His word* or *message*
ᵍ10:40 Or *tell her to help me*

[41] The Lord[1] answered her, "Martha, Martha, you are worried and upset about many things, [42] but one thing is necessary. Mary has made the right choice,[a] and it will not be taken away from her."

THE MODEL PRAYER

11 He was praying in a certain place, and when He finished, one of His disciples said to Him, "Lord, teach us to pray, just as John also taught his disciples."

[2] He said to them, "Whenever you pray, say:

> Father,[2] Your name be honored as holy.
> Your kingdom come.[3]
> [3] Give us each day our daily bread.[b]
> [4] And forgive us our sins,
> for we ourselves also forgive everyone in debt to us.[c]
> And do not bring us into temptation."[4]

KEEP ASKING, SEARCHING, KNOCKING

[5] He also said to them: "Suppose one of you[d] has a friend and goes to him at midnight and says to him, 'Friend, lend me three loaves of bread, [6] because a friend of mine on a journey has come to me, and I don't have anything to offer him.'[e] [7] Then he will answer from inside and say, 'Don't bother me! The door is already locked, and my children and I have gone to bed. I can't get up to give you anything.' [8] I tell you, even though he won't get up and give him anything because he is his friend, yet because of his persistence,[f] he will get up and give him as much as he needs.

[9] "So I say to you, keep asking,[g] and it will be given to you. Keep searching,[h] and you will find. Keep knocking,[i] and the door[j] will be opened to you. [10] For everyone who asks receives, and the one who searches finds,

---

[1] 10:41 Other mss read *Jesus*
[2] 11:2 Other mss read *Our Father in heaven*
[3] 11:2 Other mss add *Your will be done on earth as it is in heaven*
[4] 11:4 Other mss add *But deliver us from the evil one*

---

[a] 10:42 Lit *has chosen the good part*
[b] 11:3 Or *our bread for tomorrow*
[c] 11:4 Or *everyone who wrongs us*
[d] 11:5 Lit *Anyone of you*
[e] 11:6 Lit *I have nothing to set before him*
[f] 11:8 Or *annoying persistence* or *shamelessness*
[g] 11:9 Or *you, ask*
[h] 11:9 Or *Search*
[i] 11:9 Or *Knock*
[j] 11:9 Lit *and it*

When You Have God, You Have It All

You do not need to be doing something to feel fulfilled. You are fulfilled completely in a relationship with God. When you are filled with Him, what else do you need?

The Lord answered her, "Martha, Martha, you are worried and upset about many things, but one thing is necessary. Mary has made the right choice, and it will not be taken away from her."

—Luke 10:41–42

Make Sure He Is Lord No Matter What

He calls you to a relationship where He is Lord—where you are willing to do and be anything He chooses.

He said to them, "Whenever you pray, say: Father, Your name be honored as holy. Your kingdom come."

—Luke 11:2

and to the one who knocks, the door[a] will be opened. [11] What father among you, if his son asks for a fish, will,[1] instead of a fish, give him a snake? [12] Or if he asks for an egg, will give him a scorpion? [13] If you then, who are evil, know how to give good gifts to your children, how much more will the heavenly Father[b] give the Holy Spirit to those who ask Him?"

A HOUSE DIVIDED

[14] Now He was driving out a demon that was mute.[c] When the demon came out, the man spoke who had been unable to speak, and the crowds were amazed. [15] But some of them said, "He drives out demons by Beelzebul,[d] the ruler of the demons!" [16] And others, as a test, were demanding of Him a sign from heaven. [17] Knowing their thoughts, He told them: "Every kingdom divided against itself is headed for destruction, and a house divided against itself falls. [18] If Satan also is divided against himself, how will his kingdom stand? For you say I drive out demons by Beelzebul. [19] And if I drive out demons by Beelzebul, by whom do your sons[e] drive them out? For this reason they will be your judges. [20] If I drive out demons by the finger of God, then the kingdom of God has come to you. [21] When a strong man, fully armed, guards his estate, his possessions are secure.[f] [22] But when one stronger than he attacks and overpowers him, he takes from him all his weapons[g] in which he trusted, and divides up his plunder. [23] Anyone who is not with Me is against Me, and anyone who does not gather with Me scatters.

AN UNCLEAN SPIRIT'S RETURN

[24] "When an unclean spirit comes out of a man, it roams through waterless places looking for rest, and not

God Is So Good, So Good to Me

He will always direct you in ways that are best for you and for the world into which He calls you.

"If you then, who are evil, know how to give good gifts to your children, how much more will the heavenly Father give the Holy Spirit to those who ask Him?"

—Luke 11:13

---

[1]**11:11** Other mss read *son asks for bread, would give him a stone. Or if he asks for a fish, he will not*

---

[a]**11:10** Lit *knocks, it*
[b]**11:13** Gk *your Father from heaven will give*
[c]**11:14** That is, a demon that caused the man to be mute
[d]**11:15** Term of slander variously interpreted, "lord of flies," "lord of dung," or "ruler of demons" (cf. 2 Kg 1:2)
[e]**11:19** That is, your exorcists
[f]**11:21** Lit *his possessions are in peace*
[g]**11:22** Gk *panoplia,* the armor and weapons of a foot soldier; see Eph 6:11,13

finding rest, it then[1] says, 'I'll go back to my house where I came from.' [25] And returning, it finds the house[a] swept and put in order. [26] Then off it goes and brings seven other spirits more evil than itself, and they enter and settle down there. As a result, that man's last condition is worse than the first."

TRUE BLESSEDNESS

[27] As He was saying these things, a woman from the crowd raised her voice and said to Him, "Blessed is the womb that bore You, and the breasts that nursed You!"

[28] He said, "More blessed still are those who hear the word of God and keep it!"

THE SIGN OF JONAH

[29] As the crowds were increasing, He began saying: "This generation is an evil generation. It demands a sign, but no sign will be given to it except the sign of Jonah.[2] [30] For just as Jonah became a sign to the people of Nineveh, so also the Son of Man will be to this generation. [31] The queen of the south will rise up at the judgment with the men of this generation and condemn them, because she came from the ends of the earth to hear the wisdom of Solomon; and look—something greater than Solomon is here! [32] The men of Nineveh will rise up at the judgment with this generation and condemn it, because they repented at Jonah's proclamation; and look—something greater than Jonah is here!

THE LAMP OF THE BODY

[33] "No one lights a lamp and puts it in the cellar or under a basket,[3] but on a lampstand, so that those who come in may see its light. [34] Your eye is the lamp of the body. When your eye is good,[b] your whole body is also full of light. But when it is bad,[c] your body is also full of darkness. [35] Take care then, that the light in you is not

Don't Be Dependent on an Open Door

Open and closed doors are not always indications of God's direction. In seeking God's direction, check to see that prayer, the Scripture, and circumstances agree with the direction you sense God leading you.

He said, "More blessed still are those who hear the word of God and keep it!"

—Luke 11:28

[1]11:24 Other mss omit *then*
[2]11:29 Other mss add *the prophet*
[3]11:33 Other mss omit *or under a basket*

[a]11:25 *the house* implied
[b]11:34 Lit *simple* or *single*
[c]11:34 Lit *evil*

WORD STUDY

Greek word: **katabole**
[kah tah bah LAY]

Translation: **foundation**

Uses in Luke's Gospel: **1**
(Mt, 2; Jn, 1)

Uses in the NT: **11**

Key passage: **Luke 11:50**

The Greek noun *katabole* is related to the verb *kataballo* meaning *to throw* or *lay down* (used only in 2 Co 4:9; Heb 6:1). In the NT the term always refers to the beginning of something, making it somewhat synonymous with the more common Greek word that means *beginning (arche)*. An unusual use of the term *katabole* occurs in Hebrews 11:11, where the beginning of the promised seed through Abraham and Sarah is achieved by faith despite their advanced ages. All ten of the other uses of *katabole* are followed by the words "of the world" and are preceded by one of two prepositions: "from [Gk *apo*] the foundation of the world" refers to the time of creation (Mt 13:35; 25:34; Lk 11:50; Heb 4:3; 9:26; Rv 13:8; 17:8); and "before [Gk *pro*] the foundation of the world" refers to the eternal acts of God the Father in loving (Jn 17:24) and foreknowing (1 Pt 1:20) the Son, and in choosing believers (Eph 1:4).

darkness. 36 If therefore your whole body is full of light, with no part of it in darkness, the whole body will be full of light, as when a lamp shines its light on you."[a]

RELIGIOUS HYPOCRISY DENOUNCED

37 As He was speaking, a Pharisee[b] asked Him to dine with him. So He went in and reclined at the table. 38 When the Pharisee saw this, he was amazed that He did not first perform the ritual washing[c] before dinner. 39 But the Lord said to him: "Now you Pharisees clean the outside of the cup and dish, but inside you are full of greed and evil. 40 Fools! Didn't He who made the outside make the inside too? 41 But give to charity what is within,[d] and then everything is clean for you.

42 "But woe to you Pharisees! You give a tenth[e] of mint, rue, and every kind of herb, and you bypass[f] justice and love for God.[g] These things you should have done without neglecting the others.

43 "Woe to you Pharisees! You love the front seat in the synagogues and greetings in the marketplaces.

44 "Woe to you![1] You are like unmarked graves; the people who walk over them don't know it."

45 One of the experts in the law answered Him, "Teacher, when You say these things You insult us too."

46 And He said: "Woe to you experts in the law as well! You load people with burdens that are hard to carry, yet you yourselves don't touch these burdens with one of your fingers.

47 "Woe to you! You build monuments[h] to the prophets, and your fathers killed them. 48 Therefore you are witnesses that you approve[i] the deeds of your fathers, for they killed them, and you build their monuments.[2] 49 And because of this, the wisdom of God said, 'I will send them prophets and apostles, and some of them they will kill and persecute,' 50 so that this generation

---

[1]11:44 Other mss add *scribes and Pharisees, hypocrites*
[2]11:48 Other mss omit *their monuments* (see v. 47)

---

[a]11:36 Or *shines on you with its rays*
[b]11:37 The Pharisees were a major sect of Judaism. They followed the whole body of written and oral law.
[c]11:38 Lit *He did not first wash*
[d]11:41 Or *But donate from the heart as charity*

[e]11:42 Or *tithe*
[f]11:42 Or *neglect*
[g]11:42 Lit *the justice and the love of God*
[h]11:47 Or *graves*
[i]11:48 Lit *witnesses and approve*

may be held responsible for the blood[a] of all the prophets shed since the foundation of the world, [51] from the blood of Abel[b] to the blood of Zechariah,[c] who perished between the altar and the sanctuary.

"Yes, I tell you, this generation will be held responsible.[d]

[52] "Woe to you experts in the law! You have taken away the key of knowledge! You didn't go in yourselves, and you hindered those who were going in."

[53] When He left there,[1] the scribes and the Pharisees began to oppose Him fiercely and to cross-examine Him about many things; [54] they were lying in wait for Him to trap Him in something He said.[2]

BEWARE OF RELIGIOUS HYPOCRISY

12 In these circumstances,[e] a crowd of many thousands came together, so that they were trampling on one another. He began to say to His disciples first: "Be on your guard against the yeast[f] of the Pharisees, which is hypocrisy. [2] There is nothing covered that won't be uncovered; nothing hidden that won't be made known. [3] Therefore whatever you have said in the dark will be heard in the light, and what you have whispered in an ear in private rooms will be proclaimed on the housetops.

FEAR GOD

[4] "And I say to you, My friends, don't fear those who kill the body, and after that can do nothing more. [5] But I will show you the One to fear: Fear Him who, after He has killed, has authority to throw into hell.[g] Yes, I say to you, this is the One to fear! [6] Aren't five sparrows sold for two pennies?[h] Yet not one of them is forgotten in

---

[1] **11:53** Other mss read *And as He was saying these things to them*
[2] **11:54** Other mss add *so that they might bring charges against Him*

---

[a] **11:50** Lit *that the blood . . . may be required of this generation*
[b] **11:51** Gn 4:9,10; Heb 12:24
[c] **11:51** 2 Ch 24:20–22
[d] **11:51** Lit *you, it will be required of this generation*
[e] **12:1** Or *Meanwhile* or *At this time* or *During this period*
[f] **12:1** Or *leaven*
[g] **12:5** Gk *gehenna* (the valley of Hinnom)
[h] **12:6** Gk *assarion*, a small copper coin

WORD STUDY

Greek word: **geenna**
[GEH ehn nah]

Translation: **hell**

Uses in Luke's Gospel: **1** (Mt, 7; Mk, 3)

Uses in the NT: **12**

Key passage: **Luke 12:5**

The word "hell" in Luke 12:5 translates the Greek *geenna*, often rendered *gehenna*. It comes from the Hebrew *ge-hinnom*, "Valley of Hinnom," which was just southwest of Jerusalem. Human sacrifices were sometimes made there in OT times (2 Kg 23:10; 2 Ch 28:3; 33:6; Jr 7:31–32; 19:6). It later became a place for burning rubbish and was metaphorically used as the place of eternal punishment in the hereafter—never-ending fires of divine judgment as described in Isaiah 66:24 and Mark 9:47–48 (see also Jr 7:31–34).

In the NT *geenna* should be distinguished from *Hades*, which refers to the Greek concept of the netherworld or the realm of the dead. The Hebrew equivalent of Hades is *Sheol* (see Ps 16:10; Ac 2:27,31), and *tartarus* in 2 Peter 2:4 is probably another less common name for Hades. At the final judgment unbelievers are cast into *geenna*—called "the lake of fire" in Revelation (19:20; 20:10,14,15; see 21:8) and "eternal fire" in Matthew 25:41—where its occupants suffer forever. With one exception (Jms 3:6), the word *geenna* is used only by Jesus in the NT.

God's sight. ⁷ But even the hairs of your head are all counted. Don't be afraid; you are worth more than many sparrows!

ACKNOWLEDGING CHRIST

⁸ "And I say to you, anyone who acknowledges Me before men, the Son of Man will also acknowledge him before the angels of God; ⁹ but whoever denies Me before men will be denied before the angels of God. ¹⁰ Anyone who speaks a word against the Son of Man will be forgiven; but the one who blasphemes against the Holy Spirit will not be forgiven. ¹¹ Whenever they bring you before synagogues and rulers and authorities, don't worry about how you should defend yourselves, or what you should say. ¹² For the Holy Spirit will teach you at that very hour what must be said."

THE PARABLE OF THE RICH FOOL

¹³ Someone from the crowd said to Him, "Teacher, tell my brother to divide the inheritance with me."

¹⁴ "Friend,"ᵃ He said to him, "who appointed Me a judge or arbitrator over you?" ¹⁵ And He told them, "Watch out and be on guard against all greed, because one's life is not in the abundance of his possessions."

¹⁶ Then He told them a parable: "A rich man's land was very productive. ¹⁷ He thought to himself, 'What should I do, since I don't have anywhere to store my crops? ¹⁸ I will do this,' he said. 'I'll tear down my barns and build bigger ones, and store all my grain and my goods there. ¹⁹ Then I'll say to myself, "Youᵇ have many goods stored up for many years. Take it easy; eat, drink, and enjoy yourself."'

²⁰ "But God said to him, 'You fool! This very night your lifeᶜ is demanded of you. And the things you have prepared—whose will they be?'

²¹ "That's how it is with the one who stores up treasure for himself and is not rich toward God."

THE CURE FOR ANXIETY

²² Then He said to His disciples: "Therefore I tell you, don't worry about your life, what you will eat; or about the body, what you will wear. ²³ For life is more than

He Cares About What Happens to You

Anything significant that happens in your life will be a result of God's activity in your life. He is infinitely more interested in your life than you or I could possibly be.

"Aren't five sparrows sold for two pennies? Yet not one of them is forgotten in God's sight. But even the hairs of your head are all counted. Don't be afraid; you are worth more than many sparrows!"

—Luke 12:6–7

ᵃ**12:14** Lit *Man*
ᵇ**12:19** Lit *say to my soul, Soul, you*
ᶜ**12:20** Or *soul*

food and the body more than clothing. [24] Consider the ravens: they don't sow or reap; they don't have a storeroom or a barn; yet God feeds them. Aren't you worth much more than the birds? [25] Can any of you add a cubit to his height[a] by worrying? [26] If then you're not able to do even a little thing, why worry about the rest?

[27] "Consider how the wildflowers grow: they don't labor or spin thread. Yet I tell you, not even Solomon in all his splendor was adorned like one of these! [28] If that's how God clothes the grass, which is in the field today and is thrown into the furnace tomorrow, how much more will He do for you—you of little faith? [29] Don't keep striving for what you should eat and what you should drink, and do not be anxious. [30] For the Gentile world eagerly seeks all these things, and your Father knows that you need them.

[31] "But seek His kingdom, and these things will be provided for you. [32] Don't be afraid, little flock, because your Father delights to give you the kingdom. [33] Sell your possessions and give to the poor. Make money bags for yourselves that won't grow old, an inexhaustible treasure in heaven, where no thief comes near and no moth destroys. [34] For where your treasure is, there your heart will be also.

READY FOR THE MASTER'S RETURN

[35] "Be ready for service[b] and have your lamps lit. [36] You must be like people waiting for their master to return[c] from the wedding banquet so that when he comes and knocks, they can open the door[d] for him at once. [37] Blessed are those slaves whom the master will find alert when he comes. I assure you: He will get ready,[e] have them recline at the table, then come and serve them. [38] If he comes in the middle of the night, or even near dawn,[f] and finds them alert,[g] blessed are those slaves. [39] But know this: if the homeowner had known at what hour the thief was coming, he would not

God Always Gives Good Directions

Because His nature is love, I am always confident that however He expresses Himself to me is always best.

"Don't be afraid, little flock, because your Father delights to give you the kingdom."
—Luke 12:32

It's a Relationship, Not Just a Discipline

I hear many persons say, "I really struggle trying to have that time alone with God." If that is a problem you face, make the priority in your life to come to love Him with all your heart. That will solve most of your problem with your quiet time.

"For where your treasure is, there your heart will be also."
—Luke 12:34

---

[a]12:25 Or *add one moment to his life-span.* See Mt 6:27 note
[b]12:35 Lit *Let your loins be girded;* an idiom for tying up loose outer clothing in preparation for action. See Ex 12:11, 22–23
[c]12:36 Lit *master, when he should return*

[d]12:36 *the door* implied
[e]12:37 Lit *will gird himself.* See v. 35 note
[f]12:38 Lit *even in the second or third watch*
[g]12:38 Lit *finds so*

have let his house be broken into. ⁴⁰ You also be ready, because the Son of Man is coming at an hour that you do not expect.''

REWARDS AND PUNISHMENT

⁴¹ "Lord," Peter asked, "are You telling this parable to us or to everyone?''

⁴² The Lord said: "Who then is the faithful and sensible manager whom his master will put in charge of his household servants to give them their allotted food at the proper time? ⁴³ Blessed is that slave whom his master, when he comes, will find at work.ᵃ ⁴⁴ I tell you the truth: he will put him in charge of all his possessions. ⁴⁵ But if that slave says in his heart, 'My master is delaying his coming,' and starts to beat the male and female slaves, and to eat and drink and get drunk, ⁴⁶ that slave's master will come on a day he does not expect him, and at an hour he does not know. He will cut him to piecesᵇ and assign him a place with the unbelievers.ᶜ ⁴⁷ And that slave who knew his master's will, and didn't prepare himself or do it,ᵈ will be severely beaten. ⁴⁸ But the one who did not know, and did things deserving of blows, will be beaten lightly. Much will be required of everyone who has been given much. And even more will be expected of the one who has been entrusted with more.ᵉ

NOT PEACE BUT DIVISION

⁴⁹ "I came to bring fire on the earth, and how I wish it were already set ablaze! ⁵⁰ But I have a baptism to be baptized with, and how it consumes Me until it is finished! ⁵¹ Do you think that I came here to give peace to the earth? No, I tell you, but rather division! ⁵² From now on, five in one household will be divided: three against two, and two against three.

⁵³ They will be divided, father against son,
son against father,
mother against daughter,
daughter against mother,

God Gives So That We Can Pour Out

Are you trying to serve God and yet ignore something He has told you to do? Are you living your life as if God does not notice your disobedience? Do you apply God's standards to yourself as rigorously as you apply them to others?

"Much will be required of everyone who has been given much. And even more will be expected of the one who has been entrusted with more."

—Luke 12:48b

ᵃ12:43 Lit *find doing so*
ᵇ12:46 Lit *him in two*
ᶜ12:46 Or *unfaithful;* or *untrustworthy*
ᵈ12:47 Lit *do toward his will*
ᵉ12:48 Or *much*

mother-in-law against her daughter-in-law,
and daughter-in-law against
mother-in-law."[a]

INTERPRETING THE TIME

[54] He also said to the crowds: "When you see a cloud
rising in the west, right away you say, 'A storm is coming,' and so it does. [55] And when the south wind is blow-
ing, you say, 'It's going to be a scorcher!' and it is.
[56] Hypocrites! You know how to interpret the appearance of the earth and the sky, but why don't you know
how to interpret this time?

SETTLING ACCOUNTS

[57] "Why don't you judge for yourselves what is right?
[58] As you are going with your adversary to the ruler,
make an effort to settle with him on the way. Then he
won't drag you before the judge, the judge hand you
over to the bailiff, and the bailiff throw you into prison.
[59] I tell you, you will never get out of there until you
have paid the last cent."[b]

REPENT OR PERISH

13 At that time, some people came and reported to
Him about the Galileans whose blood Pilate had
mixed with their sacrifices. [2] And He[1] responded to
them, "Do you think that these Galileans were more sinful than all Galileans because they suffered these things?
[3] No, I tell you; but unless you repent, you will all perish as well! [4] Or those eighteen that the tower in Siloam
fell on and killed—do you think they were more sinful
than all the people who live in Jerusalem? [5] No, I tell
you; but unless you repent, you will all perish as well!"

THE PARABLE OF THE BARREN FIG TREE

[6] And He told this parable: "A man had a fig tree that
was planted in his vineyard. He came looking for fruit
on it and found none. [7] He told the vineyard worker, 'Lis-

God Will Help You Learn to Discern

God does not want you to merely gain
intellectual knowledge of truth. He
wants you to experience His truth.

*"Hypocrites! You know how to
interpret the appearance of the
earth and the sky, but why don't
you know how to interpret this
time?"*

—Luke 12:56

[1] 13:2 Other mss read *Jesus*

[a] 12:53 Mc 7:6

[b] 12:59 Gk *lepton*, the smallest and
least valuable copper coin in use

WORD STUDY

Greek word: **Satanas**
[sah tahn AHSS]

Translation: **Satan**

Uses in Luke's Gospel: **5**
(Mt, 4; Mk, 6; Jn, 1)

Uses in Luke's Writings: **7**

Uses in the NT: **36**

Key passage: **Luke 13:16**

The Greek word *satanas* comes from the Hebrew term *satan*, meaning *adversary, one who opposes another*, and the related Hebrew verb meaning *to withstand, accuse*. The Bible teaches that the adversary or arch enemy of God and His people is Satan, who is mentioned a few times in the OT (1 Ch 21:1; several times in Jb 1—2; Zch 3:1–2) but receives much greater prominence in the NT. The Greek word *diabolos,* meaning *slanderer,* is used 34 times in the NT to refer to this same spirit being as *the Devil.* (Three times *diabolos* is used in the plural with the general meaning *gossips* or *slanderers;* see 1 Tm 3:1; 2 Tm 3:3; Ti 2:3). Satan is the leader of the fallen angels or demons, who assist him in attempting to thwart and destroy God's plans and His people through tempting (Lk 4:1–11; 1 Co 7:5), possessing (Lk 4:31–37; 8:26–39; Jn 13:27), deceiving (Rv 12:9), and afflicting them with illness (Lk 11:14; 13:10–17). The final defeat and judgment of "the dragon, the old snake, who is the Devil and Satan" is described in Revelation 20:1–10 (see v. 2).

ten, for three years I have come looking for fruit on this fig tree and haven't found any. Cut it down! Why should it even waste the soil?'

8 "But he replied to him, 'Sir,[a] leave it this year also, until I dig around it and fertilize it. 9 Perhaps it will bear fruit next year, but if not, you can cut it down.' "

HEALING A DAUGHTER OF ABRAHAM

10 As He was teaching in one of the synagogues on the Sabbath, 11 a woman was there who had been disabled by a spirit[b] for over eighteen years. She was bent over and could not straighten up at all.[c] 12 When Jesus saw her, He called out to her,[d] "Woman, you are free of your disability." 13 Then He laid His hands on her, and instantly she was restored and began to glorify God.

14 But the leader of the synagogue, indignant because Jesus had healed on the Sabbath, responded by telling the crowd, "There are six days when work should be done; therefore come on those days and be healed, and not on the Sabbath day."

15 But the Lord answered him and said, "Hypocrites! Doesn't each one of you untie his ox or donkey from the manger on the Sabbath, and lead it to water? 16 And this woman, a daughter of Abraham, whom Satan has bound for eighteen years—shouldn't she be untied from this bondage on the Sabbath day?"

17 When He had said these things, all His adversaries were humiliated,[e] but the whole crowd was rejoicing over all the glorious things He was doing.

THE PARABLES OF THE MUSTARD SEED AND OF THE YEAST

18 He said therefore, "What is the kingdom of God like, and to what should I compare it? 19 It's like a mustard seed that a man took and sowed in his garden. It grew and became a tree, and the birds of the sky nested in its branches."

20 Again He said, "To what should I compare the king-

---

[a]13:8 Or *Lord*
[b]13:11 Lit *had a spirit of disability*
[c]13:11 Or *straighten up completely*

[d]13:12 Or *He summoned her*
[e]13:17 Is 45:16

dom of God? [21] It's like yeast that a woman took and mixed into fifty pounds[a] of flour until it spread through the entire mixture."[b]

THE NARROW WAY

[22] He went through one town and village after another, teaching and making His way to Jerusalem. [23] "Lord," someone asked Him, "are there few being saved?"[c]

He said to them, [24] "Make every effort to enter through the narrow door, because I tell you, many will try to enter and won't be able [25] once the homeowner gets up and shuts the door. Then you will stand[d] outside and knock on the door, saying, 'Lord, open up for us!' He will answer you, 'I don't know you or where you're from.' [26] Then you will say,[e] 'We ate and drank in Your presence, and You taught in our streets!' [27] But He will say, 'I tell you, I don't know you or where you're from. Get away from Me, all you workers of unrighteousness!' [28] There will be weeping and gnashing of teeth in that place, when you see Abraham, Isaac, Jacob, and all the prophets in the kingdom of God, but yourselves thrown out. [29] They will come from east and west, from north and south, and recline at the table in the kingdom of God. [30] Note this: some are last who will be first, and some are first who will be last."

JESUS AND HEROD ANTIPAS

[31] At that time some Pharisees came and told Him, "Go, get out of here! Herod wants to kill You!"

[32] And He said to them, "Go tell that fox, 'Look! I'm driving out demons and performing healings today and tomorrow, and on the third day[f] I will complete My work.'[g] [33] Yet I must travel today, tomorrow, and the next day, because it is not possible for a prophet to perish outside of Jerusalem!

Learn the Everlasting Value of Service

The world will estimate your importance by the number of people serving you. God is more concerned with the number of people you are serving.

"Note this: some are last who will be first, and some are first who will be last."

—Luke 13:30

---

[a]**13:21** Lit *into three sata;* about forty quarts
[b]**13:21** Or *until all of it was leavened*
[c]**13:23** Or *are the saved few* (in number); lit *are those being saved few*
[d]**13:25** Lit *you will begin to stand*
[e]**13:26** Lit *you will begin to say*
[f]**13:32** That is, *very shortly*
[g]**13:32** Lit *I will be finished*

JESUS' LAMENTATION OVER JERUSALEM

[34] "O Jerusalem! Jerusalem! The city who kills the prophets and stones those who are sent to her! How often I wanted to gather your children together, as a hen gathers her chicks under her wings, but you were not willing! [35] See! Your house[a] is abandoned to you. And I tell you, you will not see Me until the time comes when you say, **'Blessed is He who comes in the name of the Lord'**!"[b]

A SABBATH CONTROVERSY

14 One Sabbath, when He went to eat[c] at the house of one of the leading Pharisees, they were watching Him closely. [2] There in front of Him was a man whose body was swollen with fluid.[d] [3] In response, Jesus asked the law experts and the Pharisees, "Is it lawful to heal on the Sabbath or not?" [4] But they kept silent. He took the man, healed him, and sent him away. [5] And to them, He said, "Which of you whose son or ox falls into a well, will not immediately pull him out on the Sabbath day?" [6] To this they could find no answer.

TEACHINGS ON HUMILITY

[7] He told a parable to those who were invited, when He noticed how they would choose the best places for themselves: [8] "When you are invited by someone to a wedding banquet, don't recline at the best place, because a more distinguished person than you may have been invited by your host.[e] [9] The one who invited both of you may come and say to you, 'Give your place to this man,' and then in humiliation, you will proceed to take the lowest place.

[10] "But when you are invited, go and recline in the lowest place, so that when the one who invited you comes, he will say to you, 'Friend, move up higher.' You will then be honored in the presence of all the other guests. [11] For everyone who exalts himself will be humbled, and the one who humbles himself will be exalted."

[12] He also said to the one who had invited Him,

You Need His Word, Not Just His OK

Do not look for how God is going to bless your church. Look for how God is going to reveal Himself to accomplish His purposes.

"For everyone who exalts himself will be humbled, and the one who humbles himself will be exalted."

—Luke 14:11

---

[a]13:35 Probably the temple (Jr 12:7; 22:5)
[b]13:35 Ps 118:26
[c]14:1 Lit *eat bread;* that is, eat a meal
[d]14:2 That is, afflicted with dropsy or edema
[e]14:8 Lit *by him*

"When you give a lunch or a dinner, don't invite your friends, your brothers, your relatives, or your rich neighbors, because they might invite you back, and you would be repaid. [13] On the contrary, when you host a banquet, invite those who are poor, maimed, lame, or blind. [14] And you will be blessed, because they cannot repay you; for you will be repaid at the resurrection of the righteous."

THE PARABLE OF THE LARGE BANQUET

[15] When one of those who reclined at the table with Him heard these things, he said to Him, "Blessed is the one who will eat bread in the kingdom of God!"

[16] Then He told him: "A man was giving a large banquet and invited many. [17] At the time of the banquet, he sent his slave to tell those who were invited, 'Come, because everything is now ready.'

[18] "But without exception[a] they all began to make excuses. The first one said to him, 'I have bought a field, and I must go out and see it. I ask you to excuse me.'

[19] "Another said, 'I have bought five yoke of oxen, and I'm going to try them out. I ask you to excuse me.'

[20] "And another said, 'I just got married,[b] and therefore I'm unable to come.'

[21] "So the slave came back and reported these things to his master. Then in anger, the master of the house told his slave, 'Go out quickly into the streets and alleys of the city, and bring in here the poor, maimed, blind, and lame!'

[22] " 'Master,' the slave said, 'what you ordered has been done, and there's still room.'

[23] "Then the master told the slave, 'Go out into the highways and lanes and make them come in, so that my house may be filled. [24] For I tell you, not one of those men who were invited will enjoy my banquet!' "

THE COST OF FOLLOWING JESUS

[25] Now great crowds were traveling with Him. So He turned and said to them: [26] "If anyone comes to Me and does not hate his own father and mother, wife and children, brothers and sisters—yes, and even his own life—

WORD STUDY

Greek word: *miseo* [mih SEH oh]

Translation: *hate*

Uses in Luke's Gospel: **7** (Mt, 5; Mk, 1; Jn, 7)

Uses in the NT: **40**

Key passage: **Luke 14:26**

The Greek verb *miseo* is the basic word meaning *to hate,* the exact antonym of *love* (*agapao;* see the word study on page 165). The essence of love is caring more about others than about self, even to the point of great sacrifice—including death (Jn 15:13). Hate, on the other hand, is the opposite; it cares little or nothing about others and actually wishes them harm or even death (Mt 24:9).

With only one exception (Lk 1:71), *miseo* in the Gospels is always used by Jesus. By far the most difficult occurrence of *miseo* is Luke 14:26—difficult both to understand and to practice. In this passage Jesus seems to demand hatred, even toward one's parents, wife, children, and siblings—those whom we are specifically told elsewhere in Scripture to honor, protect, and love! Jesus' statement is best understood as the willingness to choose Him above all else. The context is Jesus' challenge to measure the cost of being His disciple (see 14:27-35). He warned those who were following Him (see v. 25) that continuing to do so might cost them their lives (v. 27) or perhaps their possessions (v. 33; see Lk 16:13). Therefore, Jesus' disciples must be willing to give up their most important earthly relationships—their own families—if these relationships stand in the way of following Him.

---

[a]**14:18** Lit *But from one* (voice)   [b]**14:20** Lit *I have married a woman*

WORD STUDY

Greek word: **metanoeo**
[meh tuh nah EH oh]

Translation: **repent**

Uses in Luke's Gospel: **9**
(Mt, 5; Mk, 2)

Uses in Luke's writings: **14**

Uses in the NT: **34**

Key passage: **Luke 15:7**

The Greek verb for *repent (meta-noeo)* and the related noun for *repentance (metanoia)* signify *a change of mind (meta,* meaning *after* or *change;* and *nous,* meaning *mind).* More than just an intellectual change of mind is in view; rather, both terms refer to a change in one's way of thinking that results in different beliefs and a change in the direction of one's life. The verb *pisteuo* (meaning *believe;* see the word study on page 227) is much more common than *metanoeo,* though both words refer to concepts foundational to salvation (Mt 4:17; Lk 15:7,10; Jn 3:16). *Repent* and *believe* may be understood as opposite sides of the same coin. *Repent* means to turn from one's allegiance to sin and unbelief, whereas *believe* means to place one's trust in Christ. Thus, when one is mentioned the other is implied. John's Gospel and his three Epistles never use *repent* or *repentance,* but *believe* occurs numerous times. On one occasion in the NT, *repent* and *believe* are used together for emphasis (Mk 1:15); similarly, *repentance* and *faith* occur together only once (Ac 20:21).

he cannot be My disciple. [27] Whoever does not bear his own cross and come after Me cannot be My disciple.

[28] "For which of you, wanting to build a tower, doesn't first sit down and calculate the cost, to see if he has enough to complete it? [29] Otherwise, after he has laid the foundation, and cannot finish it, all the onlookers will begin to make fun of him, [30] saying, 'This man started to build and wasn't able to finish.'

[31] "Or what king, going to war against another king, will not first sit down and decide if he is able with ten thousand to oppose the one who comes against him with twenty thousand? [32] If not, while the other is still far off, he sends a delegation and asks for terms of peace. [33] In the same way, therefore, every one of you who does not say goodbye[a] to all his possessions cannot be My disciple.

[34] "Now, salt is good, but if salt should lose its taste, how will it be made salty? [35] It isn't fit for the soil or for the manure pile; they throw it out. Anyone who has ears to hear should listen!"

THE PARABLE OF THE LOST SHEEP

15 All the tax collectors and sinners were drawing near to listen to Him. [2] And the Pharisees and scribes were complaining, "This man welcomes sinners and eats with them!"

[3] So He told them this parable: [4] "What man among you, who has a hundred sheep and loses one of them, does not leave the ninety-nine in the open field[b] and go after the lost one until he finds it? [5] When he has found it, he joyfully puts it on his shoulders, [6] and coming home, he calls his friends and neighbors together, saying to them, 'Rejoice with me, because I have found my lost sheep!' [7] I tell you, in the same way, there will be more joy in heaven over one sinner who repents than over ninety-nine righteous people who don't need repentance.

THE PARABLE OF THE LOST COIN

[8] "Or what woman who has ten silver coins,[c] if she loses one coin, does not light a lamp, sweep the house,

---

[a]**14:33** Or *does not renounce* or *leave*
[b]**15:4** Or *wilderness*

[c]**15:8** Gk *ten drachmas.* A silver coin equal to a denarius and, at one time, a day's wage

and search carefully until she finds it? [9] When she finds it, she calls her women friends and neighbors together, saying, 'Rejoice with me, because I have found the silver coin I lost!' [10] I tell you, in the same way, there is joy in the presence of God's angels over one sinner who repents."

THE PARABLE OF THE LOST SON

[11] He also said: "A man had two sons. [12] The younger of them said to his father, 'Father, give me the share of the estate I have coming to me.' So he distributed the assets[a] to them. [13] Not many days later, the younger son gathered together all he had and traveled to a distant country, where he squandered his estate in foolish living. [14] After he had spent everything, a severe famine struck that country, and he had nothing.[b] [15] Then he went to work for[c] one of the citizens of that country, who sent him into his fields to feed pigs. [16] He longed to eat his fill from[1] the carob pods[d] the pigs were eating, and no one would give him any. [17] But when he came to his senses,[e] he said, 'How many of my father's hired hands have more than enough food,[f] and here I am dying[g] of hunger![h] [18] I'll get up, go to my father, and say to him, "Father, I have sinned against heaven and in your sight. [19] I'm no longer worthy to be called your son. Make me like one of your hired hands."' [20] So he got up and went to his father. But while the son[i] was still a long way off, his father saw him and was filled with compassion. He ran, threw his arms around his neck,[j] and kissed him. [21] The son said to him, 'Father, I have sinned against heaven and in your sight. I'm no longer worthy to be called your son.'

[22] "But the father told his slaves, 'Quick! Bring out the best robe and put it on him; put a ring on his finger[k] and sandals on his feet. [23] Then bring the fatted calf and slaughter it, and let's celebrate with a feast, [24] because

---

God's Work Will Be Filled with His Power

Our ways may seem good to us. We may even enjoy some moderate successes. But when we do the work of God in our own ways, we will never see the power of God in what we do.

"In the same way, therefore, every one of you who does not say goodbye to all his possessions cannot be My disciple."

—Luke 14:33

Accept Your Rightful Place Before the Father

When you come to God as His servant, He first wants you to allow Him to mold and shape you into the instrument of His choosing. Then He can take your life and put it where He wills and work through it to accomplish His purposes.

"I'll get up, go to my father, and say to him, 'Father, I have sinned against heaven and in your sight. I'm no longer worthy to be called your son. Make me like one of your hired hands.'"

—Luke 15:18–19

---

[1] **15:16** Other mss read *to fill his stomach with*

---

[a] **15:12** Lit *livelihood* or *living*
[b] **15:14** Lit *and he began to be in need*
[c] **15:15** Lit *went and joined with*
[d] **15:16** Seed casings of a tree used as food for cattle, pigs, and sometimes the poor
[e] **15:17** Lit *to himself*

[f] **15:17** Lit *bread*
[g] **15:17** *dying* is translated *lost* in vv. 4–9 and vv. 24,32
[h] **15:17** Or *dying in the famine* (v. 14)
[i] **15:20** Lit *while he*
[j] **15:20** Lit *He ran, fell on his neck*
[k] **15:22** Lit *hand*

WORD STUDY

Greek word: ***oikonomos***
[oy kah NAH mahss]

Translation: ***manager***

Uses in Luke's Gospel: **4**

Uses in the NT: **10**

Key passage: **Luke 16:1–8**

The noun *oikonomos* is one of several Greek words for a servant, but this term describes someone with significant prestige and responsibility (by contrast, see the word study on *doulos* on page 108). The term is a compound of two Greek words, *oikos,* meaning *house,* and *nomos,* meaning *law;* thus, an *oikonomos* is *the law of the house,* a manager, one who runs a household. The related noun *oikonomia* (English *economy*) means *stewardship, administration,* or *dispensation.*

An *oikonomos* was given responsibility to run certain affairs of the household for the master (*kurios,* see word study on page 189), and his duties could include cooking, housekeeping, accounting, estate management, or supervising children (see Gl 4:2), depending on the needs of the master. In both contexts that Jesus used the term *oikonomos,* the steward is specifically an accountant or treasurer (Lk 12:42; 16:1–8). On one occasion the term was used by Paul to describe a city official (Rm 16:23), but he also used it metaphorically in reference to those with responsibility in God's kingdom (1 Co 4:1–2; Ti 1:7; see 1 Pt 4:10).

this son of mine was dead and is alive again; he was lost and is found!' So they began to celebrate.

25 "Now his older son was in the field; as he came near the house, he heard music and dancing. 26 So he summoned one of the servants and asked what these things meant. 27 'Your brother is here,' he told him, 'and your father has slaughtered the fatted calf because he has him back safe and sound.'a

28 "Then he became angry and didn't want to go in. So his father came out and pleaded with him. 29 But he replied to his father, 'Look, I have been slaving many years for you, and I have never disobeyed your orders; yet you never gave me a young goat so I could celebrate with my friends. 30 But when this son of yours came, who has devoured your assetsb with prostitutes, you slaughtered the fatted calf for him.'

31 " 'Son,'c he said to him, 'you are always with me, and everything I have is yours. 32 But we had to celebrate and rejoice, because this brother of yours was dead and is alive again; he was lost and is found.' "

THE PARABLE OF THE DISHONEST MANAGER

16 He also said to the disciples: "There was a rich man who received an accusation that his manager was squandering his possessions. 2 So he called the managerd in and asked, 'What is this I hear about you? Give an account of your management, because you can no longer be my manager.'e

3 "Then the manager said to himself, 'What should I do, since my master is taking the management away from me? I'm not strong enough to dig; I'm ashamed to beg. 4 I know what I'll do so that when I'm removed from management, people will welcome me into their homes.'

5 "So he summoned each one of his master's debtors. 'How much do you owe my master?' he asked the first one.

6 " 'A hundred measures of oil,' he said.

" 'Take your invoice,' he told him, 'sit down quickly, and write fifty.'

---

a15:27 Lit *him back healthy*
b15:30 Lit *livelihood* or *living*
c15:31 Or *child*

d16:2 Lit *called him*
e16:2 *be my manager; my* implied

7 "Next he asked another, 'How much do you owe?'

" 'A hundred measures of wheat,' he said.

" 'Take your invoice,' he told him, 'and write eighty.'

8 "The master praised the unrighteous manager because he had acted astutely. For the sons of this age are more astute than the sons of light in dealing[a] with their own people.[b] 9 And I tell you, make friends for yourselves by means of the money[c] of unrighteousness, so that when it fails,[1] they may welcome you into eternal dwellings. 10 Whoever is faithful in very little is also faithful in much; and whoever is unrighteous in very little is also unrighteous in much. 11 So if you have not been faithful with the unrighteous money,[c] who will trust you with what is genuine? 12 And if you have not been faithful with what belongs to someone else, who will give you what is your own? 13 No servant[d] can be the slave of two masters, since either he will hate one and love the other, or he will be devoted to one and despise the other. You can't be slaves to both God and money."[c]

KINGDOM VALUES

14 The Pharisees, who were lovers of money, were listening to all these things and scoffing at Him. 15 And He told them: "You are the ones who justify yourselves in the sight of others, but God knows your hearts. For what is highly admired by people is revolting in God's sight.

16 "The Law and the Prophets were[e] until John; since then, the good news of the kingdom of God has been proclaimed, and everyone is strongly urged to enter it.[f] 17 But it is easier for heaven and earth to pass away than for one stroke of a letter in the law to drop out.

18 "Everyone who divorces his wife and marries another woman commits adultery, and everyone who marries a woman divorced from her husband commits adultery.

God Only Blesses What He Begins

We do not sit down and dream what we want to do for God and then call God in to help us accomplish it. The pattern in the Scripture is that we submit ourselves to God and we wait until God shows us what He is about to do, or we watch to see what God is doing around us and join Him.

And He told them: "You are the ones who justify yourselves in the sight of others, but God knows your hearts. For what is highly admired by people is revolting in God's sight."

—Luke 16:15

1 16:9 Other mss read *when you fail* or *pass away*

a 16:8 *in dealing* supplied for clarity
b 16:8 Lit *own generation*
c 16:9,11,13 Aramaic *mammon*
d 16:13 Or *household servant*

e 16:16 Perhaps *were proclaimed* or *were in effect*
f 16:16 Or *everyone is forcing his way into it*

THE RICH MAN AND LAZARUS

[19] "There was a rich man who would dress in purple and fine linen, feasting lavishly every day. [20] But at his gate was left a poor man named Lazarus, covered with sores. [21] He longed to be filled with what fell from the rich man's table, but instead the dogs would come and lick his sores. [22] One day the poor man died and was carried away by the angels to Abraham's side.[a] The rich man also died and was buried. [23] And being in torment in Hades,[b] he looked up and saw Abraham a long way off, with Lazarus at his side. [24] 'Father Abraham!' he called out, 'Have mercy on me and send Lazarus to dip the tip of his finger in water and cool my tongue, because I am in agony in this flame!'

[25] " 'Son,'[c] Abraham said, 'remember that during your life you received your good things, just as Lazarus received bad things; but now he is comforted here, while you are in agony. [26] Besides all this, a great chasm has been fixed between us and you, so that those who want to pass over from here to you cannot; neither can those from there cross over to us.'

[27] " 'Father,' he said, 'then I beg you to send him to my father's house— [28] because I have five brothers—to warn them, so they won't also come to this place of torment.'

[29] "But Abraham said, 'They have Moses and the prophets; they should listen to them.'

[30] " 'No, father Abraham,' he said. 'But if someone from the dead goes to them, they will repent.'

[31] "But he told him, 'If they don't listen to Moses and the prophets, they will not be persuaded if someone rises from the dead.' "

WARNINGS FROM JESUS

17 He said to His disciples, "Offenses[d] will certainly come,[e] but woe to him through whom they come! [2] It would be better for him if a millstone[f] were hung around his neck and he were thrown into the sea than for him to cause one of these little ones to stum-

---

Better to Have a Sensitive Heart Than the Art of Persuasion

People do not naturally seek God or pursue righteousness. Only as the Spirit awakens their hearts to the Person of Christ are they able to see God.

"But he told him, 'If they don't listen to Moses and the prophets, they will not be persuaded if someone rises from the dead.' "

—Luke 16:31

---

[a]16:22 Lit *the fold of a robe;* also *lap* or *bosom* (see Jn 13:23)
[b]16:23 The Gk word for the place of the dead corresponding to the Hb word *Sheol*
[c]16:25 Lit *Child*

[d]17:1 *Traps* or *Bait-sticks* or *Causes of stumbling* or *Causes of sin*
[e]17:1 Lit *It is impossible for offenses not to come*
[f]17:2 Large stone used for grinding grains into flour

ble.[a] [3] Be on your guard. If your brother sins,[1] rebuke him; and if he repents, forgive him. [4] And if he sins against you seven times in a day, and comes back to you seven times, saying, 'I repent,' you must forgive him."

FAITH AND DUTY

[5] The apostles said to the Lord, "Increase our faith."

[6] "If you have faith the size of[b] a mustard seed," the Lord said, "you could say to this mulberry tree, 'Be uprooted and planted in the sea,' and it would obey you.

[7] "Which one of you having a slave plowing or tending sheep, would say to him when he comes in from the field, 'Come at once and sit down to eat'? [8] Instead, would he not tell him, 'Prepare something for me to eat, get ready,[c] and serve me while I eat and drink; later you may eat and drink'? [9] Does he thank that slave because he did what was commanded?[2] [10] In the same way, when you have done all that you were commanded, you should say, 'We are good-for-nothing slaves; we've only done our duty.'"

THE TEN LEPERS

[11] While traveling to Jerusalem, He passed between[d] Samaria and Galilee. [12] As He entered a village, ten men with leprosy[e] met Him. They stood at a distance [13] and raised their voices, saying, "Jesus, Master, have mercy on us!"

[14] When He saw them, He told them, "Go and show yourselves to the priests." And while they were going, they were cleansed.

[15] But one of them, seeing that he was healed, returned and, with a loud voice, gave glory to God. [16] He fell on his face at His feet, thanking Him. And he was a Samaritan.[f]

[17] Then Jesus said, "Were not ten cleansed? Where are

Remember Who's in Charge Here

Adjusting your mind to the truth God has revealed to you is one step short of completion. You must also respond to the truth in obedience. Then you are free to experience a more complete relationship with God.

"In the same way, when you have done all that you were commanded, you should say, 'We are good-for-nothing slaves; we've only done our duty.'"

—Luke 17:10

Always Be Quick to Say "Thank You, God"

Thankfulness is foundational to the Christian life. Thankfulness is a conscious response that comes from looking beyond our blessings to their source.

Then Jesus said, "Were not ten cleansed? Where are the nine?"

—Luke 17:17

[1]**17:3** Other mss add *against you*
[2]**17:9** Other mss add *I don't think so*

---

[a]**17:2** Or *cause . . . to sin.* The Gk word *skandalizo* has no real Eng counterpart; "offend," "cause to sin," or "cause the downfall of" are common translations.
[b]**17:6** Lit *faith like*

[c]**17:8** Lit *eat, tuck in your robe* or *gird yourself*
[d]**17:11** Or *through the middle of*
[e]**17:12** See 5:12 note
[f]**17:16** See 9:52 note

WORD STUDY

Greek word: **pascho**
[PAHSS koh]

Translation: **suffer**

Uses in Luke's Gospel: **6**
(Mt, 4; Mk, 3)

Uses in Luke's Writings: **11**

Uses in the NT: **42**

Key passage: **Luke 17:25**

The Greek verb *pascho* was origi-nally used in reference to experi-encing something from an external source, whether good or bad. In the NT it is always used of negative experiences and thus means *to suffer.*

The sufferings of Jesus are prominent in the Gospels, Acts, and Hebrews, and in each case *pascho* refers to Jesus' Passion—His arrest, trial, and crucifixion (Mt 16:21 = Mk 8:31 = Lk 9:22; 17:25; 22:15; 24:26,46; Ac 1:3; 3:18; 17:3; Heb 2:18; 5:8; 9:26; 13:12). In the rest of the NT, be-lievers are the ones who suffer (2 Co 1:6; Php 1:29; 1 Th 2:14; 2 Th 1:5; 2 Tm 1:12; 1 Pt 4:19; 5:10; Rv 2:10), but they do so for Jesus' sake and with His example in mind (1 Pt 2:19-23; 3:14-18; 4:1).

the nine? [18] Didn't any return[a] to give glory to God except this foreigner?" [19] And He told him, "Get up and go on your way. Your faith has made you well."[b]

THE COMING OF THE KINGDOM

[20] Being asked by the Pharisees when the kingdom of God will come, He answered them, "The kingdom of God is not coming with something observable; [21] no one will say,[c] 'Look here!' or 'There!' For you see, the king-dom of God is among you."

[22] Then He told the disciples: "The days are coming when you will long to see one of the days of the Son of Man, but you won't see it. [23] They will say to you, 'Look there!' or 'Look here!' Don't follow or run after them. [24] For as the lightning flashes from horizon to horizon and lights up the sky, so the Son of Man will be in His day. [25] But first He must suffer many things and be rejected by this generation.

[26] "Just as it was in the days of Noah, so it will be in the days of the Son of Man: [27] people went on eating, drinking, marrying and giving in marriage until the day Noah boarded the ark, and the flood came and destroyed them all. [28] It will be the same as it was in the days of Lot: people went on eating, drinking, buying, selling, planting, building; [29] but on the day Lot left Sodom, fire and sulfur rained from heaven and destroyed them all. [30] It will be like that on the day the Son of Man is revealed. [31] On that day, a man on the housetop, whose belongings are in the house, must not come down to get them. And likewise the man who is in the field must not turn back. [32] Remember Lot's wife! [33] Whoever tries to make his life[d] secure[1e] will lose it, and whoever loses his life will preserve it. [34] I tell you, on that night two will be in one bed: one will be taken and the other will be left. [35] Two women will be grind-ing grain together: one will be taken and the other left."[2]

---

[1] 17:33 Other mss read *to save his life*
[2] 17:35 Other mss add v. 36: *Two will be in a field: one will be taken, and the other will be left.*

---

[a] 17:18 Lit *Were they not found re-turning to give glory*
[b] 17:19 Or *faith has saved you*

[c] 17:21 Lit *they will not say*
[d] 17:33 Or *soul*
[e] 17:33 Or *tries to retain his life*

[37] "Where, Lord?" they asked Him.

He said to them, "Where the corpse is, there also the vultures will be gathered."

THE PARABLE OF THE PERSISTENT WIDOW

18 He then told them a parable on the need for them to pray always and not become discouraged: [2] "There was a judge in one town who didn't fear God or respect man. [3] And a widow in that town kept coming to him, saying, 'Give me justice against my adversary.'

[4] "For a while he was unwilling; but later he said to himself, 'Even though I don't fear God or respect man, [5] yet because this widow keeps pestering me,[a] I will give her justice, so she doesn't wear me out by her persistent coming.'"

[6] Then the Lord said, "Listen to what the unjust judge says. [7] Will not God grant justice to His elect who cry out to Him day and night? Will He delay to help[b] them?[c] [8] I tell you that He will swiftly grant them justice. Nevertheless, when the Son of Man comes, will He find that faith[d] on earth?"

THE PARABLE OF THE PHARISEE AND THE TAX COLLECTOR

[9] He also told this parable to some who trusted in themselves that they were righteous and looked down on everyone else: [10] "Two men went up to the temple complex to pray, one a Pharisee and the other a tax collector. [11] The Pharisee took his stand[e] and was praying like this: 'God, I thank You that I'm not like other people[f]—greedy, unrighteous, adulterers, or even like this tax collector. [12] I fast twice a week; I give a tenth[g] of everything I get.'

[13] "But the tax collector, standing far off, would not even raise his eyes to heaven, but kept striking his chest[h]

---

[a] 18:5 Lit *widow causes me trouble*
[b] 18:7 *to help* inferred
[c] 18:7 Or *Will He put up with them?*
[d] 18:8 That is, the faith that persists in prayer for God's vindication. Other translations include: *faith,*

that kind of faith, any faith, the faith, and *faithfulness*
[e] 18:11 Or *Pharisee stood by himself*
[f] 18:11 Or *like the rest of men*
[g] 18:12 Or *give tithes*
[h] 18:13 That is, mourning

WORD STUDY

Greek word: ***telones***
[teh LOH nayss]
Translation: ***tax collector***
Uses in Luke's Gospel: **10** (Mt, 8; Mk, 3)
Uses in the NT: **21**
Key passage: **Luke 18:9–14**

The Greek noun *telones* was used in reference to various levels of tax collecting personnel. A similar term, *architelones,* meaning *chief tax collector,* is used only in Lk 19:2 in the NT and probably indicates that several lesser *telones* reported to Zacchaeus.

Since collecting taxes often involved working for the Romans, such tax collectors were regarded as traitors by the common Jewish people in Israel. Also, tax collectors of all kinds could take advantage of their position to accumulate wealth at the people's expense. For these reasons tax collectors were so despised that in the NT they are often juxtaposed with sinners (Mt 9:10,11; 11:19; Mk 2:15,16; Lk 5:30; 7:34; 15:1; see 18:11; see also the word study on *sinner* on page 238), unbelievers (Mt 18:17), and prostitutes (Mt 21:31,32)—those considered at the lowest level of society. Jesus challenged this line of thinking, and especially the thinking of the Jewish religious leaders, when He told the parable of the Pharisee and the tax collector (Lk 18:9–14). In this parable Jesus taught that God will save anyone who humbly casts himself on His mercy but that the self-righteous will not receive His mercy. By God's grace, society's outcasts can become kingdom citizens (see Mt 21:31–32).

and saying, 'O God, turn your wrath from me[a]—a sinner!' [14] I tell you, this one went down to his house justified rather than the other; because everyone who exalts himself will be humbled, but the one who humbles himself will be exalted."

BLESSING THE CHILDREN

[15] Some people[b] even were bringing infants to Him so He might touch them, but when the disciples saw it, they rebuked them. [16] Jesus, however, invited them: "Let the little children come to Me, and don't stop them, because the kingdom of God belongs to such as these. [17] I assure you: Whoever does not welcome the kingdom of God like a little child will never enter it."

THE RICH YOUNG RULER

[18] A ruler asked Him, "Good Teacher, what must I do to inherit eternal life?"

[19] "Why do you call Me good?" Jesus asked him. "No one is good but One—God. [20] You know the commandments:

> **Do not commit adultery; do not murder; do not steal; do not bear false witness; honor your father and mother!**"[c]

[21] "I have kept all these from my youth," he said.

[22] When Jesus heard this, He told him, "You still lack one thing: sell all that you have and distribute it to the poor, and you will have treasure in heaven. Then come, follow Me."

[23] After he heard this, he became extremely sad, because he was very rich.

POSSESSIONS AND THE KINGDOM

[24] Seeing that he became sad,[1] Jesus said, "How hard it is for those who have wealth to enter the kingdom of God! [25] For it is easier for a camel to go through the eye of a needle than for a rich person to enter the kingdom of God."

[1]**18:24** Other mss omit *he became sad*

---

[a]**18:13** Lit *O God, be propitious, that is, may your wrath be turned aside by the sacrifice*

[b]**18:15** Lit *They*
[c]**18:20** Ex 20:12–16; Dt 5:16–20

Humble Yourself—He Will Lift You Up

God wants us to adjust our lives to Him so He can do through us what He wants to do.

"I tell you, this one went down to his house justified rather than the other; because everyone who exalts himself will be humbled, but the one who humbles himself will be exalted."

—Luke 18:14

God's Work Will Get the World's Attention

The only way people will know what God is like is when they see Him at work.

Instantly he could see, and he began to follow Him, glorifying God. All the people, when they saw it, gave praise to God.

—Luke 18:43

^{26} Those who heard this asked, "Then who can be saved?"

^{27} He replied, "What is impossible with men is possible with God."

^{28} Then Peter said, "Look, we have left what we had and followed You."

^{29} So He said to them, "I assure you: There is no one who has left a house, wife or brothers, parents or children because of the kingdom of God, ^{30} who will not receive many times more at this time, and eternal life in the age to come."

THE THIRD PREDICTION OF HIS DEATH

^{31} Then He took the Twelve aside and told them, "Listen! We are going up to Jerusalem. Everything that is written through the prophets about the Son of Man will be accomplished. ^{32} For He will be handed over to the Gentiles, and He will be mocked, insulted, spit on; ^{33} and after they flog Him, they will kill Him, and He will rise on the third day."

^{34} They understood none of these things. This saying[a] was hidden from them, and they did not grasp what was said.

A BLIND MAN RECEIVES HIS SIGHT

^{35} As He drew near Jericho, a blind man was sitting by the road begging. ^{36} Hearing a crowd passing by, he inquired what this meant. ^{37} "Jesus the Nazarene is passing by," they told him.

^{38} So he called out, "Jesus, Son of David, have mercy on me!" ^{39} Then those in front told him to keep quiet,[b] but he was crying out all the more, "Son of David, have mercy on me!"

^{40} Jesus stopped and commanded that he be brought to Him. When he drew near, He asked him, ^{41} "What do you want Me to do for you?"

"Lord," he said, "I want to see!"

^{42} "Receive your sight!" Jesus told him. "Your faith has healed you."[c] ^{43} Instantly he could see, and he began to follow Him, glorifying God. All the people, when they saw it, gave praise to God.

[a] **18:34** That is, the meaning of the saying
[b] **18:39** Or *those in front rebuked him*
[c] **18:42** Or *has saved you*

WORD STUDY

Greek word: **kurios**
[KUHR ee ahss]
Translation: **Lord**
Uses in Luke's Gospel: **104**
(Mt, 80; Mk, 18; Jn, 52)
Uses in Luke's Writings: **211**
Uses in the NT: **717**
Key passage: **Luke 19:30–34**

The word *kurios* is the twenty-second most common word in the Greek NT and the third most common noun (after the words for "God" and "Jesus"). *Kurios* can mean *lord, master* (both with reference to either deity or humans), and even *sir* (see Jn 4:11; 5:7). In the Greek OT, however, *kurios* was used to translate two important Hebrew words: *Yahweh* (over six thousand times), the personal name for God (normally translated LORD or GOD); and *adonai* (over seven hundred times; over three hundred in reference to God), a title of respect and honor (normally translated *Lord/lord* or *Master/master*).

Thus, two important ideas from the OT carry over into the NT's use of *kurios:* deity and lordship. *Yahweh* is God and demands absolute loyalty to Himself as Master. The NT teaches that Jesus, God's Son, is deity and demands loyalty to Himself as absolute Lord—His deity being the basis of His lordship. Therefore, in the NT *kurios* emphasizes either the deity of Christ (Rm 10:9–13; see Jl 2:32) or His lordship (Mt 7:21–23; Lk 19:30–34; notice also the OT quotation in v. 38 using *kurios,* referring to deity). It is likely that the two ideas of deity and lordship are so closely intertwined that the NT writers often intended both of them (for example, see Php 2:11).

Just by being in the presence of Jesus, Zacch.'s entire life became re-oriented

JESUS VISITS ZACCHAEUS

19 He entered Jericho and was passing through. [2] There was a man named Zacchaeus who was a chief tax collector, and he was rich. [3] He was trying to see who Jesus was, but he was not able, in the crowd, because he was a short man. [4] So running ahead, he climbed up a sycamore tree to see Jesus,[a] since He was about to pass that way. [5] When Jesus came to the place, He looked up and said to him, "Zacchaeus, hurry and come down, because today I must stay at your house."

[6] So he quickly came down and welcomed Him joyfully. [7] All who saw it began to complain, "He's gone to lodge with a sinful man!"

[8] But Zacchaeus stood there and said to the Lord, "Look, I'll give[b] half of my possessions to the poor, Lord! And if I have extorted anything from anyone, I'll pay[b] back four times as much!"

[9] "Today salvation has come to this house," Jesus told him, "because he too is a son of Abraham. [10] For the Son of Man has come to seek and to save the lost."[c]

THE PARABLE OF THE TEN MINAS

[11] As they were listening to this, He went on to tell a parable, because He was near Jerusalem, and they thought the kingdom of God going to appear right away.

[12] Therefore He said: "A nobleman traveled to a far country to receive for himself authority to be king,[d] and then return; [13] and having called ten of his slaves, he gave them ten minas[e] and told them, 'Do business until I come back.'

[14] "But his subjects hated him and sent a delegation after him, saying, 'We don't want this man to rule over us!'

[15] "At his return, having received the authority to be king,[f] he summoned those slaves to whom he had given the money so that he could find out how much they had made in business. [16] The first came forward and said, 'Master, your mina has earned ten more minas.'[g]

You're Not Capable, You're Chosen

An ordinary person is the one God most likes to use.

When Jesus came to the place, He looked up and said to him, "Zacchaeus, hurry and come down, because today I must stay at your house."

—Luke 19:5

Let God Change Your Whole Way of Thinking

We must reorient our lives to God. We must learn to see things from His perspective. We must allow Him to develop His character in us. We must let Him reveal His thoughts to us. Only then can we get a proper perspective on life.

But Zacchaeus stood there and said to the Lord, "Look, I'll give half of my possessions to the poor, Lord! And if I have extorted anything from anyone, I'll pay back four times as much!"

—Luke 19:8

---

[a]19:4 Lit *Him*
[b]19:8 Or *I give . . . I pay*
[c]19:10 Or *save what was lost*
[d]19:12 Lit *to receive for himself a kingdom* or *sovereignty*
[e]19:13 Gk monetary unit worth about 100 days' wages
[f]19:15 See 19:12 note
[g]19:16 See 19:13 note

17 " 'Well done, good[a] slave!' he told him. 'Because you have been faithful in a very small matter, have authority over ten towns.'

18 "The second came and said, 'Master, your mina has made five minas.'

19 "So he said to him, 'You will be over five towns.'

20 "And another came and said, 'Master, here is your mina. I have kept it hidden away in a cloth 21 because I was afraid of you, for you're a tough man: you collect what you didn't deposit and reap what you didn't sow.'

22 "He told him, 'I will judge you by what you have said,[b] you evil slave! If[c] you knew I was a tough man, collecting what I didn't deposit and reaping what I didn't sow, 23 why didn't you put my money in the bank? And when I returned, I would have collected it with interest!' 24 So he said to those standing there, 'Take the mina away from him and give it to the one who has ten minas.'

25 "But they said to him, 'Master, he has ten minas.'

26 " 'I tell you, that to everyone who has, more will be given; and from the one who does not have, even what he does have will be taken away. 27 But bring here these enemies of mine, who did not want me to rule over them, and slaughter[d] them in my presence.' "

THE TRIUMPHAL ENTRY

28 When He had said these things, He went on ahead, going up to Jerusalem. 29 As He approached Bethphage and Bethany, at the place called the Mount of Olives, He sent two of the disciples 30 and said, "Go into the village ahead of you. As you enter it, you will find a young donkey tied there, on which no one has ever sat. Untie it and bring it here. 31 And if anyone asks you, 'Why are you untying it?' say this: 'The Lord needs it.' "

32 So those who were sent left and found it just as He had told them. 33 As they were untying the young donkey, its owners said to them, "Why are you untying the donkey?"

34 "The Lord needs it," they said. 35 Then they brought it to Jesus, and after throwing their robes on the donkey, they helped Jesus get on it. 36 As He was going along,

Always Be Willing to Start Small

Smaller assignments are always used by God to develop character. If God has a great assignment for you, He has to develop a great character to match.

" 'Well done, good slave!' he told him. 'Because you have been faithful in a very small matter, have authority over ten towns.' "

—Luke 19:17

---

[a]19:17 Or *capable*
[b]19:22 Lit *you out of your own mouth*
[c]19:22 *If* supplied for clarity
[d]19:27 Or *execute*

they were spreading their robes on the road. [37] Now He came near the path down the Mount of Olives, and the whole crowd of the disciples began to praise God joyfully with a loud voice for all the miracles they had seen:

[38] **"Blessed is the King who comes in the name of the Lord.**
Peace in heaven and glory in the highest heaven!"[a]

[39] And some of the Pharisees from the crowd told Him, "Teacher, rebuke Your disciples."

[40] He answered, "I tell you, if they were to keep silent, the stones would cry out!"

JESUS' LOVE FOR JERUSALEM

[41] As He approached and saw the city, He wept over it, [42] saying, "If you knew this day what leads[b] to peace—but now it is hidden from your eyes. [43] For the days will come upon you when your enemies will build an embankment against you, surround you, and hem you in on every side. [44] They will crush you and your children within you to the ground, and they will not leave one stone on another in you, because you did not recognize the time of your visitation."

CLEANSING THE TEMPLE COMPLEX

[45] He went into the temple complex and began to throw out those who were selling,[1] [46] and He said, "It is written, My house will be a house of prayer,' but you have made it 'a den of thieves'!"[c]

[47] Every day He was teaching in the temple complex. The chief priests, the scribes, and the leaders of the people were looking for a way to destroy Him, [48] but they could not find a way to do it, because all the people were spellbound by what they heard.[d]

[1]**19:45** Other mss add *and buying in it*

[a]**19:38** Ps 118:26; *the King* in Lk 19:38 is substituted for *He* in Ps 118:26
[b]**19:42** *leads* supplied for clarity
[c]**19:46** Is 56:7; Jr 7:11
[d]**19:48** Lit *people hung on what they heard*

Be Ready to Act at a Moment's Notice

As you follow Him, the time may come that your life and future may depend on your adjusting quickly to God's directives.

"They will crush you and your children within you to the ground, and they will not leave one stone on another in you, because you did not recognize the time of your visitation."

—Luke 19:44

THE AUTHORITY OF JESUS CHALLENGED

20 One day[a] as He was teaching the people in the temple complex and proclaiming the good news, the chief priests and the scribes, with the elders, came up ² and said to Him: "Tell us, by what authority are You doing these things? Who is it who gave You this authority?"

³ He answered them, "I will also ask you a question. Tell Me, ⁴ was the baptism of John from heaven or from men?"

⁵ They discussed it among themselves: "If we say, 'From heaven,' He will say, 'Why didn't you believe him?' ⁶ But if we say, 'From men,' all the people will stone us, because they are convinced that John was a prophet."

⁷ So they answered that they did not know its origin.[b]

⁸ And Jesus said to them, "Neither will I tell you by what authority I do these things."

THE PARABLE OF THE VINEYARD OWNER

⁹ Then He began to tell the people this parable: "A man planted a vineyard, leased it to tenant farmers, and went away for a long time. ¹⁰ At harvest time he sent a slave to the farmers so that they might give him some fruit from the vineyard. But the farmers beat him and sent him away empty-handed. ¹¹ He sent yet another slave, but they beat that one too, treated him shamefully, and sent him away empty-handed. ¹² And he sent yet a third, but they wounded this one too, and threw him out.

¹³ "Then the owner of the vineyard said, 'What should I do? I will send my beloved son. Perhaps[1] they will respect him.'

¹⁴ "But when the tenant farmers saw him, they discussed it among themselves and said, 'This is the heir. Let's kill him, so that the inheritance may be ours!' ¹⁵ So they threw him out of the vineyard and killed him.

"Therefore, what will the owner of the vineyard do to

¹20:13 Other mss add *when they see him*

ᵃ20:1 Lit *It happened on one of the days*   ᵇ20:7 Or *know where it was from*

WORD STUDY

Greek word: *hieron*
[hee eh RAHN]

Translation: *temple complex*

Uses in Luke's Gospel: **14**
(Mt, 11; Mk, 10; Jn, 11)

Uses in Luke's Writings: **39**

Uses in the NT: **72**

Key passage: **Luke 20:1**

The Greek noun *hieron* comes from an adjective meaning *sacred;* thus, *hieron* refers to *the* sacred place in Jewish life, the temple. The term refers to more than just the sanctuary that contained the furnishings of the tabernacle. This was normally designated *naos* in the NT, whereas *hieron* referred to the entire *temple complex* and included the sanctuary, at least four courtyards, numerous gates, and several covered walkways.

The *hieron* was the center of activity for Jewish life in Jerusalem, and several events in Jesus' life occurred there, particularly teaching and healing. The apostles in the early church followed Jesus' example by teaching at the *hieron* (twenty-five uses in Acts). The temple complex that Jesus and the apostles knew was essentially the one built by Zerubbabel after the Babylonian exile (completed about 515 B.C.) but greatly expanded and enhanced by Herod the Great (ruled 37–4 B.C.; reconstruction began about 20 B.C.). The building project was not complete until about A.D. 65, and just five years later it was destroyed by the Romans. No temple has been built since then, but three NT passages indicate that a temple will be in use in the end times (Mt 24:15 "the holy place" is part of the temple; 2 Th 2:4; Rv 11:1–2).

them? ¹⁶He will come and destroy those farmers and give the vineyard to others."

But when they heard this they said, "No—never!"

¹⁷But He looked at them and said, "Then what is the meaning of this Scripture:ᵃ

The stone that the builders rejected, this has become the cornerstone?ᵇ

¹⁸Everyone who falls on that stone will be broken to pieces, and if it falls on anyone, it will grind him to powder!"ᶜ

¹⁹Then the scribes and the chief priests looked for a way to get their hands on Him that very hour, because they knew He had told this parable against them, but they feared the people.

GOD AND CAESAR

²⁰Theyᵈ watched closely and sent spies who pretended to be righteous,ᵉ so they could catch Him in what He said,ᶠ to hand Him over to the governor's rule and authority. ²¹They questioned Him, "Teacher, we know that You speak and teach correctly, and You don't show partiality,ᵍ but teach the way of God in truth. ²²Is it lawful for us to pay taxes to Caesar or not?"

²³But detecting their craftiness, He said to them,¹ ²⁴"Show Me a denarius.ʰ Whose image and inscription does it have?"

"Caesar's," they said.

²⁵"Well then," He told them, "give back to Caesar the things that are Caesar's, and to God the things that are God's."

²⁶They were not able to catch Him in what He saidⁱ in public,ʲ and being amazed at His answer, they became silent.

¹20:23 Other mss add *Why are you testing Me?*

When God Breaks You, You Are Truly Whole

Righteousness is not to be taken lightly, nor is it easily attained. God does not give it to people indiscriminately. He gives it to those who know they cannot live without it.

"Everyone who falls on that stone will be broken to pieces, and if it falls on anyone, it will grind him to powder!"

—Luke 20:18

ᵃ20:17 Lit *What then is this that is written*
ᵇ20:17 Ps 118:22
ᶜ20:18 See Dn 2:44
ᵈ20:20 *They,* that is, the scribes and chief priests of v. 19
ᵉ20:20 Or *upright,* that is, loyal to God's law
ᶠ20:20 Lit *catch Him in* (a) *word*
ᵍ20:21 Lit *You don't receive a face*
ʰ20:24 The smallest silver coin, worth about a day's wages
ⁱ20:26 See 20:20 note
ʲ20:26 Lit *in front of the people*

THE SADDUCEES AND THE RESURRECTION

27 Some of the Sadducees, who say there is no resurrection, came up and questioned Him: 28 "Teacher, Moses wrote for us that **'if a man's brother dies,'** having a wife, and he **'is without children, his brother should take the wife and produce offspring**a **for his brother.'**b 29 Now there were seven brothers. The first took a wife, and died without children. 30 Also the second[1] 31 and the third took her. In the same way, all seven died and left no children. 32 Finally, the woman died too. 33 Therefore, in the resurrection, whose wife will the woman be? For all seven had married her."c

34 Jesus told them, "The childrend of this age marry and are given in marriage. 35 But those who are counted worthy to take part in that age, and the resurrection from the dead, neither marry nor are given in marriage. 36 For they cannot die anymore, because they are like angels and are childrene of God, since they are childrene of the resurrection. 37 But even Moses indicated in the passage about the burning bushf that the dead are raised, where he calls the Lord **'the God of Abraham and the God of Isaac and the God of Jacob.'**g 38 He is not God of the dead but of the living, because all are living toh Him."

39 Some of the scribes answered, "Teacher, You have spoken well." 40 And they no longer dared to ask Him anything.

THE QUESTION ABOUT THE MESSIAH

41 Then He said to them, "How can they say that the Messiah is the Son of David? 42 For David himself says in the Book of Psalms:

> **The Lord said to my Lord,**
> **'Sit at My right hand,**
> 43 **until I make Your enemies Your footstool.'**i

44 David, then, calls Him 'Lord;' so how is He his Son?"

God's Word Is All We Really Need to Hear

God always finishes what He begins. Even with the extremely complex assignment Jesus received from His Father, He could shout triumphantly from the cross, "It is finished!" When it's all said and done, God has the last word.

Some of the scribes answered, "Teacher, You have spoken well." And they no longer dared to ask Him anything.

—Luke 20:39-40

---

[1] 20:30 Other mss add *took her as wife, and he died without children*

---

a 20:28 Lit *produce a seed*
b 20:28 Dt 25:5
c 20:33 Lit *had her as wife*
d 20:34 Lit *sons*
e 20:36 Lit *sons*

f 20:37 Lit *indicated about the bush*
g 20:37 Ex 3:6,15
h 20:38 Or *with*
i 20:43 Ps 110:1

WARNING AGAINST THE SCRIBES

⁴⁵ While all the people were listening, He said to His disciples, ⁴⁶ "Beware of the scribes, who want to go around in long robes, and who love greetings in the marketplaces, the front seats in the synagogues, and the places of honor at banquets. ⁴⁷ They devour widows' houses, and say long prayers just for show. These will receive greater punishment."ᵃ

THE WIDOW'S GIFT

21 He looked up and saw the rich dropping their offerings into the temple treasury. ² He also saw a poor widow dropping in two tiny coins.ᵇ ³ "I tell you the truth," He said. "This poor widow has put in more than all of them. ⁴ For all these people have put in gifts out of their surplus, but she out of her poverty has put in all she had to live on."

DESTRUCTION OF THE TEMPLE PREDICTED

⁵ As some were talking about the temple complex, how it was adorned with beautiful stones and gifts dedicated to God,ᶜ He said, ⁶ "These things that you see—the days will come when not one stone will be left on another that will not be thrown down!"

SIGNS OF THE END OF THE AGE

⁷ "Teacher," they asked Him, "so when will these things be? And what will be the sign when these things are about to take place?"

⁸ Then He said, "Watch out that you are not deceived. For many will come in My name, saying, 'I am He,' and, 'The time is near.' Don't follow them. ⁹ When you hear of wars and rebellions,ᵈ don't be alarmed; because these things must take place first, but the end won't come right away."

¹⁰ Then He told them: "Nation will be raised up against nation, and kingdom against kingdom. ¹¹ There will be violent earthquakes, and famines and plagues in various places, and there will be terrifying sights and

---

Just Watch God Work. It'll Truly Amaze You.

He does not simply wait around in order to help us achieve our goals for Him! He comes to accomplish His own goals through us—and in His own way.

"Therefore make up your minds not to prepare your defense ahead of time, for I will give you such words and a wisdom that none of your adversaries will be able to resist or contradict."

—Luke 21:14–15

Be Willing to Wait, Eager to Learn

Waiting on Him is always worth the wait. You must depend on Him to guide you in His way and in His timing to accomplish His purpose.

"By your endurance gain your lives."

—Luke 21:19

ᵃ20:47 Or *judgment*
ᵇ21:2 See 12:59 note
ᶜ21:5 A gift given to the temple in fulfillment of a vow to God
ᵈ21:9 Or *insurrections* or *revolutions*

great signs from heaven. [12] But before all these things, they will lay their hands on you and persecute you. They will hand you over to the synagogues and prisons, and you will be brought before kings and governors because of My name. [13] It will lead to an opportunity for you to witness.[a] [14] Therefore make up your minds[b] not to prepare your defense ahead of time, [15] for I will give you such words[c] and a wisdom that none of your adversaries will be able to resist or contradict. [16] You will even be betrayed by parents, brothers, relatives, and friends; and they will kill some of you. [17] And you will be hated by all because of My name. [18] But not a hair of your head will be lost. [19] By your endurance gain[1] your lives.[d]

THE DESTRUCTION OF JERUSALEM

[20] "But when you see Jerusalem surrounded by armies, then know that its desolation has come near. [21] Then those in Judea must flee to the mountains! Those inside the city[e] must leave it, and those who are in the country must not enter it, [22] because these are days of vengeance to fulfill all the things that are written. [23] Woe to pregnant women and nursing mothers in those days, for there will be great distress in the land[f] and wrath against this people. [24] They will fall by the edge of the sword and be led captive into all the nations; and Jerusalem will be trampled by the Gentiles[g] until the times of the Gentiles are fulfilled.

THE COMING OF THE SON OF MAN

[25] "Then there will be signs in the sun, moon, and stars; and there will be anguish on the earth among nations, bewildered by the roaring sea and waves.[h] [26] People will faint from fear and expectation of the things that are coming on the world, because the celestial powers will be shaken. [27] Then they will see the Son of Man[i] coming in a cloud with power and great glory.

[1]21:19 Other mss read *you will gain*

---

[a]21:13 Lit *lead to a testimony for you*
[b]21:14 Lit *Therefore place (determine) in your hearts*
[c]21:15 Lit *a mouth*
[d]21:19 Or *souls*

[e]21:21 Lit *inside her*
[f]21:23 Or *the earth*
[g]21:24 Or *nations*
[h]21:25 See Ps 46:3; 65:7; Is 17:12; Jl 2:30–31
[i]21:27 See Dn 7:13

WORD STUDY

Greek word: *orge* [ohr GAY]

Translation: **wrath**

Uses in Luke's Gospel: **2** (Mt, 1; Mk, 1; Jn, 1)

Uses in the NT: **36**

Key passage: **Luke 21:23**

The most common Greek word in the NT to describe God's wrath is *orge,* normally translated *wrath* or *anger.* Only five occurrences of *orge* in the NT do not refer to God's wrath (Eph 4:31; Col 3:8; 1 Tm 2:8; Jms 1:19,20). Mark alone refers specifically to the *orge* ("anger") of Jesus (3:5); Matthew refers to God's *orge* once (3:7); and Luke does so twice (3:7; 21:23).

A three-fold dynamic exists as an expression of God's *orge:* (1) His wrath is a present reality for everyone who does not believe in His Son (Jn 3:36; Rm 1:18–32), but unbelievers do not recognize God's wrath when they see it; (2) His wrath on unbelievers will intensify as the day of Christ's return approaches (1 Th 5:9; Rv 6:16,17; 11:18; 16:19); and (3) the complete and final demonstration of His wrath is reserved for the time of Christ's personal presence on earth as King and Judge (Rv 14:10; 19:15).

While *orge* is an attribute of God, man's *orge* is rarely appropriate. (Eph 4:26 uses words related to *orge.*) Although Paul referred to the *orge* of God in Colossians 3:6, he followed this immediately with a command to rid ourselves of such things (v. 8). The reason for this is given in James— "human anger does not accomplish God's righteous standard" (1:20). Only God's wrath is always righteous.

28 But when these things begin to take place, stand up and lift up your heads, because your redemption is near!"

THE PARABLE OF THE FIG TREE

29 Then He told them a parable: "Look at the fig tree, and all the trees. 30 As soon as they put out leaves[a] you can see and know for yourselves that summer is already near. 31 In the same way, when you see these things happening, know[b] that the kingdom of God is near. 32 I assure you: This generation will certainly not pass away until all things take place. 33 Heaven and earth will pass away, but My words will never pass away.

THE NEED FOR WATCHFULNESS

34 "Be on your guard, that your minds are not dulled[c] from carousing,[d] drunkenness, and worries of life, and that day come on you unexpectedly 35 like a trap. For it will come on all who live on the face of the whole earth. 36 But be alert at all times, praying that you may have strength[1] to escape all these things that are going to take place, and to stand before the Son of Man."

37 During the day, He was teaching in the temple complex, but in the evening He would go out and spend the night on what is called the Mount of Olives. 38 Then all the people would come early in the morning to hear Him in the temple complex.

THE PLOT TO KILL JESUS

22 The Festival of Unleavened Bread,[e] which is called Passover,[f] was drawing near. 2 The chief priests and the scribes were looking for a way to put Him to death, because they were afraid of the people.

3 Then Satan entered Judas, called Iscariot, who was numbered among the Twelve. 4 He went away and discussed with the chief priests and temple police how he could hand Him over to them. 5 They were glad, and

---

God's Strength Will Keep You Standing

God's presence lights your path so that you can see impending danger, but the god of this age can distort your spiritual vision. Ask Christ to illuminate your life and let you clearly see the state of your spiritual condition.

"But be alert at all times, praying that you may have strength to escape all these things that are going to take place, and to stand before the Son of Man."

—Luke 21:36

---

[1] **21:36** Other mss read *you may be counted worthy*

---

[a] **21:30** *leaves* added for clarity
[b] **21:31** Or *you know*
[c] **21:34** Lit *your hearts are not weighed down*
[d] **21:34** Or *hangovers*

[e] **22:1** A seven-day festival celebrated in conjunction with the Passover (Ex 12:1–20)
[f] **22:1** The Jewish ritual meal celebrating Israel's deliverance from slavery in Egypt

agreed to give him silver.[a] [6] So he accepted the offer[b] and started looking for a good opportunity to betray Him to them when the crowd was not present.

PREPARATION FOR PASSOVER

[7] Then the Day of Unleavened Bread came, on which the Passover lamb had to be sacrificed. [8] Jesus[c] sent Peter and John, saying, "Go and prepare the Passover meal for us, so we may eat it."

[9] "Where do You want us to prepare it?" they asked Him.

[10] "Listen," He said to them, "when you've entered the city, a man carrying a water jug will meet you. Follow him into the house that he enters. [11] Tell the owner of the house, 'The Teacher asks you, "Where is the guest room, where I may eat the Passover with My disciples?"' [12] Then he will show you a large, furnished room upstairs. Make the preparations there."

[13] So they went and found it just as He had told them, and they prepared the Passover.

THE FIRST LORD'S SUPPER

[14] When the hour came, He reclined at the table, and the apostles with Him. [15] Then He said to them, "I have fervently desired to eat this Passover with you before I suffer. [16] For I tell you, I will not eat it again[1] until it is fulfilled in the kingdom of God." [17] Then He took a cup, and after giving thanks, He said, "Take this and share it among yourselves. [18] For I tell you, from now on I will not drink of the fruit of the vine until the kingdom of God comes."

[19] And He took bread, gave thanks, broke it, gave it to them, and said, "This is My body, which is given for you. Do this in remembrance of Me."

[20] In the same way He also took the cup after supper and said, "This cup is the new covenant in My blood, which is shed for you.[2] [21] But look, the hand of the one betraying Me is at the table with Me! [22] For the Son of

Take What He Gives and Go with That

God does not usually reveal all the details of His will at once. Instead, He tells you enough so you can implement what He said. You must continue to rely on His guidance.

"Listen," He said to them, "when you've entered the city, a man carrying a water jug will meet you. Follow him into the house that he enters."

—Luke 22:10

---

[1]22:16 Other mss omit *again*
[2]22:19,20 Other mss omit from v. 19b *which is given for you . . .* through the end of v. 20.

---

[a]22:5 Or *money;* Mt 26:15 specifies thirty pieces of silver. See Zch 11:12-13
[b]22:6 *the offer* supplied for clarity
[c]22:8 Lit *He*

Man will go away as it has been determined, but woe to that man by whom He is betrayed!"

23 So they began to argue among themselves which of them it could be who was going to do this thing.

THE DISPUTE OVER GREATNESS

24 Then a dispute also arose among them about who should be considered the greatest. 25 But He said to them, "The kings of the Gentiles dominate them, and those who have authority over them are called[a] 'Benefactors.'[b] 26 But it must not be like that among you. On the contrary, whoever is greatest among you must become like the youngest, and whoever leads, like the one serving. 27 For who is greater, the one at the table or the one serving? Isn't it the one at the table? But I am among you as the One who serves. 28 You are the ones who stood by Me in My trials. 29 I grant you a kingdom, just as My Father granted one to Me, 30 so that you may eat and drink at My table in My kingdom. And you will sit on thrones judging the twelve tribes of Israel.

PETER'S DENIAL PREDICTED

31 "Simon,[1] Simon, look out! Satan has asked to sift you[c] like wheat. 32 But I have prayed for you,[d] that your faith may not fail. And you, when you have turned back, strengthen your brothers."

33 "Lord," he told Him, "I'm ready to go with You both to prison and to death!"

34 "I tell you, Peter," He said, "the rooster will not crow today until[2] you deny three times that you know Me!"

MONEY-BAG, BACKPACK, AND SWORD

35 He also said to them, "When I sent you out without money-bag, backpack, or sandals, did you lack anything?"

"Not a thing," they said.

36 Then He said to them, "But now, whoever has a

Today Is Preparation Day for Tomorrow

Your life as a child of God ought to be shaped by the future (what you will be one day). God uses your present time to mold and shape your future usefulness here on earth and in eternity.

"Simon, Simon, look out! Satan has asked to sift you like wheat. But I have prayed for you, that your faith may not fail. And you, when you have turned back, strengthen your brothers."

—Luke 22:31–32

1 22:31 Other mss read *Then the Lord said, Simon, Simon*
2 22:34 Other mss read *before*

a 22:25 Or *them call themselves*
b 22:25 Title of honor given to those who benefited the public good
c 22:31 *you* is plural in Gk
d 22:32 *you* is singular in Gk

money-bag should take it, and also a backpack. And whoever doesn't have a sword should sell his robe and buy one. [37] For I tell you, what is written must be fulfilled in Me: '**And He was counted among the outlaws.**'[a] Yes, what is written about Me is coming to its fulfillment."

[38] "Lord," they said, "look, here are two swords." "Enough of that!"[b] He told them.

THE PRAYER IN THE GARDEN

[39] He went out and made His way as usual to the Mount of Olives, and the disciples also followed Him. [40] When He reached the place, He told them, "Pray that you may not enter into temptation." [41] Then He withdrew from them about a stone's throw, knelt down, and began to pray, [42] "Father, if You are willing, take this cup away from Me—nevertheless, not My will, but Yours, be done."

[43] Then an angel from heaven appeared to Him, strengthening Him. [44] Being in anguish, He prayed more fervently, and His sweat became like drops of blood falling to the ground.]¹ [45] When He got up from prayer and came to the disciples, He found them sleeping, exhausted from their grief.[c] [46] "Why are you sleeping?" He asked them. "Get up and pray, so that you may not enter into temptation."

THE JUDAS KISS

[47] While He was still speaking, suddenly a mob was there, and one of the Twelve named Judas was leading them. He came near Jesus to kiss Him, [48] but Jesus said to him, "Judas, are you betraying the Son of Man with a kiss?"

[49] When those around Him saw what was going to happen, they asked, "Lord, should we strike with the sword?" [50] Then one of them struck the high priest's slave and cut off his right ear.

[51] But Jesus responded, "No more of this!"[d] And touching his ear, He healed him. [52] Then Jesus said to the chief priests, temple police, and the elders who had come for

---

¹22:43-44 Other mss omit these verses

---

a22:37 Is 53:12
b22:38 Or *It is enough!*

c22:45 Lit *sleeping from grief*
d22:51 Lit *Permit as far as this*

WORD STUDY

Greek word: *peirasmos*
[pigh rahss MAHSS]
Translation: *temptation*
Uses in Luke's Gospel: **6**
(Mt, 2; Mk, 1)
Uses in Luke's Writings: **7**
Uses in the NT: **21**
Key passage: **Luke 22:28-46**

The Greek noun *peirasmos* means *temptation* or *trial* and is related to the verb *peirazo,* which means *to tempt.* In the NT these two terms are normally used in a negative sense, indicating that the temptation would be spiritually harmful if not resisted, though there are exceptions (see Heb 11:17; Rv 2:2). Twice the verb is used to describe Satan as "the tempter" (Mt 4:3; 1 Th 3:5), and Jesus was tempted by Satan (Lk 4:2) and by His enemies (Mt 19:3; 22:18,25; Lk 11:16; see Heb 2:18; 4:15) on several occasions. The verb *dokimazo* means *to test, prove,* or *approve,* and is similar to *peirazo* but normally has a positive connotation.

Jesus used the term *peirasmos* three times in Luke 22:28-46. In v. 28 Jesus commended His disciples for staying with Him during His various "trials," probably a reference to various attacks by Satan and the religious leaders during His ministry. In vv. 40,46 Jesus told the disciples to pray that they "may not enter into temptation." The time for Jesus' arrest, trial, and crucifixion had come, and the disciples' conduct during this crisis would reveal their spiritual maturity. The context indicates that two of the disciples in particular, Judas (vv. 47-53) and Peter (vv. 54-62), failed miserably.

Him, "Have you come out with swords and clubs as if I were a criminal?ª ⁵³ Every day while I was with you in the temple complex, you never laid a hand on Me. But this is your hour—and the dominion of darkness."

PETER DENIES HIS LORD

⁵⁴ They seized Him, led Him away, and brought Him into the high priest's house. Meanwhile Peter was following at a distance. ⁵⁵ When they had lit a fire in the middle of the courtyard and sat down together, Peter sat among them. ⁵⁶ When a servant saw him sitting in the firelight, and looked closely at him, she said, "This man was with Him too."

⁵⁷ But he denied it: "Woman, I don't know Him!"

⁵⁸ After a little while, someone else saw him and said, "You're one of them too!"

"Man, I am not!" Peter said.

⁵⁹ About an hour later, another kept insisting, "This man was certainly with Him, since he's also a Galilean."

⁶⁰ But Peter said, "Man, I don't know what you're talking about!" Immediately, while he was still speaking, a rooster crowed. ⁶¹ Then the Lord turned and looked at Peter. So Peter remembered the word of the Lord, how He had said to him, "Before the rooster crows today, you will deny Me three times." ⁶² And he went outside and wept bitterly.

JESUS MOCKED AND BEATEN

⁶³ The men who were holding Jesusᵇ started mocking and beating Him. ⁶⁴ After blindfolding Him, they kept¹ asking, "Prophesy! Who hit You?" ⁶⁵ And they were saying many other blasphemous things against Him.

JESUS FACES THE SANHEDRIN

⁶⁶ When daylight came, the eldersᶜ of the people, both the chief priests and the scribes, convened and brought Him before their Sanhedrin.ᵈ ⁶⁷ They said, "If You are the Messiah,ᵉ tell us."

Embrace the Love of the Father

God's very nature is love. Never in your life will God ever express His will toward you except that it is an expression of perfect love. God's kind of love always seeks the very best for a person.

Then the Lord turned and looked at Peter. So Peter remembered the word of the Lord, how He had said to him, "Before the rooster crows today, you will deny Me three times." And he went outside and wept bitterly.

—Luke 22:61–62

---

¹22:64 Other mss read *they kept striking Him on the face and*

ª22:52 Lit *as against a criminal*
ᵇ22:63 Lit *Him*
ᶜ22:66 Or *council of elders*
ᵈ22:66 The seventy-member supreme council of Judaism, patterned after Moses' seventy elders
ᵉ22:67 Or *the Christ*

But He said to them, "If I do tell you, you will not believe. [68] And if I ask you, you will not answer. [69] But from now on, the Son of Man will be seated at the right hand of the Power of God."[a]

[70] They all asked, "Are You, then, the Son of God?"

And He said to them, "You say that I am."

[71] "Why do we need any more testimony," they said, "since we've heard it ourselves from His mouth?"

JESUS FACES PILATE

23 Then their whole assembly rose up and brought Him before Pilate. [2] They began to accuse Him, saying, "We found this man subverting our nation, opposing payment of taxes to Caesar, and saying that He Himself is the Messiah, a King."

[3] So Pilate asked Him, "Are You the King of the Jews?"

He answered him, "You have said it."[b]

[4] Pilate then told the chief priests and the crowds, "I find no grounds for charging this man."

[5] But they kept insisting, "He stirs up the people, teaching throughout all Judea, from Galilee where He started even to here."

JESUS FACES HEROD ANTIPAS

[6] When Pilate heard this,[1] he asked if the man was a Galilean. [7] Finding that He was under Herod's jurisdiction, he sent Him to Herod, who was also in Jerusalem during those days. [8] Herod was very glad to see Jesus; for a long time he had wanted to see Him, because he had heard about Him and was hoping to see some miracle[c] performed by Him. [9] So he kept asking Him questions, but Jesus did not answer him. [10] The chief priests and the scribes stood by, vehemently accusing Him. [11] Then Herod, with his soldiers, treated Him with contempt, mocked Him, dressed Him in a brilliant robe, and sent Him back to Pilate. [12] That very day Herod and Pilate became friends.[d] Previously, they had been hostile toward each other.

[1]23:6 Other mss read *heard Galilee*

---

[a]22:69 Ps 110:1
[b]23:3 Or *That is true:* an affirmative oath
[c]23:8 Or *sign*
[d]23:12 Lit *friends with one another*

God Desires to Get People's Attention

People may choose to receive Christ or reject Him. But one thing is for sure: they cannot ignore Him forever.

But they kept insisting, "He stirs up the people, teaching throughout all Judea, from Galilee where He started even to here."

—Luke 23:5

JESUS OR BARABBAS

[13] Pilate called together the chief priests, the leaders, and the people, [14] and said to them, "You have brought me this man as one who subverts the people. But in fact, after examining Him in your presence, I have found no grounds to charge this man with those things you accuse Him of. [15] Neither has Herod, because he sent Him back to us. Clearly, He has done nothing to deserve death. [16] Therefore I will have Him whipped[a] and release Him." ⌐[17] For according to the festival he had to release someone to them.¬[1b]

[18] Then they all cried out together, "Take this man away! Release Barabbas to us!" [19] (He had been thrown into prison for a rebellion that had taken place in the city, and for murder.)

[20] Pilate, wanting to release Jesus, addressed them again, [21] but they kept shouting, "Crucify! Crucify Him!"

[22] A third time he said to them, "Why? What has this man done wrong? I have found in Him no grounds for the death penalty. Therefore I will have Him whipped[c] and release Him."

[23] But they kept up the pressure, demanding with loud voices that He be crucified. And their voices[2] won out. [24] So Pilate decided to grant their demand [25] and released the one they were asking for, who had been thrown into prison for rebellion and murder. But he handed Jesus over to their will.

THE WAY TO THE CROSS

[26] As they led Him away, they seized Simon, a Cyrenian, who was coming in from the country, and laid the cross on him to carry behind Jesus. [27] A great multitude of the people followed Him, including women who were mourning and lamenting Him. [28] But turning to them, Jesus said, "Daughters of Jerusalem, do not weep for Me, but weep for yourselves and your children. [29] Look, the days are coming when they will say,

Living God's Way Will Bring God Glory

When God accomplishes His purposes in His ways through us, people will come to know God. They will recognize that what has happened can only be explained by God. He will get glory to Himself!

Then Jesus said, "Father, forgive them, because they do not know what they are doing." And they divided His clothes and cast lots. The people stood watching . . .

—Luke 23:34–35a

Always Keep the Cross in Mind

I never look at circumstances without seeing them on the backdrop of the cross. That is where God clearly demonstrated once and for all time His deep love for me.

Then he said, "Jesus, remember me when You come into Your kingdom!" And He said to him, "I assure you: Today you will be with Me in paradise."

—Luke 23:42–43

---

[1] **23:17** Other mss omit this verse
[2] **23:23** Other mss add *and those of the chief priests*

---

[a] **23:16** Gk *paideuo;* to discipline or "teach a lesson" LXX 1 Kg 12:11,14; 2 Ch 10:11,14; perhaps a way of referring to the Roman scourging (the Latin *flagellatio*)
[b] **23:17** See Mt 27:15; Mk 15:6
[c] **23:22** See 23:16 note

'Blessed are the barren, the wombs that never bore, and the breasts that never nursed!' [30] Then they will begin **'to say to the mountains, "Fall on us!" and to the hills, "Cover us!" '**[a] [31] For if they do these things when the wood is green, what will happen when it is dry?"

CRUCIFIED BETWEEN TWO CRIMINALS

[32] Two others, both criminals, were also led away to be executed with Him. [33] When they arrived at the place called The Skull, they crucified Him there, along with the criminals, one on the right and one on the left. [34] Then Jesus said, "Father, forgive them, because they do not know what they are doing."[1] And they divided His clothes and cast lots.[b]

[35] The people stood watching, and even the leaders kept scoffing: "He saved others; let Him save Himself if this is God's Messiah, the Chosen One!" [36] The soldiers also mocked Him. They came offering Him sour wine,[c] [37] and said, "If You are the King of the Jews, save Yourself!"

[38] An inscription was above Him:[2]

> **THIS IS
> THE KING OF THE JEWS**

[39] Then one of the criminals hanging there began to yell insults at[d] Him: "Aren't You the Messiah? Save Yourself and us!"

[40] But the other answered, rebuking him: "Don't you even fear God, since you are undergoing the same punishment? [41] We are punished justly, because we're getting back what we deserve for the things we did, but this man has done nothing wrong." [42] Then he said, "Jesus, remember me[3] when You come into Your kingdom!"

[43] And He said to him, "I assure you: Today you will be with Me in paradise."

[1]**23:34** Other mss omit this sentence
[2]**23:38** Other mss add *written in Greek, Latin, and Hebrew letters*
[3]**23:42** Other mss add *Lord*

[a]**23:30** Hs 10:8
[b]**23:34** Ps 22:19
[c]**23:36** Ps 69:22 LXX
[d]**23:39** Or *to blaspheme*

WORD STUDY

Greek word: **paradeisos**
[pah RAH digh sahss]
Translation: **paradise**
Uses in Luke's Gospel: **1**
Uses in the NT: **3**
Key passage: **Luke 23:43**

The word "paradise" in Luke 23:43 is transliterated directly from the Greek word *paradeisos,* which occurs in only two other places in the NT. In the Greek world *paradeisos* could refer to a garden, a grove, or a park; thus, it is the word found in the Greek OT for the Garden of Eden (11 times in Gn 2—3). Luke 23:43 and 2 Corinthians 12:4 use *paradeisos* to refer to the place where God especially manifests His presence, which we call *heaven.* Revelation 2:7 refers to *paradeisos* as the place where believers (those who "conquer") eat from "the tree of life," which is in the new Jerusalem (see Rv 22:2,14,19).

THE DEATH OF JESUS

[44] It was now about noon,[a] and darkness came over the whole land[b] until three,[a] [45] because the sun's light failed.[1] The curtain of the sanctuary was split down the middle. [46] And Jesus called out with a loud voice, "Father, **'into Your hands I entrust My spirit.'**"[c] Saying this, He breathed His last.

[47] When the centurion[d] saw what happened, he began to glorify God, saying, "This man really was righteous!" [48] All the crowds that had gathered for this spectacle, when they saw what had taken place, went home, striking their chests.[e] [49] But all who knew Him, including the women who had followed Him from Galilee, stood at a distance, watching these things.

THE BURIAL OF JESUS

[50] There was a good and righteous man named Joseph, a member of the Sanhedrin,[f] [51] who had not agreed with their plan and action. He was from Arimathea, a Judean town, and was looking forward to the kingdom of God. [52] He approached Pilate and asked for Jesus' body. [53] Taking it down, he wrapped it in fine linen and placed it in a tomb cut into the rock, where no one had ever been placed.[g] [54] It was Preparation Day, and the Sabbath was about to begin.[h] [55] The women who had come with Him from Galilee followed along and observed the tomb and how His body was placed. [56] Then they returned and prepared spices and perfumes. And they rested on the Sabbath according to the commandment.

RESURRECTION MORNING

24 On the first day of the week, very early in the morning, they[2] came to the tomb, bringing the spices they had prepared. [2] They found the stone rolled away from the tomb. [3] They went in but did not find the body of the Lord Jesus. [4] While they were perplexed about this, suddenly two men stood by them in dazzling

Follow God, or Expect to Get Sidetracked

If you will respond to Him as Lord, He may lead you to do and be things you would never have dreamed. If you don't follow Him as Lord, you may lock yourself into a job or assignment and miss something God wants to do through you.

There was a good and righteous man named Joseph, a member of the Sanhedrin, who had not agreed with their plan and action. He was from Arimathea, a Judean town, and was looking forward to the kingdom of God. He approached Pilate and asked for Jesus' body.

—Luke 23:50–52

[1] 23:45 Other mss read *three, and the sun was darkened*
[2] 24:1 Other mss add *and other women with them*

[a] 23:44 Lit *about the sixth hour . . . ninth hour*
[b] 23:44 Or *earth*
[c] 23:46 Ps 31:5
[d] 23:47 See Mt 8:5 note
[e] 23:48 That is, mourning
[f] 23:50 See Mt 26:59 note
[g] 23:53 Or *interred* or *laid*
[h] 23:54 Lit *was dawning*. Not in the morning but at sundown Friday

clothes. [5] So the women[a] were terrified and bowed down to the ground.[b]

"Why are you looking for the living among the dead?" asked the men. [6] "He is not here, but He has been resurrected! Remember how He spoke to you when He was still in Galilee, [7] saying, 'The Son of Man must be betrayed into the hands of sinful men, be crucified, and rise on the third day'?" [8] And they remembered His words.

[9] Returning from the tomb, they reported all these things to the Eleven and to all the rest. [10] Mary Magdalene, Joanna, Mary the mother of James, and the other women with them were telling the apostles these things. [11] But these words seemed like nonsense to them, and they did not believe the women.[c] [12] Peter, however, got up and ran to the tomb. When he stooped to look in, he saw only the linen cloths.[1] So he went home, amazed at what had happened.

THE EMMAUS DISCIPLES

[13] Now that same day two of them were on their way to a village called[d] Emmaus, which was about seven miles[e] from Jerusalem. [14] Together they were discussing everything that had taken place. [15] And while they were discussing and arguing, Jesus Himself came near and began to walk along with them. [16] But they[f] were prevented from recognizing Him. [17] Then He asked them, "What is this dispute that you're having[g] with each other as you are walking?" And they stopped walking and looked[h] discouraged.

[18] The one named Cleopas answered Him, "Are You the only visitor in Jerusalem who doesn't know the things that happened there in these days?"

[19] "What things?" He asked them.

So they said to Him, "The things concerning Jesus the Nazarene, who was a Prophet powerful in action and speech before God and all the people, [20] and how our chief priests and leaders handed Him over to be sen-

Examine the Prevailing Patterns in Your Life

When God gets ready for you to take a new step or direction in His activity, it will be in sequence with what He has already been doing in your life.

"He is not here, but He has been resurrected! Remember how He spoke to you when He was still in Galilee, saying, 'The Son of Man must be betrayed into the hands of sinful men, be crucified, and rise on the third day'?" And they remembered His words.

—Luke 24:6–8

---

[1] 24:12 Other mss add *lying there*

---

[a] 24:5 Lit *So they*
[b] 24:5 Lit *and inclined their faces to the ground*
[c] 24:11 Lit *believe them*
[d] 24:13 Lit *village, which name is*

[e] 24:13 Lit *about sixty stadia*
[f] 24:16 Lit *their eyes*
[g] 24:17 Lit *What are these words that you are exchanging*
[h] 24:17 *walking and looked* supplied

tenced to death, and they crucified Him. ²¹But we were hoping that He was the One who was about to redeem Israel. Besides all this, it's the third day since these things happened. ²²Moreover, some women from our group astounded us. They arrived early at the tomb, ²³and when they didn't find His body, they came and reported that they had seen a vision of angels who said He was alive. ²⁴Some of those who were with us went to the tomb and found it just as the women had said, but they didn't see Him."

²⁵He said to them, "O how unwise and slow you are to believe in your hearts all that the prophets have spoken! ²⁶Didn't the Messiah have to suffer these things and enter into His glory?" ²⁷Then beginning with Moses and all the Prophets, He interpreted for them in all the Scriptures the things concerning Himself.

²⁸They came near the village where they were going, and He gave the impression that He was going farther. ²⁹But they urged Him: "Stay with us, because it's almost evening, and now the day is almost over." So He went in to stay with them.

³⁰It was as He reclined at the table with them that He took the bread, blessed and broke it, and gave it to them. ³¹Then their eyes were opened, and they recognized Him; but He disappeared from their sight. ³²So they said to each other, "Weren't our hearts ablaze within us while He was talking with us on the road and explaining the Scriptures to us?" ³³That very hour they got up and returned to Jerusalem, and found the Eleven and those with them gathered together, ³⁴who said,^a "The Lord has certainly been raised, and has appeared to Simon!" ³⁵Then they began to describe what had happened on the road, and how He was made known to them in the breaking of the bread.

THE REALITY OF THE RISEN JESUS

³⁶And as they were saying these things, He Himself stood among them. He said to them, "Peace to you!" ³⁷But they were startled and terrified, and thought they were seeing a ghost. ³⁸"Why are you troubled?" He asked them. "And why do doubts arise in your hearts? ³⁹Look at My hands and My feet, that it is I Myself!

---

^a24:34 Gk is specific that this refers to the Eleven and those with them

God's Word Reveals God's Ways

The Bible is designed to help you understand the ways of God. Then, when God starts to act in your life, you will recognize that it is God.

Then He opened their minds to understand the Scriptures.

—Luke 24:45

Worship While You Wait

Whenever you do not seem to be receiving assignments from God, focus on the love relationship and stay there until the assignment comes.

"And look, I am sending you what My Father promised. As for you, stay in the city until you are empowered from on high" . . . And they were continually in the temple complex blessing God.

—Luke 24:49,53

Touch Me and see, because a ghost does not have flesh and bones as you can see I have." [40] Having said this, He showed them His hands and feet. [41] But while they still could not believe[a] for joy, and they were amazed, He asked them, "Do you have anything here to eat?" [42] So they gave Him a piece of a broiled fish,[1] [43] and He took it and ate in their presence.

[44] Then He told them, "These are My words that I spoke to you while I was still with you, that everything written about Me in the Law of Moses, the Prophets, and the Psalms must be fulfilled." [45] Then He opened their minds to understand the Scriptures. [46] He also said to them, "This is what is written:[2] the Messiah would suffer and rise from the dead the third day, [47] and repentance for[3] forgiveness of sins would be proclaimed in His name to all the nations, beginning at Jerusalem. [48] You are witnesses of these things. [49] And look, I am sending you[b] what My Father promised. As for you, stay in the city[4] until you are empowered[c] from on high."

THE ASCENSION OF JESUS

[50] Then He led them out as far as Bethany, and lifting up His hands He blessed them. [51] And while He was blessing them, He left them and was carried up into heaven. [52] After worshiping Him, they returned to Jerusalem with great joy. [53] And they were continually in the temple complex blessing God.[5]

---

[1]24:42 Other mss add *and some honeycomb*
[2]24:46 Other mss add *and thus it was necessary*
[3]24:47 Other mss read *and*
[4]24:49 Other mss add *of Jerusalem*
[5]24:53 Other mss read *praising and blessing God. Amen*

---

[a]24:41 Or *they still disbelieved*   [c]24:49 Lit *clothed with power*
[b]24:49 Lit *upon you*

WORD STUDY

Greek word: ***eulogeo***
[yoo lah GEH oh]
Translation: ***bless***
Uses in Luke's Gospel: **13**
(Mt, 5; Mk, 5; Jn, 1)
Uses in Luke's Writings: **15**
Uses in the NT: **42**
Key passage: **Luke 24:50–53**

The English word *eulogy* comes from the Greek verb *eulogeo*, meaning *to bless* or *praise*. The term literally means *to speak well of* someone or something, and was commonly used with the meaning *to extol*, especially of pagan gods in secular literature. In the NT, however, *eulogeo* has a distinct OT flavor, for behind it is the Hebrew term *barak*, a verb also meaning *to bless*. Thus, NT usage follows the OT precedent and has two main ideas: first, to speak well of someone by calling on God to bless that person or by recognizing that He has already done so; and second, to speak well of God, that is, to praise or thank Him.

In Luke's Gospel various people call on God to bless others (1:42; 2:34) and to praise or thank God as well (1:64; 2:28; 9:16; 24:30). Jesus called on His disciples to bless those who curse them (6:28; see Rm 12:14). Luke's Gospel ends with a threefold use of *eulogeo*: Jesus blessed the disciples at the Ascension (Lk 24:50–51—which is reminiscent of Jacob's blessing of his sons just before his death, Gn 49:28), and as a result of all they had witnessed, the disciples praised God (v. 53).

Greek Word Studies

in the Gospel of John

THE GOSPEL OF

JOHN

PROLOGUE

1 In the beginning[a] was the Word,[b]
and the Word was with God,
and the Word was God.
[2] He was with God in the beginning.
[3] All things were created through Him,
and apart from Him not one thing was created
that has been created.[1c]
[4] In Him was life,
and that life was the light of men.
[5] That light shines in the darkness,
yet the darkness did not overcome[d] it.
[6] There was a man named John
who was sent from God.
[7] He came as a witness
to testify about the light,
so that all might believe through him.[e]
[8] He was not the light,
but he came to testify about the light.
[9] The true light, who gives light to everyone,
was coming into the world.[f]
[10] He was in the world,
and the world was created through Him,
yet the world did not know Him.

[1] 1:3–4 Other punctuation is possible: . . . *not one thing was created. What was created in Him was life*

[a] 1:1 Gn 1:1
[b] 1:1 *The Word* (Gk *Logos*) is a title for Jesus as the communication and the revealer of God the Father (see 1:14; Rv 19:13).
[c] 1:3 Col 1:16; Heb 1:3
[d] 1:5 Or *grasp, comprehend, overtake* (see 12:35)
[e] 1:7 Or *it* (the light)
[f] 1:9 Or *The true light who comes into the world gives light to everyone* or *The true light enlightens everyone coming into the world.*

WORD STUDY

Greek word: **logos** [LAH gahss]

Translation: **Word, word**

Uses in John's Gospel: **40**
(Mt, 33; Mk, 24; Lk, 32)

Uses in John's writings: **65**

Uses in the NT: **330**

Key passages: **John 1:1,14**

Like the related verb *lego (to speak),* the noun *logos* most often refers to either oral or written communication. It means *statement* or *report* in some contexts, but most often in John's Gospel (and in the NT in general) *logos* refers to God's Word (that is, the Old Testament) or to Jesus' words. Thus, the primary use of *logos* is to denote divine revelation in some form or another. John used the term in its most exalted sense when he personified *logos* to refer to Christ. The *Logos* eternally existed as God (the Son) and with God (the Father)—He was in fact the Creator (Jn 1:1–3)—but He became a human being (v. 14), Jesus of Nazareth, so that He could reveal the Father and His will for humanity (v. 18).

[11]He came to His own,
and His own people[a] did not receive Him.
[12]But to all who did receive Him,
He gave them the right to be[b] children of God,
to those who believe in His name,
[13]who were born,
not of blood,[c]
or of the will of the flesh,
or of the will of man,[d]
but of God.
[14]The Word became flesh[e]
and took up residence[f] among us.
We observed His glory,
the glory as the only[g] Son[h] from the Father,
full of grace and truth.
[15](John testified concerning Him and exclaimed,
"This was the One of whom I said,
'The One coming after me has surpassed me,
because He existed before me.'")
[16]For we have all received grace after grace
from His fullness.
[17]For the law was given through Moses;
grace and truth came through Jesus Christ.
[18]No one has ever seen God.[i]
The only[j] Son[1]—
the One who is at the Father's side[k]—
He has revealed Him.

[1]1:18 Other mss read *God*

---

[a]1:11 The same Gk adjective is used twice in this verse: the first refers to all that Jesus owned as Creator (*to His own*); the second refers to the Jews (*His own people*).

[b]1:12 Or *become*

[c]1:13 Lit *bloods.* The plural form of *blood* occurs only here in the New Testament. It may refer either to lineal descent (that is, blood from one's father and mother) or to the Old Testament sacrificial system (that is, the various blood sacrifices). Neither is the basis for birth into the family of God.

[d]1:13 Or *not of human lineage, or of human capacity, or of human volition.*

[e]1:14 The eternally existent Word (vv. 1–2) took on full humanity, but without sin (Heb 4:15).

[f]1:14 Lit *and tabernacled* or *and dwelt in a tent;* this word occurs only here in John. A related word, referring to the Feast of Tabernacles, occurs only in 7:2. See also Ex 40:34–38

[g]1:14 Or *only begotten* or *incomparable;* the Gk word could refer to someone's only child (Lk 7:12; 8:42; 9:38) or someone's special child (Heb 11:17).

[h]1:14 *Son* is implied from the reference to the Father and from Gk usage (see previous note).

[i]1:18 Since God is an infinite being, no one can see Him in His absolute essential nature (see Ex 33:18–23).

[j]1:18 See v. 14 note

[k]1:18 Lit *is in the bosom of the Father*

JOHN THE BAPTIST'S TESTIMONY

[19] This is John's testimony when the Jews[a] from Jerusalem sent priests and Levites to ask him, "Who are you?"

[20] He confessed and did not deny, declaring,[b] "I am not the Messiah."[c]

[21] "What then?" they asked him. "Are you Elijah?"

"I am not," he said.

"Are you the Prophet?"[d]

"No," he answered.

[22] "Who are you, then?" they asked. "We need to give an answer to those who sent us. What can you tell us about yourself?"

[23] He said, "I am **'A voice of one crying out in the wilderness: Make straight the way of the Lord'**[e]— just as Isaiah the prophet said."

[24] Now they had been sent from the Pharisees. [25] So they asked him, "Why then do you baptize if you aren't the Messiah,[f] or Elijah,[g] or the Prophet?"[h]

[26] "I baptize with[i] water," John answered them. "But among you stands Someone you don't know. [27] He is the One coming after me,[1] whose sandal strap I'm not worthy to untie."

[28] All this happened in Bethany[2] across the Jordan,[j] where John was baptizing.

THE LAMB OF GOD

[29] The next day John[k] saw Jesus coming toward him and said, "Here is the Lamb of God, who takes away the sin of the world! [30] This is the One I told you about: 'After me comes a man who has surpassed me, because He existed before me.' [31] I didn't know Him, but I came baptizing with[l] water so He might be revealed to Israel."

[32] And John testified, "I watched the Spirit descending from heaven like a dove, and He rested upon Him.

The Way to God's Will Is Through God's Son

Knowing God does not come through a program, a study, or a method. Knowing God comes through a relationship with a Person.

But to all who did receive Him, He gave them the right to be children of God, to those who believe in His name.

—John 1:12

He Must Increase, We Must Decrease

The call to salvation is a call to be on mission with Him. In this new relationship you move into a servant role with God as your Lord and Master.

"This is the One I told you about: 'After me comes a man who has surpassed me, because He existed before me.'"

—John 1:30

---

[1] 1:27 Some manuscripts add *who came before me*
[2] 1:28 Other mss read *in Bethabara*

---

[a] 1:19 In John *the Jews* usually indicates the Jewish authorities who led the nation.
[b] 1:20 Lit *he confessed*
[c] 1:20 See v. 41 note
[d] 1:21 Probably the Prophet mentioned in Dt 18:15
[e] 1:23 Is 40:3
[f] 1:25 See v. 41 note

[g] 1:25 Ml 4:5
[h] 1:25 Dt 18:15
[i] 1:26 Or *in*
[j] 1:28 Another Bethany was near Jerusalem (the home of Lazarus, Martha, and Mary; see 11:1).
[k] 1:29 Lit *he*
[l] 1:31 Or *in*

[33] I didn't know Him, but He[a] who sent me to baptize with[b] water told me, 'The One on whom you see the Spirit descending and resting—He is the One baptizing in[b] the Holy Spirit.' [34] I have seen and testified that He is the Son of God!"[1]

[35] Again the next day, John was standing with two of his disciples. [36] When he saw Jesus passing by, he said, "Look! The Lamb of God!"

[37] The two disciples heard him say this and followed Jesus. [38] When Jesus turned and noticed them following Him, He asked them, "What are you looking for?"

They said to Him, "Rabbi" (which means "Teacher"[c]), "where are you staying?"

[39] "Come and you'll see," He replied. So they went and saw where He was staying, and they stayed with Him that day. It was about ten in the morning.[d]

[40] Andrew, Simon Peter's brother, was one of the two who heard John and followed Him. [41] He first found his own brother Simon and told him, "We have found the Messiah!" (which means "Anointed One"[e]) [42] and brought him to Jesus.

When Jesus saw him, He said, "You are Simon, son of John.[2] You will be called Cephas"[f] (which means "Rock").

By Knowing God, You Can Help Others Know Him

People know us. They know what we can do. When they see things happen that can only be explained by God's involvement, they will come to know Him.

He first found his own brother Simon and told him, "We have found the Messiah!" (which means "Anointed One") and brought him to Jesus.

—John 1:41–42a

PHILIP AND NATHANAEL

[43] The next day He[g] decided to leave for Galilee. Jesus found Philip and told him, "Follow Me!"

[44] Now Philip was from Bethsaida, the hometown of

---

[1] **1:34** Other mss read *is the Chosen One of God*
[2] **1:42** Other mss read *Simon, son of Jonah*

---

[a] **1:33** *He* refers to God the Father, who gave John a sign to help him identify the Messiah. Vv. 32–34 indicate that John did not know that Jesus was the Messiah until the Spirit descended upon Him at His baptism.

[b] **1:33** Or *in*

[c] **1:38** *Rabbi* means *my great one* in Hb but was used of a recognized teacher of the Scriptures (1:49; 3:2; 4:31; 6:25; 9:2; 11:8); see *Rabbouni* in 20:16.

[d] **1:39** Lit *about the tenth hour.* Various methods of reckoning time were used in the ancient world. John probably used a different method from the other three Gospels. If John used the same method of time reckoning as the other three Gospels, the translation would be: *It was about four in the afternoon.*

[e] **1:41** In the New Testament the word *Messiah* translates the Gk word *Christos* ("Anointed One") except here and in 4:25, where it translates *Messias.*

[f] **1:42** *Cephas* is Aramaic for *rock* (Gk *petros,* the same word used for Peter's name, as in v. 40).

[g] **1:43** Or *he,* referring either to Peter (see v. 42) or Andrew (see vv. 40–41)

Andrew and Peter. [45] Philip found Nathanael[a] and told him, "We have found the One of whom Moses wrote in the law (and so did the prophets): Jesus the son of Joseph, from Nazareth!"

[46] "Can anything good come out of Nazareth?" Nathanael asked him.

"Come and see," Philip answered.

[47] Then Jesus saw Nathanael coming toward Him and said about him, "Here is a true Israelite in whom is no deceit."

[48] "How do you know me?" Nathanael asked.

"Before Philip called you, when you were under the fig tree, I saw you," Jesus answered.

[49] "Rabbi," Nathanael replied, "You are the Son of God! You are the King of Israel!"

[50] Jesus responded to him, "Do you believe only[b] because I told you I saw you under the fig tree? You will see[c] greater things than this." [51] Then He said, "I assure you:[d] You will see[e] heaven opened and the angels of God ascending and descending[f] upon the Son of Man."[g]

THE FIRST SIGN: TURNING WATER INTO WINE

2 On the third day a wedding took place in Cana of Galilee. Jesus' mother was there, and [2] Jesus and His disciples were invited to the wedding as well. [3] When the wine ran out, Jesus' mother told Him, "They don't have any wine."

[4] "What has this concern of yours to do with Me,[h] woman?"[i] Jesus asked. "My hour[j] has not yet come."

---

[a] 1:45 Probably the Bartholomew of the other Gospels and Acts
[b] 1:50 *only* added for clarity
[c] 1:50 *You* is singular in Gk and refers to Nathanael.
[d] 1:51 *I assure you* is lit *amen, amen I say to you.* The double form of *amen* is used only in John (25 times). The term *amen* transliterates a Hb word expressing affirmation (Dt 27:15; 1 Kg 1:36; Ps 106:48; Jr 28:6). Jesus used it to testify to the certainty and importance of His words (see Rv 3:14).
[e] 1:51 *You* is plural in Gk and refers to Nathanael and the other disciples.
[f] 1:51 Gn 28:12

[g] 1:51 The phrase *Son of Man* was Jesus' most common way to refer to Himself and comes from Dn 7:13–14.
[h] 2:4 Or *You and I see things differently;* lit *What to Me and to you?* (see Mt 8:29; Mk 1:24; 5:7; Lk 8:28; Jdg 11:12; 2 Sm 16:10; 19:22; 1 Kg 17:18; 2 Kg 3:13; 2 Cr 35:21)
[i] 2:4 The word *woman* was not a term of disrespect in Gk (see 4:21; 8:10; 20:13,15), but was a striking way for Jesus to address His mother (see 19:26).
[j] 2:4 That is, the time of his sacrificial death and exaltation (see 7:30; 8:20; 12:23,27; 13:1; 17:1)

WORD STUDY

Greek word: **amen** [ah MAYN]
Translation: **assure**
Uses in John's Gospel: **50** (Mt, 31; Mk, 14; Lk, 6)
Uses in John's writings: **59**
Uses in the NT: **129**
Key passage: **John 1:51**

The English word *amen* comes from a Hebrew verb meaning *to trust, believe,* which is related to the noun for *truth, faith,* or *faithfulness.* It is common for Christians to end a prayer with the word *amen;* this occurs often in the Bible also. But Jesus used *amen* as part of a formula to introduce certain statements that He considered especially important (literally, *amen, I say to you*). This occurs thirty-one times in Matthew, thirteen times in Mark, and six times in Luke. The emphasis in Jesus' use of this term was on the certainty of what He was about to say. In John's Gospel all twenty-five sayings have the double *amen* (literally, *amen, amen, I say to you*), which seems to add a tone of seriousness to His statements. Jesus normally used these special formulae to introduce truths about God, Jesus, the Spirit, or some aspect of salvation.

Wanna miracle?
- *Do whatever He (Jesus; His) tells you - v.5*
- *Continue obeying in the natural - v.7 (fill the jars w/ H₂O)*
+ ordinary
- *Watch for His*

WORD STUDY

displays
of His
glory
- √, u

Greek word: **semeion**
[say MIGH ahn]

Translation: **sign**

Uses in John's Gospel: **16**
(Mt, 13; Mk, 7; Lk, 11)

Uses in John's writings: **23**

Uses in the NT: **77**

Key passages: **John 2:11;**
4:54; 20:30

The three main terms that describe miracles in the NT are *semeion (sign), dunamis (power),* and *teras (wonder).* One problem in studying these three words is that some English versions use the term "miracle" to translate all three words, at least in some contexts. The word *teras* is the least common of the three (sixteen times) and always refers to miracles; *dunamis* and *semeion* occur numerous times and refer to other phenomena besides miracles. The word *teras* is always accompanied by *semeion* and sometimes by *dunamis* also (Ac 2:22; 2 Co 12:12; 2 Th 2:9; Heb 2:4). The distinction between the three terms is one of emphasis: *semeion* refers to the purpose of the miracle; *dunamis* refers to the source that enables someone to perform a miracle; and *teras* refers to the reaction of the crowd when a miracle was performed. John's favorite term for Jesus' miracles was *semeion* (*dunamis* does not occur and *teras* occurs only once, 4:48), for he emphasized the purpose for these miracles: they revealed who Jesus was so that people would believe in Him (20:30–31). In contrast to the other Gospels, John's Gospel provides only seven signs (the first two are numbered, 2:11; 4:54), but he reminds us that Jesus performed many others (20:30).

[5] "Do whatever He tells you," His mother told the servants.

[6] Now six stone water jars had been set there for Jewish purification. Each contained twenty or thirty gallons.[a]

[7] "Fill the jars with water," Jesus told them. So they filled them to the brim. [8] Then He said to them, "Now draw some out and take it to the chief servant."[b] And they did.

[9] When the chief servant[b] tasted the water (after it had become wine), he did not know where it came from—though the servants who had drawn the water knew. He called the groom [10] and told him, "Everybody sets out the fine wine first, then, after people have drunk freely, the inferior. But you have kept the fine wine until now."

[11] Jesus performed this first sign[c] in Cana of Galilee. He displayed His glory, and His disciples believed in Him.

[12] After this He went down to Capernaum, together with His mother, His brothers, and His disciples, and they stayed there only a few days.

CLEANSING THE TEMPLE COMPLEX

[13] The Jewish Passover was near, so Jesus went up to Jerusalem. [14] In the temple complex[d] He found people selling oxen, sheep, and doves, and He also found[e] the money changers sitting there. [15] After making a whip out of cords, He drove everyone out of the temple complex with their sheep and oxen. He also poured out the money changers' coins and overturned the tables. [16] He told those who were selling doves, "Get these things out of here! Stop turning my Father's house into a marketplace!"[f]

[17] And His disciples remembered that it is written: **"Zeal for Your house will consume Me."[g]**

---

[a]**2:6** Lit *two or three measures*
[b]**2:8,9** Lit *ruler of the table;* perhaps *master of the feast* or *headwaiter*
[c]**2:11** Lit *this beginning of the signs* (see 4:54; 20:30). Seven miraculous signs occur in John's Gospel and are so noted in the headings.
[d]**2:14** The temple complex included the sanctuary (the Holy Place and the Holy of Holies), at least four courtyards (for priests, Jews, women, and Gentiles), numerous gates, and several covered walkways.
[e]**2:14** *He also found* added for clarity
[f]**2:16** Lit *a house of business*
[g]**2:17** Ps 69:9

18 So the Jews replied to Him, "What sign of authority[a] will You show us for doing these things?"

19 Jesus answered, "Destroy this sanctuary,[b] and I will raise it up in three days."

20 Therefore the Jews said, "This sanctuary took forty-six years to build, and will You raise it up in three days?"

21 But He was speaking about the sanctuary of His body. 22 So when He was raised from the dead, His disciples remembered that He had said this. And they believed the Scripture and the statement Jesus had made.

23 While He was in Jerusalem at the Passover Festival, many trusted in His name when they saw the signs He was doing. 24 Jesus, however, would not entrust Himself to them, since He knew them all 25 and because He did not need anyone to testify about man; for He Himself knew what was in man.

JESUS AND NICODEMUS

3 There was a man from the Pharisees named Nicodemus, a ruler of the Jews. 2 This man came to Him at night and said, "Rabbi, we know that You have come from God as a teacher, for no one could perform these signs You do unless God were with him."

3 Jesus replied, "I assure you:[c] Unless someone is born again,[d] he cannot see the kingdom of God."

4 "But how can anyone be born when he is old?" Nicodemus asked Him. "Can he enter his mother's womb a second time and be born?"

5 Jesus answered: "I assure you:[e] Unless someone is born of water and the Spirit,[f] he cannot enter the kingdom of God. 6 Whatever is born of the flesh is flesh, and whatever is born of the Spirit is spirit. 7 Do not be amazed that I told you that you[g] must be born again. 8 The wind[h] blows where it pleases, and you hear its sound, but you don't know where it comes from or where it is going. So it is with everyone born of the Spirit."

9 "How can these things be?" asked Nicodemus.

WORD STUDY

Greek word: **anothen**
[AH noh thuhn]
Translation: **again**
Uses in John's Gospel: **5**
(Mt, 1; Mk, 1; Lk, 1)
Uses in John's writings: **5**
Uses in the NT: **13**
Key passages: **John 3:3,7**

The expression *born again* comes from John 3:3, where Jesus tells Nicodemus that he must be born (*gennao*, the term used for the genealogy in Mt 1:1–17) again *(anothen)*. The term *anothen* can mean *again* or *from above*, but the meaning *again* for *anothen* occurs only in Galatians 4:9 in the NT. All other uses of the term mean *from above* (see Jn 3:31; 19:11,23; Jms 1:17; 3:15,17) or something similar (such as *top* in Mt 27:51; Mk 15:38). It is likely that Nicodemus misunderstood Jesus' use of *anothen*, thinking He meant *again* as in a second time. This is why Nicodemus responded the way he did, by a reference to physical birth (v. 4). But Jesus went on to indicate that He was referring to the other meaning of *anothen*, a birth *from above*, a birth from the Spirit (Jn 3:5,6,8).

---

[a]**2:18** *of authority* added for clarity
[b]**2:19** See 2:14 note
[c]**3:3** See 1:51 note
[d]**3:3** The same Gk word can mean *again* or *from above* (also in v. 7).

[e]**3:5** See 1:51 note
[f]**3:5** Or *spirit, wind* (see v. 8 note)
[g]**3:7** The pronoun is plural in Gk.
[h]**3:8** The Gk word *pneuma* can mean *wind, spirit,* or *Spirit,* each of which occurs in this context.

WORD STUDIES

Greek word: **monogenes**
[mah nah gehn AYSS]

Translation: **only**

Uses in John's Gospel: **4**
(Lk, 3)

Uses in John's writings: **5**

Uses in the NT: **9**

Key passages: **John 1:14,18;
3:16,18; 1 John 4:9; Heb 11:17**

English translations have traditionally understood *monogenes* to be from *monos (only)* and *gennao (beget),* thus following the Latin Vulgate *(unigenitus).* This has caused great misunderstanding since God the Son did not have an origin and was not in any sense begotten or created by God. He is Himself an eternal being. Therefore, it is best to understand *monogenes* to be from *monos (only)* and *genos (kind,* Latin *genus),* meaning *the only one of its kind.* This is much more consistent with John's five uses of the word, and support for this translation is found in Hebrews 11:17 where Isaac is called Abraham's *monogenes.* Isaac was not Abraham's only-begotten son (Ishmael was his firstborn and there were other sons through Keturah), but Isaac was the only one of his kind—the son of promise. Luke's three uses of the word (7:12; 8:42; 9:38) may refer to a special child, not just an only child, though this is not clear. In the Old Latin translation, *monogenes* was translated as *unicus,* from which we get our word *unique.* This is what is meant by *monogenes* in John's writings (Jn 1:14,18; 3:16,18; 1 Jn 4:9): Jesus is God's only Son in that His essential nature is the same as the Father's. There are many children of God (see Jn 1:12–13), but there is only one Son of God.

[10] "Are you a teacher[a] of Israel and don't know these things?" Jesus replied. [11] "I assure you:[b] We speak what We know and We testify to what We have seen, but you[c] do not accept Our testimony.[d] [12] If I have told you about things that happen on earth and you don't believe, how will you believe if I tell you about things of heaven? [13] No one has ascended into heaven except the One who descended from heaven—the Son of Man.[1] [14] Just as Moses lifted up the serpent in the wilderness, so the Son of Man must be lifted up, [15] so that everyone who believes in Him will[2] have eternal life.

[16] "For God loved the world in this way: He gave His only[e] Son, so that everyone who believes in Him will not perish but have eternal life.[f] [17] For God did not send His Son into the world that He might judge the world, but that the world might be saved through Him. [18] Anyone who believes in Him is not judged, but anyone who does not believe is already judged, because he has not believed in the name of the only[g] Son of God.

[19] "This, then, is the judgment: the light has come into the world, and people loved darkness rather than the light, because their deeds were evil. [20] For everyone who practices wicked things hates the light and avoids it,[h] so that his deeds may not be exposed. [21] But anyone who lives by[i] the truth comes to the light, so that his works may be shown to be accomplished by God."[j]

JESUS AND JOHN THE BAPTIST

[22] After this Jesus and His disciples went to the Judean countryside, where He spent time with them and baptized. [23] John also was baptizing in Aenon near Salim, because there was plenty of water there. And people were coming and being baptized, [24] since John had not yet been thrown into prison.

[1] **3:13** Other mss add *who is in heaven*
[2] **3:15** Other mss add *not perish, but*

[a] **3:10** Or *the teacher*
[b] **3:11** See 1:51 note
[c] **3:11** The word *you* in Gk is plural here and in v. 12.
[d] **3:11** The plurals (*We, Our*) refer to Jesus and His authority to speak for the Father.
[e] **3:16** Or *only begotten* (see 1:14 note)

[f] **3:16** 1 Jn 4:9,11
[g] **3:18** See 1:14 note
[h] **3:20** Lit *and does not come to the light*
[i] **3:21** Lit *who does*
[j] **3:21** It is possible that Jesus' words end at v. 15. (Ancient Gk did not have quotation marks.)

25 Then a dispute arose between John's disciples and a Jew[1a] about purification. 26 So they came to John and told him, "Rabbi, the One you testified about, and who was with you across the Jordan, is baptizing—and everyone is flocking to Him."

27 John responded, "No one can receive a single thing unless it's given to him from heaven. 28 You yourselves can testify that I said, 'I am not the Messiah,[b] but I've been sent ahead of Him.' 29 He who has the bride is the groom. But the groom's friend, who stands by and listens for him, rejoices greatly[c] at the groom's voice. So this joy of mine is complete. 30 He must increase, but I must decrease."

THE ONE FROM HEAVEN

31 The One who comes from above is above all. The one who is from the earth is earthly and speaks in earthly terms.[d] The One who comes from heaven is above all. 32 He testifies to what He has seen and heard, yet no one accepts His testimony. 33 The one who has accepted His testimony has affirmed that God is true. 34 For He whom God sent speaks God's words, since He[2] gives the Spirit without measure. 35 The Father loves the Son and has given all things into His hands. 36 The one who believes in the Son has eternal life, but the one who refuses to believe in the Son will not see life; instead, the wrath of God remains on him.

JESUS AND
THE SAMARITAN WOMAN

4 When Jesus[3] knew that the Pharisees heard He was making and baptizing more disciples than John 2 (though Jesus Himself was not baptizing, but His disciples were), 3 He left Judea and went again to Galilee. 4 He had to travel through Samaria, 5 so He came to a town of Samaria called Sychar near the property[e] that Jacob had given his son Joseph.[f] 6 Jacob's well was there,

---

[1]3:25 Other mss read *and the Jews*
[2]3:34 Other mss read *since God*
[3]4:1 Other mss read *the Lord*

---

[a]3:25 See 1:19 note
[b]3:28 Or *the Christ*
[c]3:29 Lit *with joy rejoices*

[d]3:31 Or *of earthly things*
[e]4:5 Lit *piece of land*
[f]4:5 Gn 48:22

Give God Room to Prove Himself to You

We come to know God as we experience Him. We can know about God as a Provider, but we really come to know God as Provider when we experience Him providing something for our lives.

"I assure you: We speak what We know and We testify to what We have seen."

—John 3:11a

Jesus Offers Everything That a Person Really Needs

The cross, the death of Jesus Christ, and His resurrection are God's final, total, and complete expression that He loves us.

"For God loved the world in this way: He gave His only Son, so that everyone who believes in Him will not perish but have eternal life. For God did not send His Son into the world that He might judge the world, but that the world might be saved through Him."

—John 3:16–17

WORD STUDY

Greek word: **zoe** [zoh AY]

Translation: **life**

Uses in John's Gospel: **36**
(Mt, 7; Mk, 4; Lk, 5)

Uses in John's writings: **66**

Uses in the NT: **135**

Key passages: **John 3:15–16;
4:14; 17:2–3**

What is the meaning of life? The most important aspect of life is a relationship with God. The essence of life is union; the essence of death is separation. Physical life is the union of body and spirit; physical death is the separation of the body and spirit. Spiritual life is union or oneness with God through faith in Christ; spiritual death is separation from God. Life—spiritual life—means more than mere existence. It refers to a relationship with God. This is the life that Jesus came to give us, and He intended us to enjoy the blessings of that life, that relationship, "abundantly" (Jn 10:10).

Therefore, everyone will exist forever, but not everyone will *live* forever. Unbelievers will experience death forever, "the second death" (Rev 20:14), eternal separation from God in the lake of fire. But by God's grace Christians have "eternal redemption" (Heb 9:12) or "eternal life" (Jn 3:15–16; 4:14). The phrase "eternal life" occurs 43 times in the NT—23 of them in John and 1 John—and refers to the permanence of the relationship believers have with God even now. Eternal life is knowing the Father and the Son (Jn 17:2–3). This is God's never-ending gift to those who trust in Christ (Rm 6:23). Truly, this is the meaning of *life*.

and Jesus, worn out from His journey, sat down at the well. It was about six in the evening.[a]

[7] A woman of Samaria came to draw water.

"Give Me a drink," Jesus said to her, [8] for His disciples had gone into town to buy food.

[9] "How is it that You, a Jew, ask for a drink from me, a Samaritan woman?" she asked.[b] For Jews do not associate with[c] Samaritans.[1]

[10] Jesus answered, "If you knew the gift of God, and who is saying to you, 'Give Me a drink,' you would ask Him, and He would give you living water."

[11] "Sir," said the woman, "You don't even have a bucket, and the well is deep. So where do you get this 'living water'? [12] You aren't greater than our father Jacob, are you? He gave us the well and drank from it himself, as did his sons and livestock."

[13] Jesus said, "Everyone who drinks from this water will get thirsty again. [14] But whoever drinks from the water that I will give him will never get thirsty again—ever! In fact, the water I will give him will become a well[d] of water springing up within him for eternal life."

[15] "Sir," the woman said to Him, "give me this water so I won't get thirsty and come here to draw water."

[16] "Go call your husband," He told her, "and come back here."

[17] "I don't have a husband," she[e] answered.

"You have correctly said, 'I don't have a husband,'" Jesus said. [18] "For you've had five husbands, and the man you now have is not your husband. What you have said is true."

[19] "Sir," the woman replied, "I see that You are a prophet. [20] Our fathers worshiped on this mountain,[f] yet you Jews[g] say that the place to worship is in Jerusalem."

[21] Jesus told her, "Believe Me, woman,[h] an hour is coming when you will worship the Father neither on this mountain nor in Jerusalem. [22] You Samaritans[i] worship

[1] 4:9 Other mss omit *For Jews do not associate with Samaritans.*

---

[a] 4:6 Lit *the sixth hour;* see 1:39 note; an alternate time reckoning would be *twelve noon*

[b] 4:9 Lit *the Samaritan woman asked Him*

[c] 4:9 Or *do not share vessels with*

[d] 4:14 Or *spring*

[e] 4:17 Lit *the woman*

[f] 4:20 That is, Mount Gerizim, where there had been a Samaritan temple that rivaled Jerusalem's.

[g] 4:20 *Jews* implied

[h] 4:21 See 2:4 note

[i] 4:22 *Samaritans* is implied since the Gk verb is plural.

what you do not know. We worship what we do know, because salvation is from the Jews. ²³ But an hour is coming, and is now here, when the true worshipers will worship the Father in spirit and truth. Yes, the Father wants such people to worship Him. ²⁴ God is Spirit, and those who worship Him must worship in spirit and truth."

²⁵ The woman said to Him, "I know that Messiah is coming" (who is called Christ[a]). "When He comes, He will explain everything to us."

²⁶ "I am He,"[b] Jesus told her, "the One speaking to you."

THE RIPENED HARVEST

²⁷ Just then His disciples arrived, and they were amazed that He was talking with a woman. Yet no one said, "What do You want?" or "Why are You talking with her?"

²⁸ Then the woman left her water jar, went into town, and told the men, ²⁹ "Come, see a man who told me everything I ever did! Could this be the Messiah?" ³⁰ They left the town and made their way to Him.

³¹ In the meantime the disciples kept urging Him, "Rabbi, eat something."

³² But He said, "I have food to eat that you don't know about."

³³ The disciples said to one another, "Could someone have brought Him something to eat?"

³⁴ "My food is to do the will of Him who sent Me and to finish His work," Jesus told them. ³⁵ "Don't you say, 'There are still four more months, then comes the harvest'? Listen to what I'm telling you:[c] Open[d] your eyes and look at the fields, for they are ready[e] for harvest. ³⁶ The reaper is already receiving pay and gathering fruit for eternal life, so the sower and reaper can rejoice together. ³⁷ For in this case the saying is true: 'One sows and another reaps.' ³⁸ I sent you to reap what you didn't labor for; others have labored, and you have benefited from[f] their labor."

Learn to Think the Way God Thinks

The adjusting is always to a Person. You adjust your life to God. You adjust your viewpoints to be like His viewpoints. You adjust your ways to be like His ways.

"God is Spirit, and those who worship Him must worship in spirit and truth."
—John 4:24

His Plan Takes Precedence Over Yours

God is far more interested in accomplishing His kingdom purposes than you are. He will move you into every assignment that He knows you are ready for.

"My food is to do the will of Him who sent Me and to finish His work," Jesus told them.
—John 4:34

---

[a]4:25 See 1:41 note
[b]4:26 Lit *I am*
[c]4:35 Lit *Look, I'm telling you*
[d]4:35 Lit *Raise*
[e]4:35 Lit *white*
[f]4:38 Lit *you have entered into*

THE SAVIOR OF THE WORLD

39 Now many Samaritans from that town believed in Him because of what the woman said[a] when she testified, "He told me everything I ever did." 40 Therefore, when the Samaritans came to Him, they asked Him to stay with them, and He stayed there two days. 41 Many more believed because of what He said.[b] 42 And they told the woman, "We no longer believe because of what you said, for we have heard for ourselves and know that this really is the Savior of the world."[1]

A GALILEAN WELCOME

43 After two days He left there for Galilee. 44 Jesus Himself testified that a prophet has no honor in his own country. 45 When they entered Galilee, the Galileans welcomed Him because they had seen everything He did in Jerusalem during the festival. For they also had gone to the festival.

THE SECOND SIGN: HEALING AN OFFICIAL'S SON

46 Then He went again to Cana of Galilee, where He had turned the water into wine. There was a certain royal official whose son was ill at Capernaum. 47 When this man heard that Jesus had come from Judea into Galilee, he went to Him and pleaded with Him to come down and heal his son, for he was about to die.

48 Jesus told him, "Unless you people[c] see signs and wonders, you will not believe."

49 "Sir," the official said to Him, "come down before my boy dies!"

50 "Go," Jesus told him, "your son will live." The man believed what[d] Jesus said to him and departed.

51 While he was still going down, his slaves met him saying that his boy was alive.[2] 52 He asked them at what time he got better. "Yesterday at seven in the morning[e] the fever left him," they answered. 53 The father realized

[1]4:42 Other mss add *the Messiah*
[2]4:51 Other mss read *saying, Your boy is alive.*

[a]4:39 Lit *because the woman's word*
[b]4:41 Lit *because of His word*
[c]4:48 *people* implied
[d]4:50 Lit *the word*

[e]4:52 Lit *the seventh hour;* or *seven in the evening;* see 1:39 note; an alternate time reckoning would be *at one in the afternoon*

" That I may really come to know practically, through experience for myself the love of Christ which far surpasses mere knowledge w/o experience." (Eph 1)

You Believe by Faith, Know by Experience

Knowledge of God comes through experience. We come to know God as we experience Him in and around our lives.

And they told the woman, "We no longer believe because of what you said, for we have heard for ourselves and know that this really is the Savior of the world."

—John 4:42

Jesus just says the word & it's done

this was the very hour at which Jesus had told him, "Your son will live." Then he himself believed, along with his whole household.

⁵⁴ This therefore was the second signᵃ Jesus performed after He came from Judea to Galilee.

THE THIRD SIGN: HEALING THE SICK

5 After this a Jewish festival took place, and Jesus went up to Jerusalem. ² By the Sheep Gate in Jerusalem there is a pool, called Bethesda¹ in Hebrew, which has five colonnades.ᵇ ³ Within these lay a multitude of the sick—blind, lame, and paralyzed—⌐waiting for the moving of the water, ⁴ because an angel would go down into the pool from time to time and stir up the water. Then the first one who got in after the water was stirred up recovered from whatever ailment he had.⌐²

⁵ One man was there who had been sick for thirty-eight years. ⁶ When Jesus saw him lying there and knew he had already been there a long time, He said to him, "Do you want to get well?"

⁷ "Sir," the sick man answered, "I don't have a man to put me into the pool when the water is stirred up, but while I'm coming, someone goes down ahead of me."

⁸ "Get up," Jesus told him, "pick up your bedroll and walk!" ⁹ Instantly the man got well, picked up his bedroll, and started to walk.

Now that day was the Sabbath, ¹⁰ so the Jews said to the man who had been healed, "This is the Sabbath! It's illegal for you to pick up your bedroll."

¹¹ He replied, "The man who made me well told me, 'Pick up your bedroll and walk.'"

¹² "Who is this man who told you, 'Pick up your bedrollᶜ and walk?'" they asked. ¹³ But the man who was cured did not know who it was, because Jesus had slipped away into the crowd that was there.ᵈ

¹⁴ After this Jesus found him in the temple complex and said to him, "See, you are well. Do not sin any

Trust and Obey

When you are convinced of His love, you can believe Him and trust Him. When you trust Him, you can obey Him.

He replied, "The man who made me well told me, 'Pick up your bedroll and walk.'"

—John 5:11

---

¹**5:2** Other mss read *Bethzatha* or *Bethsaida*
²**5:3–4** Other mss omit the words in brackets

ᵃ**4:54** 2:11
ᵇ**5:2** That is, rows of columns supporting a roof
ᶜ**5:12** *your bedroll* added for clarity
ᵈ**5:13** Lit *slipped away, there being a crowd in that place*

more, so that something worse doesn't happen to you." [15] The man went and reported to the Jews that it was Jesus who had made him well.

HONORING THE FATHER AND THE SON

[16] Therefore, the Jews began persecuting Jesus[1] because He was doing these things on the Sabbath. [17] But Jesus responded to them, "My Father is still working, and I also am working." [18] This is why the Jews began trying all the more to kill Him: not only was He breaking the Sabbath, but He was even calling God His own Father, making Himself equal with God.

[19] Then Jesus replied, "I assure you:[a] The Son is not able to do anything on His own, but only what He sees the Father doing. For whatever the Father[b] does, these things the Son also does in the same way. [20] For the Father loves the Son and shows Him everything He is doing, and He will show Him greater works than these so that you will be amazed. [21] And just as the Father raises the dead and gives them life, so also the Son gives life to whomever He wishes. [22] The Father, in fact, judges no one but has given all judgment to the Son, [23] so that all people will honor the Son just as they honor the Father. Anyone who does not honor the Son does not honor the Father who sent Him.

LIFE AND JUDGMENT

[24] "I assure you:[c] Anyone who hears My word and believes Him who sent Me has eternal life and will not come under judgment, but has passed from death to life. [25] "I assure you:[c] An hour is coming, and is now here, when the dead will hear the voice of the Son of God, and those who hear will live. [26] For just as the Father has life in Himself, so also He has granted to the Son to have life in Himself. [27] And He has granted Him the right to pass judgment, because He is the Son of Man. [28] Do not be amazed at this, because a time is coming when all who are in the graves will hear His voice [29] and come out—those who have done good things, to the resurrec-

---

[1]5:16 Other mss add *and trying to kill Him*

---

[a]5:19 See 1:51 note
[b]5:19 Lit *whatever that One*

[c]5:24–25 See 1:51 note

Make Sure You're Asking the Right Questions

"What is God's will for my life?" is not the best question to ask. I think the right question is simply, "What is God's will?" The focus needs to be on God and His purposes, not my life.

"I can do nothing on My own. Only as I hear do I judge, and My judgment is righteous, because I do not seek My own will, but the will of Him who sent Me."

—John 5:30

Stay in the Word and Know What God Says

When you come to understand the spiritual meaning and application of a Scripture passage, God's Spirit has been at work. This does not *lead* you to an encounter with God. That *is* the encounter with God. When God speaks to you through the Bible, He is relating to you in a personal and real way.

"You pore over the Scriptures because you think you have eternal life in them, yet they testify about Me."

—John 5:39

tion of life, but those who have done wicked things, to the resurrection of judgment.

³⁰ "I can do nothing on My own. Only as I hear do I judge, and My judgment is righteous, because I do not seek My own will, but the will of Him who sent Me.

FOUR WITNESSES TO JESUS

³¹ "If I testify about Myself, My testimony is not valid.ᵃ ³² There is Another who testifies about Me, and I know that the testimony He gives about Me is valid.ᵃ ³³ You peopleᵇ have sent messengersᶜ to John, and he has testified to the truth. ³⁴ I don't receive man's testimony, but I say these things so that you may be saved. ³⁵ Johnᵈ was a burning and shining lamp, and for an hour you were willing to enjoy his light.

³⁶ "But I have a greater testimony than John's because of the works that the Father has given Me to accomplish. These very works I am doing testify about Me that the Father has sent Me. ³⁷ The Father who sent Me has Himself testified about Me. You have not heard His voice at any time, and you haven't seen His form. ³⁸ You don't have His word living in you, because you don't believe the One He sent. ³⁹ You pore overᵉ the Scriptures because you think you have eternal life in them, yet they testify about Me. ⁴⁰ And you are not willing to come to Me that you may have life.

⁴¹ "I do not accept glory from men, ⁴² but I know you—that you have no love for God within you. ⁴³ I have come in My Father's name, yet you don't accept Me. If someone else comes in his own name, you will accept him. ⁴⁴ How can you believe? While accepting glory from one another, you don't seek the glory that comes from the only God. ⁴⁵ Do not think that I will accuse you to the Father. Your accuser is Moses, on whom you have set your hope. ⁴⁶ For if you believed Moses, you would believe Me, because he wrote about Me. ⁴⁷ But if you don't believe his writings, how will you believe My words?"

WORD STUDY

Greek word: ***martureo*** [mahr tew REH oh]

Translation: **testify, witness**

Uses in John's Gospel: **33** (Mt, 1; Lk, 1)

Uses in John's writings: **47**

Uses in the NT: **76**

Key passage: **John 5:31–39**

The Greek verb *martureo* was a legal term in the ancient world, just as *testify* is today in English. The same is true of other related Greek words, such as *marturia* and *marturion* (both meaning *testimony* or *witness* with an emphasis on that which is stated), and *martus* (*witness,* the person testifying); the English word *martyr* is derived from *martus*. The legal concept was not always in view for these words in Greek usage, and in fact the court setting is rarely involved in the NT. The general ideas implied by testifying and witnessing are always there, however, such as persons declaring certain things to be factual and providing evidence to validate their claims. John 5 is not a legal setting, but Jesus used *martureo* seven times and *marturia* four times to provide four evidences that validate His claims about Himself and His relationship to the Father (vv. 17–30): John the Baptist (vv. 31–35); the works Christ performed (v. 36); the Father (vv. 37–38); and the Scriptures (vv. 39–47).

ᵃ**5:31–32** Or *true*
ᵇ**5:33** *people* added for clarity
ᶜ**5:33** *messengers* supplied for clarity
ᵈ**5:35** Lit *that man*
ᵉ**5:39** In Gk this could be a command ("Pore over").

THE FOURTH SIGN: FEEDING FIVE THOUSAND

6 After this Jesus crossed the Sea of Galilee (or Tiberias). [2] And a huge crowd was following Him because they saw the signs that He was performing on the sick. [3] So Jesus went up a mountain and sat down there with His disciples.

[4] Now the Passover, a Jewish festival, was near. [5] Therefore, when Jesus raised His eyes and noticed a huge crowd coming toward Him, He asked Philip, "Where will we buy bread so these people can eat?" [6] He asked this to test him, for He Himself knew what He was going to do.

[7] Philip answered, "Two hundred denarii[a] worth of bread wouldn't be enough for each of them to have a little."

[8] One of His disciples, Andrew, Simon Peter's brother, said to Him, [9] "There's a boy here who has five barley loaves and two fish—but what are they for so many?"

[10] Then Jesus said, "Have the people sit down." There was plenty of grass in that place, so the men sat down, numbering about five thousand.[b] [11] Then Jesus took the loaves, and after giving thanks He distributed them to those who were seated; so also with the fish, as much as they wanted.

[12] When they were full, He told His disciples, "Collect the leftovers so that nothing is wasted." [13] So they collected them and filled twelve baskets with the pieces from the five barley loaves that were left over by those who had eaten.

[14] When the people saw the sign[1] He had done, they said, "This really is the Prophet[c] who was to come into the world!" [15] Therefore, when Jesus knew that they were about to come and take Him by force to make Him king, He withdrew again[2d] to the mountain by Himself.

Take Faithfulness Over Success

The outward appearance of success does not always indicate faith, and the outward appearance of failure does not always indicate that faith is lacking. A faithful servant is one that does what his Master tells him whatever the outcome may be.

"Don't work for the food that perishes but for the food that lasts for eternal life, which the Son of Man will give you, because on Him God the Father has set His seal of approval."

—John 6:27

---

[1]6:14 Other mss read *signs*
[2]6:15 Other mss omit *again*

---

[a]6:7 A denarius was a Roman silver coin worth about a day's wage for a common laborer.
[b]6:10 Or *they sat down, the men numbering about five thousand*

[c]6:14 Dt 18:15
[d]6:15 A previous withdrawal is mentioned in Mark 6:31–32, an event that occurred just before the feeding of the five thousand.

THE FIFTH SIGN: WALKING ON WATER

[16] When evening came, His disciples went down to the sea, [17] got into a boat, and started across the sea to Capernaum. Darkness had already set in, but Jesus had not yet come to them. [18] Then a high wind arose, and the sea began to churn. [19] After they had rowed about three or four miles,[a] they saw Jesus walking on the sea. He was coming near the boat, and they were afraid. [20] But He said to them, "It is I.[b] Don't be afraid!" [21] Then they were willing to take Him on board, and at once the boat was at the shore where they were heading.

THE BREAD OF LIFE

[22] The next day, the crowd that had stayed on the other side of the sea knew there had been only one boat.[1] They also knew[c] that Jesus had not boarded the boat with His disciples, but His disciples had gone off alone. [23] Some boats from Tiberias came near the place where they ate the bread after the Lord gave thanks. [24] When the crowd saw that neither Jesus nor His disciples were there, they got into the boats and went to Capernaum, looking for Jesus.

[25] When they found Him on the other side of the sea, they said to Him, "Rabbi, when did You get here?"

[26] Jesus answered, "I assure you:[d] You are looking for Me, not because you saw the signs, but because you ate the loaves and were filled. [27] Don't work for the food that perishes but for the food that lasts for eternal life, which the Son of Man will give you, because on Him God the Father has set His seal of approval."

[28] "What can we do to perform the works of God?" they asked.

[29] Jesus replied, "This is the work of God: that you believe in the One He has sent."

[30] "Then what sign are You going to do so we may see and believe You?" they asked. "What are You going to perform? [31] Our fathers ate the manna in the desert, just

[1]6:22 Other mss add *boat into which His disciples had entered*

---

[a]6:19 Lit *twenty-five or thirty stadia*
[b]6:20 Lit *I am*

[c]6:22 *They also knew* added for clarity
[d]6:26 See 1:51 note

WORD STUDY

Greek word: ***pisteuo***
[pihss TYEW oh]
Translation: **believe**
Uses in John's Gospel: **98**
(Mt, 11; Mk, 14; Lk, 9)
Uses in John's writings: **107**
Uses in the NT: **241**
Key passages: **John 3:16; 6:29–47; 20:31**

The Greek word *pisteuo* means *to believe, trust, rely upon,* and its related noun is *pistis (faith).* In his Gospel, John never used the words *repent, repentance,* or *faith* to describe the way people are saved. Instead, he used *believe* since this term included all these ideas. John preferred the verb form to emphasize the act that is necessary for someone to be saved—total dependence on the work of Another. John did indicate, however, that believing can be superficial; that is, it can be merely intellectual without resulting in true salvation (Jn 2:23–24; 12:42–43; see Jms 2:19). But John's main point is that complete reliance upon Jesus the Messiah and Son of God (20:31) for salvation gives eternal life to the person who believes (3:16; 6:47). Jesus used a wordplay when He said that people must do "the work of God" for salvation, for His point was that we must not try to work for it at all. We must simply "believe in the One He has sent" (6:29).

as it is written: **'He gave them bread from heaven to eat.'** "[a]

[32] Jesus said to them, "I assure you:[b] Moses didn't give you the bread from heaven, but My Father gives you the true bread from heaven. [33] For the bread of God is the One who comes down from heaven and gives life to the world."

[34] Then they said, "Sir, give us this bread always!"

[35] "I am the bread of life," Jesus told them. "No one who comes to Me will ever be hungry, and no one who believes in Me will ever be thirsty again. [36] But as I told you, you've seen Me,[1] and yet you do not believe. [37] Everyone the Father gives Me will come to Me, and the one who comes to Me I will never cast out. [38] For I have come down from heaven, not to do My will, but the will of Him who sent Me. [39] This is the will of Him who sent Me: that I should lose none of those He has given Me but should raise them up on the last day. [40] For this is the will of My Father: that everyone who sees the Son and believes in Him may have eternal life, and I will raise him up on the last day."

[41] Therefore the Jews started complaining about Him, because He said, "I am the bread that came down from heaven." [42] They were saying, "Isn't this Jesus the son of Joseph, whose father and mother we know? How can He now say, 'I have come down from heaven'?"

[43] Jesus answered them, "Stop complaining among yourselves. [44] No one can come to Me unless the Father who sent Me draws[c] him, and I will raise him up on the last day. [45] It is written in the Prophets: **'And they will all be taught by God.'**[d] Everyone who has listened to and learned from the Father comes to Me— [46] not that anyone has seen the Father except the One who is from God. He has seen the Father.

[47] "I assure you:[e] Anyone who believes[2] has eternal life. [48] I am the bread of life. [49] Your fathers ate the manna[f] in the desert, and they died. [50] This is the bread

Live in a Constant State of Availability

If you want to meet a need through my life, I am your servant; and I will do whatever is required.

"For I have come down from heaven, not to do My will, but the will of Him who sent Me."

—John 6:38

---

[1] **6:36** Other mss omit *Me*
[2] **6:47** Other mss add *in Me*

---

[a] **6:31** Bread miraculously provided by God for the Israelites; Ps 78:24; Ex 16:4,15
[b] **6:32** See 1:51 note
[c] **6:44** Or *brings, leads;* see the use of this Gk verb in 12:32; 21:6; Ac 14:19; Jms 2:6.
[d] **6:45** Is 54:13
[e] **6:47** See 1:51 note
[f] **6:49** Ex 16:12-36

that comes down from heaven so that anyone may eat of it and not die. [51] I am the living bread that came down from heaven. If anyone eats of this bread he will live forever. The bread that I will give for the life of the world is My flesh."

[52] At that, the Jews argued among themselves, "How can this man give us His flesh to eat?"

[53] So Jesus said to them, "I assure you:[a] Unless you eat the flesh of the Son of Man and drink His blood, you do not have life in yourselves. [54] Anyone who eats My flesh and drinks My blood has eternal life, and I will raise him up on the last day, [55] because My flesh is true food and My blood is true drink. [56] The one who eats My flesh and drinks My blood lives in Me, and I in him. [57] Just as the living Father sent Me and I live because of the Father, so the one who feeds on Me will live because of Me. [58] This is the bread that came down from heaven; it is not like the manna[1] your fathers ate—and they died. The one who eats this bread will live forever."

[59] He said these things while teaching in the synagogue in Capernaum.

MANY DISCIPLES DESERT JESUS

[60] Therefore, when many of His disciples heard this, they said, "This teaching is hard! Who can accept[b] it?"

[61] Jesus, knowing in Himself that His disciples were complaining about this, asked them, "Does this offend you? [62] Then what if you were to observe the Son of Man ascending to where He was before? [63] The Spirit is the One who gives life. The flesh doesn't help at all. The words that I have spoken to you are spirit and are life. [64] But there are some among you who don't believe." (For Jesus knew from the beginning those who would not[2] believe and the one who would betray Him.) [65] He said, "This is why I told you that no one can come to Me unless it is granted to him by the Father."

[66] From that moment many of His disciples turned back and no longer walked with Him. [67] Therefore Jesus said to the Twelve, "You don't want to go away too, do you?"

[1]6:58 Other mss omit *the manna*
[2]6:64 Other mss omit *not*

[a]6:53 See 1:51 note   [b]6:60 Lit *hear*

Depend on God for Everything

Do you realize that the Lord does not just give you life—He is your life?

"Just as the living Father sent Me and I live because of the Father, so the one who feeds on Me will live because of Me."
—John 6:57

You do not get orders, then go out and carry them out on your own. You relate to God, respond to Him, and adjust your life so that He can do what He wants through you.

"The Spirit is the One who gives life. The flesh doesn't help at all. The words that I have spoken to you are spirit and are life."
—John 6:63

[68] Simon Peter answered, "Lord, to whom should we go? You have the words of eternal life. [69] And we have come to believe and know that You are the Holy One of God!"[1]

[70] Jesus replied to them, "Didn't I choose you, the Twelve? Yet one of you is the Devil!"[a] [71] He was referring to Judas, Simon Iscariot's son,[2b] one of the Twelve, because he was going to betray Him.

THE UNBELIEF OF JESUS' BROTHERS

7 After this Jesus traveled in Galilee, since He did not want to travel in Judea because the Jews[c] were trying to kill Him. [2] The Jewish Festival of Tabernacles[d] was near, [3] so His brothers said to Him, "Leave here and go to Judea so Your disciples can see Your works that You are doing. [4] For no one does anything in secret while he's seeking public recognition. If You do these things, show Yourself to the world." [5] (For not even His brothers believed in Him.)

[6] Jesus told them, "My time has not yet arrived, but your time is always at hand. [7] The world cannot hate you, but it does hate Me because I testify about it—that its deeds are evil. [8] Go up to the festival yourselves. I'm not going up to the festival yet,[3] because My time has not yet fully come." [9] After He had said these things, He stayed in Galilee.

JESUS AT THE FESTIVAL OF TABERNACLES

[10] When His brothers had gone up to the festival, then He also went up, not openly but secretly. [11] The Jews[e] were looking for Him at the festival and saying, "Where is He?" [12] And there was a lot of discussion about Him among the crowds. Some were saying, "He's a good man." Others were saying, "No, on the contrary, He's

---

His Calling Will Be Bigger Than You Are

The kind of assignments God gives in the Bible are always God-sized. They are always beyond what people can do because He wants to demonstrate His nature, His strength, His provision, and His kindness to His people and to a watching world. That is the only way the world will come to know Him.

Then the Jews were amazed and said, "How does He know the Scriptures, since He hasn't been trained?" Jesus answered them, "My teaching isn't Mine, but is from the One who sent Me."

—John 7:15–16

---

[1]6:69 Other mss read *You are the Messiah, the Son of the Living God*
[2]6:71 Other mss read *Judas Iscariot, Simon's son*
[3]7:8 Other mss omit *yet*

---

[a]6:70 Or *a devil;* see 13:2,27
[b]6:71 Lit *Judas, of Simon Iscariot*
[c]7:1 See 1:19 note
[d]7:2 One of three great Jewish reli-
gious festivals, along with Passover and Pentecost (see Ex 23:14; Dt 16:16)
[e]7:11 See 1:19 note

deceiving the people." [13] Still, nobody was talking publicly about Him because they feared the Jews.[a]

[14] When the festival was already half over, Jesus went up into the temple complex and began to teach. [15] Then the Jews[a] were amazed and said, "How does He know the Scriptures, since He hasn't been trained?"

[16] Jesus answered them, "My teaching isn't Mine, but is from the One who sent Me. [17] If anyone wants to do His will, he will understand whether the teaching is from God or if I am speaking on My own. [18] The one who speaks for himself seeks his own glory. But He who seeks the glory of the One who sent Him is true, and unrighteousness is not in Him. [19] Didn't Moses give you the law? Yet none of you keeps the law! Why do you want to kill Me?"

[20] "You have a demon!" the crowd responded. "Who wants to kill You?"

[21] "I did one work, and you are all amazed," Jesus answered. [22] "Consider this:[b] Moses has given you circumcision—not that it comes from Moses but from the fathers—and you circumcise a man on the Sabbath. [23] If a man receives circumcision on the Sabbath so that the law of Moses won't be broken, are you angry at Me because I made a man entirely well on the Sabbath? [24] Stop judging according to outward appearances; rather judge according to righteous judgment."

THE IDENTITY OF THE MESSIAH

[25] Some of the people of Jerusalem were saying, "Isn't this the man they want to kill? [26] Yet, look! He's speaking publicly and they're saying nothing to Him. Can it be true that the authorities know He is the Messiah?[c] [27] But we know where this man is from. When the Messiah comes, nobody will know where He is from."

[28] As He was teaching in the temple complex, Jesus cried out, "You know Me and you know where I am from. Yet I have not come on My own, but the One who sent Me is true. You don't know Him; [29] I know Him because I am from Him, and He sent Me."

[30] Therefore they tried to seize Him. Yet no one laid a hand on Him because His hour[d] had not yet come. [31] However, many from the crowd believed in Him and

Let Others See Jesus in You

Let the world see God at work and He will attract people to Himself. Let Christ be lifted up—not in words, but in life.

"If anyone wants to do His will, he will understand whether the teaching is from God or if I am speaking on My own."

—John 7:17

---

[a]**7:13,15** See 1:19 note
[b]**7:22** Lit *Because of this*
[c]**7:26** Or *the Christ*
[d]**7:30** See 2:4 note

WORD STUDY

Greek word: **hudor** [HOO dohr]
Translation: **water**
Uses in John's Gospel: **21**
(Mt, 7; Mk, 5; Lk, 6)
Uses in John's writings: **43**
Uses in the NT: **76**
Key passages: **John 3:5; 7:38**

The English prefix *hydr-* (as in *hydrolic*) comes from the Greek word for water, *hudor*. This word often refers to literal water, of course, but *water* often has a symbolic or supernatural connotation in the Bible. This is particularly true in John's Gospel: Jesus changed water into wine as His first sign (2:1–11); Jesus offered the woman at the well "living water," which referred to Himself as the giver and sustainer of eternal life (4:7–26); the water in the pool of Bethesda had healing powers (5:2–7); Jesus washed the disciples feet to symbolize our relationship to Him and mutual servanthood (13:1–16); and when the soldier pierced Jesus' side after His death, "blood and water" came forth, symbolizing death ("blood," Jesus really died) and life ("water," Jesus will rise from the dead; see 1 Jn 5:6–8). Twice water is used as a symbol of the Holy Spirit: the Spirit effects the new birth ("born of water and Spirit"; see Jn 3:5–8), and the Spirit is the living water that Jesus promised to those who believe in Him (Jn 7:37–39; see Rv 22:1,17).

said, "When the Messiah comes, He won't perform more signs than this man has done, will He?"

[32] The Pharisees heard the crowd muttering these things about Him, so the chief priests and the Pharisees[a] sent temple police to arrest Him. [33] Therefore Jesus said, "I am only with you for a short time. Then I'm going to the One who sent Me. [34] You will look for Me, and you will not find Me; and where I am, you cannot come."

[35] Then the Jews[b] said to one another, "Where does He intend to go so we won't find Him? He doesn't intend to go to the Dispersion[c] among the Greeks and teach the Greeks, does He? [36] What is this remark He made: 'You will look for Me and you will not find Me; and where I am, you cannot come'?"

THE PROMISE OF THE SPIRIT

[37] On the last and most important day of the festival, Jesus stood up and cried out, "If anyone is thirsty, he should come to Me[1] and drink! [38] The one who believes in Me, as the Scripture has said,[d] will have streams of living water flow from deep within him." [39] He said this about the Spirit, whom those who believed in Him were going to receive, for the Spirit[2] had not yet been received,[3e] because Jesus had not yet been glorified.

THE PEOPLE ARE DIVIDED OVER JESUS

[40] When some from the crowd heard these words, they said, "This really is the Prophet!"[f] [41] Others said, "This is the Messiah!" But some said, "Surely the Messiah doesn't come from Galilee, does He? [42] Doesn't the Scripture say that the Messiah comes from David's off-

[1]**7:37** Other mss omit *to Me*
[2]**7:39** Other mss read *Holy Spirit*
[3]**7:39** Other mss read *had not yet been given*

[a]**7:32** *the chief priests and the Pharisees* refers to the Sanhedrin, the highest Jewish court
[b]**7:35** See 1:19 note
[c]**7:35** That is, Jewish people scattered among Gentile lands. They spoke Gk and were influenced by Gk culture.
[d]**7:38** Jesus may have had several

Old Testament passages in mind, and the main possibilities are Is 58:11; Jr 2:13; 17:13; Ezk 47:1–12; Zch 14:8; see also Jn 4:10,11; Rv 7:17; 22:1.
[e]**7:39** Lit *the Spirit was not yet;* the word *received* is implied from the previous sentence.
[f]**7:40** See 1:21 note

spring[a] and from the town of Bethlehem, where David once lived?" [43] So a division occurred among the crowd because of Him. [44] Some of them wanted to seize Him, but no one laid hands on Him.

DEBATE OVER JESUS' CLAIMS

[45] Then the temple police came to the chief priests and Pharisees,[b] who asked them, "Why haven't you brought Him?"

[46] The police answered, "No man ever spoke like this!"[1]

[47] Then the Pharisees responded to them: "Are you fooled too? [48] Have any of the rulers believed in Him? Or any of the Pharisees? [49] But this crowd, which doesn't know the law, is accursed!"

[50] Nicodemus—the one who came to Him previously, being one of them—said to them, [51] "Our law doesn't judge a man before it hears from him and knows what he's doing, does it?"

[52] "You aren't from Galilee too, are you?" they replied. "Search and see: no prophet arises from Galilee."[c]

[2][53] So each one went to his house.

8 But Jesus went to the Mount of Olives.

AN ADULTERESS FORGIVEN

[2] At dawn He went to the temple complex again, and all the people were coming to Him. He sat down and began to teach them.

[3] Then the scribes and the Pharisees brought a woman caught in adultery, making her stand in the center. [4] "Teacher," they said to Him, "this woman was caught in the act of committing adultery. [5] In the law Moses commanded us to stone such women. So what do You say?" [6] They asked this to trap Him, in order that they might have evidence to accuse Him.

Jesus stooped down and started writing on the ground

Your Relationship with Christ Colors Everything

Everything in your Christian life, every-thing about knowing Him and experiencing Him, everything about knowing His will depends on the quality of your love relationship to God.

"The one who believes in Me, as the Scripture has said, will have streams of living water flow from deep within him."

—John 7:38

---

[1]**7:46** Other mss read *like this man*
[2]**7:53** Other mss do not contain the verses in brackets (7:53—8:11).

---

[a]**7:42** Lit *seed*
[b]**7:45** See v. 32 note
[c]**7:52** Jonah (2 Kg 14:25) and prob-ably other prophets did come from Galilee.

WORD STUDY

Greek word: **phos** [FOHSS]
Translation: **light**
Uses in John: **23**
(Mt, 7; Mk, 1; Lk, 7)
Uses in John's writings: **33**
Uses in the NT: **73**
Key passages: **John 1:4–5;
8:12; 9:5**

The word *phos* is seldom used in the literal sense in the NT. Most often it is a metaphor referring to holiness, purity, or godliness. Jesus used the term in the Sermon on the Mount to describe His disciples and the holy standard of conduct that He expected them to model to the world (Mt 5:14–16; 6:23). In John's Gospel, however, Jesus Himself is "the light," as stated in the Prologue (1:4–5) and in Jesus' own words (8:12; 9:5). In this case, the light is revelatory and reflects God's character or holiness; in other words, *the light* refers to God's revelation or disclosure of Himself to the world in the incarnation (1:4–9). Incredibly, those in darkness prefer the darkness, at least until they accept the truth of God's revelation in His Son and believe in the light (3:19–21; 8:12; 12:46).

with His finger. [7] When they persisted in questioning Him, He stood up and said to them, "The one without sin among you should be the first to throw a stone at her."

[8] Then He stooped down again and continued writing on the ground. [9] When they heard this, they left one by one, starting with the older men.[1] Only He was left, with the woman in the center. [10] When Jesus stood up, He said to her, "Woman,[a] where are they? Has no one condemned you?"

[11] "No one, Lord,"[b] she answered.

"Neither do I condemn you," said Jesus. "Go, and from now on do not sin any more."|

[12] Then Jesus spoke to them again: "I am the light of the world. Anyone who follows Me will never walk in the darkness, but will have the light of life."

JESUS' SELF-WITNESS

[13] So the Pharisees said to Him, "You are testifying about Yourself. Your testimony is not valid."[c]

[14] "Even if I testify about Myself," Jesus replied, "My testimony is valid,[d] because I know where I came from and where I'm going. But you don't know where I come from or where I'm going. [15] You judge by human standards.[e] I judge no one. [16] And if I do judge, My judgment is true, because I am not alone, but I and the Father who sent Me judge together.[f] [17] Even in your law it is written that the witness of two men is valid. [18] I am the One who testifies about Myself, and the Father who sent Me testifies about Me."

[19] Then they asked Him, "Where is Your Father?"

"You know neither Me nor My Father," Jesus answered. "If you knew Me, you would also know My Father." [20] He spoke these words by the treasury,[g] while teaching in the temple complex. But no one seized Him, because His hour[h] had not come.

[1] **8:9** Other mss read *this, being convicted by their own conscience, went out one by one, starting with the older men to the youngest*

---

[a] **8:10** See 2:4 note
[b] **8:11** Or *Sir;* see 4:15,49; 5:7; 6:34; 9:36
[c] **8:13** The law of Moses required at least two witnesses to make a claim legally valid (v. 17).
[d] **8:14** Or *true*

[e] **8:15** Lit *You judge according to the flesh*
[f] **8:16** *judge together* added for clarity
[g] **8:20** A place for offerings to be given, perhaps in the court of women
[h] **8:20** See 2:4 note

JESUS PREDICTS HIS DEPARTURE

²¹ Then He said to them again, "I'm going away; you will look for Me, and you will die in your sin. Where I'm going, you cannot come."

²² So the Jews said again, "He won't kill Himself, will He, since He says, 'Where I'm going, you cannot come'?"

²³ "You are from below," He told them, "I am from above. You are of this world; I am not of this world. ²⁴ Therefore I told you that you will die in your sins. For if you do not believe that I am He,^a you will die in your sins."

²⁵ "Who are You?" they questioned.

"Precisely what I've been telling you from the very beginning," Jesus told them. ²⁶ "I have many things to say and to judge about you, but the One who sent Me is true, and what I have heard from Him—these things I tell the world."

²⁷ They did not know He was speaking to them about the Father. ²⁸ So Jesus said to them, "When you lift up the Son of Man, then you will know that I am He,^b and that I do nothing on My own. But just as the Father taught Me, I say these things. ²⁹ The One who sent Me is with Me. He has not left Me alone, because I always do what pleases Him."

TRUTH AND FREEDOM

³⁰ As He was saying these things, many believed in Him. ³¹ So Jesus said to the Jews who had believed Him, "If you continue in My word,^c you really are My disciples. ³² You will know the truth, and the truth will set you free."

³³ "We are descendants^d of Abraham," they answered Him, "and we have never been enslaved to anyone. How can You say, 'You will become free'?"

³⁴ Jesus responded, "I assure you:^e Everyone who commits sin is a slave of sin. ³⁵ A slave does not remain in the household forever, but a son does remain forever. ³⁶ Therefore if the Son sets you free, you really will be free. ³⁷ I know you are descendants^f of Abraham, but

Make the Sacrifices of Right Choices

Until you are ready to make any adjustment necessary to follow and obey what God has said, you will be of little use to God. Your greatest single difficulty in following God may come at the point of the adjustment.

When Jesus stood up, He said to her, "Woman, where are they? Has no one condemned you?" "No one, Lord," she answered. "Neither do I condemn you," said Jesus. "Go, and from now on do not sin any more."

—John 8:10–11

You Are Never as Free as When You're Following God

When God gives you a command, He is trying to protect and preserve the best He has for you. He is not restricting you. He is freeing you.

So Jesus said to the Jews who had believed Him, "If you continue in My word, you really are My disciples. You will know the truth, and the truth will set you free."

—John 8:31–32

---

^a**8:24** Lit *I am;* Jesus claimed to be deity, but the Pharisees didn't understand His meaning.
^b**8:28** See 8:24 note
^c**8:31** Or *My teaching;* or *My message*
^d**8:33** Or *offspring;* lit *seed* (see 7:42)
^e**8:34** See 1:51 note
^f**8:37** See v. 33 note

you are trying to kill Me because My word[a] is not welcome among you. [38] I speak what I have seen in the presence of the Father,[1] and therefore you do what you have heard from your father."

[39] "Our father is Abraham!" they replied.

"If you were Abraham's children," Jesus told them, "you would do what Abraham did. [40] But now you are trying to kill Me, a man who has told you the truth that I heard from God. Abraham did not do this! [41] You're doing what your father does."

"We weren't born of sexual immorality," they said. "We have one Father—God."

[42] Jesus said to them, "If God were your Father, you would love Me, because I came from God and I am here. For I didn't come on My own, but He sent Me. [43] Why don't you understand what I say? Because you cannot listen to[b] My word. [44] You are of your father the Devil, and you want to carry out your father's desires. He was a murderer from the beginning and has not stood in the truth, because there is no truth in him. When he tells a lie, he speaks from his own nature,[c] because he is a liar and the father of liars.[d] [45] Yet because I tell the truth, you do not believe Me. [46] Who among you can convict Me of sin? If I tell the truth, why don't you believe Me? [47] The one who is from God listens to God's words. This is why you don't listen, because you are not from God."

JESUS AND ABRAHAM

[48] The Jews responded to Him, "Aren't we right in saying that You're a Samaritan and have a demon?"

[49] "I do not have a demon," Jesus answered. "On the contrary, I honor My Father and you dishonor Me. [50] I do not seek My glory; the One who seeks it also judges. [51] I assure you:[e] If anyone keeps My word, he will never see death—ever!"

[52] Then the Jews said, "Now we know You have a demon. Abraham died and so did the prophets. You say, 'If anyone keeps My word, he will never taste death—ever!' [53] Are You greater than our father Abraham who

God Is Speaking. Are You Listening?

Does God really speak to His people in our day? Yes! Will He reveal to you where He is working when He wants to use you? Yes! God has not changed. He still speaks to His people.

"The one who is from God listens to God's words."

—John 8:47a

---

[1]8:38 Other mss read *of My Father*

---

[a]8:37 See v. 31 note
[b]8:43 Or *hear*
[c]8:44 Lit *from his own things*

[d]8:44 Lit *of it*
[e]8:51 See 1:51 note

died? Even the prophets died. Who do You pretend to be?"[a]

[54] "If I glorify Myself," Jesus answered, "My glory is nothing. My Father is the One who glorifies Me, of whom you say, 'He is our God.' [55] You've never known Him, but I know Him. If I were to say I don't know Him, I would be a liar like you. But I do know Him, and I keep His word. [56] Your father Abraham was overjoyed that he would see My day; he saw it and rejoiced."

[57] The Jews replied, "You aren't fifty years old yet, and You've seen Abraham?"[1]

[58] Jesus said to them, "I assure you:[b] Before Abraham was, I am."[c]

[59] At that, they picked up stones to throw at Him. But Jesus was hidden[d] and went out of the temple complex.[2]

THE SIXTH SIGN: HEALING A MAN BORN BLIND

9 As He was passing by, He saw a man blind from birth. [2] His disciples questioned Him: "Rabbi, who sinned, this man or his parents, that he was born blind?"

[3] "Neither this man sinned nor his parents," Jesus answered. "This came about[e] so that God's works might be displayed in him. [4] We[3] must do the works of Him who sent Me[4] while it is day. Night is coming when no one can work. [5] As long as I am in the world, I am the light of the world."

[6] After He said these things He spit on the ground, made some mud from the saliva, and spread the mud on his eyes. [7] "Go," He told him, "wash in the pool of Siloam" (which means "Sent"). So he left, washed, and came back seeing.

[8] His neighbors and those who formerly had seen him as a beggar said, "Isn't this the man who sat begging?"

Take Your Orders One Day at a Time

God doesn't usually give you a one-time assignment and leave you there forever. Yes, you may be placed in one job at one place for a long time, but God's assignments come to you on a daily basis.

"We must do the works of Him who sent Me while it is day."

—John 9:4a

---

[1] **8:57** Other mss read *and Abraham has seen You?*
[2] **8:59** Other mss add *and having gone through their midst, He passed by*
[3] **9:4** Other mss read *I*
[4] **9:4** Other mss read *sent us*

---

[a] **8:53** Lit *Who do You make Yourself?*
[b] **8:58** See 1:51 note
[c] **8:58** *I AM* is the name God gave Himself at the burning bush (see Ex 3:13–14); see 8:24 note.
[d] **8:59** Or *Jesus hid Himself*
[e] **9:3** *This came about* added for clarity

WORD STUDY

Greek word: **hamartolos**
[hah mahr toh LAHSS]

Translation: **sinner**

Uses in John: **4**
(Mt, 5; Mk, 6; Lk, 18)

Uses in John's writings: **4**

Uses in the NT: **47**

Key passages: **John 9:16,24,25,31**

One of the key doctrines of the Christian faith is that every person is a sinner and must believe in Jesus as Savior to have eternal life. This teaching is consistent with the use of the word *hamartolos (sinner)* in several places and with other related passages about sin (Rm 3:9–23; 5:12). A special use of the term *hamartolos* occurs in the Gospels and refers to those who have a reputation for being guilty of grievous sins, such as tax collectors, prostitutes, and pagans (see Mt 9:10–11; Lk 6:32–34; 7:34–39). In the aftermath of Jesus' miracle of healing the man born blind (Jn 9), Jewish leaders used the term *sinner* in this especially derisive sense to describe Jesus (v. 24). In doing so they hoped to undermine the clear implication of this miracle—that Jesus was the Messiah—and to keep people from following Him.

[9] Some said, "He's the one." "No," others were saying, "but he looks like him."

He kept saying, "I'm the one!"

[10] Therefore they asked him, "Then how were your eyes opened?"

[11] He answered, "The man called Jesus made mud, spread it on my eyes, and told me, 'Go to Siloam and wash.' So when I went and washed I received my sight."

[12] "Where is He?" they asked.

"I don't know," he said.

THE HEALED MAN'S TESTIMONY

[13] They brought to the Pharisees the man who used to be blind. [14] The day that Jesus made the mud and opened his eyes was a Sabbath. [15] So again the Pharisees asked him how he received his sight.

"He put mud on my eyes," he told them. "I washed and I can see."

[16] Therefore some of the Pharisees said, "This man is not from God, for He doesn't keep the Sabbath!" But others were saying, "How can a sinful man perform such signs?" And there was a division among them.

[17] Again they asked the blind man,[a] "What do you say about Him, since He opened your eyes?"

"He's a prophet," he said.

[18] The Jews did not believe this about him—that he was blind and received sight—until they summoned the parents of the one who had received his sight. [19] They asked them, "Is this your son, whom you say was born blind? How then does he now see?"

[20] "We know this is our son and that he was born blind," his parents answered. [21] "But we don't know how he now sees, and we don't know who opened his eyes. Ask him; he's of age. He will speak for himself." [22] His parents said these things because they were afraid of the Jews, since the Jews had already agreed that if anyone confessed Him as Messiah, he would be banned from the synagogue. [23] This is why his parents said, "He's of age; ask him."

[24] So a second time they summoned the man who had

[a] 9:17 That is, the man who had been blind

been blind and told him, "Give glory to God.[a] We know that this man is a sinner!"

25 He answered, "Whether or not He's a sinner, I don't know. One thing I do know: I was blind, and now I can see!"

26 Then they asked him, "What did He do to you? How did He open your eyes?"

27 "I already told you," he said, "and you didn't listen. Why do you want to hear it again? You don't want to become His disciples too, do you?"

28 They ridiculed him: "You're that man's disciple, but we're Moses' disciples. 29 We know that God has spoken to Moses. But this man—we don't know where He's from!"

30 "This is an amazing thing," the man told them. "You don't know where He is from; yet He opened my eyes! 31 We know that God doesn't listen to sinners; but if anyone is God-fearing and does His will, He listens to him. 32 Throughout history[b] no one has ever heard of someone opening the eyes of a person born blind. 33 If this man were not from God, He wouldn't be able to do anything."

34 "You were born entirely in sin," they replied, "and are you trying to teach us?" Then they threw him out.[c]

THE BLIND MAN'S SIGHT AND THE PHARISEES' BLINDNESS

35 When Jesus heard that they had thrown the man out, He found him and asked, "Do you believe in the Son of Man?"[1d]

36 "Who is He, Sir, that I may believe in Him?" he asked in return.

37 Jesus answered, "You have both seen Him and He is the One speaking with you."

38 "I believe, Lord!" he said, and he worshiped Him.

39 Jesus said, "I came into this world for judgment, in order that those who do not see may see and those who do see may become blind."

40 Some of the Pharisees who were with Him heard

Look for More Than Circumstances

Never, ever determine the truth of a situation by looking at the circumstances. Don't evaluate your situation until you have heard from Jesus. He is the Truth of all your circumstances.

He answered, "Whether or not He's a sinner, I don't know. One thing I do know: I was blind, and now I can see!"

—John 9:25

God Will Give You Everything You Need

God will never give you an assignment that He will not, at the same time, enable you to complete. That is what a spiritual gift is—a supernatural empowering to accomplish the assignment God gives you.

"If this man were not from God, He wouldn't be able to do anything."

—John 9:33

---

1 9:35 Other mss read *the Son of God*

---

a 9:24 *Give glory to God* was a solemn charge to tell the truth (see Jos 7:19).
b 9:32 Lit *From the age*
c 9:34 That is, they banned him from the synagogue (see v. 22).
d 9:35 See 1:51 note

WORD STUDY

Greek word: **poimen**
[poy MAYN]

Translation: **shepherd**

Uses in John: **6**
(Mt, 3; Mk, 2; Lk, 4)

Uses in John's writings: **6**

Uses in the NT: **18**

Key passage: **John 10:1–18**

The Greek word *poimen* occurs in John's Gospel only in John 10 where Jesus refers to Himself as "the good shepherd who lays down his life for the sheep" (v. 11). The sheep (believers) and the shepherd (Jesus) know each other, and the shepherd will bring all the sheep from the various folds (nations) into one flock (vv. 14–16).

The background for Jesus' use of the shepherd imagery is Ezekiel 34. God denounced the false shepherds (that is, false prophets) who led the sheep (the nation of Judah) astray (vv. 1–10). Then the LORD said, "I Myself will search for My sheep, and I will seek them out" from among the many places they are scattered (vv. 11–12). Finally, David will be the shepherd over God's people again (vv. 23–24). In using the shepherd/sheep imagery, Jesus was identifying Himself as the Shepherd of Israel, just as the LORD had done in this OT passage—a clear statement that Jesus claimed to be deity. Jesus also indicated that He would have the role of David as shepherd—a clear statement that Jesus claimed to be the Messiah. No wonder "a division took place among the Jews" (v. 19) at this time! Some even thought Jesus was demon possessed, but others took Jesus' claim seriously since He had healed a blind man (vv. 20–21).

these things and asked Him, "We aren't blind too, are we?"

[41] "If you were blind," Jesus told them, "you wouldn't have sin.[a] But now that you say, 'We see'—your sin remains.

THE IDEAL SHEPHERD

10 "I assure you:[b] Anyone who doesn't enter the sheep pen by the door, but climbs in some other way, is a thief and a robber. [2] The one who enters by the door is the shepherd of the sheep. [3] The doorkeeper opens it for him, and the sheep hear his voice. He calls his own sheep by name and leads them out. [4] When he has brought all his own outside, he goes ahead of them. The sheep follow him because they recognize his voice. [5] They will never follow a stranger; instead they will run away from him, because they don't recognize the voice of strangers."

[6] Jesus gave them this illustration, but they did not understand what He was telling them.

THE GOOD SHEPHERD

[7] So Jesus said again, "I assure you:[c] I am the door of the sheep. [8] All who came before Me[1] are thieves and robbers, but the sheep didn't listen to them. [9] I am the door. If anyone enters by Me, he will be saved, and will come in and go out and find pasture. [10] A thief comes only to steal and to kill and to destroy. I have come that they may have life and have it in abundance.

[11] "I am the good shepherd. The good shepherd lays down His life for the sheep. [12] The hired man, since he's not the shepherd and doesn't own the sheep, leaves them[d] and runs away when he sees a wolf coming. The wolf then snatches and scatters them. [13] This happens[e] because he is a hired man and doesn't care about the sheep.

[14] "I am the good shepherd. I know My own sheep, and they know Me, [15] as the Father knows Me, and I

---

[1] **10:8** Other mss omit *before Me*

---

[a] **9:41** *To have sin* is an idiom that refers to guilt caused by sin.
[b] **10:1** See 1:51 note
[c] **10:7** See 1:51 note

[d] **10:12** Lit *sheep*
[e] **10:13** *This happens* added for clarity

know the Father. I lay down My life for the sheep. [16] But I have other sheep that are not of this fold; I must bring them also, and they will listen to My voice. Then there will be one flock, one shepherd. [17] This is why the Father loves Me, because I am laying down My life that I may take it up again. [18] No one takes it from Me, but I lay it down on My own. I have the right to lay it down and I have the right to take it up again. I have received this command from My Father."

[19] Again a division[a] took place among the Jews because of these words. [20] Many of them were saying, "He has a demon and He's crazy! Why do you listen to Him?" [21] Others were saying, "These aren't the words of someone demon-possessed. Can a demon open the eyes of the blind?"

JESUS AT THE FESTIVAL OF DEDICATION

[22] Then the Festival of Dedication[b] took place in Jerusalem; and it was winter. [23] Jesus was walking in the temple complex in Solomon's Colonnade.[c] [24] Then the Jews surrounded Him and asked, "How long are you going to keep us in suspense?[d] If You are the Messiah,[ef] tell us plainly."[g]

[25] "I did tell you and you don't believe," Jesus answered them. "The works that I do in My Father's name testify about Me. [26] But you don't believe because you are not My sheep.[1] [27] My sheep hear My voice, I know them, and they follow Me. [28] I give them eternal life, and they will never perish—ever! No one will snatch them out of My hand. [29] My Father, who has given them to Me, is greater than all. No one is able to snatch them out of the Father's hand. [30] The Father and I are one."[h]

[1] **10:26** Other mss read *not My sheep, just as I told you*

---

[a] **10:19** 7:43
[b] **10:22** Or *Hannukah,* also called *the Feast of Lights.* This festival commemorated the rededication of the temple in 164 B.C.
[c] **10:23** See 5:2 note
[d] **10:24** Lit *How long are you taking away our life?*
[e] **10:24** Or *the Christ*
[f] **10:24** See 1:41 note
[g] **10:24** Or *openly, publicly*
[h] **10:30** Lit *I and the Father—We are one.*

Trust Him to Speak Where You Can Hear

God speaks to individuals, and He can do it in any way He pleases. As you walk in an intimate love relationship with God, you will come to recognize His voice. You will know when God is speaking to you.

"The sheep follow him because they recognize his voice."

—John 10:4b

WORD STUDY

Greek word: ***anastasis***
[ah NAH stah sihss]

Translation: **resurrection**

Uses in John's Gospel: **4**
(Mt, 4; Mk, 2; Lk, 6)

Uses in John's writings: **6**

Uses in the NT: **42**

Key passages: **John 5:29; 11:24–
25; Rev 20:5–6**

The Greek noun *anastasis* is derived from the verb *anistemi,*
meaning literally *to stand up* and
then by extension "to rise up."
Both words could be used metaphorically. The word *anastasis*
was common in the ancient Greek
world, but it rarely referred to the
resurrection of the dead, which is
the dominant meaning of its occurrences in the NT. Two major
events are described with the
word *anastasis* in the NT: the
physical, bodily resurrection of
Jesus in the past (Jn 11:25; Rm 1:4;
1 Co 15:12–13), and the physical,
bodily resurrection of believers in
the future (Jn 5:29; 11:24; 1 Co
15:42; Php 3:11; Rv 20:5–6).

RENEWED EFFORTS TO STONE JESUS

³¹ Again the Jews picked up rocks to stone Him.

³² Jesus replied, "I have shown you many good works from the Father. For which of these works are you ston-ing Me?"

³³ "We aren't stoning You for a good work," the Jews answered, "but for blasphemy, and because You—being a man—make Yourself God."

³⁴ Jesus answered them, "Isn't it written in your law,[1] 'I said, you are gods'?ᵃ ³⁵ If He called those to whom the word of God came 'gods'—and the Scripture cannot be broken— ³⁶ do you say, 'You are blaspheming,' to the One the Father set apart and sent into the world, because I said 'I am the Son of God'? ³⁷ If I am not doing My Father's works, don't believe Me. ³⁸ But if I am doing them and you don't believe Me, believe the works. This way you will know and understand[2] that the Father is in Me and I in the Father." ³⁹ Then they were trying again to seize Him,ᵇ yet He eluded their grasp.

MANY BEYOND THE JORDAN BELIEVE IN JESUS

⁴⁰ So He departed again across the Jordan to the place where John first was baptizing, and He remained there. ⁴¹ Many came to Him and said, "John never did a sign, but everything John said about this man was true." ⁴² And many believed in Him there.

LAZARUS DIES AT BETHANY

11 Now a man was sick, Lazarus from Bethany, the village of Mary and her sister Martha. ² Mary was the one who anointed the Lord with fragrant oil and wiped His feet with her hair,ᶜ and it was her brother Laz-arus who was sick. ³ So the sisters sent a message to Him: "Lord, the one You love is sick."

⁴ When Jesus heard it, He said, "This sickness will not end in death, but is for the glory of God, so that the Son of God may be glorified through it." ⁵ (Jesus loved

[1]**10:34** Other mss read *in the law*
[2]**10:38** Other mss read *know and believe*

ᵃ**10:34** Ps 82:6   ᶜ**11:2** 12:3
ᵇ**10:39** 7:44

Martha, her sister, and Lazarus.) [6]So when He heard that he was sick, He stayed two more days in the place where He was. [7]Then after that, He said to the disciples, "Let's go to Judea again."

[8]"Rabbi," the disciples told Him, "just now the Jews tried to stone You, and You're going there again?"

[9]"Aren't there twelve hours in a day?" Jesus answered. "If anyone walks during the day, he doesn't stumble, because he sees the light of this world. [10]If anyone walks during the night, he does stumble, because the light is not in him." [11]He said this, and then He told them, "Our friend Lazarus has fallen asleep, but I'm on My way to wake him up."

[12]Then the disciples said to Him, "Lord, if he has fallen asleep, he will get well."

[13]Jesus, however, was speaking about his death, but they thought He was speaking about natural sleep. [14]So Jesus then told them plainly, "Lazarus has died. [15]I'm glad for you that I wasn't there, so that you may believe. But let's go to him."

[16]Then Thomas (called "Twin") said to his fellow disciples, "Let's go so that we may die with Him."

THE RESURRECTION AND THE LIFE

[17]When Jesus arrived, He found that Lazarus[a] had already been in the tomb four days. [18]Bethany was near Jerusalem (about two miles[b] away). [19]Many of the Jews had come to Martha and Mary to comfort them about their brother. [20]As soon as Martha heard that Jesus was coming, she went to meet Him. But Mary remained seated in the house.

[21]Then Martha said to Jesus, "Lord, if You had been here, my brother wouldn't have died. [22]Yet even now I know that whatever You ask from God, God will give You."

[23]"Your brother will rise again," Jesus told her.

[24]Martha said, "I know that he will rise again in the resurrection at the last day."

[25]Jesus said to her, "I am the resurrection and the life. The one who believes in Me, even if he dies, will live.

Pray Expectantly

When I pray, it never crosses my mind that God is not going to answer. Expect God to answer prayer, but stick around for the answer. His timing is always right and best.

Then Martha said to Jesus, "Lord, if You had been here, my brother wouldn't have died. Yet even now I know that whatever You ask from God, God will give You."

—John 11:21–22

---

[a]**11:17** Lit *he*   [b]**11:18** Gk *fifteen stadia*

²⁶Everyone who lives and believes in Me will never die—ever. Do you believe this?"

²⁷"Yes, Lord," she told Him, "I believe You are the Messiah, the Son of God, who was to come into the world."

JESUS SHARES
THE SORROW OF DEATH

²⁸Having said this, she went back and called her sister Mary, saying in private, "The Teacher is here and is calling for you."

²⁹As soon as she heard this, she got up quickly and went to Him. ³⁰Jesus had not yet come into the village, but was still in the place where Martha had met Him. ³¹The Jews who were with her in the house consoling her saw that Mary got up quickly and went out. So they followed her, supposing that she was going to the tomb to cry there.

³²When Mary came to where Jesus was and saw Him, she fell at His feet and told Him, "Lord, if You had been here, my brother would not have died!"

³³When Jesus saw her crying, and the Jews who had come with her crying, He was angry[a] in His spirit and deeply moved. ³⁴"Where have you put him?" He asked.

"Lord," they told Him, "come and see."

³⁵Jesus wept.

³⁶So the Jews said, "See how He loved him!" ³⁷But some of them said, "Couldn't He who opened the blind man's eyes also have kept this man from dying?"

THE SEVENTH SIGN:
RAISING LAZARUS FROM THE DEAD

³⁸Then Jesus, angry[b] in Himself again, came to the tomb. It was a cave, and a stone was lying against it. ³⁹"Remove the stone," Jesus said.

Martha, the dead man's sister, told Him, "Lord, he already stinks. It's been four days."

⁴⁰Jesus said to her, "Did I not tell you that if you believed you would see the glory of God?"

⁴¹So they removed the stone. Then Jesus raised His eyes and said, "Father, I thank You that You heard Me.

Repeat These Words: "Yes, Lord."

Two words in the Christian's language cannot go together: "No, Lord." If He really is your Lord, your answer must always be "Yes."

"Yes, Lord," she told Him, "I believe You are the Messiah, the Son of God, who was to come into the world."

—John 11:27

---

[a]**11:33** The Gk word is very strong and probably indicates Jesus' anger against sin's tyranny and death.
[b]**11:38** See v. 33 note

[42] I know that You always hear Me, but because of the crowd standing here I said this, so they may believe You sent Me." [43] After He said this, He shouted with a loud voice, "Lazarus, come out!" [44] The dead man came out bound hand and foot with linen strips and with his face wrapped in a cloth. Jesus said to them, "Loose him and let him go."

THE PLOT TO KILL JESUS

[45] Therefore many of the Jews who came to Mary and saw what He did believed in Him. [46] But some of them went to the Pharisees and told them what Jesus had done.

[47] So the chief priests and the Pharisees convened the Sanhedrin[a] and said, "What are we going to do since this man does many signs? [48] If we let Him continue in this way, everybody will believe in Him! Then the Romans will come and remove both our place[b] and our nation."

[49] One of them, Caiaphas, who was high priest that year, said to them, "You know nothing at all! [50] You're not considering that it is to your[1] advantage that one man should die for the people rather than the whole nation perish." [51] He did not say this on his own; but being high priest that year he prophesied that Jesus was going to die for the nation, [52] and not for the nation only, but also to unite the scattered children of God. [53] So from that day on they plotted to kill Him. [54] Therefore Jesus no longer walked openly among the Jews, but departed from there to the countryside near the wilderness, to a town called Ephraim. And He stayed there with the disciples.

[55] Now the Jewish Passover was near, and before the Passover many went up to Jerusalem from the country to purify[c] themselves. [56] They were looking for Jesus, and asking one another as they stood in the temple

---

When You Believe, God Makes Your Life Unbelievable

Anyone who will take the time to enter into an intimate relationship with God can see God do extraordinary things through his or her life.

Jesus said to her, "Did I not tell you that if you believed you would see the glory of God?"

—John 11:40

---

[1] **11:50** Other mss read *to our*

---

[a] **11:47** The Jewish council in Jerusalem with religious, civil, and criminal authority

[b] **11:48** The temple or possibly all of Jerusalem

[c] **11:55** The law of Moses required God's people to purify or cleanse themselves so they could celebrate the Passover. Jews often came to Jerusalem a week early to do this (Nm 9:4-11).

complex: "What do you think? He won't come to the festival, will He?"

⁵⁷ The chief priests and the Pharisees had given orders that if anyone knew where He was, he should report it so they could arrest Him.

THE ANOINTING AT BETHANY

12 Six days before the Passover, Jesus came to Bethany where Lazarus[1] was, whom Jesus had raised from the dead. ² So they gave a dinner for Him there; Martha was serving them, and Lazarus was one of those reclining at the table with Him. ³ Then Mary took a pound of fragrant oil—pure and expensive nard—anointed Jesus' feet, and wiped His feet with her hair. So the house was filled with the fragrance of the oil.

⁴ Then one of His disciples, Judas Iscariot (who was about to betray Him), said, ⁵ "Why wasn't this fragrant oil sold for three hundred denarii[a] and given to the poor?" ⁶ He didn't say this because he cared about the poor, but because he was a thief. He was in charge of the money bag and would steal part of what was put in it.

⁷ Jesus answered, "Leave her alone; she has kept it for the day of My burial. ⁸ For you always have the poor with you, but you do not always have Me."

THE DECISION TO KILL LAZARUS

⁹ Then a large crowd of the Jews learned that He was there. They came not only because of Jesus, but also to see Lazarus whom He had raised from the dead. ¹⁰ Therefore the chief priests decided to kill Lazarus too, ¹¹ because he was the reason many of the Jews were deserting them[b] and believing in Jesus.

THE TRIUMPHAL ENTRY

¹² The next day, when the large crowd that had come to the festival heard that Jesus was coming to Jerusalem, ¹³ they took palm branches and went out to meet Him.

[1]12:1 Other mss read *Lazarus who died*

[a]12:5 This amount was about a year's wages for a common worker.

[b]12:11 Lit *going away*

Your First Priority: Love Him

Can you describe your relationship with God by sincerely saying, "I love Him with all my heart"?

Then Mary took a pound of fragrant oil—pure and expensive nard—anointed Jesus' feet, and wiped His feet with her hair.

—John 12:3

God's Will Is an Expensive Calling

You cannot know and do the will of God without paying the price of adjustment and obedience.

"I assure you: Unless a grain of wheat falls into the ground and dies, it remains by itself. But if it dies, it produces a large crop."

—John 12:24

They kept shouting: **"Hosanna!**[a] **'Blessed is He who comes in the name of the Lord'**[b]—the King of Israel!"

[14] Jesus found a young donkey and sat on it, just as it is written: [15] **"Fear no more, Daughter of Zion; look! your King is coming, sitting on a donkey's colt."**[c]

[16] His disciples did not understand these things at first. However when Jesus was glorified, then they remembered that these things had been written about Him and that they had done these things to Him. [17] Meanwhile the crowd, which had been with Him when He called Lazarus out of the tomb and raised him from the dead, continued to testify.[1] [18] This is also why the crowd met Him, because they heard He had done this sign.

[19] Then the Pharisees said to one another, "You see? You've accomplished nothing. Look—the world has gone after Him!"

JESUS PREDICTS HIS CRUCIFIXION

[20] Now among those who went up to worship at the festival were some Greeks. [21] So they came to Philip, who was from Bethsaida in Galilee, and requested of him, "Sir, we want to see Jesus."

[22] Philip went and told Andrew; then Andrew and Philip went and told Jesus. [23] Jesus replied to them, "The hour has come for the Son of Man to be glorified.

[24] "I assure you:[d] Unless a grain of wheat falls into the ground and dies, it remains by itself. But if it dies, it produces a large crop.[e] [25] The one who loves his life will lose it, and the one who hates his life in this world will keep it for eternal life. [26] If anyone serves Me, he must follow Me. Where I am, there My servant also will be. If anyone serves Me, the Father will honor him.

[27] "Now My soul is troubled. What should I say— 'Father, save Me from this hour'? But that is why I came to this hour. [28] Father, glorify Your name!"[2]

---

[1] **12:17** Other mss read *Meanwhile the crowd, which had been with Him, continued to testify that He had called Lazarus out of the tomb and raised him from the dead.*
[2] **12:28** Other mss read *Your Son*

---

[a] **12:13** *Hosanna* is a term of praise derived from the Hb word for *save* (see Ps 118:25).
[b] **12:13** Ps 118:25–26
[c] **12:15** Zch 9:9
[d] **12:24** See 1:51 note
[e] **12:24** Lit *much fruit*

What You Do Will Reveal Who You Are

You cannot stay where you are and go with God. You cannot continue doing things your way and accomplish God's purposes in His ways.

"If anyone serves Me, he must follow Me. Where I am, there My servant also will be. If anyone serves Me, the Father will honor him."

—John 12:26

Keep Your Focus on Today

God always will give you enough specific directions to do *now* what He wants you to do. When you need more directions, He gives you more in His timing.

"Now My soul is troubled. What should I say—'Father, save Me from this hour'? But that is why I came to this hour."

—John 12:27

WORD STUDY

Greek word: ***doxa*** [DAHKS uh]
Translation: **glory, praise**
Uses in John's Gospel: **19**
(Mt, 7; Mk, 3; Lk, 13)
Uses in John's writings: **36**
Uses in the NT: **166**
Key passage: **John 12:41–43**

The use of *doxa (glory)* in the NT
is shaped by the Hebrew word *ka-bod* that is so common in the OT.
The noun *kabod* is derived from a
Hebrew verb meaning *to be heavy.*
(A related noun, *kebed,* means
liver, the heavy organ.) Thus, to
recognize the glory of something
is to attach weight or importance
to it. The glory of the Lord refers
to His nature and holiness as manifested to His creatures, humans
and angels, both of whom can
share in that glory. Even in the
incarnation, Jesus shared in the Father's glory and especially manifested His grace and truth (Jn 1:14;
see 17:5). The greatest manifestation of God's glory happened at
the cross (Jn 13:31–32; the related
verb *doxazo* [*glorify*] is used
here), for here God's greatest work
occurred. We praise God when we
give Him glory, acknowledging
that He is of greatest importance
to us. Thus, *doxa* may often mean
praise. John 12 contains a wordplay with these two meanings.
John stated that Isaiah saw God's
glory, which refers to the prophet's vision of the LORD in the temple with the seraphs exclaiming:
"Holy! Holy! Holy! is the LORD of
Hosts! His glory fills the whole
earth!" (Is 6:3). But according to
John, Isaiah saw the glory *(doxa)*
of Jesus (v. 41). Those who refused
to confess Him did so because
"they loved praise [*doxa*] from
men more than praise [*doxa*] from
God" (v. 43).

Then a voice came from heaven: "I have glorified it, and I will glorify it again!"

29 The crowd standing there heard it and said it was thunder. Others said, "An angel has spoken to Him!"

30 Jesus responded, "This voice came, not for Me, but for you. 31 Now is the judgment of this world. Now the ruler of this world will be cast out. 32 As for Me, if I am lifted up[a] from the earth I will draw all people[b] to Myself." 33 He said this to signify what kind of death He was about to die.

34 Then the crowd replied to Him, "We have heard from the law that the Messiah would remain forever.[c] So how can You say, 'The Son of Man must be lifted up'?[d] Who is this Son of Man?"

35 Jesus answered, "The light will be with you only a little longer. Walk while you have the light, so that darkness doesn't overtake you. The one who walks in darkness doesn't know where he's going. 36 While you have the light, believe in the light, so that you may become sons of light." Jesus said this, then went away and hid from them.

ISAIAH'S PROPHECIES FULFILLED

37 Even though He had performed so many signs in their presence, they did not believe in Him. 38 But this was to fulfill the word of Isaiah the prophet, who said:[e]

> **Lord, who has believed our report?**
> **And to whom has the arm of the Lord been revealed?**[f]

39 This is why they were unable to believe, because Isaiah also said:

> 40 **He has blinded their eyes**
> **and hardened their hearts,**[g]
> **so that they would not see with their eyes**
> **or understand with their hearts,**
> **and be converted,**
> **and I would heal them.**[h]

---

[a]12:32 Or *exalted*
[b]12:32 *people* is implied from the context
[c]12:34 Ps 89:36
[d]12:34 Or *exalted*
[e]12:38 Lit *which he said*
[f]12:38 Is 53:1
[g]12:40 Lit *heart* (both times)
[h]12:40 Is 6:10

[41] Isaiah said these things because[1] he saw His glory and spoke about Him.

[42] Nevertheless, many did believe in Him even among the rulers, but because of the Pharisees they did not confess Him, so they would not be banned from the synagogue. [43] For they loved praise from men more than praise[a] from God.

A SUMMARY OF JESUS' MISSION

[44] Then Jesus cried out, "The one who believes in Me believes not in Me, but in Him who sent Me. [45] And the one who sees Me sees Him who sent Me. [46] I have come as a light into the world, so that everyone who believes in Me would not remain in darkness. [47] If anyone hears My words and doesn't keep them, I do not judge him; for I did not come to judge the world, but to save the world. [48] The one who rejects Me and doesn't accept My sayings has this as his judge:[b] the word I have spoken will judge him on the last day. [49] For I have not spoken on My own, but the Father Himself who sent Me has given Me a command as to what I should say and what I should speak. [50] I know that His command is eternal life. So the things that I speak, I speak just as the Father has told Me."

JESUS WASHES HIS DISCIPLES' FEET

13 Before the Passover Festival, Jesus knew that His hour had come to depart from this world to the Father. Having loved His own who were in the world, He loved them to the end.[c]

[2] Now by the time of supper, the Devil had already put it into the heart of Judas, Simon Iscariot's son, to betray Him. [3] Jesus knew that the Father had given everything into His hands, that He had come from God, and that He was going back to God. [4] So He got up from supper, laid aside His robe, took a towel, and tied it around Himself. [5] Next, He poured water into a basin

---

[1]12:41 Other mss read *when*

[a]12:43 Lit *glory from men . . . glory from God;* see v. 41; 5:41
[b]12:48 Lit *has the one judging him*

[c]13:1 *to the end* can mean *completely* or *always*

God Has Put You Here for a Reason

What you plan to do for God is not important. What He plans to do where you are is very important.

"For I have not spoken on My own, but the Father Himself who sent Me has given Me a command as to what I should say and what I should speak."

—John 12:49

WORD STUDY

Greek word: *didaskalos*
[dih DAHSS kuh lahss]

Translation: **Teacher**

Uses in John: **8**
(Mt, 12; Mk, 12; Lk, 17)

Uses in John's writings: **8**

Uses in the NT: **59**

Key passage: **John 13:13-14**

The Greek word *didaskalos* refers to Jesus most of the time in the Gospels but never does outside the Gospels. In the Gospels the term is used of a recognized spiritual leader with a group of committed followers or disciples (see word study on *mathetes* on page 250). John used *didaskalos* as the Greek equivalent of the technical Hebrew term *rabbi* (see note at 1:38) and the similar term *rabbouni* (see note at 20:16). The teacher not only instructed people about the Word of God but in so doing challenged them to conform to its demands. Jesus did this better than anyone else; thus, the majority of times *didaskalos* refers to Jesus in the Gospels, it is used as a title ("Teacher"). So strong was the role of the teacher in the life of a disciple that Jesus connected it with His title as "Lord" (Jn 13:13–14).

and began to wash His disciples' feet and to dry them with the towel tied around Him.

⁶He came to Simon Peter, who asked Him, "Lord, are You going to wash my feet?"

⁷Jesus answered him, "What I'm doing you don't understand now, but afterward you will know."

⁸"You will never wash my feet—ever!" Peter said.

Jesus replied, "If I don't wash you, you have no part with Me."

⁹Simon Peter said to Him, "Lord, not only my feet, but also my hands and my head."

¹⁰ "One who has bathed," Jesus told him, "doesn't need to wash anything except his feet, but he is completely clean. You are clean, but not all of you." ¹¹For He knew who would betray Him. This is why He said, "You are not all clean."

THE MEANING OF FOOTWASHING

¹²When Jesus had washed their feet and put on His robe, He reclinedᵃ again and said to them, "Do you know what I have done for you? ¹³You call Me Teacher and Lord. This is well said, for I am. ¹⁴So if I, your Lord and Teacher, have washed your feet, you also ought to wash one another's feet. ¹⁵For I have given you an example that you also should do just as I have done for you.

¹⁶ "I assure you:ᵇ A slave is not greater than his master,ᶜᵈ and a messenger is not greater than the one who sent him. ¹⁷If you know these things, you are blessed if you do them. ¹⁸I'm not speaking about all of you; I know those I have chosen.ᵉ But the Scripture must be fulfilled: **'The one who eats My bread**ᶠ **has raised his heel against Me.'**ᵍ

¹⁹ "I am telling you now before it happens, so that when it does happen you will believe that I am He.ʰ ²⁰I assure you:ⁱ The one who receives whomever I send receives Me, and the one who receives Me receives Him who sent Me."

ᵃ**13:12** At important meals the custom was to recline on a mat at a low table and lean on the left elbow.
ᵇ**13:16** See 1:51 note
ᶜ**13:16** Or *lord*
ᵈ**13:16** 15:20
ᵉ**13:18** 6:70
ᶠ**13:18** Or *eats bread with Me*
ᵍ**13:18** Ps 41:9
ʰ**13:19** Lit *I am;* see 8:58 note
ⁱ**13:20** See 1:51 note

JUDAS' BETRAYAL PREDICTED

[21] When Jesus had said this, He was troubled in His spirit and testified, "I assure you:[a] One of you will betray Me!"

[22] The disciples started looking at one another—at a loss as to which one He was speaking about. [23] One of His disciples, whom Jesus loved,[b] was reclining close beside Jesus.[c] [24] Simon Peter motioned to him to find out who it was He was talking about. [25] So he leaned back against Jesus and asked Him, "Lord, who is it?"

[26] Jesus replied, "He's the one I give the piece of bread to after I have dipped it."[d] When He had dipped the bread, He gave it to Judas, Simon Iscariot's son.[1] [27] After Judas ate[e] the piece of bread, Satan entered him. Therefore Jesus told him, "What you're doing, do quickly."

[28] None of those reclining at the table knew why He told him this. [29] Since Judas kept the money bag, some thought that Jesus was telling him, "Buy what we need for the festival," or that he should give something to the poor. [30] After receiving the piece of bread, he went out immediately. And it was night.

THE NEW COMMANDMENT

[31] When he had gone out, Jesus said, "Now the Son of Man is glorified, and God is glorified in Him. [32] If God is glorified in Him,[2] God will also glorify Him in Himself, and will glorify Him at once.

[33] "Children, I am with you a little while longer. You will look for Me, and just as I told the Jews, 'Where I am going you cannot come,' so now I tell you.

[34] "I give you a new commandment: that you love one another. Just as I have loved you, you should also love one another. [35] By this all people will know that you are My disciples, if you have love for one another."

[1] 13:26 Other mss read *Judas Iscariot, Simon's son*
[2] 13:32 Other mss omit *If God is glorified in Him*

[a] 13:21 See 1:51 note
[b] 13:23 19:26; 20:2; 21:7,20
[c] 13:23 Lit *reclining at Jesus' breast;* that is, on His right; see 1:18
[d] 13:26 Ps 41:9
[e] 13:27 *Judas ate* added for clarity

WORD STUDY

Greek word: **mathetes**
[mah thay TAYSS]
Translation: **disciple**
Uses in John: **78**
(Mt, 76; Mk, 42; Lk, 37)
Uses in John's writings: **78**
Uses in the NT: **261**
Key passage: **John 13:35**

The English word *disciple* basically means *follower*. The Greek word *mathetes,* however, comes from the verb *manthano,* which means *to learn.* Thus, a *mathetes* is primarily a learner, though being a follower is certainly included. *Mathetes* occurs only in the Gospels and Acts and refers to disciples of various teachers or rabbis, such as the Pharisees (Mk 2:18) and John the Baptist (Jn 1:35). In Jewish life there was no such thing as a *mathetes* without a *didaskalos* (*teacher,* see word study on *didaskalos* on page 249), the person the disciple learned from. Most often in the NT *mathetes* refers to disciples of Jesus, sometimes in general (Jn 6:61,66) but most often to the Twelve. Jesus stated that the single attribute that characterizes His disciples is that they love one another (Jn 13:35).

PETER'S DENIALS PREDICTED

[36] "Lord," Simon Peter said to Him, "where are You going?"

Jesus answered, "Where I am going you cannot follow Me now; but you will follow later."

[37] "Lord," Peter asked, "why can't I follow You now? I will lay down my life for You!"

[38] Jesus replied, "Will you lay down your life for Me? I assure you:[a] A rooster will not crow until you have denied Me three times.

THE WAY TO THE FATHER

14 "Your heart must not be troubled. Believe in God; believe also in Me.[b] [2] In My Father's house are many dwelling places;[c] if not, I would have told you. I[1] am going away to prepare a place for you. [3] If I go away and prepare a place for you, I will come back and receive you to Myself, so that where I am you may be also. [4] You know the way where I am going."[2]

[5] "Lord," Thomas said, "we don't know where You're going. How can we know the way?"

[6] Jesus told him, "I am the way, the truth, and the life. No one comes to the Father except through Me.

JESUS REVEALS THE FATHER

[7] "If you know Me, you will also know[3] My Father. From now on you do know Him and have seen Him."

[8] "Lord," said Philip, "show us the Father, and that's enough for us."

[9] Jesus said to him, "Have I been among you all this time without your knowing Me, Philip? The one who has seen Me has seen the Father. How can you say, 'Show us the Father'? [10] Don't you believe that I am in the Father and the Father is in Me?[d] The words I speak to you I do not speak on My own. The Father who lives

[1] 14:2 Other mss read *For I*
[2] 14:4 Other mss read this verse as *And you know where I am going, and you know the way*
[3] 14:7 Other mss read *If you had known Me, you would have known*

[a] 13:38 See 1:51 note
[b] 14:1 Or *You believe in God; believe also in Me*
[c] 14:2 The Vulgate used the Latin term *mansio*, a traveler's resting place. The Gk word is related to the verb *meno*, meaning *remain* or *stay*, which occurs forty times in John.
[d] 14:10 10:30,38

You'd Be Surprised What He Can Do Through You

I have come to the place in my life that, if the assignment I sense God is giving me is something that I know I can handle, I know it probably is not from God.

"I assure you: The one who believes in Me will also do the works that I do. And he will do even greater works than these, because I am going to the Father."

—John 14:12

The Holy Spirit Will Steer You Right

When the Holy Spirit reveals Truth, He is not teaching you a concept to be thought about. He is leading you to a relationship with a Person.

"He is the Spirit of truth, whom the world is unable to receive because it doesn't see Him or know Him. But you do know Him, because He remains with you and will be in you."

—John 14:17

in Me does His works. [11] Believe Me that I am in the Father and the Father is in Me. Otherwise, believe[1] because of the works themselves.

PRAYING IN JESUS' NAME

[12] "I assure you:[a] The one who believes in Me will also do the works that I do. And he will do even greater works than these, because I am going to the Father. [13] Whatever you ask in My name, I will do it, so that the Father may be glorified in the Son. [14] If you ask Me[2] anything in My name, I will do it.

ANOTHER COUNSELOR PROMISED

[15] "If you love Me, you will keep[3] My commandments;[b] [16] and I also will ask the Father, and He will give you another Counselor[c] to be with you forever. [17] He is the Spirit of truth, whom the world is unable to receive because it doesn't see Him or know Him. But you do know Him, because He remains with you and will be[4] in you. [18] I will not leave you as orphans; I am coming to you.

THE FATHER, THE SON, AND THE HOLY SPIRIT

[19] "In a little while the world will see Me no longer, but you will see Me. Because I live, you will live too. [20] In that day you will know that I am in My Father, you are in Me, and I am in you. [21] The one who has My commandments and keeps them is the one who loves Me. And the one who loves Me will be loved by My Father. I also will love him and will reveal Myself to him."

[22] Judas (not Iscariot) said to him, "Lord, how is it You're going to reveal Yourself to us and not to the world?"

[23] Jesus answered, "If anyone loves Me, he will keep My word. My Father will love him, and We will come to him and make Our home with him. [24] The one who

[1] 14:11 Other mss read believe Me
[2] 14:14 Other mss omit Me; other mss omit all of v. 14
[3] 14:15 Other mss read If you love Me, keep (a command)
[4] 14:17 Other mss read is

[a] 14:12 See 1:51 note
[b] 14:15 1 Jn 5:3
[c] 14:16 Gk Parakletos, one called alongside to help, counsel, or protect (see v. 26; 15:26; 16:7; 1 Jn 2:1)

WORD STUDY

Greek word: **parakletos**
[pah RAH klay tahss]
Translation: **Counselor**
Uses in John: **4**
Uses in John's writings: **5**
Uses in the NT: **5**
Key passages: **John 14:16,26; 15:26; 16:7; 1 Jn 2:1**

The Greek word *parakletos* is derived from the verb *parakaleo* (literally *to call alongside;* basically *to comfort, counsel, exhort*). It is also related to the noun *paraklesis (comfort, exhortation)*. Both are much more common than *parakletos* but do not occur in John's writings, while *parakletos* occurs only in John's writings. In all four occurrences of *parakletos* in John's Gospel, Jesus used the term to refer to the Holy Spirit as our *Counselor.* The idea is that the Spirit comes alongside to aid us in the tasks Jesus gave us as His disciples.

WORD STUDY

Greek word: **meno** [MEHN oh]

Translation: **remain**

Uses in John's Gospel: **40**
(Mt, 3; Mk, 2; Lk, 7)

Uses in John's writings: **68**

Uses in the NT: **118**

Key passage: **John 15:1–16**

The Greek verb *meno* is commonly used in the NT to mean *remain* or *stay,* such as someone staying in a specific location (Mt 26:38; Jn 1:38–39), town (Jn 7:9; Acts 9:43), or house (Mt 10:11; Lk 19:5). John's Gospel often uses the term with a spiritual significance referring to some aspect of our relationship to God, and this is always the case for the twenty-four occurrences of *meno* in 1 John. In this spiritual sense, *meno* refers to clinging to a relationship already begun or continuing a process already started. The most concentrated use of *meno* in John's Gospel occurs in John 15:1–16 (eleven times), where Jesus admonished the disciples to always cling to Him so that they can produce spiritual fruit. Not clinging to Jesus is costly (v. 6).

What does this mean?

continue in His WORD

Be intentional

doesn't love Me will not keep My words. The word that you hear is not Mine, but is from the Father who sent Me. [25] "I have spoken these things to you while I remain with you. [26] But the Counselor, the Holy Spirit, whom the Father will send in My name, will teach you all things and remind you of everything I have told you.

JESUS' GIFT OF PEACE

[27] "Peace I leave with you. My peace I give to you. I do not give to you as the world gives. Your heart must not be troubled or fearful. [28] You have heard Me tell you, 'I am going away and I am coming to you.' If you loved Me, you would have rejoiced that I am going to the Father, because the Father is greater than I. [29] I have told you now before it happens, so that when it does happen you may believe. [30] I will not talk with you much longer, because the ruler of the world[a] is coming. He has no power over Me.[b] [31] On the contrary, I am going away[c] so that the world may know that I love the Father. Just as the Father commanded Me, so I do.

"Get up; let's leave this place.

THE VINE AND THE BRANCHES

15 "I am the true vine, and My Father is the vineyard keeper. [2] Every branch in Me that does not produce fruit He removes, and He prunes every branch that produces fruit so that it will produce more fruit. [3] You are already clean because of the word I have spoken to you. [4] Remain in Me, and I in you. Just as a branch is unable to produce fruit by itself unless it remains on the vine, so neither can you unless you remain in Me.

[5] "I am the vine; you are the branches. The one who remains in Me and I in him produces much fruit, because you can do nothing without Me. [6] If anyone does not remain in Me, he is thrown aside like a branch and he withers. They gather them, throw them into the fire, and they are burned. [7] If you remain in Me and My words remain in you, ask whatever you want and it will be done for you. [8] My Father is glorified by this: that you produce much fruit and prove to be[d] My disciples.

[a]**14:30** 12:31
[b]**14:30** Lit *he has nothing in Me*
[c]**14:31** *I am going away* added for clarity and refers to the cross
[d]**15:8** Or *and become*

this is how He loves us.

fvu?

CHRISTLIKE LOVE

9 "Just as the Father has loved Me, I also have loved you. Remain in My love. 10 If you keep My commandments you will remain in My love, just as I have kept My Father's commandments and remain in His love.

11 "I have spoken these things to you so that My joy may be in you and your joy may be complete. 12 This is My commandment: that you love one another just as I have loved you. 13 No one has greater love than this, that someone would lay down his life for his friends. 14 You are My friends, if you do what I command you. 15 I do not call you slaves anymore, because a slave doesn't know what his master[a] is doing. I have called you friends, because I have made known to you everything I have heard from My Father. 16 You did not choose Me, but I chose you. I appointed you that you should go out and produce fruit, and that your fruit should remain, so that whatever you ask the Father in My name, He will give you. 17 This is what I command you: that you love one another.

PERSECUTIONS PREDICTED

18 "If the world hates you, understand that it hated Me before it hated you. 19 If you were of the world, the world would love you as[b] its own. However, because you are not of the world, but I have chosen you out of the world, this is why the world hates you. 20 Remember the word I spoke to you: 'A slave is not greater than his master.'[cd] If they persecuted Me, they will also persecute you. If they kept My word, they will also keep yours. 21 But they will do all these things to you on account of My name, because they don't know the One who sent Me. 22 If I had not come and spoken to them, they would not have sin.[e] Now they have no excuse for their sin. 23 The one who hates Me also hates My Father. 24 If I had not done the works among them that no one else has done, they would not have sin.[e] Now they have seen

continuing w/ Him remaining w/ Him produces complete joy — not remaining = you wither

Remember Where Your Strength Lies

Jesus realized that He could do nothing by Himself. Yet with the Father at work in Him, He could do anything. If Jesus was that dependent on the Father, then you and I should realize we are even more dependent on God the Father to be working in and through us.

"I am the vine; you are the branches. The one who remains in Me and I in him produces much fruit, because you can do nothing without Me."

—John 15:5

Do You Know How Much God Loves You?

God is far more interested in a love relationship with you than He is in what you can do for Him.

"Just as the Father has loved Me, I also have loved you. Remain in My love."

—John 15:9

a15:15 Or *lord*
b15:19 *you as* added for clarity
c15:20 Or *lord*
d15:20 13:16
e15:22, 24 See 9:41 note

WORD STUDY

Greek word: **_kosmos_**
[KAHZ mahss]

Translation: **world**

Uses in John's Gospel: **78**
(Mt, 9; Mk, 3; Lk, 3)

Uses in John's writings: **105**

Uses in the NT: **186**

Key passages: **John 1:10; 3:16;
16:11,28,33; 1 John 2:15–17**

The noun _kosmos_ (English _cosmos, cosmic_), normally translated _world_ and most often having negative connotations, especially in John's writings. John provides the foundational verse about the _kosmos_ in 1:10—"He [the Word] was in the world [earth; see 16:28], and the world [the universe; see 17:5] was created through Him, yet the world [unbelieving humanity] did not know Him" (see 17:25). The _kosmos_ is consistently described by John as hostile to Jesus and the things of God. The world needs the light (1:9; see 8:12) because it is in darkness (3:19). It is dead and needs life (6:33,51). The world hates Jesus (7:7) and His followers (15:18; 17:14), but it will be judged (9:39; 12:31), as will its prince (i.e. Satan; 12:31; 16:11). But as "the Lamb of God, who takes away the sin of the world" (1:29), Jesus "conquered the world" (16:33). God loved the world (despite its sins) and gave His Son to redeem the world (3:16–17). John warned believers not to love the world, for it is contrary to the things of God and is destined to disappear (1 Jn 2:15–17). This will occur when Jesus returns and "the kingdom of the world has become the kingdom of our Lord and of His Messiah," who "will reign forever and ever" (Rv 11:15).

and hated both Me and My Father. [25] But this happened[a] so that the statement[b] written in their law might be fulfilled:[c] **'They hated me for no reason.'**[d]

COMING TESTIMONY AND REJECTION

[26] "When the Counselor comes, whom I will send to you from the Father—the Spirit of truth who proceeds from the Father—He will testify about Me. [27] You also will testify, because you have been with Me from the beginning.

16 "I have told you these things to keep you from stumbling. [2] They will ban[e] you from the synagogues. In fact, a time[f] is coming when anyone who kills you will think he is offering service to God. [3] They will do these things because they haven't known the Father or Me. [4] But I have told you these things so that when their time[1g] comes you may remember I told them to you. I didn't tell you these things from the beginning, because I was with you.

THE COUNSELOR'S MINISTRY

[5] "But now I am going away to Him who sent Me, and not one of you asks Me, 'Where are you going?' [6] Yet, because I have spoken these things to you, sorrow has filled your heart. [7] Nevertheless, I am telling you the truth. It is for your benefit that I go away, because if I don't go away the Counselor will not come to you. If I go, I will send Him to you. [8] When He comes, He will convict the world about sin, righteousness, and judgment: [9] about sin, because they do not believe in Me; [10] about righteousness, because I am going to the Father[h] and you will no longer see Me; [11] and about judgment, because the ruler of this world has been judged.

[12] "I still have many things to tell you, but you can't bear them now. [13] When the Spirit of truth comes, He will guide you into all the truth. For He will not speak on His own, but He will speak whatever He hears. He

---

[1]16:4 Other mss read _when the time_

---

[a]15:25 _this happened_ added for clarity

[b]15:25 Lit _word_

[c]15:25 12:38; 13:18; 17:12; 18:9, 32; 19:24,36

[d]15:25 Ps 69:4

[e]16:2 9:22; 12:42

[f]16:2 Lit _an hour_

[g]16:4 Lit _hour_

[h]16:10 14:12,28; 16:17

→ Wow !

will also declare to you what is to come. [14] He will glorify Me, because He will take from what is Mine and declare it to you. [15] Everything the Father has is Mine. This is why I told you that He takes from what is Mine and will declare it to you.

SORROW TURNED TO JOY

[16] "A little while and you will no longer see Me; again a little while and you will see Me."[1]

[17] Therefore some of His disciples said to one another, "What is this He tells us: 'A little while and you will not see Me; again a little while and you will see Me'; and, 'because I am going to the Father'?" [18] They said, "What is this He is saying,[2] 'A little while'? We don't know what He's talking about!"

[19] Jesus knew they wanted to question Him, so He said to them, "Are you asking one another about what I said, 'A little while and you will not see Me; again a little while and you will see Me'?

[20] "I assure you:[a] You will weep and wail, but the world will rejoice. You will become sorrowful, but your sorrow will turn to joy. [21] When a woman is in labor she has pain because her time[b] has come. But when she has given birth to a child, she no longer remembers the suffering because of the joy that a person has been born into the world. [22] So you also have sorrow[3] now. But I will see you again. Your hearts will rejoice, and no one will rob you of your joy. [23] In that day you will not ask Me anything.

"I assure you:[c] Anything you ask the Father in My name, He will give you.[d] [24] Until now you have asked for nothing in My name. Ask and you will receive, that your joy may be complete.

JESUS THE VICTOR

[25] "I have spoken these things to you in figures of speech. A time[e] is coming when I will no longer speak to you in figures, but I will tell you plainly about the

---

Expect Times of Testing and Stretching

Waiting on the Lord should not be an idle time for you. Let God use times of waiting to mold and shape your character. Let God use those times to purify your life and make you into a clean vessel for His service.

"When a woman is in labor she has pain because her time has come. But when she has given birth to a child, she no longer remembers the suffering because of the joy that a person has been born into the world. So you also have sorrow now. But I will see you again. Your hearts will rejoice, and no one will rob you of your joy."

—John 16:21–22

---

[1] 16:16 Other mss add _because I am going to the Father_
[2] 16:18 Other mss omit _He is saying_
[3] 16:22 Other mss read _will have sorrow_

---

[a] 16:20 See 1:51 note
[b] 16:21 Lit _hour_
[c] 16:23 See 1:51 note

[d] 16:23 14:13–14; 15:16
[e] 16:25 Lit _an hour_

Amazing transliteration: Amen, I say to you Amen

I have to ask

WORD STUDY

Greek word: **hora** [HOH rah]

Translation: **hour**

Uses in John: **26**
(Mt, 21; Mk, 12; Lk, 17)

Uses in John's writings: **38**

Uses in the NT: **106**

Key passages: **John 2:4; 17:1**

In the NT the Greek word *hora* seldom if ever refers to a period of sixty minutes. Even "one hour" in Revelation (17:12; 18:10,17,19) should be understood as an idiom meaning *quickly* or *suddenly*. In John's Gospel a special use of *hour* occurs several times and refers to Jesus' death, though His exaltation in glory is often in view also. This meaning of *hour* first occurs at Jesus' miracle of changing the water into wine (2:4), and the final one occurs at the beginning of Jesus' prayer to the Father (17:1) just before His arrest (18:12; for others during passion week, see 12:23,27; 13:1). In between these two events, John's Gospel states on two occasions that the hour of Jesus' death had not yet arrived (7:30; 8:20). The appointed moment for His death on our behalf was set in eternity past and could not have been changed by anyone, no matter how powerful.

Father. [26] In that day you will ask in My name. I am not telling you that I will make requests to the Father on your behalf. [27] For the Father Himself loves you, because you have loved Me and have believed that I came from God.[1] [28] I came from the Father and have come into the world. Again, I am leaving the world and going to the Father."

[29] "Ah!" His disciples said. "Now You're speaking plainly and not using any figurative language. [30] Now we know that You know everything and don't need anyone to question You. By this we believe that You came from God."

[31] Jesus responded to them, "Do you now believe? [32] Look: An hour is coming, and has come, when you will be scattered each to his own home, and you will leave Me alone. Yet I am not alone, because the Father is with Me. [33] I have told you these things so that in Me you may have peace. In the world you have suffering. But take courage! I have conquered the world."

JESUS PRAYS FOR HIMSELF

17 Jesus spoke these things, then raised His eyes to heaven, and said:

"Father, the hour has come.
Glorify Your Son so that the Son may glorify You,
[2] just as[a] You gave Him authority over all flesh;[b]
so that He may give eternal life to all You have given Him.
[3] This is eternal life: that they may know You, the only true God,
and the One You have sent—Jesus Christ.[c]
[4] I have glorified You on the earth
by completing the work You gave Me to do.
[5] Now, Father, glorify Me in Your presence
with that glory I had with You before the world existed.

[1]16:27 Other mss read *from the Father*

---

[a]17:2 Or *since*
[b]17:2 Or *people*

[c]17:3 5:38; 6:29

JESUS PRAYS FOR HIS DISCIPLES

6 "I have revealed Your name to the men You
gave Me from the world.
They were Yours, You gave them to Me,
and they have kept Your word.
7 Now they know that all things You have given
to Me are from You,
8 because the words that You gave to Me, I have
given to them.
They have received them and have known for
certain that I came from You.
They have believed that You sent Me.
9 I pray[a] for them. I am not praying for the
world,
but for those You have given Me,
because they are Yours.
10 All My things are Yours, and Yours are Mine,
and I have been glorified in them.
11 I am no longer in the world, but they are in the
world,
and I am coming to You.
Holy Father, protect[b] them by Your name[c]
that You have given Me,[1]
so that they may be one just as We are.
12 While I was with them I was protecting them
by Your name that You have given me.[2]
I guarded them and not one of them is lost,
except the son of destruction,[d]
that the Scripture may be fulfilled.[e]
13 Now I am coming to You, and I speak these
things in the world so that they may have My
joy completed in them.
14 I have given them Your word.
The world hated them because they are not of
the world,
just as I am not of the world.

Focus on Your Own Relationship with God

The Scripture leads us to understand that God is saying, "I want you to love Me above everything else. When you are in a relationship of love with Me, you have everything there is." To be loved by God is the highest relationship, the highest achievement, and the highest position in life.

"This is eternal life: that they may know You, the only true God, and the One You have sent—Jesus Christ."

—John 17:3

[1] 17:11 Other mss read *protect them by Your name those You have given to Me*
[2] 17:12 Other mss read *I was protecting them in Your name. I guarded them, those you have given Me*

[a] 17:9 Lit *ask* (throughout this passage)
[b] 17:11 Lit *keep* (throughout this passage)
[c] 17:11 Pr 18:10
[d] 17:12 That is, the one destined for destruction, loss, or perdition.
[e] 17:12 Ps 41:9; see Jn 13:18; 15:25; 19:24,36

[handwritten margin note: * Do a Hb/Gk transliteration on "one"]

[handwritten margin note: Jesus prays for unity (He values it)]

15 I am not praying that You take them out of the
world,
but that You protect them from the evil one.
16 They are not of the world, just as I am not of
the world.
17 Sanctify[a] them by the truth; Your word is truth.
18 Just as You sent Me into the world,
I also have sent them into the world.
19 I sanctify Myself for them,
so they also may be sanctified by the truth.

JESUS PRAYS
FOR ALL BELIEVERS

20 "I pray not only for these, but also for those
who believe in Me through their message.[b]
21 May they all be one, just as You, Father,
are in Me and I am in You.
May they also be one[1] in Us,
so that the world may believe You sent Me.

[handwritten margin note: unity yields revival.]

22 I have given them the glory that You have given
to Me.
May they be one just as We are one.
23 I am in them and You are in Me.
May they be made completely one;
so that the world may know You sent Me

[handwritten margin note: why unity?]

and that You have loved them just as You have
loved Me.
24 Father, I desire those You have given Me to be
with Me where I am.
Then they may see My glory, which You have
given Me
because You loved Me before the world's
foundation.
25 Righteous Father! The world has not known
You.
However, I have known You,
and these have known that You sent Me.
26 I made Your name known to them and will
make it known,

Your Calling Is No
Better, No Worse—It Is
Your Part in the Body

All members of the body belong to
each other, and they need each other.

*"May they all be one, just as
You, Father, are in Me and I am
in You. May they also be one in
Us, so that the world may
believe You sent Me."*

—John 17:21

[handwritten margin note: This is what should yield unity.]

1 17:21 Other mss omit *one*

a 17:17 That is, set apart for special
use   b 17:20 Lit *word*

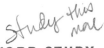

so that the love with which You have loved Me
may be in them,
and that I may be in them."

JESUS BETRAYED

18 After Jesus had said these things, He went out with His disciples across the Kidron ravine,[a] where there was a garden into which He and His disciples entered. [2] Judas, who betrayed Him, also knew the place, because Jesus often met there with His disciples. [3] So Judas took a detachment of soldiers and some temple police from the chief priests and the Pharisees and came there with lanterns, torches, and weapons.

[4] Then Jesus, knowing everything that was about to happen to Him, went out and said to them, "Who is it you're looking for?"

[5] "Jesus the Nazarene," they answered.

"I am He,"[b] Jesus told them.

Judas, who betrayed Him, was also standing with them. [6] When He told them, "I am He," they stepped back and fell to the ground.

[7] Then He asked them again, "Who is it you're looking for?"

"Jesus the Nazarene," they said.

[8] "I told you I am He," Jesus replied. "So if you're looking for Me, let these men go." [9] This was to fulfill the words He had said: "I have not lost one of those You have given Me."

[10] Then Simon Peter, who had a sword, drew it, struck the high priest's slave, and cut off his right ear. (The slave's name was Malchus.)

[11] At that, Jesus said to Peter, "Sheathe your sword! Should I not drink the cup that the Father has given Me?"

JESUS ARRESTED
AND TAKEN TO ANNAS

[12] Then the detachment of soldiers, the captain, and the Jewish temple police arrested Jesus and tied Him up. [13] First they led Him to Annas, for he was the father-in-

[a] **18:1** Or *Kidron valley,* which was east of the temple complex in Jerusalem

[b] **18:5, 8** Lit *I am* (see 8:58 note; Ex 3:13–14)

WORD STUDY

Greek words: ***ego eimi***
[eh GOH igh MEE]

Translation: **I am**

Uses in John's Gospel: **76**

Uses in John's writings: **86**

Uses in the NT: **153**

Key passages: **John 4:26; 8:58; 18:5**

The words *ego eimi* occur numerous times in the NT, but in John's Gospel they have a special meaning with two related connotations. First, *I am* often refers to Jesus' claim to be the Messiah. This is clear in John 4 where the woman at the well referred to the coming Messiah (v. 25) and Jesus responded, "I am He [*ego eimi*]" (v. 26). This meaning of *ego eimi* also occurs in Jesus' words to the disciples, "I'm telling you now before it [Judas's betrayal] happens, so that when it does happen you will believe that I am He [*ego eimi*]" (13:19). Jesus' foreknowledge of Judas's betrayal provided evidence for the other disciples that He was indeed the Messiah. Second, *ego eimi* often refers to Jesus' claim to deity and probably reflects the burning bush episode when God revealed Himself to Moses as "I am" (Ex 3:14). This meaning of *I am* occurs at Jesus' walking on the water (6:20; "It is I; see Mk 6:50; Lk 21:8), in a conversation with the Jewish leaders when Jesus stated that He existed prior to Abraham (Jn 8:58; "Before Abraham was, I am"), and at Jesus' arrest when the soldiers attempting to find Him fell back to the ground on hearing Jesus say the words "I am He" (18:5). The words *ego eimi* are also used in John's Gospel to introduce seven special titles for Jesus: (6:48; 8:12; 10:7; 10:11; 11:25; 14:6; 15:1).

law of Caiaphas, who was high priest that year. [14] Caiaphas was the one who had advised the Jews that it was advantageous that one man should die for the people.[a]

PETER DENIES JESUS

[15] Meanwhile Simon Peter was following Jesus, as was another disciple. That disciple was an acquaintance of the high priest; so he went with Jesus into the high priest's courtyard. [16] But Peter remained standing outside by the door. So the other disciple, the one known to the high priest, went out and spoke to the girl who kept the door, and brought Peter in.

[17] Then the slave-girl who kept the door said to Peter, "You aren't one of this man's disciples too, are you?"

"I am not!" he said. [18] Now the slaves and the temple police had made a charcoal fire, because it was cold. They were standing there warming themselves, and Peter was standing with them and warming himself.

JESUS BEFORE ANNAS

[19] The high priest questioned Jesus about His disciples and about His teaching.

[20] "I have spoken openly to the world," Jesus answered him. "I have always taught in the synagogue and in the temple complex, where all the Jews congregate, and I haven't spoken anything in secret. [21] Why do you question Me? Question those who heard what I told them. Look, they know what I said."

[22] When He had said these things, one of the temple police standing by slapped Jesus, saying, "Is this the way you answer the high priest?"

[23] "If I have spoken wrongly," Jesus answered him, "give evidence[b] about the wrong; but if rightly, why do you hit Me?"

[24] Then Annas sent Him bound to Caiaphas the high priest.

PETER DENIES JESUS TWICE MORE

[25] Now Simon Peter was standing and warming himself. They said to him, "You aren't one of His disciples too, are you?"

Submit Yourself Freely to His Correction

Disobedience is never taken lightly by God. At times He lets you proceed in your disobedience, but He will never let you go too far without discipline to bring you back.

One of the high priest's slaves, a relative of the man whose ear Peter had cut off, said, "Didn't I see you with Him in the garden?" Peter then denied it again. Immediately a rooster crowed.

—John 18:26-27

---

[a]**18:14** 11:50   [b]**18:23** Or *testify*

He denied it and said, "I am not!"

²⁶ One of the high priest's slaves, a relative of the man whose ear Peter had cut off, said, "Didn't I see you with Him in the garden?"

²⁷ Peter then denied it again. Immediately a rooster crowed.

JESUS BEFORE PILATE

²⁸ Then they took Jesus from Caiaphas to the governor's headquarters.ᵃ It was early morning. They did not enter the headquarters themselves; otherwise they would be defiled and unable to eat the Passover.

²⁹ Then Pilateᵇ came out to them and said, "What charge do you bring against this man?"

³⁰ They answered him, "If this man weren't a criminal,ᶜ we wouldn't have handed Him over to you."

³¹ So Pilate told them, "Take Him yourselves and judge Him according to your law."

"It's not legalᵈ for us to put anyone to death," the Jews declared. ³² They said this so that Jesus' words might be fulfilled signifying what sort of death He was going to die.

³³ Then Pilate went back into the headquarters,ᵉ summoned Jesus, and said to Him, "Are You the King of the Jews?"

³⁴ Jesus answered, "Are you asking this on your own, or have others told you about Me?"

³⁵ "I'm not a Jew, am I?" Pilate replied. "Your own nation and the chief priests handed You over to me. What have You done?"

³⁶ "My kingdom is not of this world," said Jesus. "If My kingdom were of this world, My servantsᶠ would fight, so that I wouldn't be handed over to the Jews. As it is, My kingdom does not have its origin here."ᵍ

³⁷ "You are a king then?" Pilate asked.

"You say that I'm a king," Jesus replied. "I was born for this, and I have come into the world for this: to

Obedience Is Worth Any Cost

Although obedience is costly, it is always worth the cost. In fact, whenever you are tempted to consider the cost too high, you need to consider what it will cost you not to do the will of God. The cost is even greater.

"My kingdom is not of this world," said Jesus. "If My kingdom were of this world, My servants would fight, so that I wouldn't be handed over to the Jews. As it is, My kingdom does not have its origin here."

—John 18:36

ᵃ**18:28** That is, the *praetorium*, the home of the governor of a Roman province
ᵇ**18:29** Pontius Pilate was appointed by Caesar Tiberius as the fifth governor of the province of Judea in A.D. 26. His jurisdiction included Samaria to the north, Gaza and the Dead Sea area to the south. He remained at this post until A.D. 36.
ᶜ**18:30** Lit *an evil doer*
ᵈ**18:31** That is, according to Roman law
ᵉ**18:33** That is, the *praetorium*
ᶠ**18:36** Or *attendants, helpers*
ᵍ**18:36** Lit *My kingdom is not from here*

testify to the truth. Everyone who is of the truth listens to My voice."

38 "What is truth?" said Pilate.

JESUS OR BARABBAS

After he had said this, he went out to the Jews again and told them, "I find no grounds for charging Him. 39 You have a custom that I release one prisoner[a] to you at the Passover. So, do you want me to release to you the King of the Jews?"

40 They shouted back, "Not this man, but Barabbas!" Now Barabbas was a revolutionary.[b]

JESUS FLOGGED AND MOCKED

19 Then Pilate took Jesus and had Him flogged. 2 The soldiers also twisted a crown out of thorns, put it on His head, and threw a purple robe around Him. 3 And they repeatedly came up to Him and said, "Hail, king of the Jews!" and were slapping His face.

4 Pilate went outside again and said to them, "Look, I'm bringing Him outside to you to let you know I find no grounds for charging Him."

PILATE SENTENCES JESUS TO DEATH

5 Then Jesus came out wearing the crown of thorns and the purple robe. Pilate said[c] to them, "Here is the man!"[d]

6 When the chief priests and the temple police saw Him, they shouted, "Crucify! Crucify!"

Pilate responded, "Take Him and crucify Him yourselves, for I find no grounds for charging Him."

7 "We have a law," the Jews replied to him, "and according to that law He must die, because He made Himself[e] the Son of God."[f]

8 When Pilate heard this statement, he was more afraid than ever. 9 He went back into the headquarters[g] and asked Jesus, "Where are You from?" But Jesus did not give him an answer. 10 So Pilate said to Him, "You're not

He Will Show You What He Wants You to Do

Truth is not discovered; it is revealed. Only God can tell you what He is doing or is wanting to do through your life. You will not be able to figure that out on your own.

"I have come into the world for this: to testify to the truth. Everyone who is of the truth listens to my voice."

—John 18:37b

---

[a] 18:39 *prisoner* added for clarity
[b] 18:40 Or *robber;* see 10:1,8 for the same Gk word used here
[c] 19:5 Lit *He said*
[d] 19:5 Zch 6:12
[e] 19:7 That is, He claimed to be
[f] 19:7 5:18; 19:12
[g] 19:9 That is, the *praetorium*

talking to me? Don't You know that I have the authority to release You and the authority to crucify You?"

[11] "You would have no authority over Me at all," Jesus answered him, "if it hadn't been given you from above. This is why the one who handed Me over to you has the greater sin."[a]

[12] From that moment Pilate made every effort[b] to release Him. But the Jews shouted, "If you release this man, you are not Caesar's friend. Anyone who makes himself a king opposes Caesar!"

[13] When Pilate heard these words, he brought Jesus outside. He sat down on the judge's bench in a place called the Stone Pavement (but in Hebrew Gabbatha). [14] It was the preparation day for the Passover, and it was about six in the morning.[c] Then he told the Jews, "Here is your king!"

[15] But they shouted, "Take Him away! Take Him away! Crucify Him!"

Pilate said to them, "Should I crucify your king?"

"We have no king but Caesar!" the chief priests answered.

[16] So then, because of them, he handed Him over to be crucified.

THE CRUCIFIXION

Therefore they took Jesus away.[1] [17] Carrying His own cross, He went out to what is called Skull Place, which in Hebrew is called Golgotha. [18] There they crucified Him and two others with Him, one on either side, with Jesus in the middle. [19] Pilate also had a sign lettered and put on the cross. The inscription was:

> **JESUS THE NAZARENE
> THE KING OF THE JEWS**

[20] Many of the Jews read this sign, because the place where Jesus was crucified was near the city, and it was written in Hebrew, Latin, and Greek. [21] So the chief priests of the Jews said to Pilate, "Don't write, 'The

Watch the Way Jesus Did It

When I want to learn how to know and do the will of God, I always look to Jesus. I can find no better model than Him.

So Pilate said to Him, "You're not talking to me? Don't You know that I have the authority to release You and the authority to crucify You?" "You would have no authority over Me at all," Jesus answered him, "if it hadn't been given you from above."

—John 19:10–11a

---

[1]**19:16** Other mss add (and) led Him out

[a]**19:11** See 9:41 note
[b]**19:12** Lit Pilate was trying
[c]**19:14** Lit the sixth hour; see 1:39 note; an alternate time reckoning would be about noon

WORD STUDY

Greek word: *teleo* [tehl EH oh]

Translation: **finish**

Uses in John's Gospel: **2**
(Mt, 7; Lk, 4)

Uses in John's writings: **10**

Uses in the NT: **28**

Key passage: **John 19:28-30**

Just before His death on the cross, Jesus uttered a single word of victory: *tetelestai* [teh TEHL ehs tigh], "It is finished!" (Jn 19:30). The verb *teleo* is related to several other Greek words that refer to something being finished, accomplished, completed, or coming to an end. (The same verb is translated "accomplished" in v. 28.) The perfect tense of the Greek verb Jesus used indicates that He understood His death at this point in time to have abiding or lasting results. Jesus' death on the cross on our behalf was His purpose for coming into the world. It is not surprising that Revelation uses the term eight times, more than any other NT book, to describe various events related to Jesus' second coming (10:7; 11:7; 15:1,8; 17:17; 20:3,5,7).

King of the Jews,' but that he said, 'I am the King of the Jews.'"

²²Pilate replied, "What I have written, I have written."

²³When the soldiers crucified Jesus, they took His clothes and divided them into four parts, a part for each soldier. They also took the tunic, which was seamless, woven in one piece from the top. ²⁴So they said to one another, "Let's not tear it, but toss for it, to see who gets it." They did this[a] to fulfill the Scripture that says: **"They divided My clothes among themselves, and for My clothing they cast lots."**[b] And this is what the soldiers did.

JESUS' PROVISION FOR HIS MOTHER

²⁵Standing by the cross of Jesus were His mother, His mother's sister, Mary the wife of Clopas, and Mary Magdalene.[c] ²⁶When Jesus saw His mother and the disciple He loved standing there, He said to His mother, "Woman, here is your son." ²⁷Then He said to the disciple, "Here is your mother." And from that hour the disciple took her into his home.

THE FINISHED WORK OF JESUS

²⁸After this, when Jesus knew that everything was now accomplished, that the Scripture might be fulfilled, He said,[d] "I'm thirsty!" ²⁹A vessel full of sour wine was sitting there; so they fixed a sponge full of sour wine on hyssop[e] and held it up to His mouth.

³⁰When Jesus had received the sour wine, He said, "It is finished!" Then bowing His head, He yielded up His spirit.

JESUS' SIDE PIERCED

³¹Since it was the preparation day,[f] the Jews did not want the bodies to remain on the cross on the Sabbath (for that Sabbath was a special[g] day). They requested

---

[a]**19:24** *They did this* supplied for clarity
[b]**19:24** Ps 22:18
[c]**19:25** Or *Mary of Magdala;* Magdala apparently was a town on the western shore of the Sea of Galilee and north of Tiberias.
[d]**19:28** Ps 69:21
[e]**19:29** Or *with hyssop*
[f]**19:31** 19:14
[g]**19:31** Lit *great*

that Pilate have the men's legs broken and that their bodies[a] be taken away.[b] [32] So the soldiers came and broke the legs of the first man and of the other one who had been crucified with Him. [33] When they came to Jesus, they did not break His legs since they saw that He was already dead. [34] But one of the soldiers pierced His side with a spear, and at once blood and water came out. [35] He who saw this has testified[c] so that you also may believe. His testimony is true, and he knows he is telling the truth.[d] [36] For these things happened so that the Scripture may be fulfilled:[e] "**Not one of His bones will be broken.**"[f] [37] Also, another Scripture says: "**They will look at the One they pierced.**"[g]

JESUS' BURIAL

[38] After this, Joseph of Arimathea, who was a disciple of Jesus—but secretly because of his fear of the Jews—asked Pilate that he might remove Jesus' body. Pilate gave him permission, so he came and took His body away. [39] Nicodemus (who had previously come to Him at night) also came, bringing a mixture of about seventy-five pounds[h] of myrrh and aloes. [40] Then they took Jesus' body and wrapped it in linen cloths with the aromatic spices, according to the burial custom of the Jews. [41] There was a garden in the place where He was crucified. And in the garden was a new tomb in which no one had yet been placed. [42] So because of the Jewish preparation day, since the tomb was nearby, they placed Jesus there.

THE EMPTY TOMB

20 On the first day of the week Mary Magdalene[i] came to the tomb early, while it was still dark. She saw that the stone had been removed[j] from the tomb. [2] So she ran to Simon Peter and to the other disciple, whom Jesus loved, and said to them, "They have taken the Lord out of the tomb, and we don't know where they have put Him!"

[3] At that, Peter and the other disciple went out,

Seek the Advice of Trustworthy Believers

Trust God to provide you counsel through other believers. Turn to them for counsel on major decisions. Listen attentively to anything the church has to say to you. Then let God confirm what His message is for you.

He who saw this has testified so that you also may believe. His testimony is true, and he knows he is telling the truth.

—John 19:35

---

[a]**19:31** *their bodies* added for clarity
[b]**19:31** Dt 21:22
[c]**19:35** 1:14,34
[d]**19:35** 21:24
[e]**19:36** 13:18; 17:12; 19:24
[f]**19:36** Ex 12:46; Nm 9:12; Ps 34:20
[g]**19:37** Zch 12:10
[h]**19:39** Lit *a hundred litrai* (a Roman *litrai* = twelve ounces)
[i]**20:1** See 19:25 note
[j]**20:1** Lit *She saw the stone removed*

WORD STUDY

Greek word: **pempo** [PEHM poh]
Translation: **send**
Uses in John's Gospel: **32**
(Mt, 4; Mk, 1; Lk, 10)
Uses in John's writings: **37**
Uses in the NT: **79**
Key passages: **John 4:34; 20:21**

The Greek verb *pempo* is an old and common term meaning *to send,* reaching all the way back to the writings of Homer (eighth century B.C.). In John's Gospel, however, *pempo* emphasizes that someone is being sent by another of higher rank to perform a special task. Those who questioned John the Baptist had been sent (1:22) by the Pharisees (see v. 24), but John explained that he had been sent by God (v. 33). The Father will send the Holy Spirit (14:26), and so will Jesus (15:26; 16:7). On two occasions Jesus stated that He sends His disciples (13:20; 20:21). The dominant function of *pempo* is found in Jesus' use of the term to explain that the Father had sent Him. This aspect of *pempo* occurs twenty-three times in John's Gospel and has two connotations: first, to remind us of Jesus' divine origin, that He came from heaven where He had been with the Father (5:23; 6:38-39; 7:33; 8:16; 16:5); second, to emphasize that the Father gave Him a special task that only He could accomplish, the task of redemption (4:34; 6:44; 7:16,28). In the latter case, *pempo* takes on the meaning *commission* or *appoint.*

heading for the tomb. [4] The two were running together, but the other disciple outran Peter and got to the tomb first. [5] Stooping down, he saw the linen cloths lying there, yet he did not go in. [6] Then, following him, Simon Peter came also. He entered the tomb and saw the linen cloths lying there. [7] The wrapping that had been on His head was not lying with the linen cloths but folded up in a separate place by itself. [8] The other disciple, who had reached the tomb first, then entered the tomb, saw, and believed. [9] For they still did not understand the Scripture that He must rise from the dead. [10] Then the disciples went home again.

⌐ why didnt they understand

MARY MAGDALENE SEES THE RISEN LORD

[11] But Mary stood outside facing the tomb, crying. As she was crying, she stooped to look into the tomb. [12] She saw two angels in white sitting there, one at the head and one at the feet, where Jesus' body had been lying. [13] They said to her, "Woman,[a] why are you crying?"

"Because they've taken away my Lord," she told them, "and I don't know where they've put Him." [14] Having said this, she turned around and saw Jesus standing there, though she did not know it was Jesus.

[15] "Woman," Jesus said to her, "why are you crying? Who is it you are looking for?"

Supposing He was the gardener, she replied, "Sir, if you've removed Him, tell me where you've put Him, and I will take Him away."

[16] "Mary!" Jesus said.

Turning around, she said to Him in Hebrew, *"Rabbouni!"*[b]—which means "Teacher."

[17] "Don't cling to Me," Jesus told her, "for I have not yet ascended to the Father. But go to My brothers and tell them that I am ascending to My Father and your Father—to My God and your God."

[18] Mary Magdalene[c] went and announced to the disciples, "I have seen the Lord!" And she told them what[d] He had said to her.

[a]**20:13** See 2:4 note
[b]**20:16** See 1:38 note; *Rabbouni* is used in Mk 10:51 also.
[c]**20:18** See 19:25 note
[d]**20:18** Lit *these things*

THE DISCIPLES COMMISSIONED

[19] In the evening of that first day of the week, the disciples were gathered together[a] with the doors locked because of their fear of the Jews. Then Jesus came, stood among them, and said to them, "Peace to you!"[b]

[20] Having said this, He showed them His hands and His side. So the disciples rejoiced when they saw the Lord.

[21] Jesus said to them again, "Peace to you! Just as the Father has sent Me, I also send you."[c] [22] After saying this, He breathed on them and said,[d] "Receive the Holy Spirit. [23] If you forgive the sins of any, they are forgiven them; if you retain the sins of[e] any, they are retained."[f]

pneuma "breath"

THOMAS SEES AND BELIEVES

[24] But one of the twelve, Thomas (called "Twin"), was not with them when Jesus came. [25] So the other disciples kept telling him, "We have seen the Lord!"

But he said to them, "If I don't see the mark of the nails in His hands, put my finger into the mark of the nails, and put my hand into His side, I will never believe!"

[26] After eight days His disciples were indoors again, and Thomas was with them. Even though the doors were locked, Jesus came and stood among them. He said, "Peace to you!"

[27] Then He said to Thomas, "Put your finger here and observe My hands. Reach out your hand and put it into My side. Don't be an unbeliever but a believer."

[28] Thomas responded to Him, "My Lord and my God!"

[29] Jesus said, "Because you have seen Me, you have believed.[g] Blessed are those who believe without seeing."

Obedience Is Always a Right-Now Event

The moment God speaks to you is the very moment God wants you to respond.

Then He said to Thomas, "Put your finger here and observe My hands. Reach out your hand and put it into My side. Don't be an unbeliever but a believer." Thomas responded to Him, "My Lord and my God!"

—John 20:27–28

THE PURPOSE OF THIS GOSPEL

[30] Jesus performed many other signs in the presence of His disciples that are not written in this book. [31] But

---

a**20:19** *gathered together* added for clarity
b**20:19** 14:27; 16:33
c**20:21** 13:20; 17:18
d**20:22** Lit *He breathed and said to them*
e**20:23** *the sins of* supplied for clarity
f**20:23** Mt 16:19; 18:18; Jn 9:41
g**20:29** Or *have you believed?*

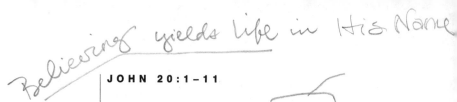
Believing yields life in His Name

these are written so that you may believe Jesus is the Messiah,[a] the Son of God,[b] and by believing you may have life in His name.

JESUS' THIRD APPEARANCE TO THE DISCIPLES

21 After this, Jesus revealed Himself again to His disciples by the Sea of Tiberias.[c] He revealed Himself in this way:

[2] Simon Peter, Thomas (called "Twin"), Nathanael from Cana of Galilee, Zebedee's sons, and two others of His disciples were together.

[3] "I'm going fishing," Simon Peter said to them.

"We're coming with you," they told him. They went out and got into the boat; but that night they caught nothing.

[4] When daybreak came, Jesus stood[d] on the shore. However, the disciples did not know that it was Jesus.[e]

[5] "Men,"[f] Jesus called to them, "you don't have any fish, do you?"

"No," they answered.

[6] "Cast the net on the right side of the boat," He told them, "and you'll find some." So they did,[g] and they were unable to haul it in because of the large number of fish. [7] Therefore the disciple whom Jesus loved said to Peter, "It's the Lord!"

When Simon Peter heard that it was the Lord, he tied his outer garment around him[h] (for he was stripped) and plunged into the sea. [8] But since they were not far from land (about a hundred yards away[i]), the other disciples came in the boat, dragging the net full of fish. [9] When they got out on land, they saw a charcoal fire there, with fish lying on it, and bread.

[10] "Bring some of the fish you've just caught," Jesus told them. [11] So Simon Peter got up and hauled the net ashore, full of large fish—153 of them. Even though there were so many, the net was not torn.[j]

God's Will Is Always Right, Though Not Always Reasonable

When you do what He tells you, no matter how unsensible it may seem, God accomplishes what He purposed through you. Not only do you experience God's power and presence, but so do those who observe what you are doing.

"Men," Jesus called to them, "you don't have any fish, do you?" "No," they answered. "Cast the net on the right side of the boat," He told them, "and you'll find some." So they did, and they were unable to haul it in because of the large number of fish.

—John 21:5–6

---

[a]**20:31** Or *the Christ*
[b]**20:31** Or *that the Messiah, the Son of God, is Jesus*
[c]**21:1** That is, the Sea of Galilee; *Sea of Tiberias* is used only in Jn (see 6:1,23)
[d]**21:4** 20:14,19,26
[e]**21:4** 20:14
[f]**21:5** Lit *children*
[g]**21:6** Lit *they cast*
[h]**21:7** Lit *he girded his garment*
[i]**21:8** Lit *two hundred cubits*
[j]**21:11** Lk 5:4–10

[12] "Come and have breakfast," Jesus told them. None of the disciples dared ask Him, "Who are You?" because they knew it was the Lord. [13] Jesus came, took the bread, and gave it to them. He did the same with the fish.

[14] This was now the third time[a] Jesus appeared[b] to the disciples after He was raised from the dead.

JESUS' THREEFOLD RESTORATION OF PETER

[15] When they had eaten breakfast, Jesus asked Simon Peter, "Simon, son of John,[1] do you love[c] me more than these?"

"Yes, Lord," he said to Him, "You know that I love You."

"Feed My lambs," He told him.

[16] A second time He asked him, "Simon, son of John, do you love Me?"

"Yes, Lord," he said to Him, "You know that I love You."

"Shepherd My sheep," He told him.

[17] He asked him the third time, "Simon, son of John, do you love Me?"

Peter was grieved that He asked him the third time, "Do you love Me?" He said, "Lord, You know everything! You know that I love You."

"Feed My sheep," Jesus said. [18] "I assure you:[d] When you were young, you would tie your belt and walk wherever you wanted. But when you grow old, you will stretch out your hands and someone else will tie you and carry you where you don't want to go."

[19] He said this to signify by what kind of death he would glorify God.[e] After saying this, He told him, "Follow Me!"[f]

---

1 21:15–17 Other mss read *Jonah;* see 1:42 note; Mt 16:17

---

a 21:14 The other two are in 20:19–29.
b 21:14 Lit *was revealed* (see v. 1)
c 21:15–17 Two synonyms are translated *love* in this conversation: *agapao,* the first two times by Jesus (vv. 15,16); and *phileo,* the last time by Jesus (v. 17) and all three times by Peter (vv. 15,16,17). Peter's threefold confession of love for Jesus corresponds to his earlier threefold denial of Jesus (18:15–18, 25–27).
d 21:18 See 1:51 note
e 21:19 Jesus predicts that Peter would be martyred. Church tradition says that Peter was crucified upside down.
f 21:19 1:43; 8:12; 10:27

WORD STUDY

Greek word: ***phileo*** [fihl EH oh]

Translation: **love**

Uses in John's Gospel: **13** (Mt, 5; Mk, 1; Lk, 2)

Uses in John's writings: **15**

Uses in the NT: **25**

Key passage: **John 21:15–17**

Although *agapao* (verb) and *agape* (noun) are normally considered the Greek words for divine love, the verb *phileo* can be used in the same way. The *phileo* word family has thirty-three terms used in the NT, including *philos (friend), philadelphia (Philadephia* or *brotherly love),* and *philema (kiss).* The verb *phileo* can refer to the wrong kind of love (Mt 6:5; 10:37; 23:6 Lk 20:46; Jn 12:25; 15:19; Rv 22:15), as can *agapao* (Lk 11:43; Jn 3:19; 12:43; 2 Tm 4:10; 2 Pt 2:15; 1 Jn 2:15). But *phileo* is also used to describe the Father's love for the Son (Jn 5:20), the Father's love for believers (Jn 16:27), Jesus' love for believers (Jn 11:3; 20:2; Rv 3:19), and believers' love for the Lord (1 Co 16:22) and for each other (Ti 3:15). Both *agapao* (Jn 13:23; 19:26; 21:7,20) and *phileo* (Jn 20:2) are used to describe "the disciple Jesus loved," and the meaning is the same. Thus, it is better not to make a sharp distinction in John 21:15–17 between *agapao* (Jesus' term in vv. 15,16) and *phileo* (Jesus' term in v. 17 and all three times by Peter). This is especially true since three other pairs of synonyms occur in this passage with no significant difference in meaning. In this context, both *agapao* and *phileo* refer to love in its purest form, so Peter's threefold confession of his love for Jesus, which corresponds to his earlier threefold denial of Him, should not be understood as a secondary form of love.

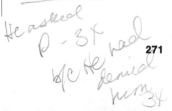

He asked
P - 3x had
b/c He denied
him 3x

271

CORRECTING A FALSE REPORT

[20] So Peter turned around and saw the disciple Jesus loved following them. That disciple[a] was the one who had leaned back against Jesus at the supper and asked, "Lord, who is the one that's going to betray You?" [21] When Peter saw him, he said to Jesus, "Lord—what about him?"

[22] "If I want him to remain until I come," Jesus answered, "what is that to you? As for you, follow Me."

[23] So this report[b] spread to the brothers[c] that this disciple would not die. Yet Jesus did not tell him that he would not die, but, "If I want him to remain until I come, what is that to you?"

EPILOGUE

[24] This is the disciple who testifies to these things and who wrote them down. We know that his testimony is true.

[25] And there are also many other things that Jesus did, which, if they were written one by one, I suppose not even the world itself could contain the books[d] that would be written. *Amazing!*

Your Part in God's Will Is Simply to Follow It

The servant does not tell the Master what kind of assignments he needs. The servant waits on his Master for the assignment.

When Peter saw him, he said to Jesus, "Lord—what about him?" "If I want him to remain until I come," Jesus answered, "what is that to you? As for you, follow Me."

—John 21:21–22

---

[a]21:20 *That disciple* added for clarity
[b]21:23 Lit *this word*
[c]21:23 The word *brothers* refers to the whole Christian community.
[d]21:25 Lit *scroll*